A
Charmed
Life

A Charmed Life

A MEMOIR

Trevor Summons

iUniverse®

A CHARMED LIFE
A MEMOIR

iUniverse books may be ordered through booksellers or by contacting:

iUniverse
1663 Liberty Drive
Bloomington, IN 47403
www.iuniverse.com
1-800-Authors (1-800-288-4677)

ISBN: 978-1-4917-7175-4 (sc)
ISBN: 978-1-4917-7176-1 (e)

Print information available on the last page.

iUniverse rev. date: 08/03/2015

CONTENTS

A CHARMED LIFE –
A MEMOIR

There are two men who influenced me to write this. Firstly, my very good friend Paul Everest wanted me to write another autobiography. I had written one – my first book – about 20 years ago and although I'm quite pleased with it as a first effort, it was rather focused on the profession from which I was about to exit. It was called *Life of a Salesman*, after the Arthur Miller tragedy of a similar name written in the 50's, I think. When I returned home from visiting Paul in Sanibel Island, FL, where he customarily takes a three month spell to avoid the start of winter back home in England, I had a go at roughing it out.

I realised at that time, I was not ready, and anyway I had given a pretty accurate description of my early life and didn't see that I could improve on it.

He had however suggested a viewpoint which caused me to give some additional thought and in the process gave me a title. He said to me on that occasion that in his opinion I had led a "charmed life!"

That's all very well and without doubt on the surface it might appear that way. The fact however is that although I have not been struck by any awful tragedy like debilitating illness in my life, I've tried pretty hard to achieve whatever success I've attained, and I've made few mistakes in recent years; well, ones that I can recognise at least.

Like Everest, I have been unfortunate however in that I never had a drive to be anything in particular, and in many ways I'm still waiting as is he I think, for that inspiration to come out of the skies.

In truth, the drive to be… fill in the blank… slowly surfaced and grew out of the job I was already doing to get by, when I was in my late twenties. But there never was an "on the road to Tarsus" moment.

The second man to inspire me to take this on is the late Christopher Hitchens, who sadly died long before his time at age 62 a couple of years ago.

In some way we shared a number of things. To begin with we were both English and immigrated to America about age 40. We were born some 25 miles apart – he in Portsmouth, Hampshire and me in Southampton in the same county.

Both our fathers were naval men – his in the Royal navy and mine by the time I was born having left the P & O.

We were both products of a staunch middle class system with all its advantages and hang-ups. We both attended English private school – still called "public" school for some arcane reason. But there the similarity ends.

Hitchens was a brilliant scholar and learned an extensive vocabulary and how to use it from a very early age. He was a rebel, although I think he would prefer the term contrarian. He went on to Oxford where he earned a degree.

Unlike me who was a knee jerk conservative. (It was a rare bird indeed who bucked that particular stripe in our circumstances.)

He went on to become a full fledged Marxist, then a Trotskyite and wrote inflammatory papers for a number of prominent British left wing magazines.

I watched him many times on television and he was a fearsome opponent in debates due to his extensive list of achievements and also the enormous number of people he had met.

He was a strong advocate for the oppressed and he traveled all over the world to witness injustices, and it seems to me to put himself in harm's way many times.

Towards the end of his life and long before he knew it was to close so prematurely, he admitted to slowly becoming more and more conservative. Perhaps he fell victim to the saying attributed to Winston Churchill: "Anyone who is not a liberal at 19 has no heart; anyone who is not a conservative at 40 has no head!"

Hitchens also became famous for his regular attacks on religion in its many forms. He had decided at school that it was all made up and he refused to kneel in his school prayers – he had seen this done by a hero of his at the time and decided to join him.

He stated strongly that the concept of believing in something that in the end would mean "entrance to an amusement park a little like North Korea where you adored the great leader for ever," was truly wrong, and in fact evil.

Even towards the end of his life when he knew he couldn't survive, he felt no last minute conversion.

His book Hitch 22 – A Memoir, was riveting, although a little too peppered with Hitchens' name dropping. It gave me the idea that perhaps I could tackle something along those lines.

I wrote a daily blog for four years – some 1400 posts. I eventually gave it up believing that I might be getting stale. The blog covered all types of things that interested me, and each week I posted two in particular; Trevor's Tirade and The Right Track. These were things that ticked me off and also a political view that might be a little different from the normal lefty position so favoured by our media.

We shall see how this turns out.

Chapter One

BEGINNINGS

Well, they're queer; but they're all very old, and so they're bound to be. 'But they're not mental,' explained Mother; adding candidly, 'Anyway, not enough to be put away."
— Gerald Durrell

Our ancestors are very good kind of folks; but they are the last people I should choose to have a visiting acquaintance with.
— Richard Brinsley Sheridan

I think there is nothing more boring in any form of biography or memoir than a tired list of ancestors. These ancestors, let's face it, are merely people, and on top of that they're all extremely old. To quote Oscar Wilde: *Relatives are a tedious bunch of people who have no idea how to live nor the remotest idea of when to die!"*

But my friend Paul Everest did me the big favour of tracking down my ancestry a few years ago, and it made for marginal interest.

I never had any illusions that I was descended from some form of aristocracy and the evidence is now in to prove my feelings correct. Against the people who came ahead of me in the family the words *(agricultural worker)* come up on most occasions. At least in a couple of cases alongside that is the definition *"inside,"* so at least they had the moxy to be employed indoors out of the British weather!

Any central search of births, marriages and deaths is limited to those who were counted in the 1810 census. If you want to know more then you have to visit the actual parishes and go through the written records. You'd have to be very keen to do that, I think.

So as for anyone else not linked by blood to our small clan, the far distant relatives are no more than just people who lived a long time ago.

1

I'm sure that if we ever came into contact we wouldn't know what to talk about. My knowledge of agriculture is pretty small.

It is said that in order to live a long and healthy life firstly you should choose healthy and long living grandparents. Well, I made a very good choice in that all my grandparents lived long lives.

I lost my favourite one, my paternal grandfather when I was 24 and he was 82. But by then I was married and my focus was on different things.

On my mother's side they both lived very long lives and my grandfather died when he was 100 plus two weeks. I guess having received his telegram from the Queen – I'm assuming in 1984 they still did this although I don't really know, and I never saw the piece of paper to prove it. Well, having got his I guess he thought it was unlikely he would ever get another and died in his sleep.

He was a grand old man however, and although I didn't see quite so much of him as the other one, he took me out and about around the Sussex lanes with him on his routes. He was the village carrier and also ran a taxi service.

He had served in the Great War of 1914/1918 and even though he had been on the front lines as an ambulance driver and also a water carrier, he never even got so much as a scratch. He was chosen for these duties as he had considerable skills with horses, having been a groom in his pre-war life. In spite of what must have been a horrific experience in the mud of Flanders, he didn't suffer at all from any form of post traumatic stress disorder. No doubt because they hadn't invented it back then.

As a side note my father had a fellow working for him back in the 60's who had a form of claustrophobia, brought on by being in the water and crushed during the Dunkirk evacuation. No one made a big thing about it, but they let him go from work a little early so he didn't have to be in the thick of the rush hour.

My maternal grandfather was a true countryman and even on occasions wore brown leather gaiters up to his knees. I've never known anyone else to do that. Mind you had we lost the war in 1939/1945, we could have had the opportunity of seeing lots of them, but they would have been polished black!

He had returned from the Great War and went immediately back to his job at some stately home in Berkshire. I have no idea who it was owned by. After a little he became restless and he decided to move to another position and this one was in Essex. It was a small joke, therefore that my mother was in fact an "Essex Girl!" The equivalent of being a "Valley Girl," out here in Southern California.

After a while, he once again became discontented with things and realised it was not the location, it was the position, and the fact that deep down he wanted to be his own boss.

One day he found an advertisement for a taxi business in the little village of East Hoathly in Sussex. They uprooted, pulled the savings out of the bank and bought it.

Somewhere along the way he also took on the business of being the village carrier, which was a sort of one-man UPS service. It was in this business's van that I used to ride along with him.

He used to pick up packages and deliver them. Often we would go to Uckfield's railway station and then we would take boxes to their eventual destination. We also would collect costumes from the famous Glyndebourne Opera and take it to a nunnery where they operated a laundry. It was several hours work each day, and I always enjoyed going with him.

The relatives on my father's side were all Welsh people. Now for some reason this was a matter of great pride to my father. He used to call himself a Welshman, even though he'd been born in the Royal Navy town of Devonport in England.

I became infected with the same nonsense when I was young and even used to put an "f" in the middle of my name instead of a "v." I eventually realised that Wales is a land of warm beer and ugly women and dropped the pretence. It's one thing to call oneself Welsh if your parents have accents, but quite another when the accent has disappeared completely and you're living in Watford!

I was fortunate to have known my paternal great grandfather fairly well. He died when I was ten at the age of 94. The doctors said if he hadn't smoked he'd have lived a lot longer.

There was a very small whiff of scandal about him in that he had married at age 19 when his wife was 21! Oh the horrors! But society was very structured back in those dim and distant days.

He looked the part of the Victorian patrician though, with a grey wool suit and a permanent pipe in his mouth. I don't think he took a lot of notice of me when we came into contact, as I think he wanted to spend all his time talking to his son and his grandson, the latter as I remember being rather in awe of him.

He was quite a mathematician I believe, and it was said he could make his own logarithms. Sadly this particular gene did not come through to me. He had run several collieries in South Wales and he was also the Provincial Grand Organist of Wales for the Freemasons. A photo of him in his regalia exists somewhere. But as the Freemasons are a secret society – much more secret in the UK than in the US – there were few bragging rights about this.

His wife, my great grandmother, was only ever in bed when I was taken in to see her. At two years older than her husband she was quite up there, and had that aura of great age that is so discomforting to the very young. On arriving at her bedside, my one fear was that I'd have to kiss her. As it was she only ever took my hand in her veiny skinny pallid one. That was bad enough.

A long way back there was a female relative who was in some type of government institution at the time of the census, so there was some sort of murk there, but so long ago that any crime was lost in the mists of time. Oh yes, and one great grandmother signed her marriage certificate with just an "X," indicating that she couldn't read or write. Perhaps she was a "looker" though!

There were a few characters on that side of the family that I knew quite well. We had a marriage between two first cousins that rocked things a bit I believe, and when great grandfather died, his Masonic jewels were removed by his eldest daughter. Great Aunt Violet. Don't you think that everyone should have one of those in the family? Particularly one that has effectively been banished.

As it happened Great Aunt Violet was quite a find. I dug her out when she was about 82, having found her living very comfortably in an old ladies home in South Norbury; not far from Croydon.

Professionally she had been a buyer for one of the London stores and travelled quite extensively to Europe. She was single and perhaps the reason for this was to be found among the several photographs of a well covered, statuesque woman she had on display in her room. In some of them this woman was dressed in the garb of an Eastern Star – the equivalent of women's freemasonry. Hence the perceived theft of the jewels.

I visited her several times when I was in the area and she actually came to my first wedding which allowed her to meet up again with her brother, my grandfather. I have no idea how the event passed and if there was some form of a reunion. I'm quite sure that her "preference" was never discussed, nor her attendance to the Eastern Star meetings. My grandfather was a lapsed Mason and didn't bother with it when I knew him, although my father did the whole thing including being worshipful master of his lodge.

One of his great disappointments with me - one of many, I'm afraid – was that I wouldn't join the society. I never saw the point, and anyway being rather anti-social the thought of regularly meeting up with people and going though some type of ceremony is even worse than hanging around chit-chatting. And for what?

Another relative who at least had some type of interest for me was Uncle Ivor. He was quite tall, extremely Welsh and wore very baggy grey flannel trousers.

It seems that in order to avoid service in the Great War, he had rubbed pepper into his eyes and as a result he had very poor vision. He couldn't be trusted in the kitchen, and would regularly misjudge the distance to the stove when he wanted a cup of tea to which he was addicted.

I cottoned on to this when I was quite young and it was an enormous delight to me when the kettle was dropped and went clanging to the floor. At which point all the grown ups would leap to their feet and rush in to see the damage.

Both my grandmothers were not only separated by about 50 miles and never met after my parents wedding, but also in their personalities.

My mother's mother, Sue, was very small but rather feisty. Her general demeanour overcame her 4' 11" height. She was in fact quite fierce. In that curious way that the older generation had of making reverse names of people's characteristics, my father used to call her "Lofty." She was OK with me but as she had three other grandchildren only a mile or two away she was focused more on them and didn't get too excited at our rather irregular visits.

My paternal grandmother on the other hand was a much larger woman with a pronounced Welsh accent. She adored me and I loved her. She was an accomplished cook and her food was something I used to dream about on my way down to see her.

She was "chapel" as my grandfather used to say, and so she didn't accompany the two of us to church. Rather she would sit in the kitchen next to the stove and cook up Sunday lunch. During her particular form of religious ceremony, as that was how I viewed the end result, she would consume bottles of Courage Light Ale. Quite how much she consumed was never mentioned, but it didn't affect the quality of the forthcoming repast.

I think I must have inherited more of her genes than the others as I too like to cook and accompany the process with beer. Courage Light Ale is not available here, so I have to make do with Coor's Lite.

The only other relative that seemed in any way remarkable was Little Vi. Obviously not to be confused with Great Aunt Vi. Little Vi had been deserted by Elwen. Obviously a blackguard, whose photograph nonetheless was still displayed on one of Aunty Dolly's shelves. I could never tease out quite went wrong there, but before he did a bunk and to use the old fashion terminology, "their union had been blessed with issue." This was in the form of my cousin David, who taught me how to pee in the fireplace.

Little Vi was one of those unfortunates who seemed beaten down by life. I have never hit a woman in my life, but frankly there was something about her that made one's fist ball up a bit. She was also infected with that slightly, wavering, lilting, lisping Welsh accent that makes most Englishmen cringe. I don't think she knew any color other than grey, which no doubt helped match her complexion. Frankly, although I never met him, my sympathies were entirely with Elwen.

In my childhood, I used to hear of friends' big family gatherings and I wondered if I was actually missing out on stuff. We lost our car at the end of the war (1939/1945). It went along with my father's job which had been repairing bombers. Could he not see the way that things were going, and once peace ensued there just wouldn't be the call for them?

I had to wait until I was about 25 before the envied large family gathering occurred. It was on the occasion of a golden wedding and the place was stuffed with people, most of whom I only knew slightly.

Such events are one of my problems in life. It's just that I'm extremely bad at small talk and I never quite know what to do. Perhaps that's one of the reasons that I've never had a party in my entire life. Not even as a child.

The family event remained a type of mystery throughout my childhood and teens. No car does rather hamper one a bit.

So immediately after WWII, we entered a period of considerable hardship, but our accommodation which had also come along with the bomber repair job at least continued. It was a rather nice flat over the top of a boys' private school, called St Georges.

There was a slight bit of awkwardness as my father had decided that this school was not good enough for his son and heir and sent me to another one. The headmaster of St Georges obviously saw this as an insult and made no effort to hide his dislike of me. But we were quite insulated from the school and as I was always going to a quite demanding school twelve miles away, I didn't spend that much time there.

My father managed to secure some sort of position in an office for about a year, but he hated it and moved on to pastures new. In fact he moved on quite a few times to various firms in various management positions. But the elusive car was far away. His financial situation was not helped by having to pay school fees so that I could advance. I always knew about this and felt bad that I rarely, if ever, measured up to his standards of excellence.

It's not that he was particularly academic, but my efforts were very poor indeed and I lived in fear of two dates that came around three times every year. The first date was the arrival of the "school report." Usually it was filled with remarks like: "Could do better;" "Must try harder;" "Satisfactory" (mostly for the unimportant subjects like art or gym ;) and the much feared "Easily led!" Total damnation!

The next bad event was a few days later when the bill came. This was when my poor father could see the price he was paying for the dismal efforts I was making. But he continued to double down and put up with it all. I shall be forever grateful.

Like most women of their time, there was never a hint that my mother should work. It just wasn't done, unless the family owned some type of business like a shop or small company, where the wives helped out.

I saw a clip of Christopher Hitchens being interview by a staunch feminist on Australian TV, I think it was. She asked him what his wife did, and he said she looked after him and the children. The woman was very put out and asked him why she didn't work. Hitchens looked askance and said he didn't believe it was the role of his wife to work to raise money as that was his responsibility.

It was an amusing thing to see as neither of them could understand the other's point of view at all. The feminist was not placated in the least by Hitchens' assertion that his wife could work if she really wanted to but he didn't think it was necessary.

7

I truly can't believe that anyone with his advanced outlook on life was quite so "old-fashioned," and perhaps he was just winding up the feminist; a branch of society with which he had few sympathies.

Later on we'll wander into the area of technological improvements in my lifetime and come to some of the things that helped women in the house. But growing up in the 40's and the 50's these had yet to arrive, and therefore my mother had to deal with all the usual tasks allotted to the distaff side of the house. It was quite a lot of work, and also considering that to buy groceries she went everywhere by bus and had to lug the stuff back in cloth shopping bags. Who knew that we were even then helping to save the planet; obviously we were a very environmentally correct family!

She cleverly balanced her responsibilities to both her men by switching her attention immediately from me to my father when he arrived back home from work at about 6:15. I never felt any resentment at this as I seemed to understand her role pretty well. But having had to put up with accounts of my day, she then had to turn the same interested ear towards my father. Her day no doubt didn't consist of much other than the same routine of keeping the family fed, and looking reasonable, and the house ship-shape; all the time while listening to the wireless as it used to be called.

It may seem very reactionary today that such positions existed in society, but after all that was the way things had always been, and my parents like everyone else's that I knew behaved in the same way. Woman simply didn't seriously enter the work place until the mid to late sixties. They could get jobs as secretaries or working in factories, but it was always seen as just filling time before they became married and had children (and in that order too!)

Of course, relatives are added to in life with the activity of marriage. I mentioned earlier that my parents' in-laws never seemed to meet after the wedding and frankly I think it might have been better had my parents not linked up with my in-laws after mine.

It was entirely my naïveté that suggested that a meet might be nice. It was not. It's not that that there was any serious unpleasantness, as there wasn't, it was more a question of the two couples being quite unsuitable.

My in-laws were extremely difficult people and in fairness, I have to say under those circumstances, they were very good to me. It must have been quite a strain.

Neither of them was at all sociable. My father-in-law was a successful shipping owner and broker. He was in fact nouveau riche. My mother-in-law behaved like it and expected to wear her wealth around her. On top of that they were quite spectacularly unhappy people and in particular with their marriage.

In the fashion of the times, they had stayed together "for the children's sake." In practice the children had both suffered from the poisonous atmosphere that had been going on for years. With my comfortable traditional middle class background, coming into their world was like a long drink from the fire hose of reality.

After meeting Veronica and during our two years courtship, I used to witness doors slamming, windows breaking and furniture crashing. Scenes I had never seen in my entire short life. It was jaw dropping. On top of that the children seemed to revel in stirring the pot of discord by enticing me to comment on the ongoing behavior in order to make some type of inappropriate judgement.

I'm rather proud to say that naïve though I might have been I wasn't that daft. But as the wedding neared, I tried to adapt to their life and eventually I was able to exist for visits to their house without being too discombobulated.

After some seventeen years of marriage when we parted, I have to say I rather missed them as a lot of the fire had gone out of them. However as the injuring party I never had the courage to re-visit and explain or see them ever again. I consider myself the poorer for that. They had been a big part of my life and outside the behavior which was only ever between themselves I recognise that they were very good to me and helped me a lot.

It is inconceivable that my in-laws would have stayed together in current times. But I have to ask would they have been any happier if they lived apart as neither of them seemed to have the social skills necessary to form good relationships.

Looking back it is very sad to recall what unhappy lives they lived. If one could arrange it they would be ideal candidates for another attempt at life.

God gives us relatives; thank God, we can choose our friends."
— Addison Mizner

Chapter Two

THE TRAVEL BUG

"I never travel without my diary. One should always have something sensational to read in the train."
— *Oscar Wilde,*

"The world is a book and those who do not travel read only one page."
— *Augustine of Hippo*

My parents met at the rail of the P&O liner S.S Strathmore in 1935. My mother as a nineteen year-old had secured a position as a children's nurse, for which she had been trained, and was on her way to work for a Mr. and Mrs. Boulter and their seven year-old son in India.

Such an adventure would be considered pretty surprising today, but things back then were very different and in modern parlance maybe it was no big deal.

I'm quite sure that had the job been located in say, France or Spain, which are considerably closer to England's shore, she would have balked at having to go to such a "foreign" country.

But India was different. India was, after all, part of the Empire and therefore part of England.

I know that her father had traveled to the Continent in order to fight in France and Belgium in WWI. I don't think his wife, my mother's mother and my maternal grandmother had ever gone abroad or even to far flung places in the UK. She seemed settled in her Sussex village and I never heard her talk of other places. This would include Scotland, Wales or even, God forbid, Ireland!

But at nineteen years of age my mother's father drove her up to the east London docks of Tilbury and handed her over to the crew of her floating home for the next three weeks.

I did ask her how she felt about such a voyage, and wasn't she scared or worried at the prospect of going to such a far distant land with what must have been a culture so different. As was normal for her generation she merely shrugged and said: "One just put up with it!"

Those six words were often spoken, and summed up an age where stoicism was thought to be desirable if not obligatory to survive in the world.

I don't know the time of the year that she went out, but I suspect it was the summer as pictures of her on board were of her wearing dresses and no top coat.

She did say that she was quite sad at leaving her family – there were five of them with two parents and three girls close in age to each other. It must have been a wrench.

It was no doubt this aura of sadness as they were leaving the British possession of Gibraltar, which caused a young engineering officer - smart in his crisp, white uniform - to come over to her as she gazed out at the departing port.

He asked her if she was feeling alright. They fell into conversation. By the time they had reach the destination of Bombay (now called Mumbai) he asked if he might call on her when the ship returned. Thus began a two year courtship of letters and occasional visits.

My mother's time in India was one of the most exciting in her entire life; the heat, the animals, the food, the millions of milling people and the sounds of the music that she called "Ogwallah."

The family for whom she worked was in the tea planting business and I believe she was treated like a member of it. I think that something caused this relationship to become tainted; perhaps they considered her departure to England after two years a breach of contract. But suggestions to contact them much, much later in the age of the Internet were met with indifference by my mother.

I remember her talking of Breach Candy – in Ceylon I believe - and also going up to the hills to visit Shimla. Mr. Boulter was obviously doing OK.

But the time came when the young P & O officer decided to pop the question. There was a pause and my mother said she would like to marry him, but there was a price. He would have to leave the sea. She had no intention of playing second fiddle to the oceans of the world.

George was sufficiently smitten to agree to the terms. In later life he often maintained that this loss was very hard for him, but in view of his reticence to make any trips abroad later I do wonder if maybe it was regret for his lost youth rather than the loss of a life at sea.

Almost from the time I could understand, the talk in the family was of foreign parts and the excitement of such places.

Along with this were the sepia photos of my mother in a swimsuit on the beach; in a white dress under a parasol; walking in a garden. There were many of them – now long since gone, I suppose.

She was a very pretty woman, and George was a handsome man with jet black hair brushed straight back in the fashion of the time. In all the pictures he was never without a cigarette in his hand. Once again the fashion of the time and a sign of desired maturity.

I'm not sure if the pair made the return trip together, but there was an incident where his future in-laws were to take tea in his cabin, when the ship re-docked back in Tilbury. His best friend, Eric Allen, whom he rather looked up to, was put on his best behavior as George arranged the Hindustani servants to flap around with cucumber sandwiches, dainty fairy cakes and hot cups of tea.

Everything was going along swimmingly, and even my mother's youngest sister, Diana, an extremely pretty girl, was having a great time.

Suddenly, the door flew open and there, looking rather the worse for wear, stood Eric Allen. He smiled somewhat inanely at everyone and then weaving his way across the cramped cabin, said: "Where's the bloody gin, George?"

So saying, he wrenched open a closet door and out fell half a dozen bottles. Everyone was transfixed. It was the start of my grandfather believing that his middle daughter was going to marry a drunk.

Granted he may have given the sauce a pretty good handling in the early days, but he developed a duodenal ulcer quite soon, which caused him to hang up his glass for the rest of his life, and apart from the occasional G & T he hardly ever drank at all.

Soon after they were married, my parents were staying with the in-laws in Sussex and right across the road was a pub called the Forester's Arms. The landlord of this fine establishment was called Bill Steele. My father knew Steele from some earlier part of his life.

Sadly Bill was a professional boozer and must have led my father astray, and I'm sure my father returned to his in-laws' home late for dinner and much the worse for wear on a couple of occasions. The die, if it was not cast by the Tilbury episode, certainly was now. The son-in-law was addicted to the demon drink. Ah, would that he could have been!

Our trips to Sussex were quite irregular – the absence of a car was tantamount in this.

But we managed to get to Southampton and the other set of grandparents more easily by train, and therefore with money so tight this was to be our destination for annual vacations for several years to come.

Around the dining room table, the talk was often of foreign parts. Also by this time my father had been to many different places in England. But it was Granddad's talk of his time with the Royal Navy that kept everyone entertained at mealtimes.

It seemed that he'd been everywhere. He told stories about visiting the West Indies, and around the various Pacific Islands.

He had served in WWI and was decorated at the battle of Jutland, which he never ever mentioned and it was only after his death that the medal was found.

All his travel was in the uniform of the Senior Service, of which he was immensely proud. I can only imagine how tough it must have been to witness the demise of the Empire for which he had fought and seen his shipmates die.

He had an irascible sense of humor and loved to tell jokes – only clean ones. Although on his regular short bus trips up to St. Mary's parish church with the incumbent clergyman, Cannon Waldegrave, I suspect the jokes were a little more colorful. I say suspect as I was always sent to the front of the bus to watch the driver. This was a pretty boring activity while these two pillars of society were chortling away for the entire journey.

During the visits, my grandmother continued to produce award winning food and smiled as her husband regaled us with his stories. Like so many of her ilk, she had never been anywhere. She had only been out of the country on one occasion. It was a day trip to Boulogne. She remembered it well but she didn't care for it.

These were happy times indeed. And I suspect in some way they kindled in me a desire to also travel the world and witness the things that were out there.

During the war we had been to a number of cities like Bristol, Brighton and Oxford, and we had lived in them while my father did his work in the aircraft industry. But once the foe had been defeated, we were stuck in Watford and there we were to stay for the rest of the next 15 years.

It could have been worse, I suppose, and it seemed to have cured both parents of any wanderlust they might have had within them.

Early on there was a trip to Wales but other than that and the trips to Southampton, it was only the 301 bus to Berkhamsted each school morning and the return trip back about 4:30 each night. No doubt the travel bug was in me, but with that existence it didn't get to flower much.

Nonetheless that was to change when I had left school and begun the first stage of my career.

Having joined Ilford Limited, the UK equivalent of Kodak, as a management trainee, I was sent away to a number of their sites to familiarize myself with the business. But it was after my two-year stint there that I went on the road and traveled to the Midlands and even further up north to see how the products of DJ Tipon Ltd worked.

The travel side of the experience was the only part that I liked. Basically as will be covered later, I was extremely shy and having to approach men many years beyond me with the idea of selling them something was very unnerving to me.

But I got to stay in hotels and move around until I was given the permanent area of Hampshire, Dorset and Sussex, and eventually I learned how to drive and gained that all important item for a salesman, a car.

Every morning, I would look forward to the day's adventure – not of selling the product - but of driving to parts of the country that I didn't know. It almost made the job worthwhile.

I had a number of mostly unsuccessful positions until in 1965 after a short spell of unemployment I went for an interview at Muzak, the background music people.

I got the job and along with it came a brand new Ford Cortina in British Racing Green. Boy, that was success indeed.

For about five years, Muzak had been a lost leader to the TV firm of ATV, but they had decided that maybe they should try and do something with the service. I was one of the people taken on to make that happen. Good luck with that!

Even though by now I was 26, I still lacked that confidence necessary to knock down some doors, but the money and the car were so good that somehow I had to hang on. I was lucky.

During my time there I traveled around the country a lot and became familiar with many of the cities and the developing motorways.

By the time I left in 1972 I knew the country inside out. My new position at Keyboard Training allowed me to build on that as their Sales Director. Furthermore the focus of the company was to franchise the concept and develop markets abroad. Traveling was an inherent part of such a plan

Naturally the first trips were to places close by, like Ireland, then Holland, France and Spain.

Vacations were taken in Greece and also around the UK and a couple of times to Belgium.

I soon recognized that doing business in a foreign country was preferable to just spending a couple of weeks on holiday there. It required an insight into the culture and also some familiarity with the language, customs and people.

I began to collect visa stamps in my passport. They were heady days.

Travel began to be a goal in itself. It was something that seemed to me to be a necessary part of my existence, along with eating and breathing.

Back in those days it was of course, a little more exciting than today. Places were very different to each other. There was a massive difference in the way societies lived and behaved. Not just the languages and food, but manners and customs. Some of these have remained in the more primitive lands. But in the days before social media and the Internet places stayed much as they'd always been and that was the way people liked it.

It was not the actual journey itself; it's always been more for me an innate curiosity as to what is around the next bend or over the next wall.

Back in the seventies, people would dress up to go on a plane, similar to going to church. But today that has gone along with church attendance. Could there be a link?

I noticed that my contacts had very little sympathy for one's condition after a long flight. Some type of comment would be made about how tired one would feel, but that was about it. Therefore it was incumbent to arrive looking fresh and awake no matter the length or quality of flight.

I had a system where I would carry the suit jacket, putting it on top of the carry on above me in the rack. Trousers would be in the same carry on along with carefully folded shirt waistcoat and tie. Half an hour before landing, the jeans I was wearing would be exchanged for the suit trousers, the shirt and tie put on and I would walk off the plane in the best shape I could be in. It was a small matter of pride, but it set the standard for the rest of the trip.

After ten years of flying around, I had to retire my trusty Revelation Globetrotter. It was a very big case with leather reinforcements on each corner to help with the rough handling of the baggage people in far distant airports.

I was asked once by a Japanese man how pieces of luggage I took with me on this particular six-week journey. I told him I had one suitcase. He was amazed as he had just returned from a two week vacation in Hawaii and had taken six cases with him.

I explained that in my case, every item I had with me would be used. Most people over packed with lots of spares that they would never use.

I also was a wash out when it came to recommending hotels. I would explain that my chosen hotel firstly had to be quiet, and then have an excellent laundry with quick service. Then it had to have first class telecommunications. This was in the days before mobile phones and roaming charges remember.

It didn't seem to matter to me the form of transportation. Either by car, boat or plane it was the travelling that used to get me up and running.

For about a year I was caring for some business in Holland. I was living on the South Coast at the time and used to drive my car to Dover, where I would board the ferry to Ostend. The journey was about three hours long, and time enough to enjoy a couple of Belgian beers and then a fine lunch. Afterwards I would retire to a pleasant cabin and take a long nap before the steward would bring in a cup of tea half an hour before docking.

Ostend was a city that I knew well as it was a favourite of my in-laws and became so with Veronica and me. It is principally a fishing port as well as a channel harbour. The dockside is lined with stalls selling all kinds of seafood and delicacies and I have stayed at some of the small hotels above the fish shops. All very simple but the food was to die for.

After getting the car off the ferry I would breathe in the atmosphere, heavily laden with the flavors of the sea.

I might pick up some langoustines before driving north through Belgium and arriving at my Dutch destination some three hours later. It was a journey that I enjoyed and took me through three entirely different cultures in one day. I still look back on it with very fond memories

At that same period of time, I had to drive all over England to visit a wide array of potential clients. Living at the very bottom of the country meant crossing London – it was before that massive circular by-pass, the M25 – and head up north. To pass the time, I would keep that day's Daily Telegraph crossword open on the seat beside me, and work on clues in my head.

I admit I would often fill in the answers while driving at high speed; perhaps the equivalent of today's great sin of texting while driving; a complete no-no.

It's very hard to explain this travel thing. Some people don't have it at all. I've met people who have only listed about four states out here in America. I made it my business to see all 50 of them whenever it has been possible.

No doubt there are people who prefer to stay in one place, which helps them feel safe, because there is no doubt that moving around all the time does promote a feeling of insecurity.

We all have felt at one time that odd experience of waking up and not knowing where one is. A life on the road makes that a regular occurrence, and to begin with it's just as unpleasant and fearful as for everyone else. However after a couple of dozen times, one accepts the phenomenon and also knows that come morning, one's location will be clear enough and there's little point in fretting about it.

I think it's all a question of picking your poison and being able to accept certain discomforts that others dislike intensely.

As a traveller, I have had to accept flights that can be long and boring. London to Tokyo via Moscow; Los Angeles to Sydney and many, many flights across the USA from one corner to another. But long ago I realised that you have to be somewhere, and let's be quite frank, an airplane seat is one of the few places where you can be on your own, undisturbed, and able to think your own thoughts and not have to do anything at all.

I have friends who become fidgety on flights and they get twitchy. A pointless exercise as is constantly checking your watch. Just accept that the entire thing is out of your hands and enjoy the ride along with a good book.

Sadly I see the encroachment of electronic devices to spoil this analysis of mine. I-phones and similar things can soon interact with you and there will be no escape from those on the ground who would like to direct your time more productively. We're not quite there yet but I can see it coming very soon.

Towards the end of my active working life, the ultimate in sophistication was a telephone credit card to be used at a public phone box on arrival at an airport. Just as I was exiting the building and my chosen career, cell phones were to become all the rage and soon made phone boxes redundant. Who would ever have seen that coming? Certainly not I!

Among my fondest travelling memories are the trips I have taken with my son, Michael.

For a couple of years we sailed on the Japanese seas on his catamaran, Milestone. On one trip we took along my 15 year-old grandson, Evan. It was extremely hot but it was truly wonderful to sail over the strange waters and sleep out on the netting – until it was time to escape the mosquitoes at dawn and head down to the by now cool cabins.

A year or two later we had to transfer Milestone down to a small marina in Nio on the southwest corner of the Inland Sea. We took along some of Michael's friends as well as a sea-going captain, Suzuki.

It was quite an adventure as we hit very bad weather out on the Pacific; but not as bad as the weather we endured halfway down the Inland Sea. Looking back we were in fact in severe danger of being swept onto the black jagged rocks which seem to be a permanent feature of Japan's coast line.

Perhaps some of the most memorable travels I have undertaken have come recently, again with Michael. But this time astride the two wheels of a Harley Davidson.

Some twenty years ago he said he was getting a motorcycle. Naturally like all good English parents I forbade the idea as being dangerous and also unsuitable in an English climate. Naturally, he ignored me and went ahead and bought a Harley Sportster. It was a bad decision only in that although by far the cheaper of the HD models it's not very practical for people of our size at well over six feet.

He changed it quite soon after and also came out to California on one of his regular visits.

He wanted to go to the local HD dealer in Marina del Rey where we were living, and while we were walking around looking at the many and beautiful machines available he poured some poison into my ear. "You ought to think about getting one of these," he said. "It's the sort of thing you'd enjoy."

Here, you might well recall the oft quoted words of many of my school reports: *Easily led!* I have to say that not immediately, but over the next few days, I began to see the wisdom of his advice and started to seriously consider what it might be like to ride one of these beauties.

Of course, I did not mention these thoughts to She Who Must be Obeyed as also being English, S.W.M.B.O. had a natural distrust and dislike of these machines.

Apart from the aforesaid dangers, they always had a strong "lower class" tang to them as they were perhaps the first step on that hard-to-obtain motorized ladder when we were growing up.

I began a system of slow indoctrination to the idea, however. This started with leaving sales literature around and also calling into the dealer when we were passing. The culmination was when we were off to watch The LA Dodgers one Sunday afternoon.

I said: "I just want to pop into the Harley dealer for something," and left the car. When I returned, S.W.M.B.O. was looking a trifle peeved. She announced: "If you get one of those things, I'm leaving you!" This was done through clenched teeth. Not a good sign at all.

I had about thirty minutes of car journey time to sell the idea, beginning with the concept that if she could find someone better than me without a Harley then I could quite understand. I then went on to mention that as I had never ridden a motorcycle in my 50 years, I was going to need lessons and a course at the California Highway Patrol. When she said those words; "You will be careful won't you," I knew I was IN!!!!

She even came along to the dealer on buying day to help me select the model – an FXRS- SP 1993 – as it happened.

I only had one more hurdle to jump. And that was my business partner, Richard.

He had a true hatred for the machines as he had lost a young brother to a M/C accident many years previously.

A week or two after I took delivery and ridden away in a very shaky fashion, I waited until we had finished a decent lunch and then suggested a coffee and a brandy at the bar. He obviously knew I wanted to raise a difficult matter, but had no idea what it might be,

"So what's going on then?" He asked. "Well, Richard," I said. "I've bought a motorcycle." "Oh God," he replied. "How big is it? Is it 500 cc's?" "No," I replied. "It's 1350!" Then after a couple of refills I tried to calm his fears and basically that was the last prejudiced bridge crossed.

There only remained the difficulty of passing the test, although in California law I was allowed to ride as much as I liked with no passenger for basically as long as I liked – except at night.

Now the practical driving test for motorcycles in CA is rather clever, and damned hard. In the UK, I believe, they follow you and tell you over a headset what to do. Out here, there's none of that. Instead there is a circle about 15 feet wide and also two lanes with orange cones about every four feet. You are supposed to ride down one lane weaving in and out of the cones, then enter the circle which has an outer ring about three feet away. You go around that one way, exit, and do another loop in order to enter the circle from the other direction.

This may sound relatively easy, but I can assure you that even now after twenty years plus and many thousands of miles, I wonder if I could do it.

The result of my first try was that on my second circle, I put a foot down and that was it, failed!

I told the fellows at the dealership and they told me to look in the paper for an advert for someone who offered a smaller – indeed much smaller – bike, which would be a hell of a lot easier. They weren't kidding. Pushing the 150cc Yamaha round the course, was a breeze, and the $100 dollars was a fee I had no problem in paying. I was finally a motorcyclist and after a year, S.W.M.B.O. came on the back with me many, many times!

Back in 2004 I went for a memorable ride with my two sons, Simon and Michael. We decided we wanted to look at Yosemite and took that wonderful road the 395.

Unfortunately Simon became sick when we were up beyond Bishop. We were camping at Benton Hot Springs and I decided that we should see how he was in the morning and then act accordingly.

He was still poorly the next day so I escorted him back to Lone Pine and put him in a Best Western hotel for a day and night with instructions to call me the next day first thing.

I felt it was a combination of de-hydration – we had ridden through some very hot desert the day before - and also just the overall wear and tear of riding. He was on a sport bike, a Triumph, which is not the most ideal for such a journey.

In the morning, after a day at the pool and drinking lots of water he was fine, but felt he should ride home although he wouldn't need an escort which I was quite willing to provide, of course.

It was an unfortunate episode and my daughter-in-law, Caroline has never quite forgiven me for deserting her husband. But the problem was that I had one son who had traveled thousands of miles to spend his one summer vacation this way, and the other one who after a 24 hour rest was in reasonably good shape, hence me leaving him to ride back alone. What would you have done?

As it happened, the ride set a standard for regular future trips for Michael and me.

We both love the American outdoors, particularly the west of the country. We both enjoy the camping experience and so for the last three years we have gone on extensive trips. Last year's was perhaps the most remarkable so far.

We rode through the nasty bit of Las Vegas and up the rte 93 to upper Nevada. From there we went to the Great Salt Lake outside the capital of Utah, thence up through Idaho and into Yellowstone. Finally we made the additional run to the Glacier National Park on the border with Canada. It was a long way and we ended up this monumental trip putting 3,570 miles on the odometers. I shall never forget it.

Over the course of my life, traveling has certainly changed. Perhaps it's due to the fact that in sixty years or so more and more people do it. It was after all only the relatively wealthy who could afford it and boarding a plane in say the 1950's through the 70's was not done by very many.

Also travelling in foreign parts was usually very safe. I've wandered along many a strange street without any fear – and some of these streets were in places now where a westerner is not only unwelcome but in positive danger.

In order to enjoy a charmed life of course, it is necessary to have lived it, and a premature end can put to rest any chance of continuing happiness.

21

I'm unaware that I've ever been in any particular danger in my life. A price of 200 pounds was on my head every time I went to Belfast in Northern Ireland, which I did several times in the 70's, but other than that I've always been pretty safe.

There was one occasion however in Tehran in the October of 1978. I was there to investigate the possibility of doing business with several local and American companies.

At the time there were rumours of trouble brewing from Islamic fundamentalists, and there were a number of troops around in trucks parked at various strategic locations. But the Shah was known to be a stern ruler who had things well tightened up in his kingdom.

One evening I was invited to join a group of others going to a restaurant outside the city. We were all in one car and driving along when one of the occupants suggested that rather than driving all the way to restaurant A we should go to one that we were about to pass. This other restaurant B was quite new and full of "trendy" people.

A short discussion ensued and eventually it was decided that we should continue on to A for some particular reason and we passed an interesting evening there.

The next day we heard that restaurant B had been blown up. As it was in a basement the damage to the diners was enormous and almost certainly I would if not killed have been gravely injured.

It is impossible to know how many other times I have been close to danger, as one never truly knows what is around the corner as you pass along life's road. But this event has always stayed with me. As it happened the Shah left his country just four moths later and the revolutionary sheik from Paris arrived; things have never been the same in that totalitarian country since.

This chapter began with my telling the tale that my parents met at the rail of a ship going out to India. It was a remarkable beginning for a romance and talk of it began a desire in me to travel as much of the world as I could.

It's therefore fitting that I should close this part with standing at the rail of an even larger ship forcing its way through the waters of the Pacific, just outside San Francisco.

Several years ago, S.W.M.B.O. suggested that we should go on a cruise. I was horrified. I had always imagined the experience as being locked up in a floating jail surrounded by drunks in polyester leisure suits continuously dancing the Conga.

However as all men realise, a happy wife is a happy life, and so I succumbed to the idea as ungrudgingly as I could and followed her up the gangplank of one of Carnival's big ships.

Within a day I was a total convert to the idea and now feel that any year I don't get out on the ocean is a missed year. I have yet to witness the dreaded Conga line either. A nasty little bout with the "noro" virus did mean we forewent the annual cruise for about three years, but we soon got back into it with no other recurrent symptoms.

When my father died his ashes were put into the water of the Mudeford Run in Hampshire. This fast-paced water empties and fills Mudeford Harbor where he retired and where he was very happy.

I like to think that his spirit along with some tiny microscopic parts of him has circulated around the oceans of the globe since and that perhaps he is aware of me when I lean on the rail of one of our cruise ships. Like most men of my age and my generation, I regret that we didn't have as many conversations of importance as we should have, and it is at those moments out on the deep leaning on the rail that I think fondly of him.

> *"But that's the glory of foreign travel, as far as I am concerned. I don't want to know what people are talking about. I can't think of anything that excites a greater sense of childlike wonder than to be in a country where you are ignorant of almost everything. Suddenly you are five years old again. You can't read anything, you have only the most rudimentary sense of how things work, you can't even reliably cross a street without endangering your life. Your whole existence becomes a series of interesting guesses."*
> — *Bill Bryson,*

Chapter Three

EDUCATION

"Education is an admirable thing, but it is well to remember from time to time that nothing that is worth knowing can be taught."
— *Oscar Wilde*

"Schools have not necessarily much to do with education...they are mainly institutions of control, where basic habits must be inculcated in the young. Education is quite different and has little place in school."
— *Winston Churchill*

Recently I saw a report on TV where a group of people had gathered together to collect books for school age children in order to help them to read. The number of mid-level children not able to read was somewhere north of 50%.

This report came a day or two after we had returned from a cruise where one evening, we were sitting at a table for six, and two of the women – of middle age – announced that they were school teachers. There then began a ten-minute airing of credentials on where they had attained their various degrees and in what subjects. One of the husbands felt it necessary to announce that he was an engineer with qualifications from some imposing school.

I was halfway into a somewhat forgettable piece of fish when the women's eyes came to rest on me.

I was probably about twenty years their senior all around, and I simply said that I was sorry but I had left school at age 16 with rather poor results, and it was a huge stroke of luck and also a wonder to my friends and relatives that I had neither been in prison nor unemployed for any length of time. I was basically therefore written off as one of the unwashed, but it didn't bother me too much.

These were school mistresses after all. They spent all their time with children. And if the recent reports are anything to go by they're not doing it very well either. Or is that just sour grapes?

Not having impressed anyone with my grades or achievements at school, I sometimes worry what are today's similarly affected students to do with their lives.

In the mid-fifties it was quite normal at around 16 to leave school, accept a job that was not too repellent to you and then hopefully find your way in the world, and maybe achieve some success.

Universities were called "Redbrick" if they were in some out of the way town or city, and proper ones were simply Oxford, Cambridge or at a pinch London. A qualification from say Brighton didn't mean a thing to those in the know, and only people destined for the toughest and most demanding careers would go to "Oxbridge." Way outside of nearly everyone's vision and therefore not getting a degree was quite comfortable for the great unwashed.

Today it seems that your degree is out front and center, but has it really helped with our lives? It seems not too much.

We hear all the time of young people over-qualified and underutilized in their selection of jobs. And the same can be said of the selection process.

In spite of highly qualified human resources departments' insistence on the highest standards, the best that any interviewer can hope for is a fifty/fifty success rate.

I was told this sad fact by a senior executive from the Xerox company who had hired and fired hundreds in his career with that prodigious firm.

I've hired quite a lot of people in my life as well, and I think I've pretty much made up my mind in the first few minutes whether this person has any chance at all.

It comes down to instinct, but there have been failures. I refer to the spectacular case of one, let's call him Bob Brown.

We were needing a good representative in New York, a notoriously difficult place for outsiders to do business.

I was aided in this venture by Patrick Allen who was overseeing things and helping a poor Limey try not to screw things up too much.

Patrick had had a long and impressive record in US corporate affairs and not only did I respect his judgement but he became one of my closest American friends.

We went through several applicants and then this big fellow walked in with a presence as large as his 6' 3," 235 lb frame.

He had been in some impressive jobs and was currently selling a high ticket item to large firms. Patrick and I spend a good half an hour with him and then broke for a little rest.

"Let's see how he handles the eating irons," Patrick said.

We met up with Bob at the Cattleman's Restaurant on 5ᵗʰ Avenue. A surprising choice looking back as N.Y is hardly the ideal setting for anything western. But it turned out to be a good choice with steaks all round and some red wine to go along with it.

Bob was good over lunch and we enjoyed his company and his talks about the city we were currently in. We offered him a trip to California to seal the deal.

Quite what happened between leaving him outside the Cattleman's and his arrival at LAX I cannot ever figure out. When he came through into the baggage hall he seemed to have shrunk about four inches, looked pale and was wearing a creased cheap suit. His first words to me were could he call his mother as soon as we got to the office? He was about 40, as I remember.

He did nothing on the way to the office apart from generally jabber away about silly things. My first impressions were gradually re-forming, and I was forced to admit that a great mistake might have been made.

When we arrived, the plan was that we would shuttle him right away into Richard's office to "meet the chairman!"

Once again he seemed to shrink a little as I opened the door and introduced him. The interview only lasted about five minutes and out he came again once more. Richard followed and said: "Can you get him a phone, he wants to call his mother."

I didn't need to look at Richard's face as I knew from the tone exactly how this information was going down with the "chairman."

As the phone call was set up, I went into see Richard and he asked me if I was sure about this fellow. I said that I wasn't any more and obviously the New York air had done something to my brain as this didn't seem the self-assured man with whom we had shared lunch.

We had a rather difficult five minutes with Bob to tell him that we didn't feel we wanted to progress his acceptance any further and we called for a cab to take him to the airport.

It didn't seem to faze him in the least and he parted from us quite happily. On reflection, I'm sure similar situations had happened to him on previous occasions. He had a "front" for interviews and could sustain such for some time, but underneath he was just a mother's boy who lacked any backbone. A sad business all round.

I mention this episode as a counter to my earlier suggestion that perhaps we had gone overboard in trying to over-professionalize the selection process. In defence, I'm sure Bob Brown would have sailed through such a modern form-generated procedure, however.

The fact is that over the years, the gut feeling, shoot from the hip, fire breathing executive (possibly chomping on a cigar) has gone out of favour.

Perhaps it was never much good, but in the late fifties and early sixties this was the image that was put out there for successful executives to follow. It seems rather silly looking back on it now.

Part of this image was that good men were born with abilities, although a lot of effort was put into helping younger ones coming up the ladder to develop such skills.

But the most intransigent – and I certainly include here "the chairman" – never bought into "self-improvement."

Before I came into his world and during my Muzak days, I worked for a totally different type of manager, Stan Lea. He became my sales manager and was very much of the thinking type. He also believed that we should all take courses on various business subjects to aid our careers and improve our skills. I soon found such courses to be of great assistance.

But for all the learning, there is no doubt that some type of intuition in finding the right people is vital for success. I'm proud to say that there were very few Bob Brown episodes in my business life.

But all this is about later education, not the type that sets children on the right (or wrong) path to life.

How is it possible to produce children in California who can't read or write? We spend as much and in some cases more than other states or countries in the world, and yet there is always the drum beat for more and more funding.

Let us examine the way my generation was dealt with. Before the voices are raised about different times and a more complicated society, let us just remember that my time was immediately after the horrors of WWII and a society that was still groping with a loss of a generation from the effects of war; and this was not long after the previous one that ended in 1918, which had butchered even more.

I shall always be grateful to my father for the supreme sacrifice of paying for my education. I never set foot in a state school, and from the earliest all my teachers were rewarded on results – or I suspect they were.

Results are what drive private education. It's a simple matter, in order to attract children who can be paid for; the school must show that they can teach children to a high standard. If not they will not survive in a competitive business. Education is after all in the private sector just another business.

The English "Public" School system was set up in the late 18th century. It was designed to give the sons of gentlemen a sufficiently rounded education that they could go on to manage the empire. This important aspect was run by men who all understood each other, had learned the same skills and could effectively communicate with each other on a level playing field. By the time I joined its ranks, as a very doubtful recruit, the thing had been working pretty well for 150 years.

The public school man was much derided as time went by. The old school tie – as a badge of entrance – was a derisive term used by those who lacked its ownership. The Old Boy's Club too was joked about quite openly. Also by the time I was old enough we no longer had an empire to administer and we were just like everyone else in the civilised world.

Nonetheless, the system truly worked and I'm so very grateful that I went through it as even with someone not gifted with much studency, there was enough discipline, and can one say guilt, to make a silkish purse out of a sow's ear.

To begin with the entire education system was based on Christian ideals. Also there was an inherent belief in the fact that little boys were not much better than young animals, and in order to produce men of character and decency they had to be trained. This included physical discipline and lots of organised sports.

Now in today's liberal world I can already hear the whining setting up about what about those who can't do sports, and other tough bars to leap? Well, in those cases, a note from a doctor could get one out of the activity, but the shame of doing so back then was sufficient to stop all but the most challenged from using that exiat.

There was also no escaping long hours of work. We were at school six days a week, with three afternoons devoted to sports. There were also two gym periods, and a couple of sessions of CCF work. One in full army uniform. (CCF is the equivalent of ROTC.)

Each morning began with fifteen minutes worship in the school chapel, complete with psalms and hymns, accompanied by a full wind organ and choir. Then lessons of 45 minutes duration would start, with classes being held in rooms where the teacher remained and the boys moved from class to class. Yes, boys, as there were absolutely no females in the school at all apart from maids and one music teacher; all of whom seemed to have been selected for their extreme ugliness as well as an hirsuteness that made our developing acned chins truly envious.

The system was designed to allow those gifted boys to float to the top while the rest of us were punished, beaten and generally cajoled into something resembling a reasonably well-behaved example of humanity.

I recently heard of the childhood of the writer Rudyard Kipling. It seems at the tender age of six he and his three year old sister were sent away to England from India where his teacher family lived and where he was born. He was sent to a boarding house in Southsea, Hampshire, a town I knew very well. His new guardians were a kindly man, but a shrew of a fundamentalist Christian wife. She earnestly believed that little boys were "full of sin, and constantly lied!"

In fact that was the view of most in the teaching profession and they believed it was their job to beat the sin out of boys and punish them harshly for lying.

It seems really harsh nowadays, but were their views so totally wrong, as we shrink from their methods? I came in on the backside of that attitude, and it was tough; but had it been a lot more lenient, then I'm sure I would have taken advantage.

Recently on one of our long motorcycle rides, and sitting around the camp fire, Michael and I were talking about a mutually known man and I remarked that I didn't think he'd had a particularly happy childhood. Michael said he didn't think any boys had particularly happy ones – it was always difficult.

It set me to thinking and I realised that most boys are naturally unruly and unless they are one of the gifted ones, anti-learning. As society insists that we adopt civilised behaviour, this totally goes against the grain.

For myself, I was never happier than when lessons ended and I could rag around the grounds with all my pals. Maybe even pushing the envelope of behaviour and all the while wishing like hell I could be a grown up and not have to have all these wretched restrictions. Perhaps that is the natural way for boys, to just want to be men, but without having to go through all the learning to get there.

But Berkhamsted School knew all about me and my friends' little ways, as they had been dealing with such small ruffians since the school had been founded in 1541 – yes, that was over four hundred years before I first walked nervously though the Lytch gate across the gravel quad in 1950.

Dean Incent had been at Henry VIII's court and had upset His Majesty over some trifle – no doubt a choice of female who his nibs had set his heart on. It was not the Godfather who had invented the concept of an offer he could not refuse as one only has to look into medieval history to see it being handed out regularly.

Incent was offered the chance of opening up a school in a far distant old Roman town or face another alternative. He made the wise choice.

Like all public schools, Berkhamsted was applying a template to what they believed was the ideal man. Someone who was loyal; courageous; decent; modest; a good loser; honest; sober, and also an applied scholar.

For those of you with small boys in your vicinity, you will immediately recognise that these traits do not come naturally. They have to be taught and in the case of the most recalcitrant forced upon unwilling students.

In fact, I believe that all the characteristics that were deemed desirable by the authorities – and still are, of course – were completely opposite to what came naturally to boys. I'm not sure about girls but from the get-go they seem to be much more "civilised."

It's always dangerous to generalise in such matters, so to avoid the hate mail piling up in my email in-box, perhaps I should state that this overall opinion is made on the majority.

Apart from one woman on the faculty, and she was locked away in the music school teaching a variety of instruments, we only had men who taught us. As will be seen from a future chapter on business, most of the middle aged men who were available for work came directly out of the armed forces. This included the teaching profession.

The military has a certain way of looking at things; they too work on producing a template of conforming behaviour. The firing line is no place for a non-conformist let's face it; and so most of my school masters had a rank before their name, although "Berko" was notoriously liberal and worked hard at avoiding such badges.

I use the term liberal, but it would not be thought that way by today's progressives, who find any form of standardisation of acceptable behaviour unacceptable. Except in thought, of course! Today, freedom from rules is the way to go and whatever happens we should not pass judgement on others' views, morals or behaviour. Such a philosophy would have been totally repellent to any of my school masters.

It should also be noted that my generation was raised in the "little boys should be seen and not heard" philosophy. We were not encouraged to speak out on anything. And it was quite customary for even the most loving parent (and I include my doting mother here) to say: "Nobody's interested in hearing what you've got to say, Trevor!"

Hence by the time we hit our teens, most of us boys were rather shy and pathetic. The "modest" part of the template was therefore not too hard to attain.

Our lessons were taught the old fashioned way, by rote. We had one master we nicknamed Poona, who taught French. He was quite old and no doubt had served in the Indian Army hence his name. He had all his lessons written out in wavering script in exercise books. They never varied. He was not an inspiring teacher. I failed dismally in both written and oral French.

But generally our masters were caring in the subjects they taught and they produced good results. And all this with only books, a blackboard and chalk to emphasis their points. From time to time a bamboo cane about three feet long was also used. Not an iPad or Google in the entire establishment. And yet, I am sure there was not one boy out of the entire 600 who was unable to read or write. So what price progress?

One decidedly different attitude in all our education was the complete lack of focus by any of those in charge of us, and I include prefects both house and school, on self-esteem.

There were very few "attaboys" in my upbringing either at home or at school. There was a reason for this. I didn't deserve any.

This might be considered strange as the motto of the school was *Virtus Laudata Crescit*, which means: *Greatness increases with praise.*

I was an acceptable athlete but not good enough to make the top teams outside of some field events. I was appalling at cricket and used to get fed up in rugby. My running was good because of my physique, but mostly I was at best average.

No one felt it necessary to scream and holler during my average performances as they never warranted it. I don't think anyone was the least concerned about how I felt inside. Mostly those in charge assumed I was a bit of a disaster inside like most of their pupils. The important thing was to ensure that on the outside I showed all the attributes listed above.

The top performers were lauded of course, but they were pretty few, and everyone knew who they were and that they were destined for heights not open to us. At least we weren't to be disappointed.

Our elders and betters knew that the world was a very difficult place to enter, and if we could exhibit most of those aforementioned valuable attributes then it didn't matter a damn if we were churning up inside with insecurities. Is it really any different today? In spite of being cheered senseless for mediocre performances at every step of the way, when under pressure at the all important interview are today's teenagers any more confident? Or if they are, is it helping them?

As the time for departure loomed for us 16-year olds, we were expected to sit for exams to set us on the road to a worthwhile position in society. About six weeks before the final papers were presented to us, we had "mock" exams. It was during this time that I finally understood that my behaviour up to now had not been exactly in my best interest. I had been told over and over, but had I listened?

The result was that I began to actually study, but it was too late. When my results came in it was a sad and dismal day. It was many years before I could shake off the feeling of failure as I tried to fit into society.

However looking back I realise that the money that my poor father had spent on me had not been completely wasted. I might not have been able to win a scholarship to Jesus College, Oxford, which is what he would have liked for me, but it seems that the system that had worked for so long had given me a template that became a standard in my own life; namely loyalty; courage; decency; modesty; the ability to be a good loser; honesty, and over the years in an effort to catch up, an application to scholarship.

The more eagle eyed might spot the absence of the goal of sobriety from this list. Well, in fairness I did give the wallop a good thrashing in the middle years, but apart from a few Coor's Lites of an evening even that has conformed to Berkhamsted's somewhat rigid template.

> *"Wisdom is not a product of schooling but of the lifelong attempt*
> *to acquire it."*
> — *Albert Einstein*

Chapter Four

CAREERS

Just remember, Trevor, that no one in business is indispensible!
— *J.G. Summons (My Father)*

"The crowning fortune of a man is to be born to some pursuit which finds him employment and happiness, whether it be to make baskets, or broadswords, or canals, or statues, or songs."
— *Ralph Waldo Emerson*

Back in the mid-fifties, gowns, mortarboards and the playing of Elgar's Pomp and Circumstance March Number One were parts of life that meant nothing to the 1950's UK schoolboy leaving for the next chapter of life.

I don't know if this play-acting is now an English part of life as it is in the USA, but back then mortarboards and gowns were worn by masters and students at the more famous universities. As for the famous march, well, it was thought of as a second national anthem and always played with much gusto at the Last Night of the Proms in the Albert Hall each year. It had nothing to do with college graduation or any other activity.

Therefore there were no ceremonies to celebrate the closing of this particular chapter of one's young life. It was a normal end-of-term day except that for many of us it was the end-of-school day.

In my own case, even that last day was not to be as traditional as the rest of my pals. I had been caught smoking in public by one of the house prefects, and in co-operation with many of his colleagues, they were out to get me and give me a beating.

This was a traditional punishment in those days and I had endured it many times. Oh, I can hear the liberal whining: Oh, it's so unfair to pass judgement on another; Oh, it is so demeaning: Oh, it strips a boy's self esteem away, etc., etc. All of which is true and exactly the reason for such punishment.

However, I felt it extremely unfair to get "six-of-the-best" on my last day and I set about avoiding it. This entailed quietly gathering my things and doing a bunk as quickly as possible. The end result was that I was chased up Berkhamsted High Street by a group of prefects while I jumped on the bus and waved a triumphant vulgar sign at them as I passed by.

Quite amazingly, I was chastised for this avoidance of punishment by my old house-master when I returned a couple of months later to obtain my "O" level results. He seemed to think that I should have remained long enough to receive my beating. I disabused him of that idea and took my dreadful results away with thoughts of a questionable future muddling though my head.

Now some sixty years along the path, I wonder what those thoughts might be in the modern world. Here I would be once again, a teenager with mediocre scholastic results and the entire unknown world stretched out before me as I begin my journey.

Frankly with so much knowledge gathered over the years, the idea is terrifying and I have to admit I have pondered the same question over and over across the time span. What shall I do?

The awful fact is that I have no more idea of what my game plan should be now than I did then. Exactly what should an unqualified young person do who has very little scholarship and no particular bent at anything? A few years into my stumbling beginning, I watched a TV drama about two young men who were facing similar challenges. One was a man who decided as he liked clothes, he would accept a job in a men's store. The other went into engineering.

The first young man immediately began to earn money and had an extensive wardrobe. He was the life and soul of parties and he even had a junky car to drive around in. The other was dreadfully short of money and his road to some acceptance seemed very long and arduous.

But eventually as in the Tortoise and the Hare, the second man earned his qualifications and soon took a position in society where he was far ahead of the first, who was still making about the same money and driving the same junky car.

The analogy wasn't lost on me, and acted like a beacon during my flailings towards whatever success I might hope to acquire.

Looking at young people today, I see very little difference in their challenges to mine at that time. In fact I only see the problems being more concentrated.

The subject of class is not talked about much. Certainly out here in the US, it is wrongly attributed to money and a type of flashy behaviour, which it certainly is not.

In the UK, class is deemed to be position in society and although much as been said that such a thing is finished, I have yet to see its demise.

There are three basic classes; the upper class, the middle and the lower. Everyone, even Americans, knows this and behaves accordingly. Where it becomes difficult is when extremely large amounts of money are injected into the mix. This would be for film actors, rock stars and sports personalities and the like.

Exactly where do you put such people as Madonna, George Clooney and Kobe Bryant? Personally in any discussions regarding class, I think it's best to exclude them as they are anomalies.

Taking the US, where class is to some extent said not to exist, the people at the top work really hard to stay in charge. Here, their money ensures that they educate their children, their political contacts work to keep the status quo and the financial policies continue to keep them making money when most of the rest of us don't keep enough money to be able to take advantage of the increases in the stock market.

A somewhat simplistic summary, but you get the idea. Let's face it, the people in charge in Washington D.C. would never send their children to the state schools there, who have about the worst reputation in the entire nation. No, from the very start, these privileged kids' names are put down for the finest schools so that they can continue with the paths their parents have selected for them.

This statement is not some form of communistic manifesto, just a stating of the facts that we are all faced with. And were things any different in the USSR? Really?

As it is best to exclude excess money from any discussions of class, then also it is best to remove excessive talent too from such discussions. If a child is exceptionally brainy or shows some form of gift that the rest of us lack, then they too are likely to advance up the scale and settle into the top bracket. It's just the way things are and frankly should be; such talents benefit all of us.

But for the rest what is the plan when there is not excessive money, talent or that most important of all ingredients for life, a dream or motivation? There lies the real challenge to solve.

Such was my case, and I can tell you that the early days were anything but charmed; they were in fact quite miserable.

I suspect that back in those days, with choices of occupations being far less than today, it was no easier. Is it simpler now with so many opportunities? Imagine entering a small café in England with a friend who has invited you to lunch. The problem is you don't have much of an appetite. The menu is given you and on it is printed the day's selections: Roast beef; shepherd's pie; salad, or hamburger. It wouldn't take too long to make a selection. As you're not too hungry maybe the salad.

A few days later you are in California and staying in Marina del Rey. The choice of another friend is to meet you at the Cheesecake Factory overlooking the beach. Here the menu is the size of a telephone directory. With all the jet lag, you're not hungry here either. Does the size of the menu make you feel any hungrier? You see my point.

Back in my days to use the analogy again, the lack of choice didn't make my selection any easier, or any more difficult.

There were certain things that even early on didn't appeal to me. Working for eight hours a day in an office was pretty high on the list of things I didn't want to do. Manual labour was certainly not even on the list, even low down. It would have been almost impossible to work in a factory as my middle class background would have precluded that. I neither had the desire nor the understanding of how that type of work happened.

It was my poor, and I use the term deliberately, father who came to the rescue. He decided that I should become a civil engineer. Even now I find the concept laughable. Of all the subjects I failed at in school, mathematics was at the very top. I had a horror of arithmetic and avoided it like the plague. I can only imagine the type of bridges I would have built, and the crooked roads I would have laid down. Monstrous!

But my father managed to pull a few strings and I was accepted into the civil engineer's office of London Transport, who ran all the buses and underground trains in the capital. This was his firm as well, but in a different location.

It was a tough introduction to the world of work, but frankly I enjoyed it. I didn't know what was really going on there, but I enjoyed the companionship of the men and also going out on the tracks with them. Here, levels and theodolytes were used and even though the weather was getting cold, I enjoyed seeing the men working on the railway lines and being in some type of managerial position, even if it was at a student level.

Eventually of course, the time came to declare my poor school exam results, and it was not pretty. I was marched into the office of the chief civil engineer himself.

He was a tall crusty man in a dark dusty suit. The air was full of tobacco smoke as he drew on a big pipe continuously. He asked me to sit down and proceeded to lecture me on how many young men he had in his office begging to be allowed into commerce. Now here was the conundrum. I quite liked the job I was doing, even though it wasn't that marvellous. Also I knew that although I could perform it, in order to do it permanently I had to gain qualifications, and that meant long hours of study, which meant the bane of my life, mathematics.

All this was going though my head as the chief droned on and on and eventually told me that I could no longer work there. I was in fact sacked! Ah, the first of too many such occasions, I'm afraid. Hardly an early ingredient of a charmed life!

Losing my position with London Transport didn't upset me much – how could it when basically all I wanted was to do very little. But my father must have been upset, although in his resignation of the overall lack of talent by his son he didn't get too cross about it.

I'm quite certain that his altruistic desires for me were not entirely selfless. Like most men, I am sure he would have liked to boast that his son was up at Cambridge doing rather well actually. Or perhaps studying physics or pharmaceuticals or bloody well anything.

He accepted that none of the professions was within my grasp and then attempted to maneuver me towards that perennial dry dock of the hopeless, the civil service!

Now I knew very little about this sector of society, except that once I heard the words, "very secure with a good pension," I knew it was not for me. What 17 year-old is in the least bit interested in a pension?

At that time I had a girlfriend, of whom my father deeply disapproved, as he believed that such a distraction was only going to further distort my indolent mind. He was right in so many ways, but testosterone is a very powerful drug.

My girlfriend's father was the Industrial Sales Manager of Ilford Limited. This firm was in competition with Kodak and provided a full range of photographic products to all markets.

Perhaps this relationship was the start of my charmed life in the young adult stage.

Once he heard that I was looking for a job, he said to me, and I shall never forget the words: "Why don't you become a rep?"

As I didn't know what that was he explained the position of representing a company by going out to see the customers and making sure that they were happy with the products. It seemed a pretty decent way to spend the day and so I said what would I get? He said, and again I've never forgotten the words: "About a thousand a year and an A40."

Now a thousand a year man was the sort of level that people looked up to. It was the salary of a bank manager; one of the senior members of society. And an A40 was a new car by Austin that was a real trail blazer (for the Brits!)

My head spun with the possibility that I could actually hit that level of success, and so quickly.

He soon realised that not only had I bought into his suggestion, but that my youthful enthusiasm might need a little tamping down. "Of course, you'll have to be trained, but I can arrange an interview with our office manager quite soon."

"How long before I could get the A40?" I asked him. He said it would probably take a couple of years. This seemed a pretty long time to one of such tender years, but perhaps I could shave a bit of time off that. The car was acting as a very strong incentive now and even outpaced the thousand a year.

As good as his word, I went along to the interview and passed with flying colors. I joined on November 1st 1956 and started as a management trainee. This entailed visiting all the departments in the company and learning what each did and how the entire process worked.

One of the visits that I had to make was to a depot, from where the firm's products were distributed. I was in fact sent to Coventry! It was close and had all the necessary aspects to teach me that side of the business.

I was escorted into the manager's office and sat down opposite him while we both lit up cigarettes. He was a short energetic man constantly twisting around on his swivel chair.

"So, what do you know about the war, Summons," he said.

It had been only eleven years since the end of it so it was still very much on people's minds.

I said that I knew as much as most people my age.

He fixed me with a glaring eye and said he had been at Bergen Belsen Concentration Camp with the RASC. This was the Royal Army Service Corps who were often used for clean up jobs and other assorted duties.

"Yes, I went in on the first day," he said. "Have a look at these." And he threw a brown envelope across the desk at me. "Go on have a good look, it'll teach you something about the people we were fighting."

Now at 17 I had already seen a number of these types of photos of the terrible things that the Nazis had inflicted on Jews and other sections of their population that had been deemed "undesirable," through the Nuremburg Laws. But there were some 100 pictures in this selection, and it was as a tough job looking at all of them. But this slightly maniacal individual wasn't going to let me off lightly; he wanted me to see the lot. It was a difficult fifteen minutes. I remember very little else of the visit to the depot.

I enjoyed my time with Ilford, although I got stuck in a couple of areas that were boring and I didn't enjoy the long days. I also had one of the worst commutes possible.

London was developed as a great series of circles; each being added to by successive ages, from Roman through WWII to modern times. The spokes of the wheel largely were designed to bring people into the center and of course, out again.

My home was still in Watford, at about 11:00 on the clock face and Ilford's head office, not surprisingly located in Ilford, Essex, was at about 3:00 on the same clock face. I therefore had to take a train into the center and another out to the east. It was long, complicated and tiring. Many times I traveled with Ron Dumpleton, who was my entry to the firm and my girlfriend's father.

He was a very nice man who always spoke as he felt and had learned. There was no side to him and he obviously saw me as a future husband to his daughter. Therefore my progressing in the firm had something of self-interest for him.

After two years, however, I became bored with things and decided it was time for the A40 and the upgrade to the thousand a year, which was so far out there as to still seem a dream.

I met with the general manager who disabused me of my early desires. "We'd never put anyone on the road until they were at least 21," he said. Disaster. What was I to do? That was two years away and that seemed a lifetime. I had already been there, performing various clerical tasks that were very boring, and I had heard all the chatter that went on with the reps and how they were respected in the company. I wanted to be one of them.

Once again my father came to the rescue. He knew a company that might be prepared to take me on. He was the methods research engineer for London Transport; he was a sort of practical efficiency expert. As such he used to meet with many firms who wanted to introduce their products to London's traffic monopoly.

One of these companies was called D.J.Tipon Ltd. It was located at 83, Piccadilly, London W.1. A very prestigious address.

I met up with sales director, Stewart Staples, who was a most imposing man. He had a large office and was wearing a fantastic suit. He had a lot of charm and invited me into his office for a decent cup of coffee served by his glamorous secretary whom he called Marine.

I was to find out later that she was really called Maureen and she hated the way he said it.

I was bewitched by the entire scene and couldn't wait to get my feet under this particular table.

After awhile the owner, Mr. Donald Joseph came in. He was the DJ bit of the firm's title. He seemed a decent enough fellow, but he asked me why I wanted to be a salesman. Now maybe here is another part of the charmed bit. My answer in truth was "I believe that the work's not too hard and I might get a thousand a year and an A40, Sir!" Of course, I didn't say that as I instinctively knew that was not cool. But I didn't really know the reason. I was floundering.

Had Donald Joseph applied the most basic selling technique at this moment he might have been spared a not particularly worthwhile employee. That technique is written in hard stone: When you ask a closing question; Shut Up!

As it happened he immediately followed up his question with the answer: "I'll tell you why you want to be a salesman; you want to make more money than being an engineer or a bank clerk."

"Exactly, Sir!" I replied. And in truth that was my idea all along. But my original answer had I ever used it was perhaps rather artless.

But I was "in!"

My girlfriend's family were not very happy at my leaving the old man's company, and no doubt his ability to help and protect the future father of their grandchildren. In fact the relationship ended within a few months, as after about three and a half years, it had run its course. Pastures new all around.

My new career began outside Coventry Railway Station. There I was met by my new boss, one Arthur Astley, a large rotund man with, as I was to find out, a distinctly personal method of selling. He had been a colour sergeant in the Grenadier Guards, and he'd learned his craft by basically bullying people.

He drove a white Austin Cambridge – several rungs above the much desired A40, I might say. It had no radio and for some reason he allowed a circular tin of Castella cigars to roll around on the back parcel shelf. I never saw him smoke these famously cheap cigars, and I found the noise very annoying; but he obviously liked it.

As we drove away from the station entrance, he pulled rapidly to a stop. He had seen a woman hesitating at the curb of a Zebra crossing. He wound the window down – there were no electric windows in those far off days – and shouted at her: "I don't wish to be rude, Madam. But when you step on that crossing, you are the law!"

I remember the words as if it was yesterday. And it was an introduction to this man's style.

Next he asked me to tell him about myself. I said "I left Berkhamsted School two years ago…" To which he jumped in and said: "Well, I went to a council school."

Sadly, the scene was set.

Now in fairness, I have to say that things could have been a little difficult for Astley. He was an army NCO in a company of army officers. He had never been a part of my interview, simply told he had a new man on his team and he rather resented me, I think. Looking back I quite understand.

On top of that I was useless. I was 19, and had very little idea of what to do with the only man I could ape being a bully twice my age.

Also we were in an industry which was not exactly soft and fuzzy. We were selling polyester resin to coachbuilders; in other words small businesses that beat out the dents in people's cars and then resprayed them. I had no idea about any of it and the businesses were dirty, noisy and right outside any area I had ever known about.

Astley didn't help in the introduction of the sales business to me either. We marched straight into several places and he proceeded to shout and bully the occupants into using our products before he left – rather like a quick and brutal tornado, or a scene from the Tasmanian Devil cartoon. I was appalled and horrified. And I was with him for a week.

Now one thing Astley did know was how to push teenagers around. After all he'd been doing it in his army days for years. He knew exactly all my little weaknesses and traits – laziness, sleepiness, timidity, the list was endless – but we were somewhat stuck with each other.

I tried to get along with him but my only feeling when we at last parted at the end of the week was supreme relief.

I spent two years under his wing, and I can truthfully say in all that time, I never learnt a thing from him.

I did perhaps learn some negative things in how not to behave, and certainly how not to sell our products.

After I left I never heard of him again and I never wanted to either. He had plagued me for the entire time and it's something of a testament to my doggedness I suppose that it took me two years to quit.

Any such autobiography as this is likely to produce the memories of all the jobs and the characters that have been encountered. In my earlier book on my selling life I did just that, but this time around I'll leave the details of the following situations out as this volume is a little wider in its scope than a list – many of them frankly appalling.

I was 25 before I had any true idea of how the selling world was structured. It's not one world either. It has many levels and initially I wandered around rather lost in most of them. I also wasn't much good.

I tried selling to retail shops, and wholesalers. I had a stint, which was pretty dreadful, in office equipment; I even tried the building industry. It was a long list and mostly rather unsuccessful.

Perhaps rather unfairly the world of selling has been called "The Mecca of the Unskilled." And in fairness it's a business that can only be learned by doing it. Some people are definitely not cut out for it and yet they are often given the chance.

Salesmen in general are thought of as being highly outgoing, exuberant, and gregarious people. Many of them fall into these categories, but from my experience the most effective are quite reserved, thinking types, who shun groups except to grow their contacts. Like any other profession the facts are often different to the perceived image.

Unfortunately, my innate shyness and reserve was a big handicap for me, I struggled with what the American marketers referred to as "call reluctance."

It was often joked that the first stage of selling is walking up and down outside the buyer's office praying he can't see you.

That stage stayed with me a long time. And to some extent it's still buried deep inside me. I don't like initial contacts and I don't like answering the phone or making initial calls if I can avoid it. Some things don't change.

Of course, I have overcome my shyness with time, and that horror of all horrors, cold calling, is not required of me these days. But if one lacks the courage to do that one is being hampered in a world of necessary contact.

I don't think this shyness of mine was completely unique and certainly I did my best to hide it from my colleagues. I met a salesman when I was working for 3M who suffered as well and he had a very good reason to do so. We'll call him John Jones; he had a quite pronounced stutter.

I suspected that he suffered from shyness as he did everything to avoid sales meetings when they regularly occurred at 3M house in Wigmore Street. He would lay out all kinds of reasons for not turning up and I found out that his great fear was having to speak in front of our group of salesmen. I can't say I enjoyed it much either.

Nonetheless he was a very effective salesman when left to his own devices. I had to join him one day and his technique was quite unique.

He was a tall and very handsome man of about 27 and he would enter a shop quite diffidently, lay his samples on the counter and begin to speak to the manager in a very quiet tone. At this time his stutter would kick in and with his quiet voice I noticed that people would lean in towards him and listen very carefully to what he said. I even think that John increased the stutter for greater effect. It was quite magical.

He was often with us when we went on our regular sales drives out into the country towns around London. It was rather like a cloud of locusts swooping down on fields of awaiting nourishment. The provinces in many ways are nowhere near as hardened by life as Londoners are, who have heard it all before. It's the same as New York and say, Little Rock.

We would arrive in a small town and be directed to go off and see as many outlets for Scotch Tape as we could find and then meet up at an arranged hour to gather all the orders

Being in a group would often help me overcome some of my fears and anyway one just couldn't sit and tremble with one peers all around; and they were a noisy and boisterous lot.

It was on one of these early skirmishes that I was teamed with Paul and saw his technique. It was wonderful to watch but I couldn't replicate it.

On this particular occasion we were staying at the Old Ship Hotel in Reading. We had had a good day and as usual with young men the evening beckoned with thoughts of women.

Now back in 1960 or thereabouts, sexual encounters were not that easy. We were in pre-pill days and it was a very unwise young lady who would be prepared to "go all the way" with a passing salesman, no matter how attractive – and we were all very attractive!

This evening we were having a few beers when one of our number mentioned that there was a club not far way in Swindon. I'm sure there was one in Reading, but it was to Swindon that we decided to go and find women.

As we were making our plans it was noticed that John Jones was sitting very close to a pretty woman who was somewhere to the north of 35. They were engaged in quite intimate discussions with their heads together and we couldn't help winking at John as we left the bar.

Our evening was as to be expected rather poor with many suggestions to the fairer sex being roundly rejected, and so at about 11:00 we returned to the hotel.

It had been a long day and so we all retired to bed to rejoin for breakfast at about eight to hurl ourselves once again at the unprepared shopkeepers of the town.

Paul came in at a few minutes afterwards and one of our number remembered his liaison the evening before. "How did it go with that mysterious woman you were with last night, Paul?"

John said it had gone extremely well and in fact they had spent the night in his bed before she had to go off early to her business meeting.

There were lots of: "Oh, sure." "No chance." And "You're having us on."

But John insisted it had all happened really well. Better than could be expected.

By now our faces were turned to him to hear all about the gory details. How the hell did you manage that, we wanted to know. As mentioned this was not the normal experience for us young men back in those dark days.

"Well," he said. "I d-d-d-decided to sell it to her."

"How the hell did you do that," asked one of the group.

"Well, I told her that I'd j-j-j-just come back from Saudi Ar-r-r-r-abia where I'd been working with the Sheik t-t-t-t-there.

"I t-t-t-told her that while I was t-t-t-there I was shown a m-m-m-most fantastic way of m-m-m-making love. It was t-t-t-truly mind b-b-b-b-blowing. Also that I'd never tried it in the six months t-t-t-that I'd been back here. And after a few c-c-c-cocktails, she bought it."

We started laughing as we knew that John had never been anywhere near the Middle East. And we demanded to know how he behaved when he had to perform.

"Oh I just d-d-d-did it straight m-m-m-missionary."

"Well, what the hell did she say about this wonderful way you knew?"

"W-w-w-well, afterwards she said is that it, then? And I said yes, isn't it f-f-f-fantastic? And she said that everybody does it that way. I just said I was really d-d-d-disappointed as I thought I had l-l-l-learned something new. Then we fell asleep."

In 1965, I joined the English franchise holder of Muzak and it was here that I finally began to shake the bounds of failure off myself and gain some confidence.

Here I was taught a trick to overcome my shyness with this bête noir of cold contact. I shall write a chapter about this lucky moment in my life as it requires some deeper work than being stuck in a general chapter about careers.

But having once learned this way, I blossomed and in the process became motivated towards success, and I like to think that I achieved some of that in my own way.

Once I had established myself as a producer and not one of the others who were generally looked down upon and eventually replaced, which had certainly happened to me many times, I began to hunger for more of what was working for me.

About the time I made my first trip to America, I met a man called Peter Jansen. He was very impressive.

Peter was Dutch South African and had devoted himself to the world of business. His father had been a successful executive with the

Pfizer Corporation and Peter himself had worked for that company, before his father died rather suddenly at about age 60.

Peter's entire family had lived in Holland during the time of the Nazi occupation and he and his father had been hidden under the stairs by Mrs. Jansen until she could sell her jewels and get them out. Peter and his father had the dark looks that betrayed their Jewish heritage, although Mrs. Jansen was not, I believe.

They went to S. Africa and then after the war back to Europe and England.

At the time I met him, Peter was the general sales manager for a pharmaceutical company and he drove around in a large, powerful Jaguar, the ultimate status symbol. Our families were similar and it was through our eldest sons and a kindergarten that we met up, and began to talk about life, and of course, business.

Peter was an enthusiastic businessman, devoted to that world. He had gone around the actual sales aspect, but was fascinated by it. He was always asking me how I did what I did, and I remember one thing which I told him and which he never forgot.

I said that when I went in to meet a new client, I used to pause for a split second as I went through the door and imagine that I filled that entire frame. He told me many years later that he had used that thought many times over his extremely successful career.

Peter was rather surprised and disappointed at my overall lack of knowledge about business, and insisted that I read two books on the subject. The first one was the bible of the time, The Theory of Management by Peter Drucker, and the other was Macgregor's Theory X and Theory Y.

I found them a little hard going but I did read them and learned a bit from them, I think.

He also told me that if I wanted to gain real success in business I had to get into management. It was all very well going along selling lots of stuff and reaping the rewards, but I would be much more successful if I made the change into management and let others do the heavy lifting for me.

I saw the sense, but there were no management openings for me in Muzak. I had to bide my time.

I well remember his dedication when he took a position with a world renowned management consultancy firm. His reason for joining was that by doing so he would be exposed to many different types of companies, and not only learn from them but perhaps be able to join them.

His initial training took place about twenty minutes drive from where he lived. After a couple of weeks, one weekend I found out that he was not driving back and forth but staying at the hotel provided. He even stayed out over Friday nights and returned to the hotel on Sunday evening. I questioned him about this, and he said there was so much to learn he couldn't afford the time or the distraction of home life during the six weeks he was on the course. I immediately recognised that I lacked such dedication.

Of course Peter and I slowly drifted apart; particularly when I left for America. He went on from strength to strength and eventually bought a small company, built it up and went public, depositing a very large amount of money in his bank account.

I never had the drive or ambition to do that but I never felt jealous of him. I last had lunch with him beside the Thames in Marlow and we relived old times. I was living happily in Southern California and he had a huge house in the most desirable area of suburban London.

He could have bought and sold me many times, but sadly he died like his father, prematurely at age 59.

He had finally retired from his company and accepted an outside board position for another company in the City of London. At his first board meeting on the Tuesday four days after leaving his previous firm, he collapsed off his chair and was dead before he hit the ground. It was a very sad business indeed.

By the time I was 32, I was enjoying success. I had already been to America and had tried to emigrate there, as will be covered later. But I was becoming a little stale and needing a new challenge, when once again perhaps I was to be lucky with my running into Martin Knights.

He had taken over as the Sales Director of a firm called Keyboard Training Limited. My current boss had heard that KTL had not been saying flattering things about our background music service in one of our key markets, namely "mechanised accounts." What we then called punch rooms.

As a result he had called the head of that company to see if something could be done.

Ever the entrepreneur, Richard Littlehailes, the chairman, agreed to come along to see if there might be some mutual business that both firms could do together. However he was delayed by going to the USA to launch his business there. Therefore Martin was selected to fill in for him.

On the allotted day, Stan asked me if I'd like to join them to talk about what KTL did, and as it was to be at the L'Epee D'Or, just across the road at the Cumberland Hotel – a favourite four-star restaurant - I readily agreed.

Martin was a charming fellow and explained what KTL did. They trained keyboard operators in the computer industry – data entry girls. This they did by putting in consultants to train each operator on site, to increase speed and improve accuracy.

We all got along famously and the result was that they would agree to put our service, Muzak, into their training facility in Putney, and we would mention them favourably when the matter came up.

Tileman House, Upper Richmond Road was close to the very center of Putney. KTL's training center there was a form of back up service for ones and twos who had missed the central training which was always carried out at a client's premises. These girls – and in 99.9% of cases they were usually girls aged about 17 through 25 - would come along to learn how to operate punch card equipment effectively. The courses usually lasted about two weeks.

Keyboard Training had been founded by Richard's wife in the sixties. He had been a typewriter salesman at the time and she ran a typing school in Putney. He had sold her several machines, and they became "involved."

The story goes that one day he was at a large insurance company arranging a new sale, and he happened to ask why they needed so many typewriters. The answer was that there was so much work and the standard of typing in London was so poor that the only way they could get it all done was to hire more typists and buy more typewriters. Good business for Richard!

On a walk through the workrooms, mostly called typing pools back then, Richard noticed that the wastebaskets were overflowing with spent paper.

"Why don't you teach these girls to type properly?" He asked the buyer, the germ of an idea forming in his mind.

His question wasn't just an empty one, as Ann taught typing in her Putney School and was open to the idea of exporting her training skills to firms rather than just having the girls come to her.

Ann had been a European typing champion – yes, they actually had competitions for it. Her secret was that she never had to look at the keys and was able to concentrate fully on the copy and never made mistakes.

She had invented a color coded system where the keys of the typewriter were covered with colored dots masking all the letters. Alongside the keyboard was a chart laid out in the same colored way, but on this one the student could write the letters and numbers. It then caused the eye to become confused. When looking at the keys there were no letters, but by looking away the letters were visible – therefore typists from the get go had to look away.

It became the system that allowed many of us to earn a damned good living around the world and also taught touch keying to many thousands of people over the course of forty years; my own daughter included.

Within a year, Richard returned from the States and saw that KTL needed a good sales manager and mentioned to Martin the fellow he had talked about a year earlier, when they were struggling a bit and couldn't afford me.

We all had lunch together and I agreed to join the company on November 1st 1972. It was a heady day.

This is written 16 years after I retired from the full time workforce. I can't say I've missed it, and I don't remember too many details of the negotiations I managed all over the world. They were in such diverse places as Iran; Bahrain; Japan; Spain; Holland; Finland, and all over America.

Many of the people I looked after I remember very well, but the actual sales, not too much.

Neither can I admit to a feeling of uselessness, which I believe is the reason so many men die quite soon after they hand in their tools.

Taking up the small challenge of writing a weekly column and other articles that crop up from time to time, has no doubt assisted in not feeling like I went into it all cold turkey.

The fact is that of all the stages in my life, I think retirement is the most satisfactory and enjoyable.

I believe that not everyone is gifted with the ability to be on his or her own, with no particular occupation, and with only the delightful company of a wonderful wife. But if such a position was available in earlier life, then I would have volunteered for it immediately.

I was very fortunate to stumble into a profession that allowed me to exploit the minimal talents I had and see much of the world at other people's expense. And so perhaps in that way I have led a charmed "working" life.

One of the most successful TV comedies of the 70's was The Fall and Rise or Reginald Perrin, starring Leonard Rossiter. I happened to look it up the other day on You Tube. I found it rather depressing. It showed a man who had acquired all the trappings of success with a stock broker house in suburbia and a nice wife and a commute by train up to the city.

It was a life so many of us aspired to. I'm so grateful that I didn't succeed.

> *"There are moments when one has to choose between living one's own life, fully, entirely, completely - or dragging out some false, shallow, degrading existence that the world in its hypocrisy demands."*
> — *Oscar Wilde*

Chapter Five

BOB AITCHESON

"Tell me and I forget, teach me and I may remember, involve me and I learn."
— *Benjamin Franklin*

"The best teacher is not the one who knows most but the one who is most capable of reducing knowledge to that simple compound of the obvious and wonderful."
— *H.L. Mencken*

As mentioned earlier, even at the age of 25, I was still suffering from "call reluctance." It is a strange thing to have if one is a salesman, but it was borne out of an innate shyness. I have noticed that such shyness is quite prevalent in people of my culture and age. No doubt due to an excessive amount of "little boys should be seen and not heard" syndrome.

Most of our parents didn't like us up front and central to discussions and from my point of view that suited me just fine.

But when it came to meeting new clients, and particularly when I had no appointment beforehand, the act of walking through the door was almost impossible.

Arthur Astley detected it straight away and when he asked me to "perform" after a couple of days out in the field he saw that I just wasn't up to the task; and particularly not in front of him

Therefore, he chose a slightly different route. He sent me into a panel shop, as those businesses were called, on my own, while he sat outside.

I can still remember the slow walk to the doors through which I had to pass and thence find the boss and tell him my story. It still gives me an uncomfortable feeling after all this time.

Astley sat, plump in his gleaming white Cambridge, while I crossed the Rubicon. The difference between me and Caesar was that he only had to do it once; I had to do it several times a day.

Now here is where it became strange. Once I had opened the door and asked for the boss my fear evaporated. The only similar feeling I can find is the one while sky-diving. There, one is taken up to about 10,000 feet and told to get in the door. It is a moment of sheer terror. But with a queue behind one and no time to procrastinate, once the command "Go, go, go," is given one just falls out. Once that happens all the fear disappears and you float down after the chute is opened.

For me cold calling was very like that. The selling bit was actually quite easy, it was the getting in – or in this case going through – the door that took the courage.

I had one job, with 3M, that entailed nothing but cold calling. Every day was a misery. Occasionally we would go out in teams and to some extent that seemed to help, knowing that not only were others having to face the same fear as me, but at the end of the day one was expected to account for one's time and success. Pride helped alleviate the horror of it all.

And yet, once again, the moment I started talking to a prospect, I was fine. My instincts and training took over.

Back in my skydiving days, after I had done five jumps I asked one of the instructors if she still felt any fear. She had completed some 2000 jumps and, yes, she said she still felt it when she had to go out of the door. All the instructors were called "jump masters" and as you will see in the Tirade chapter I have an aversion to calling women "master". I therefore used to call this pretty little Asian woman, my "Jump Mistress." She never seemed to mind at all.

I reasoned that if she still had that fear after 2000 falls, then mine was not going to diminish any time soon. Skydiving was also one of those annoying activities where you had to hurry up and wait. It took place in very out-of-the-way places, with at least a two-hour drive. I decided to leave the inconvenience and the fear behind. At least I had done it, I could now honourably withdraw.

Not so easy when it's your way of life. Even if you didn't actually choose it but it had hold on you. What possible alternatives could there be? Coal mining?

Frankly it is a miracle that I had managed to survive for so long - about six years - lugging this problem around. I had only been out of work once in all that time, and had managed to obtain several positions although lack of experience didn't always help me make the correct choice.

Of course, my fear was something that I never discussed with anybody and in some way didn't even think about it myself.

I've heard it said that in order to achieve success, you have to leave your comfort zone. Well, there were days I frankly couldn't manage it and days where I coaxed myself through the figurative and also actual doorways of potential customers.

My opportunity with Muzak was one of those big moments in my life. As well as a terrific company car, the firm seemed to be something a little better than most of the previous ones I had worked for.

The sales were divided into two separate divisions, work area, where we sold background music and sound systems to premises where people were at work; and then there was the public area, which was basically pubs, clubs and restaurants.

It was a high-ticket item with a five-year contract and sales were extremely slow. The firm had gone through several metamorphoses. At one time they even had a couple of knights on the team in order to attract the attention of the higher echelons of society.

They had tried everything to promote the idea of background music and they did have some serious competition in the public area. But there were not exactly hoards of salesmen roaming around selling to factories and offices.

It was also not one of those products where you had any chance just walking into a company and hoping to sell the idea right off the bat. So it seemed my bête noire of cold calling was unlikely to raise its head.

I managed to cling on to the job for a year. I had sold about three deals in that time and that was three more than a number of my colleagues. But the company naturally wanted a lot more.

In order to achieve some increase, they decided to recruit a couple of professional sales managers to the firm, and after all the usual rumours and innuendos, two were selected.

The new public area sales manager seemed very like the original type of man Muzak had always hired. He was a very nice fellow, who had expensive suits and always tucked a handkerchief in his sleeve.

He had been a POW with the Japanese and had a mangled hand to prove it. He seemed a little like a Hurrah Harry, but he did a good job for a long time with them.

The work area sales manager was something of a secret however, and nothing about him leaked out.

However, he sent for all the salesmen on a very rainy day. We were summoned to ATV house at Marble Arch and one by one we were sent for into his office.

I remember the occasion very well. I was wearing my best custom tailored suit. It was a brown three-piece with a pink shirt and brown knitted tie. To compliment the entire ensemble were a highly polished pair of brown Chelsea boots.

Bob Aitcheson was standing looking out of the window at the pouring rain. He turned around as I entered. He said: "Lovely day for cold calling!" Oh boy!

"In fact Summons, this is not a good day for it. It's best to do it when it's not raining!"

I was somewhat upset at the tone and the man was definitely a little intimidating.

I found out later that he had come from a company whose reputation was rather tarnished. They were management consultants who were known to force people into deals that were too expensive and from which there was no escape.

He was around fifty; about six feet tall, with a dark charcoal grey suit, white shirt and dark tie. He was obviously an ex-military man, and wouldn't you know it he had a slightly mangled hand like the public area fellow. Apart from that slight deformity they were as different as chalk and cheese.

Continuing his monologue as he left the window and sat down he said. "And you can cold call this product too you know, Summons. They've said it can't be done, but I know otherwise. We're going to show them how to do it." Like I said before, Oh boy!

"Now I've looked at your record and I think there's a remote possibility that we can turn you into an effective salesman of this product, if you're prepared to work with me. Up to now there's been too much negotiating and not enough selling! What do you say?"

Of course, I replied positively while inwardly thinking how best I could escape this somewhat scary person.

"Right then, to begin with we're going out to cold call and I'll show you how it's done. We'll meet on Wednesday at 9:00. But when we do you'll wear a dark suit, a white shirt and a dark tie. Also black shoes. Frankly, Summons, if you wear that you won't upset anybody, and at this stage I don't think you can afford to take that chance, do you?"

I mumbled something and after shaking hands, I left the office with my head a little wobbly. Who the hell was this guy and what was all this nonsense about cold calling?

It was a few days before the allotted date and it was noticeable that in that time, a number of my colleagues no longer turned up at their desks. It seems a big shake up was going on and lots of people were let go. Also a couple of the men knew better than to tangle with the new sales manager, and just gave up the ghost and left of their own accord.

But there was something about Aitcheson, and I did as asked and met him on the outskirts of Reading, Berks as agreed.

We drove in his car to a large seed merchant. Not exactly high on the list of potential customers I would have thought. "This'll do," he said.

We got out of the car and I reached behind the seat for my briefcase, which contained all the brochures and paperwork about the services and products we offered.

Aitcheson go out and retrieved his bowler hat (derby) and a rolled umbrella. Nothing else. He was swathed in very dark grey suite and a brilliant white shirt and dark tie, with highly polished black business shoes.

He looked at me standing there with my briefcase and said, "Put that back in the car, we don't want to look like salesmen, for God's sake!"

I did as asked and followed him as he strode purposely into the reception area. "Let me do the talking," he said. "Don't say anything."

I rather hung behind him as he removed his bowler hat and with what I can only describe as a somewhat threatening gesture placed his umbrella across the receptionist's desk. "My name's Aitcheson, I'd like to make an appointment to see your managing director. What is his name please?"

After the umbrella gesture, the receptionist was sitting well back and spoke the name somewhat reverently. "Mr Jackson, Sir."

"Would you please tell Mr. Jackson's secretary that I'm here and I would like to make an appointment."

"I think Mr. Jackson's in a meeting at the moment, Sir."

"I'm sorry, I can't see him now I'm far too busy, hence my wish to make an appointment, please let his secretary know I'm here."

With that Aitcheson removed his umbrella, turned away and indicated we should move to another area of reception. The receptionist looked a little flummoxed but eventually picked up her phone. Aitcheson stood at ease. I watched in awe.

I was more flummoxed than the girl. I had never seen such a display of arrogance in my life, and it was all done with that heavy air of authority born of the English officer class.

Once we had moved to a neutral corner and with his back to the receptionist, Aitcheson winked at me and gave me a huge smile. It was hard not to grin back. But I remained poker faced.

The offices were obviously above reception and there was a stone staircase to reach them as well as an elevator. After a few moments, a middle aged woman in a smartly tailored blue suit came down the stairs, high heels clicking, and greeted us. In her hands was a desk diary of the type executives used to keep all their engagements. Aitcheson agreed on a time the next day, gave thanks all around and we walked out of the building.

It was a procedure he had done hundreds of times before without thinking, but I was a changed man - forever!

Perhaps it is best at this moment to look at a little bit of history. These events took place fifty years ago and that's a lot of water under the bridge. Business back then was conducted much as it had been fifty years before that. Not too many changes.

There were no computers, no cell phones, no Internet and no social media. It must be hard for young people to imagine such a world. What ever did people do with all that time they must have had on their hands?

Social mores have altered enormously and also the structure of the work place. Few women were in positions of authority. I'm sure feminists must have kittens just thinking of how repressed their sisters back then must have been.

And yet we had several female members in my family and I don't remember any of them being victimised. The fact is that until the advent of the birth control pill in the early sixties, women could not be relied upon to be there in six months, a year, or a decade. It was very hard to imagine them building a career as they would very likely be married and pregnant and wishing to leave. It's just the way things had always been.

At the time, there were many salesmen on the road. It was a normal way to do business with regular follow ups to existing customers, and calls to prospective ones.

I doubt today you would get very far using Aitcheson's techniques, as over the years barriers have been erected to stop such frontal attacks. To begin with there is now the question of security. A guard house protects even the reception area of a major business and I doubt Deputy Dawg would be impressed with a tightly furled umbrella and a bowler hat.

Dress too has changed allowing a far more relaxed appearance. I note that back in the UK suits are still very much the norm in London, but is that the case everywhere?

In the US, only the very top people seem to wear suits and so the wheel seems to have come full circle. The bosses dress up and the hoi polloi wear crap. This is progress?

Cold calling I am sure has gone the way of other strange habits consigned to the dark ages. Towards the end of my career I employed a very talented fellow who did nothing but make appointments for a team of half a dozen salesmen.

He would send out letters, and three dimensional marketing pieces designed for senior executives to read. Then he would make follow up phone calls to try and set appointments. He had a full time secretary and it was quite an expensive operation. It was not a job I would have cared for, but he was excellent at it.

None of my sales team had made a cold call at any time in their careers with me.

I did do it out here in the US on a couple of occasions. Once was in Houston at the main electrical company in the center of town. I had a fellow with me who was thinking about becoming an agent when we were still experimenting with such an idea.

He was a fairly tough type of guy who'd been around the business world a fair bit. As an aside he had held a large dinner party for me and about twenty of his friends at his large house on the outskirts of town. I was put at the top of the table and just about the time everyone was seated he came up to me and said: "Would you like to say grace?"

Once again I was indebted to my father and his supreme sacrifice, whereby I had studied Latin for many years. We said grace everyday at school and so it was quite easy to trot out that formula. I bowed my head and said: "Benedictus, Benedicat!" And proceeded to tuck in. "Is that it?" Someone asked. In between bites, I said, "Yup, that's it!"

To this day I've never quite figured out whether he had done it to throw me off course, or he just assumed I would be able to say it. Very few Brits could say it in any language, as it's not a part of life there.

On that visit, he and I were walking down one of the main streets in the center of the city and I happened to notice this huge building we were approaching. I asked him what it was and he told me it was the Texas Electrical Company or some such title. I asked him if they would make a good prospect for our services. He said they would be the very best.

I said that we should have a go and see if we could get in there. He balked a bit at such an approach, so I said, it won't take long, let's go inside.

Now these were pre-security and pre-paranoia days and so there was a receptionist at the desk. "What's the name of your computer manager, please?" Now I have to say that the English accent has always been a huge benefit as it seems to transfix a lot of Americans. Also in the south, they are naturally polite. She told me the name and I said would you be so kind as to call his office and tell him I would like to make an appointment for tomorrow. I gave her my card, she made the call.

I was quite surprised when the answer came back that we could go on up. I said I was very sorry but we couldn't see him to day as we were very busy, but some time tomorrow we'd like to talk to him

Back came the reply that ten o'clock would work for him. I said we'd be back and left the building.

Once we were outside, my contact said he'd never seen anything like it except with IBM who also had the same degree of arrogance. It was great, but wasn't I flying out first thing in the morning. I said yes, I was, but he wasn't! Now he had to bone up on the products!

But to return to Bob Aitcheson. Once we were in the sanctity of the seed merchant's car park he asked me what I thought. I said exactly what was in my head: "It was bloody marvellous!"

I also added that I thought it had a lot to do with the bowler hat. He laughed and said that it was a prop and it helped. "You see, Trevor, only officers, senior executives or building foremen wear bowler hats, and I hope they don't think I'm a foreman!"

I agreed it most unlikely that such a mistake would be made.

We made a number of similar calls that day, mostly to unlikely clients for our particular services; it was just his way of teaching me this little technique.

At the end of the day he asked me if I would like to try it out myself. I was pretty pumped up and said I'd actually like to have a go.

I think we called on a regular company providing some type of clerical service, like temps, and I did exactly what I had seen done earlier, minus the hat and umbrella of course.

To my surprise, once the receptionist made the call a door opened after a few minutes and a man came out. "I'm the managing director, what can I do for you?"

Well, that hadn't happened before, but at least after a year, I was pretty fluent with Muzak's story and immediately went into it.

I think it impressed Aitcheson as he stood silently while I explained the advantages of background music in a clerical setting and how Muzak used the stimulations of music to increase productivity.

Unfortunately this company was really very small with most of its staff outside, so we didn't get very far. But it was quite a good learning experience for both of us.

Aitcheson was an old fashioned sales manager. He believed his place was out with his salesmen, and not sitting in some office pouring over statistics and expense sheets. He told me once that it was very easy to spot any man who was fiddling his expenses. "You simply line up all the sheets and the one whose fiddling stands out like a boil on a baby's bum!"

I always remembered that too and put it into practise when I rose up through the ranks: I also repeated this sage advice, hoping it was as effective for my charges as Aitcheson's advice was to me. I never tried fiddling expenses!

Every week, Aitcheson would leave for the north to look after his other salesmen, this left his office empty and he suggested that I use it. The firm had closed its Oxford Street premises and all the southern salesmen were given desks in Willesden where the engineering department operated.

Now I had no problem with the engineers, in fact I was quite fond of a number of them, but Willesden? Puhlease!

I'm a little ashamed that I never once set foot in this new office. After all everyone else did, but the prospect of sitting in Aitcheson's

West End office overlooking Marble Arch with access to all the nice pubs and restaurants was too good and for three weeks out of the four, I stayed there.

By this time, I was having some exciting success. Now that my confidence had been dragged out of me, and I didn't feel scared most of the time, I became a new man.

I think Aitcheson was quite pleased with his prodigy, as we would talk for long periods on the phone discussing various tactics for landing sales.

A part of this was also his offer that if I managed to close some particular deals by a certain time, he would buy me a bowler hat, as I was so certain it was a talisman that would work for me.

As I achieved this sales goal I went along to Simpson's of Piccadilly and bought a grey bowler, and it became a trade mark for me for several years.

A Muzak sale took some time – Perhaps three or four months. There were surveys and contracts and frankly it needed some skill to steer the entire process through while not letting the contact get wobbly if things took a poor turn.

I seemed to have a natural aptitude for the process, and kept a list with me at all times of those deals that could close in the foreseeable future.

But Bob Aitcheson was not to last very long however. He was dismissed about six months into his tenure with Muzak. I think he was far too abrasive, and being away from his office for such lengths he couldn't protect his turf. I never found out why he was dismissed, and I was sorry he went as we had become fast friends and I rather missed him.

I heard that within a matter of a few weeks, he had joined our competition – Reditune. They sold machines for pubs, clubs and restaurants, and had a decent business, but they were definitely down market. I'm sure Aitcheson didn't care. I didn't hear of what happened to him for a long time.

Except one day seven years later I was walking along Putney High Street about lunchtime. A bus stopped and down jumped the man himself, almost bumping into me.

For a moment I didn't recognise him. Still the same dark suit, white shirt and dark tie, with polished black shoes, but the entire ensemble looking a little the worse for wear.

"Mr. Aitcheson?" I asked. It's funny, but I never called him Bob in all the time I knew him; although he always called me Trevor. "How are you?" It took a moment for him to recognise me, it had been quite a long time and I think I had changed quite a bit as well.

"It's Trevor," he said, and stood beside me on the pavement. He was older of course, as well, and the years had not been too kind to him. He must have been about 55 or 60 by then I guess, but I never really knew.

"Can I get you a drink?" I asked him, and he declined on the grounds that he was on his way to an appointment – (By bus, I asked myself?)

"I'd like a word with you, though," I said. "I'd like to thank you for what you did for me. You see I was really struggling with a problem of innate shyness and had no idea of how to cure it.

"I've just come off a business trip to Japan, the USA, and also Holland and Spain. I'm the sales director of a good company and what you taught me helped me overcome a fear of prospecting and allowed me to use my talents. I couldn't have done it without your help. You opened the door for me."

He looked a little askance at this outburst, and also a little embarrassed. He said that he was delighted that he'd been able to help, and hoped we'd meet up again when he had more time. We shook hands and off he went. I never saw him again.

Thinking back on this street side meeting, I realised that what I'd said to him was not as important to him as it was to me. Bob Aitcheson was like a great number of men from that generation. He had been in the army as a major – his injury to his wrist was from a bullet received in the Ardennes, although he never dwelt on it. As an officer, he was obliged to help any of his men if they needed it.

When he demobbed, he went into sales as many of them did, and he still clung to the same code of conduct.

I'm sure over the years he had helped many young salesmen who like me lacked confidence. He had a system that he had honed and he merely put that into place with me, having felt that it was worth his time. This guidance was something he did naturally, and I suspect he didn't feel too much about it, although I'm sure he was pleased and rewarded me with the bowler hat, and the use of his office.

But sadly Bob Aitcheson was what was called rather harshly a "one-trick pony," although he certainly taught me that trick and opened up my potential.

Was this a case of luck in meeting him, and it helping me towards that charmed life? I guess as much as any influential person in any life it must have been.

> *Leadership is giving out far more than one expects in direct return. The rewards are intangible, yet priceless.*
> — *T Jay Taylor*

Chapter Six

SALES

A salesman, like the storage battery in your car, is constantly discharging energy. Unless he is recharged at frequent intervals he soon runs dry. This is one of the greatest responsibilities of sales leadership.
— R.H. Grant

Sales are contingent upon the attitude of the salesman, not the attitude of the prospect.
— W. Clement Stone

Having spent 40 years in sales, it may come as a surprise to find that I don't dwell on a long list of sales for which I was responsible – a type of Hall of Fame. The fact is though that all sales however large or small are merely a series of successful relationships.

They may be as short as convincing a shopkeeper to give Scotch Tape a try in his already overcrowded business, or as long as the difficult process of converting a large business from manual labor to Optical Character Recognition.

Salesmen (and women) are often given a poor reputation as in some cases they are seen as people who convince others against their will to part with their (or their company's) resources.

Although that might on the surface appear the case, it is more likely that the salesman is merely the instrument that helps the buyer to arrive at an informed and correct decision. Often this is done against the wishes of colleagues and sometimes even against the wishes of the salesman's own company.

I remember on one occasion having to convince my firm that having dollar signs on computerized accounting equipment was not helping anyone. British accountants for some strange reasons prefer the pound sign! I was met by the factory manager with the remark: "Why can't you people sell what we've already got!" The redesign took only a few hours and solved the annoying problem once and for all.

It would be wrong to say that up until my timely meeting with Bob Aitcheson, I had learned nothing from the ten years of experience I had gained from kicking unsuccessfully around the business world.

I remember hearing one American executive say that ten years experience was truly nothing more than one year multiplied by ten, which I think is merely parsing things a little.

But my problem was only at the very start of things in the sales cycle; once I'd passed that "trepidatious" first step I was usually fine and had all the confidence in the world.

There was one momentous occasion with 3M when the fears of the opening were so great I couldn't face doing anything for two whole days. I cowered in various places like book shops or, forgive me, the cinema, nursing my embarrassing complaint.

Having eventually to produce the dreaded weekly report and now with a three-day back fall to make up, I had to face my demons and just get on with it. If only it were that easy every day, but fear of another pink slip outdid my usual terrors.

I started out early that morning and in a few hours had done rather well. I pushed on through the lunch hour. By mid afternoon high on success and Snickers bars or the equivalent, I realised that I was about to pass a company record that was always being held out to us. The figures today mean nothing but by five-thirty, when all respectable salesmen should be at home watching the news, I was within sight of this remarkable goal.

I actually turned in an eleven-hour day with large amounts in the sales record book. I felt rejuvenated and only slightly let down by the realisation that I had to divide the total by three to make up for my two previous days absence.

Also if Garth Jesamine, my sales manager at 3M had ever known what a producer he had on his hands he would never have forgotten it and been on my case all the time. I had to accept that this was a private affair and was never to be disclosed.

Unrealistic goals are the bane of many a salesman.

When at Muzak and winning a lunch from the then sales manager, I suggested a concept to him that had always rather bothered me.

"Suppose I came in every Monday morning with a fortnight's business, clean and signed," I said to him. "But you knew that I had a set of expensive golf clubs in the car and sported a year round tan. Also I could never be reached in business hours. It was obvious that I was not working much but just seemed able to produce twice as much as anybody else. How would you feel about that?"

I wasn't quite at that level but I was doing pretty well and outpacing the rest of the sales force. Hence the lunch.

I won't give the man's name, but his reply was all I expected it to be. "Well, Trevor," he said in his acquired mid-Atlantic accent, "it would be my duty to encourage you to put in a regular effort to capitalise on your ability."

I smiled and inwardly thought: "Bollocks!"

This man was one of a type; usually underweight, excessively hard working and prematurely bald. I don't know why but lack of hirsuteness always seemed to be the case with these types. He was about 40 and most days would dash off clutching his well worn sports bag to spend his lunch hour swimming many lengths of the local pool before returning to the office sweaty and pink.

He professed to only sleeping four hours a night as he had so much work to do, and was constantly restless.

One day during his lunch hour, one of my colleagues happened to visit the local squash club for a couple of games with a friend. He was walking along the corridor and looked into what he thought was an empty court, only to see this infamous over-active sales manager fast asleep curled up on his gym bag.

Back then in the sixties this self-promotion of over-activity was not the way to get on in English business, and the sales manager didn't last long after that episode.

But you can learn from negative lessons as well as positive ones.

Muzak was one of those products that had to be sold using a demonstration. It was a well tried method of getting the prospect out of his office onto your ground; all the while allowing him to see the service in full operation with happy smiling faces of relaxed and highly productive employees.

I had joined the firm with another much older salesman called Andrew. He was extremely distinguished looking and always completed the Daily Telegraph crossword puzzle.

He never went out of the office if he could help it, and hardly ever produced the regular weekly list of potential clients that was required by management.

Andrew had been around the block a lot and knew that most of this prospecting effort was a total waste of time and he had no desire to do any of it. He watched as the rest of us spun our wheels in a fruitless search for business. He stayed close by the phone waiting for the day that one phone call came in and he would be on it, like a bromlikite.

I personally don't know what a bromlikite is but my father was always saying it so it must be true.

There was one occasion when Andrew happened to be in the restroom and I was sitting at my desk when a call came in. It was a genuine enquiry, and I jumped on it immediately. I didn't tell Andrew but when I eventually converted it to an order of some size he was furious when he found out about the source. I hadn't poached it as we didn't have set territories; just a sort of melee. Andrew however really believed that any incoming enquiry was rightfully his.

But his experience did teach me one thing, as before the evidence of my stealing what he genuinely considered to be his inquiry, we were quite good friends and he talked to me a lot about his experiences.

One day he came in from doing a demonstration. He was looking pleased with himself.

I asked him about the situation. He had been talking for some time to a shirt manufacturer in the East End of London.

I asked him how the "dem" went, and he said it was great. "Where did you take him?" I asked.

"Oh I took them to London Finance," he said.

"But that's in the city; it's an office isn't it? Why did you take a factory manager there instead of the meat pie factory?"

The meat pie factory was a well known plum industrial account in the East End and was much spoken of and boasted about by management.

He just smiled and said he preferred the office one. I thought he was crazy.

Soon it came to be my turn to take a potential client out. It was a furniture factory not far from the meat pie factory - perfect.

On the allotted day, I collected my prospective client from his office and drove the mile or two to the large industrial building where these pies were made.

As we exited the car, there was a rather unpleasant odour of meat extract covering the entire atmosphere. We entered the building and the receptionist told us to help ourselves and showed us the door to the factory entrance.

Now I can assure you that if the odour was bad the sight of stewed meat in great metal canisters was far far worse. Slopping around in gravy and wearing rubber boots, the workers didn't seem to be enjoying their work at all. Furthermore there was not a whisper of the type of music likely to sooth their savage breasts.

I excused myself and went back to reception and asked the woman where the music rack was located – it was behind her in a small room. I immediately located the on/off switch and turned it on.

Returning to the factory floor, my prospect had wandered around to where the pastry side of the pie business was snaking around the edges of a large conveyor belt. It was exceedingly unappetising, but the music was at least now audible and I hoped doing its job.

We made the mistake of asking a couple of the girls nearby what they though of the music that was playing and they were rather forceful in their views. "Bloody awful," was the answer, "we always turn the bloody stuff off!" Pretty much game, set and match! The drive back was very dismal and the suggestion that I get back with him probably sounded rather insincere. I think he felt rather sorry for me.

I mentioned the disastrous events to Andrew who merely smiled and leaned back in his well worn chair. "Didn't you check it out beforehand?" He asked. I replied that as it was so well spoken of by our management, I assumed it was a wonderful place to go. His smile broadened. "Well, now you know. Never take anyone to a place you don't know intimately. Also you need to talk to all the people you're likely to ask."

He then told me that in spite of seeming a poor match, his visit to an attractive office for a shirt manufacturer was done in the full understanding of the golden rule of all demonstrations. Take them out to have a nice experience, and to a place that makes them want to be a little like that for their own businesses.

Back then most British companies didn't spend money on making their places pretty. Air conditioning and potted plants were not the order of the day, but nice pictures on the walls and a pleasant atmosphere were nonetheless to make their way in. They were a sight better than the smell of meat and snaking carpets of grey pastry.

I learned a great deal from that experience and I can still see the horror of the insides of such a place to this day.

I didn't touch a meat pie for months afterwards.

Sometime after this sorry event, I read a book about American senior salesmen. In it their practises were explained and the incredible amount of care they took with outings for potential and existing clients.

It was never too much trouble to visit say, the restaurant where you intended to have lunch. Here you'd meet the maitre d' and point out the table where you would prefer to be sat and look at the menu and meet the waiter who would serve you. Having acquired a potential client, you don't just turn up to a place and hope for the best. I had certainly learned that lesson in spades.

But it wasn't always possible to do this research, particularly if the "dem" had to be done abroad.

During my three year sojourn away from the keyboard training business, I was involved in OCR. Optical Character Recognition was and for all I know still is an exact science. It's most acceptable form is the reading of machine printed fonts like checks and receipts.

My position was outside banking and government agencies and the pickings were few. However I had managed to dig up a rather unique and unknown company located just to the south of Gatwick airport in Surrey.

The business was built on the need of casual building contractors to have an annual vacation. These men wandered from site to site and often due to the temporary nature of their work, they didn't have a way to build up the credit for an annual holiday.

A system was devised back in the forties, I think it was, where companies who employed such labor, would provide a stamp every week to each of these men. Such stamps, similar to postage stamps, would be stuck in a book to be redeemed after a year for the cash needed to pay for a vacation.

Over the years the value of the stamps had increased greatly making the theft of them a target for ill-intentioned.

The collection of books and the counting of the stamps was very labor intensive and was all done by hand. Just imagine if such work could be done by machine and also such a machine could not only count the stamps, but calculate the value as there was a division for those under 18 and those over.

Having unearthed this opportunity, it was my job to make it happen with instructions to our factory, located in deepest Pennsylvania as well as guiding the client towards stamp design that was machine readable.

As many of the stamp stickers were out on rainy, windy building sites, stamps sometimes were stuck in upside down or sideways, and sometimes after several attempts had Scotch tape to hold them in. Could we read those? And could we read every stamp's serial number? And could we tally it all up and assign each stamp to each contractor? The list went on.

After several months working on the answers to these questions and after many weeks of people sticking stamps in books in every way imaginable, we had several suitcases of them ready to go to the factory for a big demonstration.

On reflection, perhaps I should have insisted on several of these books being sent out ahead of time. But the factory was quite confident and in fact said that the various tasks set them were quite simple ones. Also time was of the essence as the client and my company were anxious to complete this sale.

Flights were booked and Mrs. "L" and her general manager as well as my assistant Simon and I were ready to throw ourselves into a day of total success and glory to the sound of cheers from every compass point.

I had been warned that the factory was not an attractive place to visit – it had in fact been an old cinema. It was quite serviceable, but there was no way to avoid its somewhat decrepit looks.

I had arrived a couple of days earlier and checked out the site and the impression was as reported; this place looked grim, but once inside things took on a more pleasant appearance. At least there was no meat or odour either.

On the day of the dem, I drove the five of us, complete with heavy and loaded suitcases of cards to the factory. I drove up the road and in rather a hurry swung into the parking lot with no warning and parked as close as I could to the actual building, thereby hiding the full view of the place.

Mrs. L had never been to the States before and was all of a twitter. She was a lady of great charm but Irish irascibility so we all had better look out. The GM as he was called was a nice fellow who had totally bought into the great savings that could be had by going the OCR route. We just had to pull off the dem successfully and all would be well.

The machine was located on the second floor in a well lit room with several technical types hanging around, all with sufficiently obsequious expressions and as many cups of coffee and cookies as our hearts desired. The president too was on hand to give the formal greeting and to be available if such was necessary.

Everyone had been primed to do their bit and I was very pleased with the way things had gone so far.

We loaded up the hopper with many hundreds of cards. The machine sat awaiting the go command; the computer consul was given final instructions to calculate the various fields, and then in a grand gesture, Mrs, L pressed the red button.

All went well for a few seconds. Then there was a distressing grinding sound and a little wisp of grey smoke came out of the side of the machine. Then the noise grew and a few cards came out of the exit. They were missing several stamps, and were bent as well. The machine stopped with a lurch.

I had visions of the meat pie factory all over again. Mrs. L was the first to react. "Get the president up here immediately," she spat. We offered calming cups of coffee, but she was not to be calmed. Eventually El Presidente arrived and was full of apologies and generally did a fine job of quieting everyone down. He summoned the chief engineer who appeared complete in long tan coat with instruments in his top pocket.

Unfortunately like so many of his breed his demeanor was very negative, and he had that sort of "I told them this just wouldn't work," look on his face.

We retired for an early lunch and met back up again to hear the fate of our experiment. It would take at least two weeks to get everything working right, but we were not to be worried as it was a relatively simple thing to do. Now we had enough cards to work with.

We eventually flew back to London, and a month later an impressive enough dem was held to allow the deal to go through. All the calculations were correct and OCR was brought to the Surrey countryside.

Working for these early companies also taught me several things about management. From the age of about 33 I was no longer just a salesman, I had to look after, guide and coach salesmen (and women.)

Muzak had been a very generous employer and I brought that philosophy to Keyboard Training as well.

I realised that good salesmen are a true asset to any company and they are not to be treated with disdain. If you've got a good team then it is up to you to nurture them and encourage them to stay.

I always tried to pay them a little more than they would hope to receive elsewhere, and also to tell them not to work so hard that their thinking process would be affected.

Nearly all statistics on business show the 80/20 rule has not changed much in my career. That is that 80 percent is produced by 20 percent of the sales force. Also I have found the reverse to be true, that 80 percent of the work is wasted and only 20 percent is actually productive.

I was very successful in weeding out the effort that was useless and I have always encouraged my teams to work that way. One thing you can say however is that you have to think a lot about the various deals that you have in your hopper, and keep on trying to move them along and improve them.

I must have been OK at this as although I have found it necessary to dismiss staff from time to time, I never had one leave me on their own wishes.

An old colleague called me the other day to just talk about the old times and how people were doing. He's a bit younger than me and still in corporate life. He moaned about how difficult things seemed to be these days and how long orders took to finalise.

I sympathised with him as towards the end of my corporate life, I was feeling the same pressure – things just took so long.

I think the final confirmation of how tough it was going to be occurred when I was completing a deal in Columbus, Ohio. Just before we agreed, one more meeting was requested. To my horror 16 people were present and we had to go through the entire business again.

Naturally a few points were raised, as anyone at the table seemed to have the authority to raise an objection while at the same time they had no authority to agree to our terms.

Unfortunately I am convinced this is in many ways due to the enormous number of women in middle and sometimes higher management positions.

Whereas men used to be lauded for making quick decisions and gained the reputation as fire-breathers, women have not been encouraged to behave so. They are natural consensus builders and feel vulnerable making decisions that might come back to haunt them.

After so long now in these positions men have seen how it's done and have copied this behaviour. No doubt it has benefited business with this caution, but for those of us in sales it's been a tough time. I'm glad I'm out of it!

> *Kites rise highest against the wind, not with it.*
> — *Winston Churchill*

Chapter Seven

AMERICA I

"[Americans] were, for one thing, so smitten with the idea of progress that they invented things without having any idea whether those things would be of any use."
— *Bill Bryson*

America has never quite forgiven Europe for having been discovered somewhat earlier in history than itself.
— *Oscar Wilde*

Growing up in post war Britain must have been pretty depressing. Of course, at the time, none of us kids knew anything different; we'd lived through the bombings, the blackouts, and of course, the rationing.

I was lucky in that although my father's work in the aircraft industry meant he was often posted close to targets for the Luftwaffe – our first home was bombed out when I was a baby – we never received a direct hit.

We lived in a block of flats in Brighton for a time and that was opposite a searchlight and ack-ack battery. Unfortunately, searchlights were among the primary targets for any accompanying fighters on a bombing run, but I guess Brighton didn't offer much of a place to drop expensive bombs, unless some German didn't like piers of which the famous seaside town had two.

The ration when compared to today's full super-markets is remarkable in its paucity. One egg a week, two ounces of butter, two ounces of cheese eight ounces of sugar, and one pound of meat was the entire amount allowed by the authorities for one person.

Britain is an island and can't completely sustain itself and with the Battle of the Atlantic in full swing, it's a miracle that the US ships managed to get through at all. It was two or three years before the Allies could protect the convoys coming from the well stocked food baskets of the American mid-west.

We were allowed to grow our own food, and vegetables were widely available, as were horse meat and whale meat shops.

My mother tried us on whale meat sausages a couple of times; they were pretty nasty, but she drew the line at horse meat.

There were such things as dried eggs, which were yellow powder, and could be scrambled or made into omelettes; I don't think they tasted like real eggs at all. Also a product called POM was a form of dried and powdered potato. Again like the dried eggs, it seemed to have a funny aftertaste.

There was the rumoured "black market," of course, where pretty much anything could be had for the right price. There were whispers of petrol coupons being exchanged for steaks, and steaks being exchanged for petrol coupons. I was too young to understand such whispers.

Fruit was almost impossible to obtain, except for apples which were constantly foisted on us. To this day, I can't say I'm particularly fond of them and rarely eat them.

Oranges and other exotic fruits were virtually impossible to find, and for the first six years of my life I thought a banana was about three inches long, half an inch thick and brown. It was a dried banana.

Milk food for babies was called National Dried Milk and continued to be a staple well into the seventies. It was what passed for today's formula.

And yet, studies have shown that the ration was surprisingly effective and very healthy. Maybe a jump start on the current vegan craze.

Sweets were on ration until 1953, eight years after the war ended. The ration was removed once before then in 1950, and the public went so crazy queuing that they had to put them back on in a couple of days. Such is the draw of sugar.

Country people of course, managed to do quite well, knowing as they did how to catch rabbits and hares and also live off the land. There were fewer of them of course, too. Lots of them kept chickens and therefore knew how to collect eggs

To this day a roast chicken still seems something of a treat although we probably have one every ten days or so. Mushrooms too were not available except in those expensive shops where my poor mother's limited ration card and limited funds reduced her shopping efforts to keep her family fed.

Clothing was rationed. Every piece was labelled with a small "utility" tag. This was two black circles about the size of a dime with a quarter of the piece cut out of each side.

On the face of it this early childhood may look to be the antithesis of a charmed existence, and yet, as with us all in the struggle against the Nazi foe, the difficulty of life in general pulled us all closer together.

Recently on the evening of the tragedy of 9/11 we made a trip to the local bar, and it was obvious that even such a localised attack on the other side of the continent had the effect of drawing together a highly disparate population; also confirming the feeling was the tremendous number of Stars and Stripes on display for weeks afterwards. Such is how people behave in a crisis.

Every evening, my parents would get close to the radio, to listen to the news. Afterwards my father would fiddle with the dial and change to the BBC broadcast to the Continent. Here messages would be sent to resistance groups in all the occupied countries. If found to be receiving these, individuals there would be taken by the Gestapo never to return – a high price to pay for such resistance.

We performed our own small act of rebellion. My father would sometimes tune into Lord Haw Haw as he was called. This man, William Joyce, was a former Irishman who had turned himself in to the Germans to help with their propaganda. Most nights he would begin his broadcast with his recognisable nasal snarl: Jairmany calling! Jairmany calling!

He would then begin to list the damage we Brits were suffering, and naming people who had been killed and the relatives who were mourning them. It used to drive my father nuts to hear his jeering tones, and he was always asking: How does he know all this stuff?

To a "straight up and down man" like my father it was incomprehensible that English people could actually be passing information on to the Germans.

Listening to his broadcasts was frowned upon by the authorities, but no one was ever dragged away to cold damp cells that I remember.

Joyce was captured in 1945 when the Allies overran Berlin. He was hanged in Wandsworth Jail nine months later, being the penultimate person to be so executed for a crime other than murder. On the first of May of that year, he gave his last broadcast. By the sound of him, he'd been dipping into the schnapps supply rather enthusiastically.

You can hear his broadcasts today by looking them up on You Tube – a marvellous invention.

As England slowly began to clear away the bomb damage from its streets and people started to live life again we boys began to hear of how life was in other places.

In our short time on earth we had been bombarded by our elders' talk of life "before the war;" frankly it drove us mad, as we had no idea what this paradisiacal life could be like. On railway stations there were machines that once took coins and gave out chocolate. That of course was "before the war." These mysterious relics reminded us all that there had been a better time, but it was impossible to imagine – and chocolate? That was almost as impossible to imagine as the machine that provided it.

There were empty cigarette machines too, but they were also totally empty, but of course, totally full "before the war!" How funny that having won the peace, in a few decades such machines would be banned from our lives, in order to protect us. We are so lucky!

Slowly though, life began to normalise, or so we thought. We had a long way to go. There were TV's in some of the rich people's houses, and I myself first saw the medium when the then Princess Elizabeth married Philip, in 1947. The novelty of the occasion soon wore thin to two eight year olds. My friend called House, had a most wonderful attic where he actually had a trapeze from which we could swing.

It was 1953, when Princess Elizabeth was now queen and was to be crowned that most of us who could afford it, obtained a TV to watch the ceremony.

Until then America was some far distant place where American's came from. Most middle class people had memories of their presence during the war. When they were to be sent Winston Churchill remarked that they were: over-paid, over-dressed, over-sexed and over here! It was a view shared by many.

I didn't come into contact with any Americans that I was aware of during the war. Perhaps we were never located near them. My mother had few opinions about them, but my father took the aforementioned attitude as well as adding: "They'll probably be OK in a few hundred years."

I think he genuinely believed that for a nation to work it had to be around for at least a thousand years.

A few magazines circulated at the end of the 40's and into the 50's. There must have been some little bump in the family's fortunes as we all of a sudden began to receive the National Geographic Magazine every month.

It came from America and was full of all kinds of stuff. The contents I used to look for however were the advertisements. What things they had over there. TV's with round screens, washing machines – my mother was still washing everything by hand and drying them on a line outside.

There were adverts of trains going through amazing countryside with mountains and lakes – not like the boating lake in Watford's Cassiobury Park, which spent most of its time drained.

The trains were very long and some of the coaches had glass roofs with people sitting inside staring out at the remarkable scenery. This was a magical place it seemed to my pre-teen eyes.

Then there were the ads for cars. Long and sleek and in the brightest colors. Ours were still mostly in black or dark green or blue. I don't think my dad took the magazine for more than a year, but it was enough time to light a fire deep in me.

Once we had our first television set for the coronation in 1953, the lids were permanently lifted from most of our eyes. We had American programs and although everybody pretended to look down their noses at them, we all watched.

By the time I was getting out of my teens, programs such as Route 66 were a regular weekly series that we lads were glued to. Buz and Tod's adventures across the country taking jobs where they could and having adventures; these were so far away from our damp lives as to be almost the stuff of fantasy. Yet we knew that's how Americans lived.

Into my twenties with a wife and new baby, the programs if anything became better. Our weather continued in its English way, while golfers in California strode around emerald green courses, in short sleeves with the sparkling Pacific as a backdrop, while we had to put another lump of coal on the fire. It was quite a change.

After my "Road to Tarsus," moment with Mr. Aitcheson and I began to find success, I won a little competition in the company which gave us some pretty nice prizes. I was thrilled. Such an aspect of the profession had never been on my radar before.

After Aitcheson left, we were on a big sales competition again. This time it was for two prizes; the first was a trip to New York to attend the international conference; the second was a trip to Munich to look around that operation.

Unfortunately, I was destined to have an operation in early April that year, which was halfway through the length of the competition's timeframe which was to close on the 31st July.

The procedure meant a week's stay in hospital and then at least two weeks convalescence. Such a break of a month meant I did not spend a lot of time thinking about this race to the top of the sales charts.

They weren't kidding. A hernia operation, believe me is not something you can just shrug off. I needed the time in hospital. My father-in-law having arranged a vacation in the South of France very generously suggested I might like to come along to aid in the convalescence.

We flew down to Nice and went to the Hotel des Belles Rives, which was a small hotel in Juan les Pins.

I had never seen anything like it; it was quite the most beautiful place I'd ever been. Let no-one tell you that the South of France is not the very best place for a sunshine and great food holiday.

All thoughts of my potential sales went straight to the back of my head and I revelled in the luxury of this couple of weeks.

The Internet is a dangerous thing! In the process of editing this I had a quick look via Google at the Hotel to see if it was still there some 45 years later. It is and also I found out that it had been the home of author Scott Fitzgerald and his wife Zelda. They may have been long gone when I was there, but it remains clear in my mind as the utmost in luxury.

It was May 1st when I made my way back to my office, which was now permanently at Head Office in Marble Arch.

Everyone was very kind and after a day or two I began to look at how the sales figures were shaping up.

My opposite number on the public area side was a fellow called Ken Faulks. He was a very dedicated salesman and worked extremely hard. It's true that some of his deals were a little shaky, but overall he was a very valued provider for the company. We weren't really rivals as our markets were so totally different. He worked for the man with the handkerchief up his sleeve and now with Bob Aitcheson gone, my boss was Stan Lea.

Stan had been raised in a pub in the Midlands, and had served for the last few months of the war on board a Royal Navy ship. He was the exact opposite of Aitcheson. He read a lot, was interested in all kinds of subjects and had a great love of the English canal system about which he was quite an expert.

He was much more of a coach, and would give small pieces of very valuable advice at times, and once I'd got used to his style, I sought out his opinion.

It seemed that in my absence, Faulks had not set the sky alight. By their nature public area deals were usually a lot smaller than work area, and he'd only been doing his normal with the amounts adding up, but not to a great degree.

I wrote down all the deals I could possibly close before July 31st, and using an average of Faulks forecasts, I could see that with a little tail wind I could get pretty close to him.

With the South of France tan fading from me and the injury now gone, I spent all my time concentrating on my deals and, granted with some luck, I closed all the ones I had planned and also a few extra.

On August 1st, the day after the end of the competition, I was sent for by the MD. He asked me how much I had sold in the six months and I told him to the last shilling – we were still using pounds, shillings and pence, back in those days.

"Do you know how much Ken Faulks has sold?" He asked.

I said at the last count it was a couple of thousand pounds less than my target.

"Well, you may not know then, that he came in this morning with a very big order from Heron Garages, which puts him well over the top."

I was somewhat shocked, also it was obviously not worth pointing out that the competition closed the day before. I stood rather dumbfounded.

"But after such a terrific effort on both your parts, it would be rather cheeseparing to only select one of you for the top prize, so we're going to send you both to New York."

I couldn't remember the word "cheeseparing" being used about me before, but I thanked him very much and said I really would like to go there, as it was a sort of dream for me.

(It should be noted, that the deal which had made Faulks the winner, developed a lot of contractual problems and was eventually cancelled! – Just pointing that out!)

The company were first rate in their treatment of both Faulks and I. They put us up at a very good hotel on Park Avenue and gave us ample spending money. The general manager too came over as well and he also gave me his remaining funds when I told him I wanted to stay a few extra days.

Muzak, or Planned Music Limited as the franchise was called, had always treated their staff in a very generous way, and throughout the rest of my career I tried to emulate them. It wasn't always easy.

The day of departure eventually arrived, and after a long flight on a BOAC 707 we arrived at Kennedy and took a taxi to the hotel. On the way the taxi driver spent the entire time trying to convince his four passengers that he had managed to cram into the cab that after all we would all have had to pay him so it was only right that we did so – the fare should be quadrupled. It didn't work!

As we alighted from the rather hostile atmosphere of the cab outside the hotel, a man was standing holding open the door. As we climbed out to the sidewalk he held his hand out in the accustomed manner for a tip. Foolishly I gave him a coin and he went on his way. He was merely a passing pedestrian who saw a chance to gain a little extra that day. Welcome to New York! Have a nice day!

The atmosphere in the city was electric. The noise, the traffic and the smells of the place gave me a churning gut from the moment I stepped out of the taxi.

New York has perhaps some of the finest restaurants in the world, and yet every time I have been there my appetite seems to vanish; it's the energy of the place that seems to upset me.

We were part of a large international conference that was held by Muzak and all its franchisees. There were several hundred of us there, with a fairly busy schedule. But not so busy that we couldn't get out and see the city.

Faulks was an amicable companion and we enjoyed everything we saw. The conference was held at the Waldorf Astoria on Park Avenue just to the north of the famous Pan Am building. They had only just stopped the helicopter shuttle from Kennedy to its roof a couple of months before as it was considered unsafe. I was rather sorry as I would have liked to have seen the take offs and landings.

The Pan Am building was a bastion of coolness when we walked from our hotel on the west side of Park Avenue to the conference each day. It was like walking into a freezer, from the steaming August weather outside. Boy was it hot! But we loved it.

At night one could hear that characteristic thrump thrump as the taxis rode over the bumps in the streets, and there was the constant sound of horns blowing. I never got tired of the atmosphere.

We took a helicopter tour of the city departing from Pier 14 and flying out towards the East River across the tops of the skyscrapers. It was the first time for me in such a machine and the experience was exhilarating, even though going over the roof with so much air conditioning, the flight was rather bumpy.

Within a few days we were attracting the attention of a number of the larger franchise holders. It was obvious that we were considered important assets and also fair game to poach.

I also could see that whereas salesmen were not too high on the societal scale in the UK, out here, even the president of the entire company called himself their chief salesman,

At the time, most English corporations were run by engineers, accountants and perhaps administrators. If you came out of the ranks of sales, then it would be likely that the PR department would no doubt invent a fancy title from your past to cover up your previous lowly status.

However, out here, salesmen were lauded – at any rate that was the case back in 1969.

I note that today, the US has sadly followed the UK in the attitude about salesmen (and obviously I include women in this craft.) Furthermore, most of them will find it hard to climb the ranks of the executive ladder if they don't have an MBA or something similar. And yet, one truth has never altered: salesmen are the only people bringing any income into the company, while everyone else is spending it!

Shortly after I returned from my New York trip, I spent an afternoon with my next door neighbour. He was a veterinary surgeon who worked in the animal husbandry section of the Ministry of Agriculture.

He asked me what exactly it was that I did. In the fashion of the day, I said I was an area manager – one of the euphemisms often used by salesmen to heighten their status. "Oh, he said, you're a company representative."

I concurred with a slight lowering of the head. He smiled widely and said: "I remember once, when I was young and I was in the north with my old professor. We were staying at some hotel and I happened to notice that there were a great number of young men in the place. They were all very well dressed, and they seemed to be handsome, friendly people.

"I mentioned to my professor that perhaps they were shooting a film there as there were so many attractive young people around." He said to me that they weren't actors, they were company representatives. I replied: "Oh, you mean they're just salesmen."

He took me to one side and said, "You obviously don't understand. These men have all been hand-picked by their companies. The best person to represent a company is the managing director, but he has so many duties he can't do it. These men have all been chosen as the next best thing to go out into the world and be the personal representatives of their managing directors. That's why they look and sound so good; they're the best that can be found."

This coming from an academic was quite a life lesson. It rather staggered me, but frankly it spoke volumes and I have told nearly all the salesmen who have worked for me about it over the years. I hope it's been as inspirational to them as it was to me.

As my time in New York wound down, I had received several tempting offers from various owners of Muzak franchises. I found one of them to be very attractive, the one in Washington D.C. The boss was called Al Smith and he said he would really like me to come out to his city and run a division doing what I was doing in London. By the time I returned to Heathrow, I was hooked. America was for me!

I had only been to New York at this stage, and I wasn't about to make a big change without some knowledge of the area to which I would be moving job, family and Golden Retriever, George.

I therefore cashed in an insurance policy to return to the US on my own dime and see what a position in the nation's capital would be like.

My return trip was about five weeks later on board a short lived aircraft, the VC10. Their slogan was "Try a little VC tenderness!"

I had for some time in the sixties developed a slight fear of flying, but two cross Atlantic flights had cured me of that. It's tough to be scared for five hours when nothing is happening!

The VC10 was called a pilot's plane and it carried me safely across the water back to New York where I had some contacts.

After a couple of days, I travelled down to Washington to meet Al Smith again at his office on K Street, which was to become infamous as the street with all the lobbyists.

He was a short, lively man, with a nice set of premises and as far as I could tell a tremendous potential for work area business. He offered me a decent salary and some expenses to help with my moving. All it needed now was to gain the visa to acquire the green card.

We went to see a baseball game at Robert Kennedy Stadium which was the home of the Washington Senators. Now since gone. I believe the franchise was sold and the team became the Montreal Expos. The Nationals are now the capital's baseball team, and not doing badly either.

It was here that I first came upon my introduction to racism. There's a chapter on this later, but it was at this ball game that I was confronted by it.

We were sitting about halfway up in the seats and a few rows down were a group of very young black children. They were all very well behaved but like all kids jumped about a bit.

Al leaned in to me and said: "They're real cute aren't they? Too bad they have to grow up!"

I was pretty amazed. I had never heard this type of thing before, but managed not to show my feelings in front of my future boss.

We sat in the sun in the afternoon and I developed the fiercest headache I can ever remember. I took it all the way back to New York and swallowed several aspirin before it left me.

Al Smith was as good as his word and also sent me every week, the local paper so I could look at housing and furniture. We looked at passages on the Queen Elizabeth II so we could take George as well.

All the forms for the visa were completed, with photographs and references, and then began the long wait.

I had told my bosses at Planned Music that I had returned to the States and that I had accepted a position. They were extremely gracious about it saying that it was not just the firm's responsibility to pay me in exchange for my time, but also to help me develop as well. It was another lesson, which I tried to put into practice for the rest of my career.

The end of the year slipped by, and phone calls to the embassy about my status were useless.

I have told my American friends that in spite of people running over the border, this is a very tough country to come into legally, and I stress the word legally.

Basically, there are certain preferences that are considered. I was sixth preference. The first preference is being born an American and wanting to reclaim your citizenship. The second is being married to an American, the third is having American parents; fourth is being exceptionally skilled in the arts or the sciences, and five is skilled labor. Mine was unskilled labor – number six, only one from the bottom, number seven. I dread to think how long those poor wretches must wait.

I hung on for thirteen months and of course, after all that time, the concept of moving out of my comfort zone and relocating, had lost a lot of its appeal. Also the new position of becoming sales manager for Keyboard Training Ltd was close.

When the call from the embassy came, I ignored it.

I joined KTL two days later.

Ours is the only country founded on a good idea
— John Gunter

Chapter Eight

AMERICA II

You know what made us the biggest, meanest, Big Mac eating, calorie-counting, world-dominating kick-ass powerhouse country in the history of the human race? The pursuit of happiness. Not happiness. The pursuit!
— *Will Fergusson*

Part of America's genius has always been its ability to absorb newcomers, to forge a national identity out of the disparate lot that arrived on our shores.
— *Barack Obama*

"Mr. Summons. Mr. Trevor Summons!" The voice at the American embassy in Grosvenor Square London W.1 came over the loudspeaker.

It was mid-November 1982, seven months after I had applied again, for a visa to live in the United States and 12 years since I had last done it.

I went up to the window and a smartly dressed man spoke to me. "You have already been granted a visa back in 1970, why are you applying for one again?" I have something of a horror of bureaucrats. They have all the power and a system that has been honed over the years to protect their decisions, right or wrong.

There was nothing for it, with my new family already over in the States I was a trifle vulnerable at this point. Nothing for it but to explain.

"Well, back in 1970 I had been waiting for 13 months for a visa to come and absolutely no way of knowing how long it would take. So I had to turn down the opportunity in Washington D.C. and accept one in London. I'm sorry if it's caused confusion."

"Oh, I quite understand, so you never collected it, then?"

"No, I suppose I should have told someone, but frankly I didn't know who to contact at the time."

"Oh, that's fine then, here's your passports back, and you're in the system now."

I walked out of the embassy feeling a little light headed. I hadn't anticipated any problems and I was rather taken by surprise at the clerk's information. Boy, they keep those records for a long time.

Back then getting the green card process was a little easier than now. In 1982 I had used a lawyer to "walk my documents" though the embassy, and it wasn't necessary for the entire family to apply in person at the USA embassy. Hence the fact that I was on my own. Today, I believe everyone has to be present.

But now that I had the piece of paper in the passport saying that an application had been accepted, not the actual green card itself of course, I was effectively treated (as were the entire family) as if we had the card. It isn't green either by the way!

We were all free to come and go in and out of the country as we liked.

America is a very big country and people with no paperwork exist quite happily and safely without ever leaving its boundaries. But I was too old to start playing those games. It had to be legal or nothing. And fortunately for me, Richard, who was already here, knew a lawyer and how the system worked.

This had been a whirlwind year, and it's almost the stuff of storybooks.

My stint with KTL, had ended in 1979, six and a half years after joining them. We had split the company into one that sold a machine to provide the training, and leaving behind the traditional consultancy team and sales force in a separate company.

I found myself in the very odd situation of being the sales director of two competing forces. It was understood that I would never sell out the other side and they were quite happy working that way. I'm sure nothing in Drucker's or Macgregor's books ever came up with such a strange set of circumstances.

Richard had seen great success with his years in America in the late sixties, and he was driven to create a company with the same amount of prestige as he had then. It remained a dream all the time I worked with him.

Unfortunately I never believed that teaching people keyboard skills could ever be made that large, as the market was never that enthusiastic about the service. A hard fact but true. At least it kept competition away as it was a very tough market to sell to.

In 1978, Richard met a man who had been the CEO of the largest computer company in the UK. He was a personable and effective businessman. After many discussions, Richard invited this man, Russell, to join our company as our CEO. His brief was to bring the company up to the sort of standard where we could go public.

At the time I was flying all over the world keeping the various agencies and franchisees up to standard. I'd been doing it for about three years, and frankly I was getting a little stale.

It also wasn't doing much for my marriage. I was gone for six week journeys and then staying at home for two weeks before going off for another six weeks. The strain on my home life was beginning to show.

After one of my trips, I went into the office to see Russell, at his request. He said that although he wouldn't fire me, he felt that my time at KTL was pretty much done. He felt I would be doing myself a big favour by leaving and going into something where I could exploit my talents.

I was pretty shocked, but over the weekend I realised that what he had said was true. I had made myself partially redundant, and the firm could do without me. I had trained a replacement for my sales management position in the UK, and the franchisees were either going to make it or fold - it happened that they fell about 50/50.

Part of Russell's suggestion was that he'd give me six months salary and also set up an interview with a company he knew and who needed a good sales manager.

I had been earning pretty good money, but as with most English middle class people, there was little opportunity to acquire any "keeping" money. It all went on stuff and of course, England was one of the highest taxed countries in the world.

This was the first time I had ever managed to get my hands on a decent lump and it was a feeling I liked very much.

The company I went to was a disaster. On paper they looked to be ideal, but they were behind the times in technology and were saddled with a factory producing things that nobody wanted. They were also located in one of the most depressing areas of Southern England. They were between the offal factory and the pork pie factory in a small county town, with poor weather. It was my second unfortunate experience with meat pies; and I was batting 0 and 2!

In order to cut back on expenses, the chairman had insisted that half the electric bulbs be taken out which caused a gloomy feeling to add to the generally depressing and smelly atmosphere.

I didn't like the place much to begin with, but the MD was a very decent chap and I got along well with him.

Four weeks into my employment, they fired the MD. Oh boy! A senior manager from the holding company took over duties and he was of the fire-breathing type. Lots of noise, but very little of use.

I'd been around the sales world for quite a while now. I was 40, and at the top of my game. The time was past where I would just stick it out and hope. I knew better than that.

I had used a very good recruiting agency for a few years and knew the boss of the outfit well. One day, scanning the Telegraph I noticed an advert for a company selling optical character recognition equipment. It was also being handled by the recruiters that I knew.

The pay looked great and apart from the fact I knew nothing of the subject, it looked tailor made for me.

I called my contact. "Alan, this company selling OCR, it looks up my street. The place I'm in is horrible, get me out!"

"I already had you tipped for this," he said. "But I wanted to let a little activity pass before I put you forward. Give me a week or two."

As good as his word, Alan, came back to me in a fortnight and said I was to meet the MD of the OCR company later that week. "Try not to screw it up!!!" He said with a laugh.

As it happened it was like leaving a cold bath and getting into a warm shower when I joined OCR Scandata.

They were located in Twickenham and were a first class outfit selling high end OCR machines to the banking industry also the insurance industry and the government.

They had decided that to expand the firm they needed to open a new division and that would be to the Direct Mail and Catalogue business. Plus other industries if I could find them.

It was a fine job with very good pay and I had an assistant who had been doing the job before me. Surprisingly, he wasn't resentful of my taking over his job, and him being demoted.

The first duty was a long day going through all his current negotiations and seeing exactly how much chance we had of closing any sales.

Ian was a nice fellow, with a pleasing air about him. But he wasn't a salesman. OCR Scandata had figured that out. He had a pile of folders abut three feet thick and he truly believed every one of these represented a good chance of a sale.

I sat with him in the conference room and we began to divide up the folders into three piles: the ones that would be worth following up; the ones that had a small chance but not immediately, and the final pile, the ones that were useless.

By lunchtime, there were none in the first pile, a scattered few in the second and a huge lot in the throw out pile.

There are two types of salesmen: grafters and prima donnas. The first are the easiest to manage. They work hard and pursue every lead with equal enthusiasm. The prima donnas have the skill to produce a great deal more, but in the process they are the ones who are likely to cause you the most grief. They overspend, don't tell you where they are going, cause problems internally, and have been know to get women into trouble. But they can be extremely creative. Most companies hate them.

Ian was of the former type. He equated hard work with results and confused his efforts with closing sales. He rarely had done this as his prospect list showed he hadn't a clue which ones would actually turn into customers. We ended up that day with about three potential customers.

After visiting them we only had one, and that turned rancid in a few weeks. There just weren't any bones and none with any meat on them. We had to start from square one.

I reported my findings to the MD and he completely understood our problem.

This is a memoir and not a sales manual and so I shall skip over my progress with this company and simply say that eventually I found one very hot prospect who turned into a good customer, but the time they signed the deal I had left for America and my life had changed once again. At least I had done all the necessary work, they merely had to make sure they didn't screw it up; and they didn't. They were a great outfit and treated me very well.

Now we may be coming to a part of the tale where I have to admit to a huge piece of luck and which perhaps could be said to be responsible for Paul Everest's charge of me having a charmed life.

In late September 1981, I had been gone from KTL for two and a half years. I had managed to earn decent money in the world of sales management and also done a good job for the two companies that had employed me. I felt happy with my efforts. There was a problem.

As I had written earlier, Richard had a dream that he wanted KTL to be bigger and more successful that we had managed to make it.

It was the duty of any company to expand as if it doesn't then it is likely to contract and eventually fall to competition or inactivity.

OCR Scandata was no different. However the way they wanted to do it was by opening up another division. Here was the problem; the direction they wanted to go didn't actually exist.

In KTL's situation, the market didn't exist for any more keyboard training and neither did it for Scandata. They had the banking, insurance and government sectors tied up and they were really the only markets for this very expensive and problem fraught technology.

I was running a division that had virtually no potential. I felt a bit like a kicker on an American football team. I was spending a long time sitting on the bench with few opportunities to use my skills

The company was great with the only problem being that they were owls and I was a lark. I would be in the office at seven most mornings and everyone else would come in about nine-thirty. It didn't affect my business but it was an odd situation.

One Saturday morning, I was feeling a little miserable. My marriage to Veronica had ended a couple of years ago, I was living in a rented house in Littlehampton and although Veronica and I were still very friendly and I saw Michael my son who was then 15 regularly, my life lacked any future.

I decided that I needed a little cheering up and went to The Lamb in Angmering, which had been my "local" since we had moved down from Surrey to Sussex.

I rarely if ever went there at lunchtime, but this day I drove over and went in to the saloon bar as usual.

There was a man, called Peter, whom I recognised standing by the fireplace. He always wore an RAF tie and he was a very decent chap. I bought a pint and went over to him,

We started chatting and in the way of pub ethics I looked around to see who else was there.

I was surprised to see sitting at the bar, a very pretty woman whom I had known some years ago when Veronica and I used to go in early evenings for a drink. She was called Yvonne and as usual she was wearing a wonderful outfit full of color, which was her trademark.

When she used to come in two or three years earlier, it would always be with her husband who was mostly the worse for wear.

I'm sure that nearly everybody who knew him then would agree with my description; a world class, twenty-two carat wanker!

But he was not with her; she seemed to be talking with some other man, so I excused myself from Peter, and went straight over.

Now, I didn't mess about. I put my elbow right next to the man she was with and leaned into speak to her. She was a real quality woman and at my advanced age, there was little point in hanging about.

"Good heavens, how lovely to see you," I said.

"It's great to see you too," she replied with a big smile. She looked lovely but there is no doubt that she looked a little tired.

"I haven't seen you in a long time, what have you been doing?" I asked.

"I'm just about to get divorced," she said. I told her I was already divorced and perhaps we could get together and have dinner one evening.

She said that was a great idea and I said if she gave me her phone number I'd call next day and set it up for the following week.

The guy she was with didn't take a lot of notice of my intrusion, and I ignored him. It turned out his name was Trevor, for heaven's sake!

That evening, Veronica came over to leave Michael with me for a day or two and I took her out for a drink. It was at a hotel on the big grass surround opposite the beach. It's gone now, ploughed under and with something nasty in its place. I do wish people would leave places alone.

We went in and after some usual discussions about how we were both doing, I raised the fact that I had bumped into Yvonne. "You remember that pretty little blonde who used to come in the Lamb with that wanker, Reg?"

"Oh, yes, I remember her,"

"Well I'm thinking about taking her out, what do you think?"

"I think you'd be very wise."

I remember this conversation very clearly, not that I needed Veronica's blessing, it's just that I didn't have too many friends at the time, and I still considered her to be one of my closest.

I called the number Yvonne had given me the next day. She sounded as if a cold might be approaching, but she agreed to come out for dinner on Tuesday next. I chose a restaurant very close to the big client I had at that time. No point in being silly! Salesmen are supposed to put things on their expenses aren't they?

She really wasn't very well at all with a bad head cold.

We sat at a quiet table for two and ordered something with some decent wine. We told each other about our lives. She had a regular boyfriend – the one I had seen was someone who wanted her to work for him, right!

I had a girlfriend too and we soon found out that for different reasons, we were neither of us happy with our current relationships. I felt very sorry for her with her bad cold, but could see that she was a terrific woman and the germ of an idea began to form in my mind.

Towards the end of the meal she asked me if I liked clocks. It happens that over the years I had acquired several of them into a small collection. She also asked me if I knew anything about L.A.

Apart from the Cockney joke about living in Little 'Ampton, my only experience was of passing through the airport on my way to Japan some years earlier.

"I've got something to show you back at my house," she said.

On the drive back, during which she struggled with her cold, she told me about an encounter she'd had about a month before.

Feeling pretty unhappy with her life she took the advice of one of her friends and visited a Mrs. Arnold, who lived in neighboring Worthing. Mrs. Arnold was an aurologist; she read auras.

After her visit, her friend said to write everything down as otherwise she was likely to forget it all.

When we arrived at Yvonne's house, she showed me the paper of Mrs. Arnold's predictions.

Among several items about her children and other things, this was written down: *You will be very influenced by a person with the initial T; you'll be surrounded by clocks; you'll be married within a year, and you'll be living in L.A.*

My attitude was well, we can all see the "T" bit, but this is our first date; yes, I collect clocks; married in a year is a bit strong, and as for L.A. I know nothing about it.

I left her letting the paper go out of my mind, but the other idea in front of my thoughts.

The next morning I called her to find that she was much better, and I asked to come over to see her.

On arrival we first spoke about this other Trevor, who was wanting her to work for him in a sales capacity. It was one of those nasty jobs that required a lot of cold calling and with very little reward as I could see. I recommended declining.

Then I put this suggestion to her. "We are both rather unhappy with our current situations. Let's drop both these people who are causing us sadness and while we get over them, we'll support each other and if something good comes out of that we'll be even better off. But if that doesn't happen at least we'll be shot of our problems."

We talked it over for some time, and during this time it came out that while she was married to the infamous Reg, she was never allowed to wear jeans. We lived in the country and so I said cocktail dresses (Reg's preferred outfit for her) were all very good, but if we just wanted to slip down to the pub for a couple, then jeans were the way to go.

I suggested that I collect her the following day and I'd drive her to London to buy her the first pair of jeans. It was to be a Thursday.

In between, we both made uncomfortable phone calls to our soon to be ex's and prepared for the following day.

Yvonne's cold had gone, and she was looking great as we set off for the city.

We made a number of stops and enjoyed a nice lunch before we turned back to the coast and the village of Angmering. On the way, I began to feel a little drowsy.

Now I have to admit to a small family failing. All the men seem to need an afternoon "kip," as it's called. Forty winks, my father and grandfather referred to the ten or fifteen minute nap. It's not always easy in a commercial life, but I've nearly always managed it.

The Chinese, I believe say that if you hold a small bell in your hand and then lean back in the chair and close your eyes, when the bell hits the floor, and you've only been asleep for a micro-second, that is enough. Well that may be OK for the Chinese, and it may be all you can manage in a boring board meeting - if you've managed to get your secretary to collect you for an important phone call - and you've stretched out on the sofa in your office – and she's awakened you after ten minutes, but a micro-second, forget it!

We had just driven around the Dorking by-pass, and were close to where Michael went to school. There was an excellent parking lot at the bottom of Box Hill, I pulled in.

Yvonne looked at me quizzically. No doubt she thought I had some nasty business on my mind. I said: "I really need to get my head down for ten minutes, I hope you don't mind." I let the seat down and she did the same with hers.

After a few minutes I could hear that she was breathing regularly. Good Girl! Fifteen minutes later we were back on the road again.

"So you have no trouble with a short nap after lunch, then?"

"Not at all!" A great little asset here, I thought.

We arrived back in time to collect Simon from his school bus. He was seven and had a bit of an attitude. He'd not had a very happy childhood with his parents coming to the end of their marriage, and I'm sure the introduction of a new man into his life could not have been easy.

Early that evening, we went to The Lamb in the village. Alan and Iris, the landlords, were mutual friends of ours and we thought we should let them know our plans.

The evening wore on and we had rather a lot to drink. The result was that I didn't want to drive the ten miles over to L. 'A! And stayed the night in Yvonne's comfortable home.

The next day I gave my landlady Mrs. Ray notice, and moved my stuff into Yvonne's.

Yes, rather sudden, but we had no doubts about it. The village of course, were outraged, but we ignored it as we regularly went to the pub - Yvonne sporting her new jeans - and smilingly faced them down.

I tried to fit in to the household which took a little effort, with a daughter of 19, who was not well and a seven year old with an attitude.

But the days rolled by and then the months. It was Christmas time already

Now since I had left, KTL, I had not had much contact with my previous partners. I hadn't seen Richard in years and I'd only seen Martin a few times.

Just before Christmas, Martin called me, which was quite unusual. Furthermore he asked me out to lunch which was even more unusual. We set a date for the next day or so, and I thought little more about it.

The morning of the lunch date, he called me to cancel. Something had come up. With the holidays it was difficult making another date, so I just asked him: "How's Richard doing these days?"

"Oh, he's living in Los Angeles - L.A."

The expression someone walking over one's grave is not often a true happening. But when I heard these words, I came out in goose bumps. "Martin, does he want me to come out there with him?"

"Yes, I rather think he does."

I went into the living room and said to Yvonne: "Well, the L.A. connection has finally fallen into place."

I explained the situation with my old boss and what Martin had told me.

About a year earlier, Richard had gone out to the US, as he was unhappy with the results being produced by Advance Systems Incorporated, the US agents.

The firm was run by an irascible Lancashireman of whom we were quite fond. But the sales were miserable.

Richard had done a deal with Tom Duerdon which allowed ASI to keep a portion of the company, but meant that Richard could take over control.

He was as usual needing someone to handle the sales function and during a meeting where Martin had gone out to California, my name came up.

As said earlier, my position with Scandata kept me underutilised and I knew that my prospects there were limited, so eventually I would have to seek pastures new.

When I heard the news from Martin, my immediate reaction was how soon can I go, but reason told me to look at it carefully. "When's Richard coming back to the U K? I asked. He was due in early February.

My experience with America had broadened over the years. With KTL I had been across the pond many times to help set up the sales force and assist with their training.

The furthest west I had ever been was Chicago, but I had been around the New York, New Jersey, Pennsylvania, Delaware and Massachusetts area quite frequently. I had also spent a lot of time visiting clients and had learned some of the differences with US businesses.

I still thought of it as a wonderful place, and had always wanted to go there for more time than a general business visit. Perhaps this was my chance.

Yvonne and I talked at length about the possibility of moving to the US.

There were some complications, Sue was still not well and Simon's attitude had not improved. I quite understood that he didn't want a new Daddy, and purposely I asked him to call me Trevor, in the hope that he wouldn't have to think of me as a replacement.

Looking back, I'm not sure if that was the right idea, but I stuck to it and the situation exists to this day.

Richard, Martin and I met up as agreed in February. It was quite like old times. We had lunch in a small Italian restaurant in Barnes, and Richard explained that they were waiting for a big order to come in, which would finance my re-location.

I explained that I would not be coming alone, and Richard didn't see anything wrong with that. He always was quite a traditionalist.

I made the trip over via World Airways (They no longer carry passengers these days, only freight). I arrived at the Imperial Terminal in LAX which caused some confusion with Gill Cargill who was to meet me.

This terminal is located on the south side of LAX and is entirely separate from the main building and only accessible from a different direction. Poor old Cargill naturally went to the usual international arrivals building and couldn't find World Airways. He arrived late in a bit of a panic.

I on the other had with no-one to meet me, I just waited as patiently as possible. I knew nothing of the area and Richard had gone out of town for a few days – no doubt to let Cargill and me see who could pee up a tree the highest.

I'm not sure quite what Richard had in mind as it was obvious that he wanted me to report to Cargill, who was a very charming black guy, somewhat like Benson in the series Soap.

Once he arrived we went off to get something to eat. He chose a particularly odd place called Dina's, famous for their fried chicken. Not my first choice when ending a twelve hour flight across the Atlantic and the entire width of America.

We settled into a plate of this stuff and Cargill seemed to really like it. I found out he was somewhat addicted to fast food of the greasy type.

As stated earlier he was a charming fellow, and was full of all the things that we could do with the company. He had been one of the earlier ASI salesmen and he also had worked for IBM.

After we'd had all we wanted and were talking of this and that he told me my hotel was just across the street. I said: "OK, boy, let's go!" He grabbed my arm and said: "Listen, out here we just have babies and men; there's nothing in between!"

I was rather shocked and said to him: "Look, just remember that I'm English. I don't have the type of prejudices you Americans are used to, so don't start getting uppity with me." I think we needed a higher tree to pee up against!

Over the next few days we discussed this entire racial thing. On one occasion, we went into a tavern and he refused to sit at the bar. "Some time ago, I was sitting at a bar and some jerk hit me over the head with a bottle. I never saw it coming." This apparently had stayed with him, as I'm sure it would have stayed with me.

I realised that basically we English were not immediately prejudiced on the basis of color. We didn't like the French, were suspicious of the Germans, thought the Spanish were dodgy, couldn't understand the Scandinavians, but as for color we rather took it as it came.

He explained to me how it all worked out here, and to some extent what it was like being black. I found it all very difficult and realised that one had to tread very carefully.

A little later on in our time together, he introduced me to a man called Terry Edwards. Terry was extremely black, tall and good looking. He was born and raised in a small town in Minnesota and told me that they were the only black family in the area. As a result he had to learn to be black when he moved to Southern California. A really odd situation, but it was very educational.

Both Terry and Gill were products of an anomaly of IBM's about ten years before. The company had been examined by some governmental board. They had been reported as not being fair to "minorities." That means blacks. As a result they had rushed around to find people of color who could fill minor management positions where so far they had been very absent.

The ones that I met were all good guys and I liked them all. They taught me what they could of how things worked out here, and put up with my ignorance, forgiving my occasional mistakes.

On our first day out, Cargill and I had to drive down to Costa Mesa to a large insurance company. It was raining hard and we got lost. Not a difficult thing to do as I was to find out later.

We knew we were not far away and we had plenty of time so Cargill suggested we stop at a bar to find our way. It was about nine in the morning.

It was a very small place in a strip mall. There was a small OPEN neon light in a window, but otherwise it was rather dark; particularly with the rain coming down. "Come with me," he said. "You'll learn something here."

We sprinted across the street trying to keep dry and rushed into the bar. It was as dark inside as out, but as we came through the door there was quite a commotion at the far end with men jumping up and rushing out the back door.

"They think we're the migra!" Cargill whispered to me as he asked the barman where our customer was located.

Once we got outside, he explained that mostly this area had a lot of agricultural workers, who were mostly illegals from Mexico.

"Two guys coming through the door like that, particularly one black one white, looked like we were from the Immigration Service – La Migra! I thought you'd enjoy that." I obviously had a lot to learn.

The following day we took a trip to San Diego, where we were hoping to set up an agency. It was one of those occasions where I sat still and watched and tried to adapt my three year-old knowledge of the products and services to a newer method and also a newer culture. But it was a great experience and an interesting challenge.

On our way back we stopped for a coffee at Oceanside. This is a small seaside town with fine beaches and a type of surfer atmosphere. There was a public phone box close to the small group of shops and I excused myself while I made a call to England.

I think it was quite late in the evening, when Yvonne picked up the phone. "Hi, it's me," I said. "This place is terrific. I think we should do it. Can you get down to the registry office and book a wedding for say April 15th?"

I suppose that is a form of proposal, in a way. But I never had any doubts about it. Fortunately Yvonne didn't balk at the immediacy and began to make plans.

She did go out one evening with some of her girlfriends, who seemed intent on putting her off the idea. After all it had only been six months since we had become an item. They said it wouldn't last. Well as of this writing, it has only been 32 years, so maybe they were right.

We haven't seen any of them since our first trip back after six months of living here.

The company was not doing particularly well. But I will say this about Richard, he's never been known to spend money on unnecessary stuff. He was sharing offices with some contacts of Cargill. These were in a very nice new building. As most of these people, who were engaged in some type of scam, I'm sure, didn't come in until late in the afternoon mornings were fairly quiet.

But my introduction to KPI (as the company was called out here) was in the mid afternoon. Richard was sitting at his desk smoking a cigar in a room surrounded by black people all talking nineteen to the dozen. It was one of the funniest sights I've ever seen, with him trying to maintain an air of sophistication in this shambles.

A large deal had been sold to Farmer's Insurance Company which was going to pay for me, and also some new premises. The latter would be fixed before I came out. I don't think there was any more room in the black people's office!

But it was good to see Richard and he took me early one morning to see David Gardner, who was acting as the company's lawyer.

We drove over to Wilshire to see David and he explained the visa process. Once we were here, we would fill in some forms which would then be sent over to London. When the time was right I would need to go over and his firm there would walk our applications through the embassy.

It wasn't necessary for all four of us to be there, just me, in case of any problems.

But between then and now, we had quite a lot to do. The concept of me reporting to Cargill was briefly discussed, but it didn't seem a real problem. After all I had known Richard for ten years and he was the one hiring me. After a couple of days I had moved from the hotel into his comfortable apartment in Playa del Rey.

My ten days in California were very busy. Cargill was of enormous help as he had the street knowledge and took care of where we were to live and how we were to get around and all the other details when people re-locate.

Americans often move quite long distances for their jobs and so they know how it's done. It reminded me of one difference in the cultures.

During my time with KTL, we were selling our consultancy business to the newspaper industry. Back in the mid-seventies, the provincial newspapers were changing over from Linotype hot metal machine to computer typeset. It was a big change and there were some inherent problems.

To begin with most Linotype operators had to serve a seven year apprenticeship and closely guarded their skills and positions. They were heavily unionised.

KTL offered a service where each man would be interviewed; they would be given an aptitude test and finally a dexterity test. This was to select similar skills.

The dexterity test would often show up that men had lost fingers in the huge machines that set the type in hot metal. Part of the job was the maintenance of their machines, which were cumbersome and often jammed.

The unions were not happy at these changeovers as it meant that the workforce would be reduced by about half – computers were so much faster.

We talked to other places in the industry where men who had been laid off because of the changeover, could be employed.

At the Glasgow Record, we gave a presentation to the entire labor force of 150, who were engaged in typesetting work and explained that not only was a company in Reading prepared to offer them similar work, but they would pay to have them re-located.

At the end of the talk, we had a desk set up to take names and addresses of men who wanted to use this opportunity. Not one man volunteered. None of them was prepared to move. Quite a culture difference to the USA.

Cargill found us a very good place in Marina del Rey, just half a mile from where the office was to be located on Admiralty Way. It caused some raised eyebrows as Oakwood Garden Apartments had a vague reputation where single "activity" was known to occur. I never witnessed any unpleasantness in my time there, although there were quite a few older singles, who milled about in a sort of gang for aged Yuppies.

I kept in touch with Yvonne and could see that the arrangements for the wedding were progressing well. Just as well, as that's not my kind of thing.

Eventually I returned home, put my notice in at Scandata, who once again behaved with considerable class about the entire business.

On the day of the wedding, which I think was a Friday, the house was in an uproar. Bags had to be readied as the day after the ceremony, we were to board World Airways mid-day for our emigration to California.

A friend of Yvonne leant us his Rolls Royce, which is the one and only time I've traveled in one. We had to ride over to Worthing to the registry office. My parents and assorted relatives were there, together with Paul Everest, my best man. He had chosen the exact same suit as me – a grey double breasted. We had both been to the same clothiers and never talked about the possibility. Would men ever?

I don't suppose anyone cared; if they noticed at all. Yvonne's relatives were all "out of town." None of them approved of the indecent haste of the event, or her choice of man. But there was nothing anyone could do about that.

After the civil ceremony which was particularly unmemorable, we went back to the place where we had first met and also met up again six months ago on October 6th 1981, The Lamb in Angmering.

The reception had an open bar and unfortunately both Yvonne and I took full advantage of it. But wait, I was paying for it.

We both awoke in the middle of the night with the most dreadful head aches. Proof that beer, champagne, and whiskey do not mix. It was the last time we made that mistake.

The next day we had a sad little parting from Michael and I gave him Yvonne's DAF car. It wasn't a bad going away present to a seventeen-year-old though. He would be coming out to see us in a couple of months once he'd finished his school term.

At 1:15 p.m. we took off from Gatwick watching the green landscape of England disappear below the DC10's wings. I had absolutely no regrets and no doubts as to our future.

We arrived in America at DWI, in the afternoon. We lined up to go through passport and customs and presented our passports with B1-B2 visas in them. These were the standard tourist/visitor visas at the time.

How long do you intend staying in the United States, the official asked: "Oh a couple of weeks," I replied.

I should point out that at the time of this cursory examination Yvonne was in the front wearing a mink coat; Simon was next to her with a big teddy bear. I told them both that people in mink coats and with teddy bears don't enter the United States illegally. Also we were travelling on to California, which as far as the official was concerned was virtually a different country. However, as this was the entry point we had to go through the interrogation here.

As I told him about a couple of weeks, a porter was pushing his cart containing our luggage behind us. It contained 14 suitcases, eleven pieces of hand luggage and by now Simon had tired of his Teddy Bear and had put that on the top as well. The official ignored this as he stamped our passports. It was now up to David Gardner, the lawyer.

Richard and Edmée met us at LAX and drove us down to the Marina along Lincoln Boulevard, a street I was to become very intimate with over the next few decades.

It was dark, and it was congested and hot. There were the usual collection of signs, wires and neon overhead and generally it was pretty rough. I couldn't resist opening the window and calling over to Yvonne with the old Morecombe and Wise remark: "What do you thing of it so far?"

She wasn't amused. Neither was she impressed with our accommodation. Oakwood had put us in the rear of the building. Not only that but it's only outlook was into the parking lot, with exhaust pipes pointing at our windows. I assured her that I would do something about it the next morning. We were pretty tired.

The next day, we walked over to the beach to have some breakfast. Every one was a little groggy but they served cocktails and after one of those for the adults we felt a lot better. The weather was brilliant.

I called into Oakwood's office to talk about our apartment. I must have been in a lucky/charmed state that day as the manager's unit was just empty and would we like that? I had a look; it was overlooking the swimming pool with a nice balcony on the second floor. Yes, that would be wonderful. We moved in right away.

On Monday morning, my duties began. KPI had moved out of the shared place and Richard had his own office in which he could smoke his cigars. We were on the fourth floor of the Marina Towers looking out over L.A. and on a clear day to the mountains beyond. It was a great place and a wonderful office.

Cargill walked me down to the social security office and told them to fix me up right away with a social security card. We also did the same for Yvonne. At the time I had no idea how important this card was as it is your true identity for being in the United States, and later on they were to be stamped with NOT FOR EMPLOYMENT across them. Ours looked just like every other American's.

Unfortunately within three months of our arrival, the UK company had seriously gotten into trouble. It was foundering. Things looked pretty bleak.

It was at times like these, that Richard really came into his own. We needed the UK company to help us financially and to lose it would put us in some jeopardy. Richard flew to London and effectively sold the firm to the company that wanted it and they agreed to keep all the employees in place as well as paying us for one year. It was a masterly job all around.

Once he had done what seemed impossible, we focused like mad on getting enough sales to make us successful. But I was aware of a growing discomfort within me.

California was marvellous. The weather, the pace of life and the excitement of a new place were wonderful. But there was this uncomfortable feeling inside me.

I happened to mention this to our lawyer, David Gardner. "Ah yes," he said. "The same thing happened to me soon after I came out here." David had already passed his law degree in England, but needed to do so out here in order to gain American qualifications.

"I was using a local small printing company to do all my paperwork copies and one day I noticed an error with their bill. It was quite obvious that they were trying to cheat me." This type of behaviour in the UK was almost unheard of but out here, it did happen. There was a different morality.

"The moment I saw this and understood what had happened, I was cured."

I asked him what he meant by cured, and he told me that for some weeks, he'd been throwing up many mornings, and he didn't understand why.

I told him I had a constant uneasy feeling in my stomach and perhaps it was the same problem. Basically it was a tenseness that we never felt back home.

"What you have to realise. Trevor," he told me. "Is that this is a foreign country. Furthermore it's more foreign to us than even France, Germany or Spain. There, due to the language, we treat it as foreign, but here we imagine it's the same as England, which it definitely is not."

I felt a lot better after this, as it made a lot of sense. This was not England. It was riskier and there was a level of desperation that floated over everything.

People think that Los Angeles is laid back. Nothing is further from the truth. Many of the people here have failed elsewhere in the US. If they were to fail here, where do they go from California? Hawaii? I think not.

This is a very big country and can afford to make a number of mistakes, but there is a level of competition that runs through everything. And it seems to be getting worse.

The UK was a welfare country. It would not have been easy to have starved, there was a safety net. Out here, the safety net was a lot smaller back in the early 80's, and the feeling of performing difficult feats with the net removed needed a change in attitude.

Over the last three decades things have changed. Perhaps it's a naturally progression that with a degree of wealth people demand more security. Socialism has seeped into the way of life here and what appeared impossible back then has become the norm now.

But if you are given just enough to survive, then the drive to succeed is diminished. Back then there were more people trying to make it, and make it big!

Marina del Rey was a wonderful place for two people plus two children to begin a life in America. To begin with it was quite a small place with definite boundaries to give one a sense of security. There was the ocean on one side, Lincoln Boulevard to the east, Washington to the north and Culver to the south.

Some years later I was having a morning coffee on Washington Boulevard, and I happened to be admiring a classic Harley Davidson gleaming in the early sunshine. I had just ridden my newer model to Laughlin and back and was feeling quite pleased with myself.

I asked the rider if he'd been there and he laughed and said he never left the Marina. I imagined he was joking, with such a wonderful machine, but no, he really meant it. "I never cross Lincoln," he said.

We had everything we needed within these borders but it was quite easy to visit the many other areas of the massive city of Los Angeles and its environs. The 405 Freeway was very close which gave access to the outer reaches and the 10 gave us a route to the inner city and beyond to the east.

But we had arrived in mid-April and we so enjoyed the life in this small community and we tended not to stray far from home for our enjoyment. On the other hand I was anxious to explore the entire area, and my business encouraged me to do so.

I had inherited a wall sized map of LA and I used to gaze at it during the day to become familiar with the territory. I don't know what happened to the map but I saw one only the other day and it brought back memories.

Many mornings I would head out to San Diego. We had a number of leads there, one of them being General Dynamics. Back then I could leave my office at 8:00 a.m. and walk through General Dynamics' door for a 10:00 appointment. It would take three hours today, and I wouldn't fancy it.

On my way I would sometimes dictate my thoughts on life out here to my friend Paul Everest in England. He would send me a small tape back. A little later when Michael first moved to Japan we would do the same thing. There was no email then. None of us had any idea how much that would change all our lives.

We were pursuing the plan of appointing agents to sell our service. It was a good idea to try and avoid the on-going expense of paying for our own dedicated sales force. However, the service was difficult to sell and we never had a lot of success doing it this way.

We had to wait for a year or two before we could afford our own team and that was when we began to surge ahead. The early days were not easy for us, and in the process, we collected a number of law suits.

In America it is possible to sue anybody for anything. If A believes B has done him wrong; he only needs to find a lawyer who will represent him and go to court. Even if the lawsuit is frivolous then the expenses are paid by both parties.

We had a friend who was sued by a large company on the grounds that he had infringed their copyright. The friend won, but in so doing came close to bankruptcy. Several attempts have been made to stop this practise by introducing "loser pays" laws, but the lawyers lobby is so strong that they have always failed.

There never was a law of contingency in England at the time. I heard that this has altered somewhat these days. But basically here certain lawyers exist on the basis that if they win for a client they take a portion of the winnings. It encourages such frivolous attempts.

It took me a long time to get used to adverts for lawyers on TV suggesting that if you took a certain drug and it upset you they, Honest Joe and Partners, would get you millions in compensation. It was quite eerie and frankly unsettling.

I soon figured out that here in America you could get rich by working hard, having some talent, and also by suing someone. Not quite the game, old chap. Hardly cricket!

But as David Gardner had so wisely said: "this is a very foreign country." We were finding that out. And in so doing, writing checks to him to protect us.

The biggest problem in our service was that people did not like doing it very much. Learning to type requires building up muscle memory and that takes a lot of exercises and drills.

It's boring, and people would much rather do other more interesting stuff. Our methods needed at least an hour a day and if possible two.

On top of that the world of central data capture was disappearing and in its place data was being collected at users desks, which meant lots of data capture but in smaller groups or in individual small offices.

For some years, Farmer's Insurance Company, whose business had effectively paid for my relocation to America, continued to be a very valued customer.

But eventually instead of insurance claims being sent to their large offices located in different places around the country, they decided to decentralise.

This meant that claims would not only be processed locally, but by the actual agents who were responsible for them.

Although we tried to interest Farmers in setting up training for these agents, frankly they were not going to pay to train those agents who were all independent businesses.

But America is a very big place and not every company was like Farmers. There was plenty of business opportunity to go around for quite some time.

During all this we revelled in the climate. Who, out of rainy old England, would not?

We enjoyed our time at the pool on the weekends and also learning how to live in a different culture. But one day in mid-May all of a sudden, there were thick clouds when we woke up. Clouds? What is going on?

As soon as I arrived in the office, I asked the girl who was looking after accounts, what had happened to the weather. She was of Japanese parentage from Hawaii, and as such the weather was not exactly of a prime concern to her. She said: "Oh it's like this every year from now until September."

I have to say I rather panicked, but she was quite certain that this was normal and we'd get used to it.

What she was referring to was the famous "June Gloom" that visits the coast of California. It does actually last right through the summer, but usually clears away in the late morning.

It might have been overcast, but those with white English skins had best look out as the ultra violet still comes through as a few of us found out to our lobster skin costs.

By the end of the summer, it was agreed that although we were still very green around the edges of this new life, we wanted to stay. We therefore went back to England and sold Yvonne's house, put all the visa papers in order and returned to continue with our adventure in California.

We continued to live in Oakwood Garden Apartments, but found that although it was a very friendly atmosphere, it was all on the surface. There were few opportunities to forge lasting friendships, which with a full family we didn't worry about too much.

People often asked us what we missed most about England to which we answered that it was only the pubs and the easy access to the Continent that we missed.

We had plenty of bars around for an early evening drink which had become our habit, but they seemed to lack the same atmosphere that a village pub provided.

I thought about why this was and came to the conclusion that most California bars were lock-up businesses. English pubs were for the most part run by a tenant and his wife who "lived over the shop." The full name for pub is public house, and it is in fact someone's house that has been opened to the public.

A bar out here is often a very attractive place which has been designed to affect a particular atmosphere to appeal to a particular clientele, but it could never be confused with someone's home.

Similarly its customers tend to visit on occasions but not be regulars. Nonetheless this is a small criticism and one we overcame with little difficulty.

108

Also with perfect weather people tended to gather outside in public places and not in each other's homes. I'm sure this also keeps people from becoming very close, with a lack of the personal entertainment side missing.

The Marina was a tourist magnet and was often full on the weekends with all kinds of people wanting to enjoy the seaside air and the harbour attractions. There were plenty of places to go and just along Washington was Venice Beach with extensive sands and other amusements.

A walk along Venice Boardwalk would stimulate any visitor to the area. It seemed over the years to have attracted the strangest and the most bizarre.

There was the chain saw juggler, and the man on roller skates who played a guitar while singing in a high pure tenor voice. There were all types of vendors selling all types of wares, and by mid-afternoon it was jam packed. We took many a Sunday stroll there and enjoyed the craziness of the place.

Like so many others arriving from other parts, we began to start considering our health a little more then we had before. The wine was the first to go.

Booze is rather expensive in the UK and in California it's relatively cheap. One can buy very large bottles of table wines for very little. It's easy therefore to quaff the stuff down with no little voice in your head reminding you that there is a cost to all this.

We gave the wine up; the liquor was to follow a few years later. And on the last day of December 1982 – a not very original date – we gave up smoking. We both have said looking back that it was the best day's work we ever did.

Overlooking a large pool we used to watch new renters arrive to the area. Many of them were on long term contracts in California. Many of them came from other states. We used to smile as they made their first tentative steps out to the pool area. Often they were enormous people from the mid-west, who rarely if ever were seen in public in minimal clothing.

Over the course of the next few weeks we noticed many of them began to visibly shrink. They had become very conscious of their shapes and were now eating salads and drinking diet drinks, instead of regular large Cokes and huge T-bone steaks.

It was the California way.

As too seemed to be the fashion of driving small dark colored import cars. I had been doing my best with a particularly revolting GMC model called a Pontiac Phoenix. A nasty golden thing with plastic seats and the fiercest air-conditioning I had ever experienced. It was a horror. At least it was American. I could not see why people liked these small Hondas and Toyotas. What was the appeal in the land of the large land yacht?

For a week or two I drove past a local car merchant and noticed that they had on offer a massive hunk of metal. It was a 1976 Eldorado which they were knocking down a little each week.

Eventually I couldn't stand it any longer, it was there taunting me. I had a word with Richard to make sure he wasn't particularly devoted to the Pontiac and went in to see the salesman. I drove out in the biggest piece of metal outside of the military that could be driven. It was fantastic and everyone called it Big Bertha!

I see one occasionally at car rallies and shows, and I do regret that I no longer can be the only white man seen driving that particular model in LA! It was probably my most favorite ride.

At the same time, Yvonne bought a Lincoln Continental from a dealer along Lincoln Boulevard called Lucky. You can't make this stuff up.

Each morning, because by now Yvonne had joined the firm, we would fire up sixteen huge cylinders to take us the half a mile to the office. Saving the planet was not required back then. Gas was under a dollar a gallon. And for a few cents extra you could actually have someone else pump it for you. When was the last time you saw a "Full Serve" station?

I do understand how America can upset many people. I believe it is a combination of jealousy and also uncertainty how America has managed to be so lucky in its fortunes.

One of the phrases that adds to much of the confusion is the phrase "American Exceptionalism." It certainly smacks of boasting, which for a fact in the English culture is not to be tolerated.

I feel it is incumbent of me at this stage to explain the phrase as it means and not as our current President thinks it is meant.

He took issue with "American Exceptionalsim" as being lording it over other cultures. He said that the Belgians thought of themselves as exceptional. The French believed they were exceptional. They had every right to think that way and America wasn't any better than other countries.

Over the years to be exceptional has come to mean above the rest, but in fact an exception is merely something that is different.

The history of humankind has been as the Astronomer and philosopher Isaac Asimov said: "A dark turbulent stream of folly with occasional flashes of brilliance."

In truth humankind has overwhelmingly been ruled by tyrants, torture, fear, poverty, hunger and cruelty. When America became independent, the leaders wanted a country that was different to all those regimes of the past.

The declaration stated quite clearly that **We hold these truths to be self-evident, that all men are created equal, that they are endowed by their Creator with certain unalienable Rights, that among these are Life, Liberty and the pursuit of Happiness. — That to secure these rights, Governments are instituted among Men, deriving their just powers from the consent of the governed...**

Therefore it was an exception to be so founded.

> *So, then, to every man his chance--to every man, regardless of his birth, his shining, golden opportunity--to every man the right to live, to work, to be himself, and to become whatever thing his manhood and his vision can combine to make him--this, seeker, is the promise of America.*
> *— Thomas Wolfe*

Chapter Nine

ENGLAND

He was born an Englishman and remained one for years.
— *Brendan Behan*

*We have really everything in common with America nowadays
except, of course, language.*
— *Oscar Wilde*

I have touched on several aspects of England earlier in this memoire,
but it is such a big part of my life that it does deserve a separate chapter.
Also Americans are still quite fascinated by it and so I know they will
forgive me for any repetition.

Throughout its earliest history, the islands that make up Great
Britain were a troubled place. Along with all the other nations in those
pre-Roman days we were fraught with internecine quarrels and regular
fights between the many kingdoms that struggled to hold onto a very
precarious existence. Such was life back then.

But England prevailed from its arguments in defence against a
common enemy and eventually over several thousand years became one
people and then we successfully exported the idea of such to many parts
of the world. An early attempt at franchising!

There is a general misconception that the English are at heart a
peaceful, law-abiding people, but that is not the case. I believe we are
as warlike as any other bunch of hooligans if we're given the chance,

We have nonetheless managed to apply a veneer of charm and
niceness which in some cases can be quite thick indeed. But it's best not
to scrape away too much or you can get hurt.

As explained in the chapter about education, I believe the aim of
most of English society for their children was to train them to have

certain moral beliefs. These were loyalty; courageousness; decency; modesty; being a good loser; honesty; sobriety, and also to be an applied scholar.

Naturally most people failed to acquire all these in full force, but there was a definite attempt to measure up to the mark, and if one did not there was an accompanying feeling of guilt. Mostly we all recognised that it was because we had not tried hard enough.

I am sure that growing up in the war years must have moulded many of us into over zealous little patriots, but frankly I don't see that as any bad thing.

If you are fighting against a vicious enemy you need as much backbone as possible; and things looked pretty bleak in the early days. Fortunately I was too young to appreciate the dangers we were facing at that time.

Having lost an entire generation of the best of our young men in the First World War, we were in the process of losing even more in the second. And this time we were losing women and civilians as well.

And yet we were never in any doubt that somehow England had earned its position of being a great power, and at the time perhaps even the greatest in history.

By the end of the hostilities, of course, most of the stuffing had been knocked out of us and it was time to hand over the reins to anther power, namely America. I am sure it must have been terribly galling to have to accept this for my father's generation and the earlier one too.

After all we had managed to rule an empire "on which the sun never set!" Our atlases were covered in the bright rich pink of the Empire and slowly we had to watch that color fade and in many cases vanish all together.

We had managed to acquire such possessions not by being particularly decent chaps, but by having a very large navy and also by getting first dibs on various places. And although no one wants a conqueror, our empirees didn't seem to resist that much.

If your life is one of brutality from your own kind, then if some group of red-coated men with guns and long knives attached, enter your domain, then perhaps things might just change for the better. Most people in the world had pretty rotten lives and the English were not that bad, well I don't think so.

There has always been one nasty skeleton in our closet however. I refer to the emerald isle to our west – Ireland. And that is a bad scar on our history.

I have an Irish son-in-law, and on his first visits to us we "got into it" a bit. He is actually Irish, from Dublin. Not the American type who say they are Irish because some poor wretch escaped from the brutality of the English rule and washed up on the Eastern Shores of the USA a couple of hundred years ago.

Up until I was about 30, I generally believed that we English were a pretty wonderful lot. Good with children, kind to animals, gifted in the arts and faster than striking snakes. Well, that was to change when my old boss leant me a copy of The Reason Why by Cecil Woodham-Smith. Perhaps it wasn't a life changer, but it was definitely a thought changer.

I didn't take a lot of notice of history at school, having slept through most of the "Corn laws;" "the Agricultural Revolution;" the Elizabethans," and "Gladstone and Disraeli." Mostly I found it terribly boring, until the last few months of school when it suddenly came alive for me.

Afterwards when I took my failed history exam results out into the world, I read as much as I could but somehow ignored the parts about Ireland. The book I was leant changed all that. It was truly an eye opener.

The book is not only about the infamous charge of the Light Brigade, but about the entire history of English rule in Ireland and the structure of the British army at the time. I was truly transfixed by the account and how we had managed to turn what was an unmitigated disaster into something approaching pride in the behaviour of a few idiots.

To begin with we need to understand the attitude to the military at the time. In the mid-nineteenth century the position of officers was considered to be crucial in maintaining the realm and the developing empire.

Professional soldiers were not much respected; in fact they were generally treated with suspicion. Two hundred years earlier, they had been the class that had rebelled against the crown and taken over the country, led by one of their rank, namely Oliver Cromwell.

It's not much talked about but the British Civil War of 1642 to 1651 was a very bloody conflict between the parliamentarians (The Roundheads) and the royalists (The Cavaliers.) It resulted in the beheading of King Charles I and the exile of his son, who eventually became Charles II.

Statistically it was as bloody as the American Civil War and left scars that went extremely deep.

One of the outcomes was that in future it was decided that the very people who had brought this revolution, namely the military, must never be allowed to do so again. One way to maintain this position was to only allow those with the most to lose to run things. In other words if you wanted to progress in the Army, you had to buy your way up the ladder. And it wasn't cheap.

The only exception was the army in India, who were after all a damned long way away and unlikely to be able to produce the mojo for any revolution.

The three senior participants at the debacle that became known as the Charge of the Light Brigade were Lord Raglan, Lord Lucan and Lord Cardigan. The latter was a particular fool who happened to have inherited not only his family's massive fortune and title, but also an enormous ego. His primary claim to fame was the invention of the woollen garment so favored by late middle aged men.

The film of the same name which stars Trevor Howard as Cardigan and John Gielgud as Raglan also had David Hemmings in the role of Captain Nolan.

It is not to be confused with the movie starring Errol Flynn which is total fiction.

But what has all this to do with Ireland? Well, it so happens that Lord Lucan had made most of his money from his estates in Castlebar in Ireland, and he was the epitome of a slumlord with almost total disregard for the plight of his tenants.

Ireland has had an unhappy history and as I said to my future son-in-law when he mentioned that all the problems to do with his country could be traced to the British; "Well, how far back do you want to go?"

Because it could be said that it was Dermot McMurrough who started it all. He was the Irish King of Leinster, but was dispossessed of his kingdom after some hanky panky with another king's wife. Upset by this loss of status he realised that back in 1167, Ireland was in something of disarray and its many kings were an easy target for any well organised army. He approached the King of England, Henry II and suggested that if he organised a group of his knights then the entire land might be his.

He would of course, be well rewarded and be a type of regency in absence.

It was also helpful for Henry to give some of his more unruly knights not only some new estates, but keep them out of the way of the court where they were a mischief.

Henry did as suggested and effectively took complete control of the large island to the west of his kingdom.

Now it should be understood that for an island nation, England, its defences are largely naval. If however there are bases to the west under the control of foreign elements who might strike at any time, the resources of the Royal Navy have to be split and weakened. Ireland was a very important place from a tactical point of view.

However, Ireland in those far off days was a long way from where the power existed in the royal court, and the knights who were given large estates soon tired of the silent land with its strict religious conformity and lack of amusements.

As a result, the new lords of Ireland began to spend less and less time there and gave over the running of their estates to agents and other bodies who would make sure that rents were paid on time and moneys collected.

The Irish too were not helping themselves with their practices. Even the crude birth control of the time was frowned upon and children were the result of the poor and miserable conditions. Also they adopted the Continental practise of dividing the land left by dying parents and attempting to live off smaller and smaller patches.

When the potato disease hit in the mid 1800's the situation existed whereby a family of four could well be living off a piece of land ten feet by ten feet and even smaller.

The land was rich but even so, it required a super effort to feed a family purely off the two crops of potatoes grown each year. The odd pig owned in a type of cooperative helped boost the miserably plain diet, but the part that was owned by the family was often mortgaged to help buy other necessities.

When the first potato crop failed it meant that a family might just be able to survive with the potatoes that had been stored underground, but it was a difficult business. When the second crop and then the third and fourth rotted and died in a black scourge across the entire country it spelled ruin.

As a result one million escaped to America while another million starved. The remaining four million tried to hang on as best they could.

During this time their English landlords remained dependant on rents being paid, and those like Lord Lucan, who had little to do with his estates became furious that his income was declining.

He developed the nickname of the Exterminator as he invented a machine that was able to demolish an entire house with just the power of horses - sometimes with the occupants still inside. Many of these poor wretches were suffering from cholera, which accompanied the potato famine.

This was a mere 170 years ago and therefore it is still part of Irish folklore and buried deep alongside the other troubles of a rebelling population regularly put down by unfeeling masters.

It is a long and sorry history and it is no wonder that the Irish hold resentment at those not too far off days.

But I still blame it all on Dermot McMurrugh!

The Reason Why does a masterly job of explaining how it was possible to order a 650 man brigade of light cavalry armed only with swords and pistols into the face of 16 inch guns and 5,250 well armed Russian artillery.

It was not a question for the men to answer as "they were not to reason why, theirs but to do or die..." But more a question of what kind of maniacs could order such a charge?

Of course, it was all a big mistake with senior officers up on a bluff, not truly aware of the situation and then a hyped up twitchy junior officer below seething with resentment at a superior whom he felt was unqualified to be serving alongside him.

A badly written order handed over by an hysterical out-of-breath Captain Nolan completed this recipe for disaster and off they went.

Lord Cardigan, who was in charge of the Light Brigade, was a total fool but not a coward. Once the order was given he barely hesitated due to his ego. "If they want me to charge the guns, then I'll charge 'em!" was his mindset as he spurred his horse into action. He led this amazing suicide mission with barely a thought for what was bound to happen.

It must have taken the Russians a few moments to fully realise what was going on. But onwards came the cavalry into the face of their huge guns and even though many were literally blown away, the others continued.

Cardigan himself was in a rage as Captain Nolan had broken all etiquette and charged off ahead of his commander and it seemed that he was himself leading this affront. In fact he was killed very early on and it was his panicked horse that went on alone.

Cardigan reached the enemy lines unscathed, rode through them and then in the agreed fashion turned around swishing his sword right and left and returned through his bedraggled ranks to reach safety with not a scratch on him.

On that day, the 25th October 1854 the British suffered 278 casualties from their mad dash, but managed to write this entire effort into their annals as a great military adventure – similar to Dunkirk!

It's obvious that the concept of progressing officers through the higher ranks with their money alone had many unintended consequences.

Such is history and as previously mentioned the quote by Isaac Asimov says it all: A dark turbulent stream of folly, with occasional flashes of genius.

It's easy to blame those struggling to make life better for us in the past, but in fairness they were just trying to do the best they could with what they knew. And in the process they had to deal with all the many prejudices and egos that come along with life.

I'm sure that if one was able to take the very best of every society and meld it into one, things would be better, but perhaps that's what our leaders try to do from time to time.

In the case of England however, there is a certain something that has remained unique. Maybe it's being an island, perhaps it's the difficult climate, possibly it's the mixture of cultures that years ago gave the land its homogeneity.

Nonetheless there are quite obvious differences in the people and the culture, which outsiders don't always appreciate.

To begin with there is the North/South divide.

There is a sort of dotted line that runs across from one coast to another. It's just to the north of Darlaston which is a few miles north of Birmingham.

Remember now I'm talking about England here and not including Scotland, which is a totally different place entirely.

Back in the days of the post Roman raiders England was defenceless, and it was not until King Alfred managed to negotiate with the Danes that the country was able to stand independently at all.

Around 870 AD, Alfred who was King of Wessex and based in Winchester, agreed to a line with the Danes called the Danelaw. It stretched from approximately Liverpool to London. Everything to the north and east belonged to the new rulers, the Danish; the south and west was England – the land of the Angles.

To this day there are changes in vocabulary in the north, and the accent is decidedly different.

I have to say I have never felt comfortable in the north. I wish I could explain it, but it is one of life's little mysteries.

The climate is harsher and the architecture is darker. The accent of Yorkshire which is the predominate one, grates on my ear, whereas the softer country Lancashire tongue is quite pleasant, but not the urban, which is truly awful.

And yet, the people of the region don't consider Lancashire and Yorkshire to be the true north. That distinction belongs to Durhamshire, Northumberland and Cumberland; truly remote areas and perhaps the real England of old.

Whereas I usually feel a sense of discomfort in the Lancashire/ Yorkshire part I feel amazed on the rare occasions that I visit the far north.

These are tough areas. The climate is harsh and the people are harsher, but in an admirable way. There is not the natural antagonism of the north and south from them I feel, but more an interest in how things are "down there." They have an independence of spirit that is quite palpable.

I had the misfortune to have to go and live in Lancashire when I was about 21. I had been promoted to the position of senior representative for Lancashire and Westmoreland, which included the Lake District.

In those days, the motorway ended at Coventry and the rest of the journey had to be taken on trunk roads and surface streets. It took me about seven hours to travel from north London where my parents lived to Preston, on the western edge of Lancashire.

My father gave me a list of the towns I had to travel through and one Sunday at about nine I set off.

I was given a particularly unfortunate van to use as a company vehicle, and its brooding presence was not improved by the painted application of happy smiling baby faces and little stars – the product was baby food! Dear me!

I was destined for "Reigate, 16, the Boulevard, Preston, Lancs" and the abode of one, Mrs. Facer. On the face of it, it didn't sound like a bad address, but it was the usual pebble-dashed, semi-detached horror from the "between the wars" era, and sat gloomily facing out onto a canal, which was euphemistically referred to as a river.

This new home away from home had been selected for me by the outgoing rep, Roger Taylor. He was to meet me that evening at some pub in the center of town.

Mrs. Facer was a large, pleasant woman who had a desire to change every bit of her house over the coming months. I was shown to an upper room, which remained sacrosanct to some degree, although the dust from the permanent collection of contractors did manage to seep in.

On the date of arrival she was having the front and back room pushed into one. Once this had been achieved she embarked on having the kitchen altered, it was one of the jobs that was likely to see no end.

Quite what had befallen Mr. Facer was never discussed, but it was obvious that she was enjoying what he had left her when he slipped his cable. He was no doubt pleased to go and therefore able to get some peace.

I was destined to stay here for three months before my employer blessedly fired me for being unsuitable for the position. They were absolutely correct, and I'm only surprised it took them so long. I knew it from the first day. I was the epitome of a square peg in a round hole.

I still feel a little guilty about it all, but although it didn't exactly poison me for the "north" it didn't help me either. I found the people overly friendly, the constant gloom of the climate depressing and the accent awful and grating.

I made one dreadful trip to the seaside town of Blackpool. About five miles away I stopped the van on a hill to overlook the famous lights of the promenade. I got out of the car and was able to detect a quite strong odor of fish and chips. On their own they can make a pleasant supper, but to have the entire atmosphere of a large town poisoned by their flavour might put them permanently off anyone's menu.

I was looking for the opportunity to meet a young lady for I was at the age. In the habit of the day I made my way to the Wintergardens. I had found out that this was where the best public dances occurred. It was a massive place with swirling couples, and to my surprise lots of very attractive girls. It was noticeable that most of them had paid particular attention to their hair. It had been done in a far more lavish way than their counterparts in the south.

Unfortunately once they opened their mouths all image of sophistication vanished. They just didn't appeal and I only ever attempted the trip once. It was a dismal experience. I recognised very early on that the north was not for me.

In later life I had an office in Bradford, across the Pennines in Yorkshire, and although by then my position was better, I never looked forward to going there and seeing my rep, who nonetheless taught me many things about the area. They are different up there, I can tell you!

There are other geopolitical societal differences in the country as well. Take the far south west; perhaps the most attractive and unspoilt area of the country.

It's hard to place the actual border with the rest of the county, but Dorset is not a bad place to begin.

I went there firstly with my first girlfriend, her BFF, and her uncle, who was quite a young chap. We stayed at a bed and breakfast (the men in one room and the girls in another!) In Corfe Castle.

It is a small village with the wreckage of a castle high above on a steep little hill. Oliver Cromwell had destroyed the castle as it was a potential defence against his forces. He did a lot of damage that lad!

The center of the town has changed little since I was there over 60 years ago.

Keeping up the tradition of destruction, the Ministry of Defence used the tiny village of Tynham for target practice just before the D-Day landings. The residents were told to leave and they have never been allowed to return due to unexploded ordinance. There are a couple of times a year when visitors can look at the place from protected vantage points. I'm glad to have done this.

Further down the leg that extends towards America you come to the far point of Cornwall. Here, the people are strongly related to the Welsh and the Irish as they are Celts.

Generally they are small and dark and have only just stopped using their own language. The coastal fishing towns are quaint and small with tourism as the main business. This stops the locals from being too upset over "townies," who do at least swell the wallets.

The atmosphere is totally different to the rest of the country and generally the climate is less unpleasant, although it does get its fair share of rain.

Before we left England, we lived in a small village in Sussex. It was right in the middle of the sunshine triangle – if proof was necessary you only had to see the number of greenhouses there.

It was suburban/country as it was easy to commute to London from there as it was less than 60 miles from the capital. It was slowly losing its country identity, but there was just enough agriculture around to slow that inevitable progress. It was always a joy to drive back over Long Furlong and see the many sheep grazing and the cows working hard on their cuds.

Like all places, England has changed enormously over the years. It's still there, in its spirit, but in a different form. I'm sure old men from time immemorial have complained at the direction that life is going. Today I think the changes are faster, and the same goes for my country of origin.

I am shortly going back to London, which perhaps has changed the least in my lifetime. It's a massive bustling place that I have been fortunate enough to have spent a great deal of time in. I have in fact never lived in it though.

I look forward to the experience as it is always stimulating to spend time there. But in truth London is not England.

The politics of England are much the same as other western democracies. Basically Conservatives and Labour represent the Republicans and the Democrats. There are two houses within Parliament, with the upper one being non-elected.

This gives rise to a certain amount of class envy as The House of Lords encourages the class system to perpetuate itself. Lords from way back sit in the upper house and also certain "life" peers are appointed.

Like the Senate in America this house can slow down the rate of legislation, but unlike America it cannot halt it. If Parliament passes a bill three times it will automatically go into law over any objection of the Lords.

It is the fervent hope of the left that they will be able to eradicate the House of Lords and replace it with an elected one. The current membership seats the heirs of many of the original barons who forced King John to sign the Magna Carta back in 1215.

In spite of tough tax regulations that take away much of the wealth of the aristocracy with death duties, they still hang on, and basically are tolerated by the rest.

Unlike the French, these peers have a tradition that the eldest of the line inherits the title and estate, leaving them with the responsibility of caring for their siblings. The French on the other hand divide the inheritance and the titles equally, which gave rise to the many counts and viscounts which in part created the French Revolution in an attempt to rid themselves of such burdens. They also behaved in very autocratic ways, which is always going to cause problems and resentment.

The class system is much misunderstood in England, and it's very hard to describe to outsiders. It betrays itself in the oddest ways.

A couple of years after coming out here, we happened to be in a small café in Big Bear for lunch one day. A woman was talking in a quite loud voice to one of the staff and I recognised her accent immediately.

As she left I spoke quietly to her and said: "Are you from the New Forest?"

She looked harshly at me, and said: "Oh, no, I'm from Totton."

Now this was the equivalent of being an American in London and asking someone they heard if they were from Hermosa Beach and being told that no, they were from Marina Del Rey; a distance of about ten miles.

The woman was perturbed at my recognition and denied my suggested placement as she did not want me to think of her as being a "forest dweller." Very low class. Mind you if you've been to Totton, you'll know that it's no great shakes!

English ears are remarkably well attuned to accents. When I first came out here, I think I could place someone within about a thirty mile radius of their origins. I am not unusual. Although these days I don't have the fine tuning that goes with living in, let's face it, a quite small place.

No only does an accent betray one's geographical location to another, but it also puts you in a class position.

The George Bernard Shaw play Pygmalion, later turned into the musical My Fair Lady shows how it might be possible to train a working class woman into a lady. Professor Higgins attempted to do it. But one false syllable will forever show that you are a fraud. It's a very hard thing to do. The upper class never make a mistake as it's bred into them.

And so it is easy to see that along with everyone else, England is a much divided nation; it always has been.

However there is one institution that brings everyone together and that is the monarchy. Of course, even with that there are detractors who would do away with such an anachronism. Mostly though that is based on envy of the position and a lack of understanding of the benefits.

Perhaps nothing separates the UK and the USA as the position of the top job. America has its President, England has its Queen.

The President has lots of power, the Queen has virtually none, and yet, she is guaranteed to draw a very large audience whenever she appears.

Elizabeth II came to the throne in 1952, after the death of her father George VI. He himself was a very popular man as was his wife, also named Elizabeth, thence the Queen Mother, who died at the ripe old age of 101.

The British Royal Family has been there in one form or another for thousands of year, well certainly as long ago as 500 A.D.

There have been a few hiccoughs along the way particularly in the belief of how God should be worshipped. It was the dreadful interpretation of such beliefs and the subsequent punishments that gave rise to the freedom of religion, and the separation of church and state that is so heavily stressed in the American Constitution.

One of the more recent wobbles that happened to the Royals was the affair of the Prince of Wales, with the American twice-divorced Wallace Simpson in the late thirties.

This gave rise to the abdication of the then King Edward the VIII, who gave up the throne as he could not face the responsibilities "without the support of the woman I love."

He was on a boat the very next day out of the country, and never once returned officially. He lived in exile in various watering holes on the Continent and was something of an embarrassment to the country as a whole.

My father and grandfather could barely speak of the outrage they felt he had caused, and the Duke and Duchess of Windsor as they were known, were from their departure merely a note in the gossip columns of the European papers.

If one could just recognise for example that during the war, the country made him the ambassador to Bermuda, that tiny speck on the west coast of the Atlantic. Surely it must have occurred to the Germans to row ashore, and kidnap the ex-king and hold him up for ransom. Surely he had some worth. But they never bothered. I think that shows how little regard with which he was held.

After the Duke died, the widowed Duchess was allowed to visit England, but she was furious that the Royal Family refused to bestow on her the title of Her Royal Highness. The bloody cheek!

It is that sense of total conservativeness that brought about another small bump in the road of the Royal fortunes.

I was asked once if I thought Princess Diana would ever leave the Prince of Wales. I answered positively that there was absolutely no chance. So much for my understanding of such matters.

It has been quite traditional for the heir to the throne, the Prince of Wales, to marry a young woman, provide a couple of children and thence go about his business with various mistresses. It goes back a long way.

As for the marriage of Charles and Diana, he quite understood this, but she never did. The result of him continuing to consort with a previous girlfriend caused the lovely young princess considerable unhappiness, and also gave the rest of the country much concern.

I don't think England has ever quite forgiven him, although he is tolerated.

After the awful tragedy of her death in that tunnel in Paris in 1997, the country went into mourning; quite forgetting that her future was bound to be a mixed bag of scandals and difficulties. No wonder thoughts of assassination entered the minds of the conspiracyists.

There was a big debate as to what the Queen's role should be in the matter of a funeral, state or otherwise. The fact remains that the royalty are even more conservative than the church, and they immediately went to their centuries old play book to find that as she had divorced Charles, Diana was no longer a royal. Therefore she did now warrant any attention by the family. The Queen disappeared to Balmoral Castle in Scotland and tried to forget about it.

I have been a loyal subject. (technically not so since my Americanisation in 1992!) for over 60 years. In all that time I have never seen the Queen put a foot wrong nor do anything that might be considered questionable.

She has performed her duties flawlessly and with good grace and humor. For those jealous ones who thing she has it easy and should be thrown out, just imagine the dreadful task she has.

Everyday she is to face long lines of gazing faces, shaking the hands of minor dignitaries and eating truck loads of rubber chicken, before moving on to the next event. She always has to be dignified, and in a good mood, and all the while pretend to be interested in the arrangements that have been put out on display for her.

I'm sorry, but no castles or servants could make up for that daily round of horrors.

But it was clinging to that traditional play book that brought the royalty to its lowest level.

I can still remember the sight of the Queen when she finally returned from her sojourn in Scotland. As she entered the gates of Buckingham Palace, she had the car stopped and got out to see the enormous piles of flowers laid to rest in memory of her late daughter-in-law.

I don't think until that moment she had fully realised how important Diana was to the people; and also how powerful the emotions were of the population at large.

Since then the stature of the Royals has gradually increased with the emergence of the Queen's grandson, William and his attractive wife Kate, the Duke and Duchess of Cambridge. Even Prince Harry has done a pretty good job for what is usually the naughty role of the future Duke of Kent as he will become.

Once again I shall stick to the playbook in order to answer the question: Will Charles step aside to allow his more popular son, William, to assume the role of King, when Elizabeth II eventually dies?

I believe that is most unlikely to happen. Charles will become Charles III, as he has been waiting in the wings all his life. It is inevitable.

The advantages of a monarch are one), that it is a job that is totally out of the hands of craving politicians, and two) it creates a form of paternal feeling over the land. In this current time of course, maternal.

It is like having grandparents who live a distance away and whom one hasn't seen in a long time. But the feeling exists that even though it has been a long time, they still love you and it might be possible to see them if they could just make room in their very busy schedules. It's pure fantasy of course, but then so is the statement that the White House is the People's House. Just try going up and ringing the door bell. You'd be better off just jumping the fence!

> *This royal throne of kings, this sceptred isle,*
> *This earth of majesty, this seat of Mars,*
> *This other Eden, demi-paradise,*
> *This fortress built by Nature for herself*
> *Against infection and the hand of war,*
> *This happy breed of men, this little world,*
> *This precious stone set in the silver sea,*
> *Which serves it in the office of a wall*
> *Or as a moat defensive to a house,*
> *Against the envy of less happier lands,--*
> *This blessed plot, this earth, this realm, this England.*

— *William Shakespeare*

Chapter Ten

LONDON

When a man is tired of London, he is tired of life; for there is in London all that life can afford.
— *Samuel Johnson*

When it's three o'clock in New York, it's still 1938 in London.
— *Bette Midler*

About three years ago we took our sixteen-year old grandson over to England. We thought he might like to see one half of his heritage – the other one which would be from his mother's side is Filipino.

Part of the trip included my taking him up to the capital to show him around for three days and two nights.

It was a wonderful experience (at least for me) as I hadn't spent much time in London for many years. I was delighted to find that I hadn't forgotten my way around or forgotten what was available.

Looking back I realise that I have never passed more than a handful of nights in London, as I always lived outside and consider myself a "suburbanite." Perhaps the best of both the world of the country and the town – or the worst, depending on your point of view.

Both my sons I'm sure would consider themselves "cityfolk" as they both live in extremely large cities and wouldn't have it any other way.

But it was my lot to have to schlep in and out in one form of transport or another, and I've never learned that other interesting life of actually living in a city neighbourhood so that one learns the inner secrets of an area.

Nonetheless I have been fortunate to have learned the city in many ways, and most of my opportunity came about through my job in selling.

Initially, before they awarded me a salesman's bag (somewhat unwisely as you will have read in Chapter Four) I began my work with London Transport, located just to the southwest of St James Park, at 55 Broadway.

Naturally with lunchtimes I was able to explore that area and spread down to Victoria nearby. But I also learned a lot about the underground network – the Tube – as we had to go out and about throughout the network as it was our jobs to attend to various maintenance aspects. I was only there for about three months but my time on the Tube was invaluable.

Next I spent time in Ilford, and although not exactly in London it was a close suburb to the east of the city. After some time I was transferred to High Holborn and their main London showroom. I was there for about a year and in that time managed to get out and about around that central area.

My commute was into one of the large railway termini, Euston to the north. Now I seem to have developed a loathing of buses at about this time, as I had a fifteen minute walk down Southampton Row to reach High Holborn. I'm sure there were plenty of buses, but I never chose one as I preferred to walk.

I could never figure out the routes with buses, as they seemed to always be swinging off on some wretched detour or other and that always annoyed me.

So I adopted a rule in London and also in other large metropolitan areas like New York or Tokyo, or Los Angeles for that matter that if I could not catch a train, or afford a taxi I would walk. It works for me!

The place where my desk sat at Ilford's Holborn showroom has been run over by millions of tires since they pushed a road through there in the early sixties. On the rare occasions I've returned to that spot, there is nothing to remember, and the traffic is fierce coming out of Theobald's Road.

It was a good place to learn something of the mysteries of the capital's workings, however, and I enjoyed my short trips into the West End and other fascinating places nearby.

For a couple of years I spent time selling in other parts of the country before I returned to London to work for 3M.

Here I was the lowest of the low, selling Scotch tape to retailers all over London.

In the UK, Scotch was not a known brand and we were up against the generic product, Sellotape. As Americans will talk of Scotch tape when they mean sticky tape, the Brits say Sellotape. It's hard to sell against such brand recognition, but somehow we managed.

Part of the job was to visit small retailers located throughout the city, and that really meant the immediate suburbs and slightly beyond.

Usage of the product meant that we didn't call back to shops for a long time and we would just gobble up the territory and move on; somewhat like locusts!

But this rather tough and lowly selling position did introduce me to areas that I might never have visited on my own, and give me an understanding of the many different aspect of the city.

Our bibles for finding business were A to Z books that were handed down from salesman to salesman. Remember, no GPS, no IPads or IPods or cell phones back in those days. But these little books had been drawn with red ink wherever there were parades of shops, or in American "strip malls." It might sound crude, but it worked very well. But you better not lose the book, as there was no "cloud" backing you up!

It was around 1962 that I was with 3M and found myself in all types of locations. Everybody needs tape at some time, and even poor districts were targets for us. We had sales managers who made sure we didn't just go for the rich places either.

In fact looking back some of the meanest places stick in my memory the firmest. Places like the East End docks. These were not the newly fashionable Yuppy places that they have become. Back then the Isle of Dogs and Wapping were pretty grim. Even 17 years after the war, there was a lot of bomb damage that was in need of repair. But still we battled on with our little company-owned red vans.

I will always remember one small shop down in the dock area. It was tiny and sold only newspapers, confectionery and cigarettes. On the counter right in the middle was a wine glass with cigarettes splayed out. Also there was a house brick, whose indentation held some loose matches. For those really poor and really desperate for a smoke they could purchase one "fag" and one match for a penny!

But wait, haven't cigarettes become so expensive in New York that "loosies" are sold out on the street. And I thought there had been progress!

London has developed since Roman times when it was Londinium. It has grown out in rings building out from the center. From the West End and The City, more communities have grown up. Places like Chiswick in the west and Leyton in the east. There is St. John's Wood in the north and Clapham in the south.

I always think of London being in the shape of a lemon on its side – slightly wider than taller, although that may have changed a bit in the last thirty years with developments.

I also believe that like a magnet, the draw of London is more attractive the closer you are to the center. People in Kensal Rise for instance surely think that a trip into the center to see a film is barely more than just down the road.

If you move out to the west and say, Hounslow, it's no doubt easier to go further out to visit Staines. The draw is much less. We lived about 25 miles from the center growing up, and a trip to London was quite a rarity.

Once you get even further then you begin to see the capital in almost an antagonistic light. People in Birmingham or Bristol see it as somewhere they never go to and don't particularly like. It's almost foreign to them. But they are wrong as it a most wonderful place, if you don't panic.

Los Angeles is often accused of not having a true downtown – it's said it's just a collection of communities. Well, the same could be said of London, in its growing periods.

At the time of the Great Fire of London, there was the center – the City as was, and then large expanses of greenery immediately outside that border.

Today most of the greenery has gone and houses have filled those spaces. Nonetheless London preserves its green reputation with parks large and small. There is no ignoring Hyde Park or Green Park. And all around there are little squares with some public and some private access.

The Green Belt as it's been called is about Watford now and yearly suffers from the assault of developers and the need to expand the city's reach. It's a never ending fight and once the bricks are laid down, there's never a retreat.

As it's true to say that New York is not America, the same can be said of London. It's a society in itself, and has multicultures within it.

Apart from my stint with 3M and short trips out to the East End, I would have to say that the eastern areas are those where I'm least familiar. My father-in-law had an office in Aldgate High Street, which

I used to go to occasionally, but there was not a lot to do down there and no good reason to visit.

On my trip three years ago with my grandson, I asked him if there was anything in particular that he would like to see. He thought on it for a bit and then said he'd like to go and see where Jack the Ripper operated. I was quite impressed and quite pleased as I would never have made that trip myself.

We caught the tube and would have been on time if a fight had not broken out in one of the carriages. It required the police to intervene and created quite a delay. In all my years, such an event had never occurred before. But it meant that we had missed the deadline for our meeting with the guide and the rest of our group.

But with the magic of cell phones we were told exactly how to meet everyone and we only missed about ten minutes of the guided walk.

There have been considerable changes in the East End since the manic killer stalked his helpless victims. It was a time of flickering gas lamps and shady characters, prostitutes – of which the Ripper chose several as victims, and "toffs" who were looking for a little "action" away from the scrutiny of their own class.

The Luftwaffe too made a difference in the layout of this depressed part of London and then there were the immigrants. It seems that all new arrivals had to be bloodied in the East End. Jews, Chinese, Eastern Europeans, and now Hindus and Muslims; forced to live cheek by jowl.

Today, the Chinese and the Jews have moved on into the main stream of society leaving the Indians and the Pakistanis behind to try to make the same journey.

Our walk was perfect. It was mid-November and there was a slightly damp fog over the city. Although many of the buildings and archways where Jack stalked his victims have altered out of all recognition, the guide had brought along photos to show us how it was back then, together with a non-stop bloodthirsty commentary, which was just what a 16 year-old teenager was looking for.

I can still feel the chill as the guide recited the ghastly disembowelling of his five victims: Mary Ann Nicholls; Annie Chapman; Elizabeth Stride; Catherine Eddowes and Mary Jane Kelly.

It's a long time since those murders were committed in 1888, but the atmosphere of a dark, gloomy and foggy East End can still remind one of how it was.

We were quite glad to escape down into the Tube once more and emerge in the western part of the city where the lights were bright and the pubs welcoming for a late night beer and hot dog.

Like most big cities that have been around for a long time, London's skyline doesn't change very much. It still has the Tower of London, the Thames, the various bridges and since about 1960 the Post Office Tower.

This was quite a sensation when it opened. Muzak had put background music into the top revolving restaurant. It was always fun to go up there. The waiters got confused with where their diners were as it turned fairly quickly and they forgot the position of the tables.

During the seventies, the problems with the Irish Republican Army and their placement of bombs in tourist places caused the tower to close to viewers and diners alike. Today it's barely even thought about, being used simply as a repeater station for cell phones.

Two new buildings have been erected since I left England in 1982. There is now The Gerkin in the far end of the City of London, and recently The Shard which sits across from the Tower and I believe is the tallest building in Western Europe, well at least England.

Noel Coward said many years ago, that he was amazed that along with the high rise buildings came a corresponding lowering of morals. I'm not so sure about that as during the Victorian age, morals may have seemed apparent on the surface, but you didn't have to dig very far down to find it was a pretty grim place – especially for poor women.

About the time I joined Muzak, parking meters had been introduced into central London for about a year. Once again the politicians and the bureaucrats assured us that it was to help earn sufficient income to erect large public parking structures.

It's been fifty years and we have yet to see any evidence of those wonderful plans. Once these same public servants become used to an income stream they just can't do without it.

In the 60's, London had lots of empty spaces left after WWII's bomb damage and one company had made use of them. National Car Parks used up a lot of these bomb sites and with the donation of a peaked cap they employed a lot of old men to collect the fees for parking on a place that had only needed the minimum of levelling.

There was also an underlying element of crime in the parking game – Heathrow was still struggling with it in the 70's.

London was not the only city to have parking problems of course. I particularly enjoyed the spirited approach in Madrid, Spain.

Here, any small level piece of ground was fair game in that overcrowded city. As you walked towards a cross section you very often had to squeeze between parked vehicles well ahead of the crossing area as cars were bumper to bumper on the curve. Often cars would be driven straight up on the sidewalk in order to acquire a little more space.

They introduced wardens just before my duties in that city came to a close, and I was able to witness the average "madrileño's" attitude to a parking fine.

An obviously well-heeled gentleman had just exited from an expensive restaurant to find a meter-maid sticking a fine under his wiper blade. Furiously, he pulled it out and tore it into small pieces before hurling it in her face.

The intrusive London meters stopped just outside what was considered the West End and most of my colleagues at Muzak parked at Lancaster Gate and "tubed" in.

I could see the way the wind was blowing and with the daily increase in traffic and the fact that any sales calls could be done by tube in the center, I used to leave my car at Shepherd's Bush. It was faster than slogging it up the Bayswater Road. No doubt the contagion of meters has now spread to even these outer limits; and still no sign of the promised parking structures.

About ten years ago, I was in the upper north of suburbia and having a rental car we needed to go to the South Coast to end our stay in England.

We wanted to meet up with a friend in the West End and so a drive was required to get there and beyond.

As I threaded my way down the Edgware Road, it suddenly struck me that it had been so many years since I had actually driven in the West End.

Furthermore had it been a weekday, I would have had to have paid for it. That is now the rule. Little stickers have to be displayed in car windows to prove that you have paid your fee for the privilege of taking your car into central London.

However since the last couple of years at Muzak, I rarely needed to drive there. Once again the public system was so good that it was faster and cheaper – certainly today – than the car commute with the horrors of parking meters at the end.

Unlike here, the "feeding" of meters was illegal. Sales meetings were regularly interrupted by fellows having to go out and swap their cars around.

One unfortunate decided to chance a feed and had to push between two people actively talking next to his car. He elbowed between and stuck some coins in the slot only to find out the two people were actually wardens. I'm surprised they didn't slap the cuffs on him and drag him away.

On that last drive into the West End, it reminded me how good driving skills are in the capital.

Considering that many of the roads were originally laid down by the Romans two thousand years ago, and that they haven't changed much in size, it's amazing the thing works at all.

There are now many bus lanes on the inside of main roads. You really haven't known traffic congestion until a huge double-decker London bus swooshes up alongside you at a traffic light with a couple of inches to spare.

If you've had to deal with a Friday night's traffic leaving London just before a public holiday, then you are equipped to deal with pretty much any sort of motoring problem anywhere in the world.

I remember arriving in Bahrain once to be collected by my friend Paul Everest who was stationed there for a few years. Apart from the fact that his car looked like a rusting hulk – it was only a year or two old, but the high salt content of the Gulf area stripped paint from cars very quickly – the road ahead looked very dangerous.

Arabs seem to have needed more time to learn the intricate art of driving, having been jogging along on a small donkey's back until quite recently.

As we left the confines of Manama Airport, we faced a very big roundabout. Everest charged into it scattering people, cars and donkeys right and left. "Don't worry about it, these buggers have never been around Hyde Park Corner at 5:30 of an evening. They're hopeless!"

This same sporty attitude is at the heart of all London drivers. They have to have it or quietly go crazy with the stress of the endless jams. Also there is a camaraderie among them. Naturally one tries one's best to get a few feet ahead of one's rivals on the road. But if it's obvious that it can't be done, then one waves any waiting cross traffic ahead. It has to be like that or the entire metropolis would stop completely.

As we stood in the crypt of St Paul's cathedral at the edge of The City, my grandson said to me: "Do we have to look at any more churches, Grandad?"

I sympathised with him as I had taken him into about four since we had arrived in England.

Although a mostly secular society these days, the great churches of London are still a very important part of its structure. I can't resist them.

St. Paul's is perhaps one of the finest examples of cathedral that you can visit.

I had wanted to see Admiral Lord Nelson's tomb, but left it as I could see the wandering attention of a teenager was becoming evident. There's always next time!

And that perhaps is a feeling that is always there in London. It is so big that even natives can't expect to know every piece of it.

No doubt, London "cabbies" come as close to that goal as anyone can.

In order to pass the taxi-driver exam, potential cabbies have to spend a couple of years "on the knowledge." This means riding a small moped around every street and alley to learn all the routes they are likely to need when plying their trade.

Their exam entails sitting in front of experienced drivers and answering questions like: "Which is the quickest route from Waterloo Station to Putney at 5:30?" Or, "How would you handle a Royal visit interrupting your route from Victoria to Marble Arch?" Tricky stuff!

I've been in other cities like New York, where the cabbie has asked me the best way to got from A to B. Never in London.

Of course, if you don't want to use a cab or the tube, or heaven forbid a bus, you can elect to ride a Boris Bike.

I am going over to London in a few months to stay with Michael, and I hope I get the chance to try one of these out.

Named after the mayor of London, Boris Johnson, Boris bikes are plain, rather heavy looking bicycles kept in racks that are available with a regular subscription. They're of use for people who arrive at say a station and have only a short distance to travel, where they are able to deposit the bike in another rack.

I do wonder if they will survive as with the narrow roads, and congestion, are bikes really a safe way to get around; and then there's the climate.

As well as being the seat of government which is in the Houses of Parliament alongside the River Thames at Westminster, it is also the regular home for the monarchy.

Buckingham Palace, that huge square edifice at the end of The Mall (pronounced as in "pal" not as in "all") is the natural center of the capital, the country, and dare I say it, the empire.

Here on the famous balcony royalty greets its subjects and on extremely rare occasions they are joined by "commoners." Such a one was Churchill. It's a hard gig to get to for the average fellow.

The signal as to whether the Queen is in residence is if the royal standard is aloft over the palace. It's rather a gaudy piece of fabric, divided into four quarters with lions rampant and a couple of other creatures as well. It means a lot to the Royal College of Heraldry, but not much to the rest of us.

Parliament is on the other hand something that most Brits are familiar with. It's just across the road from Westminster Abbey, where all the kings and queens of England have been crowned since William the Conqueror first wrested the title from his cousin Harold.

The Abbey is a genuine Gothic building, whereas the Houses of Parliament are a replica. They were built in 1870 after a fire had destroyed the original buildings in 1834. The new architect was Charles Barry but it is Pugin who made the buildings of the "vertical gothic" style that is so recognisable.

There is an old joke that Lloyd George, the former prime minister once won a bet from a young boy, when staying at his parents' home. Parliament was easily within view and he bet the boy that he couldn't see Big Ben from there. The boy bet the PM a shilling that he could, and lost.

Big Ben is actually the bell that hangs at the top of the Elizabeth Tower and not the tower itself.

But that area of the city is so important from the history of the country that it is a magnet to visitors and locals alike. It's hard not to get swept up in the atmosphere of it when swirling around in the traffic.

A short step up the road is Downing Street and the home of the Prime Minister, Number 10.

When I was first starting out, Number 10 was only across the park and a short walk from the office. It was easy to access from Horseguards' Parade through a short passage, or directly from Whitehall. Today that is not possible and access is denied to all but invited guests.

I think it's sad that all the way through the crises of Victorian anarchists and two World Wars, that Downing Street was open to anyone and even possible to have a photo taken against the famous front door (usually with the cooperation of a friendly policeman on duty outside) but with the advent of the vicious IRA bombers that privilege ended. You cn barely see it through the iron barricades.

Walking up Whitehall past the many government offices you reach the Cenotaph. This is a stone memorial in memory of the nation's dead from the wars. At 11:00 am on Remembrance Sunday (the closest Sunday to the 11th of November when the armistice ended the conflict of WWI) the sovereign lays a wreath on behalf of a "grateful nation" for the ultimate sacrifice made by all those who died. It was King George V who suggested a two minute silence be observed across the land as the clocks struck the hour at which the war ended. I think it has subsequently been reduced to one minute – so that people can catch up with their e-mails and the latest post on Facebook!

Some time in the late sixties I was passing the brand new Paternoster Square which abuts St. Pauls Cathedral. As I came down the steps to the west entrance there were quite a lot of people standing around. I heard from the buzz, that Her Majesty was about to turn up for some celebration.

Sure enough eventually a large Daimler limousine rolled around the semi circular driveway and out she got. She was wearing a bright lemon yellow costume. Naturally I didn't make a scene, but I'm certain she knew I was there.

The only other time I saw her in person was when I was about 13 and she had just come to the throne after her father George VI had died. We had the day off at school as she was to drive along the A41 and we were expected to line the road and cheer.

We did so and the car did come past. It wasn't gong very fast, but it was too fast to really see her in any detail and I'm sure she didn't spot me on that occasion.

One of the photographs we brought over from England is a picture of Yvonne with the queen. Yvonne was accepting an award for horseback riding from Her Majesty, but I do like to point out that although she was officially the queen, the coronation had not yet occurred; so it doesn't really count, does it?

Our upcoming visit to London is fast approaching. I am really looking forward to it. There is a touch of sadness however as the reason there is room at Michael's house is that his mother Veronica died in 2013. It was very sad as she had struggled with Parkinson's disease and she had a miserable time of it for the last couple of years.

She was a terrific woman and a great friend to both Yvonne and I over the years since we parted. I was lucky to have had the chance to meet up with her with Evan when we made our trip there in 2011, and the three of us had lunch. Her short term memory was beginning to go, but she remembered things from decades ago quite sharply.

On this trip we shall try and remember her and also make a few trips to areas that I haven't been to in years. I hope however to recall some of my favourite places that perhaps Yvonne might enjoy.

> *I've been walking about London for the last thirty years, and I find something fresh in it every day.*
> — *Walter Besant*

Chapter Eleven

POLITICS

The majority is never right. Never, I tell you! That's one of these lies in society that no free and intelligent man can help rebelling against. Who are the people that make up the biggest proportion of the population -- the intelligent ones or the fools?
— *Henrik Ibsen*

The radical invents the views. When he has worn them out the conservative adopts them.
— *Mark Twain*

I don't think I took much notice of politics until I was about 45. To begin with in my childhood I was a knee-jerk Conservative like my parents. I certainly didn't give that any thought at all.

At school we had the son of a Labour MP and he had a pretty rough time. Fortunately we were merely echoing the grumbles that we had heard from our parents and so he never truly had to defend his father's positions at all.

Looking back however, I do wonder why his father sent him to a private school as surely all good socialists believe in the power and righteousness of the state and should therefore allow the state to educate their offspring.

I should have liked to ask him for his parent's reasons.

Labour and Conservative governments came and went. After the war, Churchill was voted out of office and to this day I've never found out why the man who basically singlehandedly motivated us through such terrors should have been so shabbily treated.

I have heard that it was the soldiers' vote that tipped the scale and in all fairness, he was associated with the two greatest conflicts known to man.

And so in 1946 Labour came in with all the zeal of true believers. I remember my father storming around a little, but it was only years later that I understood how upsetting it must have been for him and his like-minded conservative friends to find out that all the various railway companies were now to be run by the government and that health care, courtesy of Aneurin Bevan, was to be the way of the future.

Clement Attlee was an uninspiring figure with a rather tremulous voice. His arch rival, Winston Churchill was told by one of Atlee's supporters that Clement was a very modest man; to which he replied: "He has so much to be modest about!"

Eventually Churchill came back and served out his terms with some distinction.

Every April the Chancellor of the Exchequer would announce the new budget for the year, and to my father's horror it would contain that bane of all working men, an increase in the tax on cigarettes and beer. Petrol too would be increased but as my father didn't have a car, he didn't care about that.

He would be glum for several days. But the big alterations in the direction of the country didn't seem to upset him too much.

I suspect that the loss of the British Empire must have hit nearly everyone quite hard; particularly the jewel in the crown, India.

Anthony Eden, who had been a foreign minister with Churchill during the war was Prime Minister in 1956. It was then that we had some problems with Nasser, the dictator of Egypt. He not unreasonably wanted to control his country's major asset the Suez Canal.

This seemed extremely unreasonable to most English. After all we'd been running it for years, and the Egyptians were notoriously unreliable. They might even start charging us for sailing our ships through there. Whatever next! The fact that it was the French who actually built the thing was never mentioned.

We went to war and we were doing rather well, but the days of such gunboat diplomacy were past, and America waved a yellow and then a red card at us for unsportsmanlike behaviour and we had to be sent off the pitch of the world stage.

Slowly the entire empire became unravelled. Kenya, Malaysia, all those nasty little sundrenched countries in Africa that Englishmen had sweated, fornicated and died in were now chiefdoms in their own right.

And we were still trying to clear away much of the bomb damage from our streets. It took a long time.

I'm sure it's a very unusual young man of late teens and early twenties who pays much attention to what's going on beyond the scope of his sweaty little palms.

I was no different. I was basically aware that things were better when the Tories were in and worse when Labor took over.

I automatically liked Eden, Macmillan and their cohorts, and disliked Gaitskill, Brown and the socialists who were mostly in opposition.

I joined Muzak in April 1965, and one month later Labour was swept in to power with a crouching little north countryman called Harold Wilson.

Immediately there were tremors throughout the business community. Labour was to stop business expenses being tax exempt unless you were entertaining foreign buyers.

I remember a cartoon in a morning paper. It showed a group of well dressed businessmen getting off a bus outside the Savoy Hotel. The Jamaican bus conductor was offering himself to the crowd so that they could put their lunches down on expenses.

Nationalisation or public ownership had been the norm in several sectors of British society for some time now. The railways, the stock exchange, the electrical grid, water works, gas companies all were under the control of some bureaucracy. It was fairly benign, and none of us found there to be any particular inconvenience.

The bêtes noires of English society however were the unions. These were quite monstrous, and truly impacted our lives each year.

The system was designed so that unions could come out "in sympathy" with their fellows if a disagreement existed. Throughout the late sixties and particularly early seventies, the problems would begin with the miners.

Joe Gormley, who was the leader of the miners' union, would each January appear on the steps of the Coal Board just south of Hyde Park, looking grim.

He had been a miner and had that skin that looked like he had not been able to remove all the soot from it.

He would come out in his folksy way and tell everyone that he couldn't agree with the management, and that the lads would have to talk about it.

There would be a few more negotiations and then they would go out on strike. The argument was always: "how would you like to be down the pit, hacking away at the face with a pickaxe, breathing in the stale air in dangerous conditions?"

The truth was that by then for every face worker, there were scores of others working above ground, and even below, things had much improved for the health and safety of all concerned.

This dance around the may pole would happen every January to take advantage of the extreme winter conditions for the rest of us, and then the other unions would come out "in sympathy."

It would be the truck drivers, followed by the electrical unions and then the boilermakers, etc. etc. It was the most miserable time for everyone.

The country would grind to a halt. During one crisis we were even rationed to a three-day week. Here, we were not allowed to use any power in our offices at all. I had a paraffin lamp on my desk and managed to do with that. But even in an overcoat with gloves, it was damned cold, with no heating on.

It took Maggie Thatcher to ban sympathy strikes and then the eventual demise of the coal industry to stop the annual spiral into misery.

About that time I came out to America and left all that stuff behind. I forgot about Labor and Conservative labels, imagining that those days were behind me and that in America people were different.

How wrong I was.

The fact is that people seem to divide naturally into two types. As Horace Walpole put it in the 18th century: "The world is a comedy to those who think; a tragedy to those who feel."

If you remove any personal or family ties, then you can see this difference when a tragedy occurs. I remember once, when the famous Dale Earnhardt crashed and died on the NASCAR racetrack. It was all over the TV's in a bar one Saturday lunchtime when were having a drink. One local, a particularly tough guy, I thought, was transfixed in front of one of the TV's with tears streaming down his face. He must have been a liberal. I cannot think of any sports personality that would have me in such a state.

When we are born, we can only feel, as we don't have too many thoughts. I believe it was the goal and duty of our parents and school teachers over the subsequent years to help us overcome most of these feelings and replace them with thoughts.

I find it interesting that most liberal people like to ask others how they feel, and rarely how they think.

When we arrived in America, Ronald Reagan was the president. Of course we were so involved in trying to make our business succeed that we didn't pay a lot of attention to what was going on in the country.

However it was impossible not to notice how the media goaded Reagan at press announcements, and there was the general air of superiority over him. He was just a cowboy/actor/ex-governor etc. He wasn't as dismissed as Gerald Ford, whom it was said to have difficulty walking and chewing gum at the same time. You may remember the countless times the picture of him was shown stumbling down the steps of Air Force One, I think it was.

With the exception of Nixon, who was just considered a crook, all Republican presidents have been considered by the media as fools. Whereas all Democrat ones are thought to be the smartest people alive.

Why is that? Perhaps it's because most of the media are well to the left. And why is that? Sadly, journalism is no longer the reporting of facts. I'm sure that the vast majority of those entering journalism colleges are there because they "want to make a difference!"

As soon as they sit their little impressionable backsides down in their first class they will be greeted by a professor who also wants to make a difference.

Making a difference usually means changing our very natures, and then after we've truncated all the natural aggression and greed of mankind, we should hand it over to our betters to deal with. In today's liberal world that usually means the government.

Liberals seems to love big government and high taxes and lots of regulations that will clamp down on business, which as we all know is just a bunch of rich capitalists who want to rip us off.

Unfortunately many of the capitalists do want to rip us off, but unlike the bureaucrats who control our lives, these same businessmen must provide a service or goods that people want and need or they will go bust. Bureaucrats don't have to be that efficient, they never go bust, and they truly will go for ever.

I think the first political feelings I ever had were in 1954. I was unaware of it at the time but it was the first time I had seen the potential of political extremism.

The BBC used to put on a Sunday Theatre production every week. It was usually an hour and a half of drama and it was a firm family favourite to sit in front of our small black and white TV to watch.

We had only had TV for a short time since it was bought when the Queen was to be crowned a year earlier. There was no choice for a couple of years as the BBC was the only program aired.

The Drama on the Week on December 12th was a production of George Orwell's "1984."

Orwell, whose real name was Eric Blair, had been writing for a dozen years with mixed results and a very mixed income. He had been the son of a British civil servant in Burma. Among his duties was the overseeing of the drug trade the Brits encouraged to add to the Empire's coffers. It's not just street thugs that can figure this stuff out!

Orwell returned to England after finding life as a colonial very disturbing and unsettling. He didn't like the life and hated being involved in what he saw as injustice.

With few skills outside of writing, he found himself on the streets, and then tried to live in Paris, where again he was down and out – the name of one of his books.

He went to Spain to fight for the International Brigade against the Fascists. The "Internationals" were communists, and Orwell found a similar view of the world to his own among their ranks.

Unfortunately, he also found that this world view was not to be messed with. The strict ideological attitudes held by the leaders and the several ranks below them meant extreme cruelty and total obedience. It was worse than life under the British Raj.

He came into contact with the opposite side and found that they too were the same. Inflexibility and strict adherence to a set of beliefs was what kept the entire thing ticking.

At the tender age of 15, I had no idea of such beliefs and when the scenes of life in the far future – George Orwell had written his novel in 1948 and transposed the last two numbers thinking that 1984 was sufficiently far ahead as to be a good date – I was completely transfixed.

It turned out that the entire watching public was too. Nobody had ever seen anything like it and even in parliament, questions were asked.

The next day the play was all over the news and on everybody's lips. A few boys had seen it at school and we all talked animatedly about it.

It was the custom of the BBC to repeat the Drama of the Week again on the following Thursday and there was a lot of controversy about whether or not to show this play again as it had been so upsetting.

Eventually the decision was made to air it, and it was done live back in those days. Nearly everyone who had a TV set was glued to it, and my family also wanted to see it again.

The cast was led by Peter Cushing as Winston Smith, with Yvonne Mitchell as his secret girlfriend, Julia. Andre Morell was his inquisitor and Donald Pleasance was Smith's hapless neighbor.

There had been rumours of brain washing in the Korean War where American POW's were treated badly and forced to accept the ideology of their captors. We knew that one or two of the Germans in WWII were found to be evil, but this was altogether far, far worse, than anything we had ever heard about or even dreamed in our worst nightmares.

I find fewer and fewer young people are familiar with 1984. Perhaps with Hollywood pumping out horror flick after horror flick, the horrific atmosphere of Orwell's world is pretty tame. But in peaceful suburban Watford, Hertfordshire, it was a wake up call of monumental proportions.

For those not familiar with the plot, it is pretty simple. In the far distant time, Winston Smith is not happy with his life, which he sees as empty and dangerous; dangerous because he doesn't like it. No-one in 1984, within the party is allowed to think differently. That would be a thought crime. There is a special Thought Police who regularly drag people off if they are even charged with such transgressions.

Every room of every house is wired with two-way TV's; here every aspect of ones life is scrutinised. But Winston has a secret corner where he believes the TV's can't see him. Closeted away there he begins to write a journal criticising life under the regime.

Sex is forbidden except for procreation and is strictly controlled. But Winston falls for Julia. They meet for regular trysts in the territory ceded to the "proles." These are the people outside of the party and who make the crumbling society function. They are the virtual slaves and workers of that modern day.

But Big Brother is always watching and inevitably they are betrayed. Also Smith's journal is known to the authorities. They are both arrested and taken for interrogation. Separately they are tortured until they eventually, not only give up each other, but try to have the other one take their punishment.

The play ends with both Winston and Julia seeing each other by chance in a dreary café called The Chestnut Tree. They hardly acknowledge each other, while a crackling distorted song plays: "Underneath the spreading chestnut tree, I sold you and you sold me!"

The entire play was in black and white of course – we were at least a decade away from color – and this only added to the sense of desolation and hopelessness.

It was truly unforgettable and the later movie with Richard Burton and John Hurt never quite measured up to it.

It affected me deeply and even nowadays I see events in our western societies that remind me of the way things could go.

After this watershed, like most teenagers I was too involved with my own life to concern myself with such matters. Life had to be achieved and there were lots of things to be attracted to; not towards a lot of boring old men in dark suits droning on and on.

Some time in the mid-sixties I read my first Alexander Solzhenitsyn book. I think it was the trilogy The Gulag Archipelago. The Orwell play came back again in my mind. Solzhenitsyn's account of how life operated in Soviet Russia under Stalin made me realize that Winston Smith's hell on earth really did exist here.

And yet his book One Day in the Life of Ivan Denisovitch showed that a man could overcome such dreadful adversities if only for one day.

I really now understood why totalitarianism was so frightening. The prospect of having to live within the collective was completely abhorrent to me.

And in fairness, England's Labor Party and the USA's Democratic Party were a long way from that; at that time anyway.

All my life we always had one particularly evil enemy against who we were engaged in perpetual struggles.

Until 1945, it was the Nazis, then immediately afterwards we had the spectre of the Soviets. The latter was still in place when we came to the USA. In fact although we were further away geographically the danger had always seemed closer to the Yanks.

When the Berlin Wall came down in 1989, it was as if a great weight had been lifted off all our shoulders. We were finally free to pursue our dreams and live in peace. Sadly, the dream was not quite as perfect as we had all imagined.

By now I was becoming more interested in how the political system in America worked. Like most everything else that was viewed from Europe, it was bigger, badder and infinitely more complex that what we had witnessed back home.

We became American citizens in 1992 and attended an "intimate" little ceremony of some 5,000 people at the Convention Center in downtown Los Angeles.

We were given little flags to wave at the appointed moment and before the ceremony we had the pleasure of watching on a very large screen in the corner of the hall, a video of Dwight Yokem sitting on a tractor's fender singing "Proud to be an American."

It wasn't exactly a goose bump moment. Then in came the judge in the same kind of robe that all my schoolmasters wore, but without the fancy cowl they used for high days and holidays. He was of Chinese heritage and his accent was so thick that we hardly understood the words. But we managed as everyone else did and after reciting the Pledge of Allegiance we were Americans.

We had given up our green cards beforehand. But the importance of this magic document was so great that I kept a copy for many years; not quite believing that if we were stopped by the police or immigration, we could simply say were citizens and were inducted in LA, California.

We shuffled out of the hall into the fierce sunlight and were met by a desk from each political party. The Democratic one had a life-sized cut-out of Bill Clinton playing his saxophone. The Republican one was a simple desk with red, white and blue trimmings and a couple of forms to sign. We did that.

We rode home on my brand new Harley Davidson FXRS-SP with our flags flying. We were Americans (and Republicans, all in one day!)

About this time I discovered a talk radio host called Rush Limbaugh. Forgiving him his rather odd Christian name, I found his views mostly in agreement with mine. They also seemed to be the exact opposite of what I was hearing on the TV and reading in newspapers.

Limbaugh singlehandedly brought out the voice of all the conservative Americans who felt they were alone in the country that they loved.

After the sixties revolution the way forward seemed to all belong to the left. Once you began to dwell on these matters, it began to be depressing. How could the rot be stopped?

Limbaugh and a number of other talk show hosts elucidated views that were traditional while continuing a drumbeat of opposition to liberal ideas.

In response, the libs did what they always do; they appealed to the law to shut down this persistent voice.

Several attempts were made to start liberal talk radio. All of them failed. Yes, all of them. None of the plans worked out in the long run. Air America was an entire liberal radio network designed to present an exclusive liberal view. It lasted a few years but its audience declined to the point where even the most fanatical of its backers couldn't pretend anymore.

The legal battle was started to make alternative views on the public airwaves mandatory. In other words the scheme was that if a broadcaster was to offer a political opinion then an opposite opinion must follow. You can only imagine the shambles in a broadcast booth trying to measure fair time equally – and the lawsuits that would result.

As the TV networks were mostly left leaning (while all the time pretending to be independent, of course) such a fair balance concept would be equally idiotic in a TV studio.

Gradually the idea fell away, and talk radio continued to be the voice of conservative America.

Why should this medium be so successful for conservative minds? My theory is that such ideas have been given a great deal of thought and appeal to more thoughts rather than feelings. Feelings, which are the driving force of most liberalism, don't come over too well in just the medium of sound. They do far better when accompanied by pictures – hence the preponderance of touchy-feely programs on TV. It's where they belong.

Most of the main stream media hated Limbaugh and continue to do so. Within a year or two he became the most listened to talk show host in America with an audience of anything from 15 to 20 million daily. These numbers are of course disputed by liberals, but one thing you can say is that he hosts the most successful radio show in the world on a three hour a day basis. Monday through Friday. Liberals hate him.

Most of the opposition towards Limbaugh is along the lines of: "Well, he's just an entertainer." Well, they should have been so successful.

Even a fairly good fan begins to acquire an understanding of what Limbaugh is likely to say on any topic. I don't hear him as much as I used to when I was out driving around the country, but he still makes a lot of sense.

When he was just starting out, he wrote a column for the Sacramento Bee. In it he listed what he called the 35 undeniable truths of life. They are readily available on the Internet and I recommend reading them through. If you don't know Rush and his views, they will at least give you a taste of his wit and mentality.

Rush Limbaugh is not the only radio talk show host out there making sense. I often listen to a man called Dennis Prager. He is a former rabbi and teacher. I often refer to him as the thinking man's Limbaugh, but that's not really fair to Limbaugh.

Nonetheless he talks very fairly and I have heard him have his mind changed with a particular argument from a caller.

So after I started paying attention, I soon found out that there really wasn't any difference between the political parties of my youth than in my new adopted land.

You had the left and the right. Conservatives, Republican, Democrats or Socialists, they were much the same. It took a long time to figure out that the right wanted you to be on your own, with the skimpiest safety net. The left wanted the government to take care of you from cradle to grave.

You pays your money and you takes your choice!

When I came out here in 1982, there was still the chance of getting your hands on some "keeping money," I fear that this opportunity has now passed. Unless some elected party can reverse the trend of high taxes and overregulation, I fear we are destined to go the way of Europe.

The left often states that the deck is stacked against the middle class. But it is the left's policies that have made the middle class irrelevant and much, much poorer. Just ask the many twenty-somethings who have been forced to give up the dream of buying a house and having a couple of cars in the garage while putting some money away for the children's education.

Today, in New York, there are ten agencies you have to visit to acquire a permit to open a business. What madness is this when everyone knows we desperately need jobs? To overcome the difficulty of such a labyrinth, guess what the bureaucrats did? They opened up an eleventh department to help you steer your way around all the paperwork.

Locally here in Big Bear we have seen a couple of similar situations where bureaucracy is unstoppable. Firstly, when I managed a condominium complex of some 65 units, we had two swimming pools and two Jacuzzis. Every summer on a couple of occasions, an inspector would arrive with little bottles and a towel. They were there to make sure our water facilities were safe.

I have no problem with this, but eventually the regulations became so stringent and the agency so harsh, that a number of public pools were closed down.

Do you think any of the inspectors were let go? Exactly!

When we first arrived here, I noticed a number of older citizens driving around wearing peaked hats and with magnetic signs stuck on their car doors. These proclaimed the occupants to be a Citizen Patrol.

Not a bad idea in an area with lots of retirees and also lots of empty properties belonging to absentees.

These old people would happily drive around and keep an eye on things. They paid for their hats as well, I believe.

It didn't take long before some civil servant saw this as a great career building opportunity.

Soon these old self-funding men – they were usually men – were in nice county-owned, brand new cars with signwriting on each. They had matching uniforms as well and eventually they were seen assisting the police in some of the duties the police didn't want to do.

Naturally there would now be a complete department to handle citizen patrols and of course, there would be recruitment and training courses; lots of training courses.

What had started out as a great idea now was under the control of some bureaucrat with a big department and a full budget including all those most sought after benefits. Ah, yes, the bennies!

The end result of all this activity and cost is that today, we rarely if ever see a citizen patrol out doing what they were intended to do. It is just as it was before anyone thought of the concept.

From time to time I get talking to young people about the way things are. You may find it surprising that I don't often voice an opinion on them. I'm much more interested in how they see the world around them and how they want society to be when they're my age.

Often I would like to recommend a certain book to them but I never do because I think you have to be well over forty – and maybe fifty – before you tackle it. It is Atlas Shrugged by Ayn Rand.

She wrote it in the mid-fifties and it is the story of the producers of a society basically going on strike. Her prescience is quite remarkable as she foretold the advance and the power of a central government and its accompanying bureaucracy.

With great deliberation, John Galt contacts all the job creators of his society to disappear and start their lives anew in a part of Colorado. Here they can escape the stultifying regulations that a socialist government has foisted on them.

Ayn Rand has been accused of promoting selfishness, and on the first run through it does look that way. But her philosophy, called objectivism, was more than that. She believed that what man had in his mind was priceless and belonged to him alone. It was up to him to exploit it to the best of his ability. If he didn't do this, then trying to help everyone else was pointless. It's a simple idea, but it has caused a great deal of difficulty in being adhered to.

Some years ago a young female relative of Yvonne's came over to stay with us for a few days. We got into a number of conversations. Over dinner on her last night, she asked me what the difference between a liberal and a conservative was. I said I'd need a few hours thought on that one and allowed the ideas to ruminate overnight.

The next morning I wrote this out and gave it to her to read. I think she took it with her.

I've looked at this over a number of years and I've even sent it to liberals for their comments. I've never heard back from them. So whether my screed is beneath their contempt or it's on the mark. I'll leave you to decide.

CONSERVATISM/LIBERALISM

A quote of Bill Armey the ex-leader of the House: *"Conservatives believe it when they see it; Liberals see it when they believe it."*

"If it feels good, do it!" "Why can't we all just get along?"
(Anon, 1960's) (Rodney King, 1992)

Conservatives generally believe that the problems in the world are caused by the weakness of man, and that such weakness can be controlled by discipline and laws, for the benefit of all.

Liberals tend to believe that the problems of the world are caused by economic inequalities, and that such problems can be eradicated by re-distributing wealth. I.e. Taking from the rich (achievers) to give to the poor (non-achievers.)

Conservatives believe that most people, if left alone by government regulations, will succeed through hard work and desire.

Liberals believe that unless the government 'levels the playing field' those with benefits and talents will strip away from the rest of the pack.

Conservatives believe in competition, liberals don't. They believe it causes loss of self-worth and self-esteem. Conservatives tend not to use those terms.

Conservatives believe that if one is attacked one should strike back. Liberals believe that if one has a greater understanding of one's attacker, one can win him over with argument and reason.

Conservatives believe that given the right opportunities, everyone can succeed. Liberals believe that most people need some help - preferably from the government.

Conservatives believe that crime should be punished, as it will send a message to other criminals and act as a deterrent. Liberals believe that crime is mostly caused by wrongs done to the criminal, and can be 'cured' by understanding.

Conservatives believe in a strong military to deter attack. Liberals believe such a military only provokes one's enemies, and also causes a too aggressive stance by the nation.

Conservatives believe that in the love of God all men are equal. Liberals believe that without help many people can never become equal.

Conservatives believe that communism failed because it worked against man's natural competitiveness and brought everyone down to the lowest possible level. Liberals believe that communism would have worked if they had run it and it hadn't been crushed by American imperialism.

Conservatives tend to be optimistic, liberals pessimistic.

Liberals believe that we all have the right to be happy. Conservatives know that happiness needs work and the better one is prepared, and the more disciplined one is, the better chance of such happiness.

Conservatives tend to say: "I think that..." Liberals are more likely to say: "I feel ..."

Conservatism tends to be masculine in its outlook, and liberalism feminine.

Conservatives believe in individualism, Liberals believe in collectivism.

Liberals see themselves as enlightened and smart; they see conservatives as stuffy, and mostly dumb.

Conservatives see themselves as moral and custodians of successful Western culture; they see liberals as naïve and childlike.

Conservative heroes: Churchill, Thatcher, Reagan, and George W. Bush.

Liberal heroes: Ramsey MacDonald, Roosevelt, Kennedy (both Robert and John F.), Johnson (Who introduced the Great Society in 1964 and for which we are all still paying!) and Bill Clinton.

Conservative successes: World War II, Korea, American capitalism, private education.

Liberal successes: The Welfare State; Vietnam; equal rights for women and blacks; abortion rights; the British National Health Service?

Conservative failures: Suez Canal War; probably World War I; The unacceptable face of capitalism - namely greed; the attack by Argentina on the Falklands; privatizing British Rail.

Liberal failures: Communism; state education; the British National Health Service!

Dr. Charles Krauthammer says: *"Conservatives believe that liberals are stupid; but liberals believe that conservatives are evil!" This therefore exonerates them from attacking and using immoral methods to strike down such evil. It's for the common good (or for the sake of the children!)*

> *"The last thing I ever wanted was to be alive when the three most powerful people on the whole planet would be named Bush, Dick and Colon."*
> — *Kurt Vonnegut*

"All comparisons are odious!" (Anon)

Having lived in America now for over thirty years, I do have a couple of suggestions regarding the political process.

Whereas I have the utmost respect and admiration for those framers of our constitution who wrote such a magnificent document so many years ago, I do believe there was a provision that could have been added.

There are term limits for presidents, mayors and other positions of power. Why not for senators and congressmen?

We have so refined our system that now we have a professional class of politicians who do nothing but write laws for all of us while finding ways to avoid them themselves.

Ted Kennedy never had a proper job in his entire life. People like Nancy Pelosi and John Boehner have been there for years. Surely this is not healthy. With the electorate being lazy, 90% of incumbents are re-elected term after term. Can't we try and get some new blood spilling along the halls of Washington D.C.?

I have one other suggestion which is perhaps not acceptable to the left, who seem to revel in their side's ignorance.

Should we not have an electorate who have at least some knowledge as to how the country functions?

When I took my citizenship exam, I had to answer ten questions, with a pass mark of 50%. These were not hard. For instance, what are the three branches of government? Who is the Attorney General? What is the name of the Vice President? How many seats are there in the Senate?

Surely for those people lining up to vote, with the voting cards already being so large, adding these types of questions at the beginning would only ensure that the people casting their vote had at least the basics of citizenship?

When the machines tally the score, those with half their answers wrong would immediately have their votes eliminated. Enough with the low information voters putting in their requests for free stuff!

This is written the morning after the mid-term elections of 2014. It appears that the Republicans have managed a sizeable victory to take over the Senate and increase their hold on the House and also new governorships. But it is the mid-terms after all and I remember the drubbing Bill Clinton received in 1994, George W Bush in 2006 and now Obama.

It seems that half way through a second term any president has problems.

My problem however is that now the Republicans have taken control, what will they do with it? Or are they just Democrat-lite?

In 1994, when Newt Gingrich took over control of the House of Representatives, he had a Contract with America. In that document the incoming neo-cons as they were called, promised to shrink government. One of the casualties of such shrinkage was to be the Corporation for Public Broadcasting. It's still there. I believe the Departments of Commerce, and Education were also on the chopping block. No change there either.

A couple of decades ago the editor of National Review, John O'Sullivan, who was an Englishman in spite of his Celtic name, made a statement that I've never forgotten. He said that any organisation or group that was not specifically conservative would eventually drift left.

I have remembered this because I have noticed that it is true. I am sure that when the American Civil Liberties Union (The ACLU) was founded in 1920, its aims were specifically conservative. Over the years however they have become so far to the left as to be virtually anarchistic.

It seems that the natural state of comfortable people living without fear of anything causes them to become more and more liberal. The wealthy east and west side of New York no doubt shows this to be the case.

I heard this liberal mindset described the other day as "naïve hope." And it is difficult to refute the claim. It was the same attitude that caused Chamberlain to be taken in by Hitler. Surely it can't have been that hard to realise the man was a self-serving dictator who wanted to control Europe.

That is not to say that Chamberlain was a bad man. He wanted peace with all his heart, but he allowed this feeling of naïve hope to take over his reasoning.

Since Obama took office, I have noticed that the entire country seems to have drifted further to the left. It gives in on nearly every front in the naïve hope that it's going to help the world to like us more.

We have apologised to the Muslims, taken sanctions off the table with Iran, pulled out of Iraq, allowed Putin to annex the Crimea and play games along the Ukrainian border, while we removed our missiles from E. Europe. Now we have opened up diplomacy with Cuba. None of these things has resulted in any improvement in our position; none of them has caused the world to hate us less or stop their plans for our demise. The attitude of naïve hope has only made us weaker in the belief that somehow we've done the right thing.

The most recent action has been to allow that little pipsqueak Kim Jong Un to hack one of Hollywood's studios and effectively blackmail us into removing a film of which he disapproves.

And today the Tea Party is one of the most hated groups in the entire country because they are concerned at this overwhelming slide into weakness, over-taxation and regulation. And the dislike includes that coming from the Republican Party who seems to feel threatened by this presumption.

I just have this unsettling feeling that when the Republicans take over both houses of Congress in 2015, they'll just think it's their turn with the money, when we desperately need to change direction and earn back our credibility.

It will be an interesting two years however with Obama left alone in the White House. Of course, his unpopularity is just racism!

Recently I was asked why Obama did not attend the march in Paris to protest the shooting of unarmed journalists at the magazine Charlie Hebdo. Furthermore he did not even send the Vice President or the Secretary of State. The absence was noted all around the world and even his normal supporters in the left leaning main stream media were discombobulated and embarrassed.

I wrote this reply about Obama's attitude, which I believe to be the same as most of those who frequent faculty lounges in America's academia.

None of the actions of the current occupant of the White House are surprising to those of us who always recognised him for what he is - an old fashioned socialist/pacifist from the 1930's. We knew this before he even became the frontrunner in 2007.

As such he is extremely uncomfortable with blaming those he considers victims of American imperialism. He truly believes America gained its prominence and wealth through the exploitation of other people including Muslims, with whom he strongly identifies. He and his cohorts are not even able to say "Islamic Terrorists," maintaining that there are lots of other types. His latest position is that the recent batch of incidents are the work of people who are merely using Islam as a front. They are not really Muslims.

Therefore it would have been very difficult to have joined a march in solidarity with the others who all blame Islamic religious fervor for the murders of the 17 innocent French citizens.

And there was football on TV!

Also some of his pals didn't make it there either - Raul and Fidel Castro; Kim Jong Un; Hu Jintau or Vladimir Putin. Yesterday in explanation, Jimmy Carter said that "On returning from a (17 day tax payer funded Hawaiian) vacation, there's a lot of stuff to do; a lot of things on the desk." Thank you, Jimmy - always an insightful fellow to listen to!

It was a sad and embarrassing day to have to see the administration actually state they might have preferred a different approach. About as close as they have ever come to an apology.

> *The one thing our Founding Fathers could not foresee -- they were farmers, professional men, businessmen giving of their time and effort to an idea that became a country -- was a nation governed by professional politicians who had an interest in getting re-elected. They probably envisioned a fellow serving a couple of hitches and then eagerly looking forward to getting back to the farm*
> *— Ronald Reagan*

Chapter Twelve

RELIGION

Too many people embrace religion from the same motives that they take a companion in wedlock, not from true love of the person, but because of a large dowry.
— *Hosea Ballou*

I'm for decency -- period. I'm for anything and everything that bodes love and consideration for my fellow man. But when lip service to some mysterious deity permits bestiality on Wednesday and absolution on Sunday -- cash me out.
— *Frank Sinatra*

In polite company the two subjects considered unmentionable are religion and politics. Well, we've already broken the first taboo in the previous chapter, so here goes with the second.

In 1939, when I was born, there was no doubt that England was a Christian country. Most people if you asked them would admit to being Christian, and most attended church regularly.

Now 75 years later I wonder what the percentage of attendees is, and also the number of people who think of themselves as Christian.

On my infrequent trips back to the UK, I am always slightly disturbed by the number of closed churches and even by the ones turned into other businesses – restaurants, cafés and even bars!

But I suspect this general conversion to atheism or agnosticism only reflects my own stumbling journey down the cloistered halls of belief.

Growing up, it was taken for granted that one went to church on Sundays or had a pretty good excuse for not doing so. Those who found this excuse however would always make the effort for high days and holidays like Christmas.

Morning Service (Matins) was a cheerful occasion with everyone dressed up and the vicar smiling from the pulpit. There was something comforting about the rote of the service and the patriotic-like "marchiness" of the hymns.

We never had any doubts that God was in fact an Englishman, even though his son we were told had a decidedly Semitic background.

I read somewhere years ago an article by an American who said he always envied the English as they prayed as if it was one Englishman talking to another. Being a member of the Church of England was quite comforting.

Of course, we had Catholics in the country and they were viewed as being rather different, if not slightly dangerous. My father actually believed that they were under the orders of the Pope who could ask them to strike down a Protestant when he saw fit. I never quite bought into it.

I had a friend who lived opposite my grandparents. He was called Bobby Silcocks and he was a Catholic. He was about a year younger than me and I found him to be quite normal except when I heard about confession.

We had reached the interesting stage of some spirited games with a number of the local girls that took the form of "doctors and patients." We were making pretty good progress, when he dropped the bomb that he confessed these "sins" to the father each Friday when he entered the confessional box. It was a jaw dropping moment for me.

I used to cross the road when I walked past the Catholic Church after that, and I certainly would look away when the priest in his flowing cloak passed by. I also thereafter viewed Bobby's friendship with something approaching caution.

Looking back it seems to me that the Catholics had built up a system that the KGB would have given their eye teeth to create. Here you had a perfectly submissive population actually willing to tell you all their intimate secrets, and with no need of torture or other coercion. It seems masterly to me.

Occasionally, we would go to Evensong which was never my favourite. I never liked the basic assumption that as the day was ending we might not make it through the night and so better prepare for that eventuality. The singing of the Nunc Dimitus always depressed me.

And yet being a part of this huge historical tableau was a comfort in itself. How could one have doubts? After all some of the best (and worst) people who had walked the earth before us, were involved in this great progression of worship.

Of course, doubts would enter in, but one of the great secrets of religion is that if you keep the parishioners coming, their faith will continue and even grow. It builds a sort of dependence. Like a drug.

The practitioners of the various sects know this, of course.

For a very short time I attended a boy's Christian club called The Crusaders. It was run by the father of one of my friends. The meetings took place in a creaking, dusty hall in the center of town and the adults were obsessed with attendance.

We were all divided up into teams; each with the name of a racing car. I think I was in the Alfa Romeo team.

At least half of the meeting was devoted to swarming around the board where a race layout was illustrated. Each team's car would advance with the number of attendances of each member. My friend was some high rank like a commissar, as he had been to every meeting since the beginning of time.

I went a few times but I couldn't see the point of it; with the total absence of a motor car in the family my interest in seeing an Alfa Romeo progress around a cardboard track was minimal.

On our way to church we often used to pass a strange little chapel tucked away behind some thick fir trees. The board outside proclaimed it was The Christadelphians. Naturally I asked my father who these people were and why didn't we go there instead of St. Andrews so much further away. I was naturally a lazy child and always anxious to cut down on the foot commute we were forced to take if wanted to go anywhere.

My father hissed his answer though clenched teeth: "They're low church!" This was said in the same tone as if they were suffering from the dreadful curse of cancer. "Divorce" was the other word said in similar manner. It also warned me not to mention it again.

I was aware that around the town there were other edifices proclaiming their interpretation of the Word of the Lord. We had Baptist churches, Methodist churches, Unitarian churches, Seventh Day Adventist churches, and there was some weird outfit who just called themselves "Friends."

Also padding around the outside of all this outpouring of exaltation was The Salvation Army. They actually had uniforms and played brass band music in the town center. I rather liked them, but knew better than to suggest a closer liaison to my all-knowing father.

So there was generally a lot of religion going on in the small suburban town of Watford growing up.

There was no respite from it at school either. Hymns and prayers always started off school days at both preparatory and main school. Everybody took part unless they were among a small band of oddities.

At Berkhamsted we had a couple of Muslims and a couple of orthodox Jews. They were absent during our chapel mornings, but apparently ignored the prayers on Wednesdays when we had an assembly in Dean's Hall. I don't know whether they joined in with the hymns as everybody liked those, especially the rousing ones.

I firmly believe that Christianity does no harm to growing boys. Girls maybe don't need it as much as they seem to be perfect from the outset. But boys should have a little fear put into them instead of it coming from their peers. I see no harm in it being delivered by an all seeing Deity.

The force of religion did no harm to people who were struggling against the Nazi menace, and none of us gave a thought to the fact that there were Germans on their knees each Sunday praying like billy-oh for our demise. As the old saying goes: There are no atheists in a fox hole!

At the start of this memoir I invoked a man I rather admired, Christopher Hitchens. He was an avid atheist. He didn't water down his views with the intermediate stage of agnosticism, he went full bore straight off the bat.

Some of his debates are still to be found on You Tube and they are often very entertaining.

When he was diagnosed with terminal cancer in his late fifties, he did not, as so many do, begin to question his views. Rather, he said he'd hate the prospect of ending up in a sort of permanent Disneyland paying constant tribute to the Great Leader, like in North Korea.

My own views have altered quite dramatically, although I lack Hitchens' firm convictions.

Hitchens rebelled very early in his life. He did so in many different ways as well, whereas I was rather comfortable with the status quo all around.

My shrinking Christianity came about exactly through the danger so feared by my old friends in the Crusaders – neglect.

Quite simply, around my early thirties, I felt my life was going in a direction that made overt Christianity difficult, and I would put my somewhat infrequent church visits on the back burner. It proved fatal.

I made a similar decision with the Beethoven String Quartets. They didn't appeal to me very much when I was learning all I could about music, so I decided to wait until I was older. The result is I can never tell the difference between the A major and the G minor!

As stated earlier, religion needs constant feeding or it will wither and die. It died with me. But I don't feel bad about it.

I'm also quite pleasant when it comes to people who profess their faith. After all there's an outside chance they might be right and there is no need to make things worse with the Almighty by trying to change others around.

On the occasions that we get proselytizers at the door, I'm pretty kind; only asking the most innocent of questions. I have a neighbour who is a retired Greek Orthodox minister. He's even gentler than me. I often warn the callers in advance that he's in their business too.

One of the recurring questions I always had of my faith was: What about all those other religions around the world? Are the lamas, spinning their wheels on top of the mountains of the Himalayas, just in fact spinning their wheels? Does it matter to an attentive deity if one goes to a Catholic or a Methodist church? Does Buddha listen to Christians' requests as well as his own flock or do they reach Him further down the pile?

Where do Hindus fit in? Do they really have gods like elephants with lots of arms?

And what about all those poor unfortunate buggers in the jungles of the world, hopelessly burning effigies or fancy fires in the vain hopes of pleasing whatever gods they have. I always feel a bit sorry for those types of people as it's hardly their fault that they have been left in the spiritual darkness.

If man is made in God's image, did he not make them too? And how come they're to spend their eternities in hell for just being located where they are?

It's all very complicated, but I do believe with the gradual – rather rapid recent – progress of mankind over the years, religion is likely to have a tough time of it.

One of the major benefits of all religions has always been that life will get better for you when you die. Of course, you have to be a member of a particular team in order to cash in on these benefits, but if you do, things will be great. It helps with this of course, if your life is particularly rotten.

In the case of Muslims, the heavenly embrace of 72 virgins is a big draw. Does that work however for the sheiks and emirs who rumour has it already have access to plenty of them?

Many years ago I spend a little time with my old boss Stan Lea. He had retired from commerce and owned a pub in Somerset, called The Bull Terrier; it was a fine establishment.

We had a drive around and went to look at Wells cathedral. It is set in a slight hollow in the middle of the small city. As we stood looking at the west door Stan mentioned how things might have looked in the middle ages.

"The entire west wall was then covered in gold leaf," he said. "Just imagine the average peasant living in a rain soaked hovel looking at that wall. As the sun went down, they would have been blinded by the blaze. Truly it was the house of God."

In all the time I've known him, Stan has had a habit of saying quite fascinating things like that.

Of course, during the reformation, all the gold was stripped from the churches, but nonetheless the image has always stayed with me.

One of the interesting facts about such cathedrals is that although they preached the true God, they still allowed many little reminders of evil creatures and phantoms that the people continued to hold on to.

The fact was that back in those far off times, the church wanted to keep its control on the congregation. You couldn't be letting them run around doing what they wanted after all.

My mother was a country girl. She seemed to take her Christianity quite seriously, but as usual put her own gentle spin on it. She also had a cart load of superstitions that no doubt had been learned in the small village where she was born. Crossing your fingers if you went under a bridge with a train going over above was one where you made a wish that was certain to come true.

She never allowed spilled salt to go without a pinch being thrown over her left shoulder; a superstition coming from the fact that the devil lurked on your left side all the time. The left side being considered to be bad and very unlucky. Sinister in fact means left.

She really liked black cats, which for some unknown reason are different to American black cats that are basically bad. It used to be a regular occurrence to have someone let a black cat cross a newly wed couple's path as they came out of the church. Not a lot of call for that out here.

Coal merchants and chimney sweeps also seemed to have some type of magical draw; whereas gypsies were generally avoided. My grandmother called the faux gypsies "didicoys." I never heard anyone else do so. These were basically travellers who had no Romany blood in them at all. Gran would shoo them away from her doorstep, but the real McCoy were treated with some reverence and concern.

These quaint ideas that no doubt went back hundreds of years seemed to live comfortably alongside staunch Christianity. It's hard to fathom. Except it was further confirmation of the fact that the church authorities were more than happy to have their devotees cowed.

I think my father, who had been the instigator of the regular Sunday morning church visit, lost his faith along the road. I think it happened later to him than me and also caused him some distress.

Of course, we didn't discuss this, as his generation didn't do that type of thing.

I understood that many of the changes that the church underwent didn't sit too well with him, and frankly I never quite caught on to the new liturgy and the newer hymns.

Here in America, Christianity is an odd business. We have television evangelists who are megastars. They command massive audiences of thousands, and frankly I've never seen one yet who didn't scream "phoney" out of the TV.

My favourite was one, Jimmy Swaggart. He used to stomp up and down, when he wasn't playing mushy stuff on the piano. It seems he was a first cousin to Jerry Lee Lewis, so music must have been in the blood.

One Sunday, he burst into tears to confess that he had sinned. It appears that one of his parishioners had caught him coming out of a cheap motel after his usual weekly tryst with a not too attractive prostitute. The confession was great fun to watch. You could almost see him looking around to see how it was going!

But a couple of years later he was back stomping around and begging for money to be sent to him. It was reported that he had a proof department in the basement of his mansion, so that he could process the cheques faster. The entire operation was run by his wife. No news as to her view of the "prossie!!

My latest bête noir is a particularly loathsome creature called Joel Osteen. This hideous example of con man preaches to literally hundreds of thousands of supplicants in a massive auditorium in Texas.

He has that type of permanent sneer on his face like the cat that got the cream, or on the face of a second-hand car salesman who knows he's about to land yet another sucker. These types of odious evangelists are prevalent out here and one wonders how they manage to con anyone.

Some years ago we had another one called Orel Roberts. He had a massive campus and university somewhere in Texas, I believe. One day he made an announcement that he was desperate for money – as usual! He had been told by God, that if he didn't get the final million dollars by Wednesday, God would strike him and lift him up to heaven.

Some stupid car dealer in Florida sent him a damned check on the Tuesday. You would have thought that at least he might have waited until Thursday to see what might have happened.

Locally we went through a rough patch in that we had twice as many churches – or pretending to be churches – than bars. Fortunately, perhaps with some divine intervention the balance has been somewhat redressed.

I have often been approached by various parishioners to join their congregation. I always have the same response. Firstly I thank them very much, but being English, I don't go to churches that have been built after 1600. It just doesn't work for me.

Mostly they smile and wander off. I don't think they quite get it.

But really, I once was asked to go to a church locally. I asked where it was located and they told me in the small community of Fawnskin. As usual I asked them when the church was built, and they told me there wasn't actually a building, they had their Sunday services in a field. Now I ask you!

One other disagreement I have with many religions is that where dietary or clothing restrictions apply.

I have, it seems, too great a respect for the Supreme Being than to believe that what a devotee puts in his stomach or wears on his frame can possibly influence His decisions as they lie before Him.

I was in one of Los Angeles' best Jewish delis the other day. As I was munching down on what I had been fancying for some time – a pastrami on rye – I realised that something was wrong. It just wasn't that tasty. In fact as I thought back over my experiences in these types of establishments, it seemed to be a problem with Jewish food in general. Unless that is you keep away from the real orthodox stuff.

As I pondered this it suddenly struck me; they don't mix dairy and meat – Bingo, no butter or mayo. Similarly the lack of pig meat would be a real game changer should I be attracted to that form of worship. The same goes for Islam, of course. Also the women's dresses for both lots leave a great deal to be desired. Are these fellows so unsure of themselves that they have to dress their women like dowdy frumps or even hide them altogether?

Surely the Great Architect of the Universe didn't want his most beautiful human creations totally hidden from view. What's the point of all that work? Mind you there are a few that maybe shouldn't be put on display but that's another thing entirely.

I had a Jewish friend who was once married to a fairly orthodox woman. She loved lobsters though. Now apparently this is another no-no in the Jewish faith, which due to the readiness of food poisoning in pre-refrigeration days is also on the forbidden list.

They lived in Beverly Hills and when the urge was upon her, she would have her husband drive her fifty miles up the coast to where she could chow down on the delicacy without fear of begin seen – not by God but by the neighbors. Sort of odd when you think about it as what's the real point if it's man you're afraid of, and not the Bloke upstairs who is supposed to have levied the taboo in the first place.

Let's talk about this entire banning thing; we have refrigeration these days, so how about easing some restrictions. How about letting Hindus of the hook by "undivining" cows. Their lamb is suspiciously like goat most of the time. A good T-bone might "beef" them up a bit!

It's the same with Catholics and birth control. I get that while everyone was butchering each other and eating stuff that was killing them, keeping the numbers up was of prime importance, but again times have changed; when is enough enough?

I know somebody who is on a fast for a month. Now this is not to lose weight or benefit themselves, but purely for the sake of the Deity that they worship. They're not allowed any meat but purely fish for the entire Lenten period. But then because they are under a different calendar from everyone else they're not quite in sync. It's all very confusing.

And yet, if you think about it there is not one branch of Christianity where the apple is banned. Bearing in mind that is where all our problems are supposed to have begun you would think this fruit would be the first thing on the forbidden list.

I think the final nail in the coffin of my organised beliefs was reading a novel about the building of Stonehenge. I think it was by Bernard Cornwall, but I may be wrong. Basically it showed how the monument had been built by primitive men.

As I remember it there were two competing ideologies, one worshiping the sun and the other the moon. Two monuments to these twin deities were planned and enormous efforts were made to erect them.

I realised that this had been the struggle throughout the time that man had walked on the earth that they were trying desperately to find out why they were there and hoping they could find the best formula of offerings to gain favour with whoever had made it all happen.

As the novel unfolded it showed how much unhappiness and effort was expended and it was rather sad that this foolishness had taken over so many lives and ruined them in the process.

If I have to admit my direction in the religious area, I suppose I'm most comfortable with being a "deist." It's a form of Christianity that was very popular during the founding of America.

Basically it is a belief that the whole of creation was founded by God, but He is not concerned with the results of His work. It makes sense to me, and apart from a very few conversations – always outside by the way, so maybe those field worshipers are onto something – I try not to worry Him with the normal type of problems.

I would like to find out the reasons for His creation of such annoyances in life as mosquitoes, cancer, the suffering of children and of course, liberals. It would seem such an easy thing to just halt such horrors.

A man's ethical behavior should be based effectually on sympathy, education, and social ties and needs; no religious basis is necessary. Man would indeed be in a poor way if he had to be restrained by fear of punishment and hope of reward after death.
— Albert Einstein

And if there were a God, I think it very unlikely that He would have such an uneasy vanity as to be offended by those who doubt His existence
— Bertrand Russell

Chapter Thirteen

GUNS

The fascination of shooting as a sport depends almost wholly on whether you are at the right or wrong end of the gun.
— P.G. Wodehouse

It is one of the great joys of home ownership to fire a pistol in one's own bedroom
— Alfred Jarry

I thought that this chapter ought to be part of America II, as nothing seems to divide Europeans and Americans more than the subject of gun ownership. Europeans tend to look down on the Wild West attitude of their ex-colonials and also point out the appalling carnage of many of our inner cites.

They do this while conveniently sweeping under the rug the fact that Switzerland has a law that requires much of its citizenry to be armed. And they are not exactly known to be a wild and crazy crowd. The percentage of homes with guns in this peaceful country almost exactly equals the USA.

The framers of the American Constitution were without doubt some of the finest legal and political minds that ever walked the Earth. They produced a document, now close to 250 years old that has served this nation well.

One of the guiding principals that these amazing men worried over was not the lawlessness of the population, but the lawlessness of the government. It was to be, remember:. *A government of the people by the people.*

Scholars have long argued that "*...A well regulated militia being necessary to the security of a free state, the right of the people to keep and bear arms shall not be infringed*" should mean that such arms should be restricted to the armed forces. But what part of THE RIGHT OF THE PEOPLE SHALL NOT BE INFRINGED, is not understood by these individuals?

The Supreme Court of the United States has ruled *that the right vests in individuals, not merely collective militias,* so that should be that, but still we have zealots who want to change the constitution.

Progressives, as liberals much prefer to be called these days, having dirtied the water for so many years by their activities, are always wanting to tinker with gun control laws.

Liberals love four things above all else. They love big government, big taxes, stringent regulations on business, and gun control laws. They ignore completely that in those cities that have the strictest gun control the murder rates are among the highest in the country, and in some cases, the world.

As usual Washington D.C., that bastion of liberalism as well as the home of where laws to control the rest of us are constituted, became a bellwether for taking the guns out of private hands.

The resulting legal cases went all the way to the top and eventually the ruling was made. As recently as 2008 in District of Columbia v. Heller (2008), the Supreme Court handed down a landmark decision, expressly holding the amendment to protect an individual right to possess and carry firearms.

Note the word "individual," That should finish the argument but any short reading of The National Rifle Association's monthly magazine will show you that the fight is far from over. The liberal dream of a gun free America is still high on their list of objectives. It will never end.

And yet, let us look at some of the facts concerning this troublesome issue – troublesome for liberals, not the rest of us, of course.

There are approximately 315 million people living in America. There are approximately 300 million guns. That's a lot of hardware!

Most legal gun owners are law abiding and keep their guns safe, oiled and loaded. They are there for our protection, not to create mayhem and havoc. In a place where it's quicker to get a pizza delivered than a police patrol to arrive, believe me we need a little extra help.

Police seem to be far more involved in collecting revenues to fund their pensions and benefits by cracking down on drunk drivers than actually protecting the populace. They also love to catch anyone straying over a double yellow line!

Locally, we no longer can enter our police station. If you want to contact them you have to pick up a phone hanging outside and it is answered thirty miles away down the hill in San Bernardino. The operator there will decide where the call should be sent. In fairness the old motto that used to be on the doors of police cars "To Protect and Serve," is no longer displayed on the vehicles driven by Big Bear's Sheriffs. Perhaps I could suggest an alternative slogan: "To Collect and Re-Distribute!"

Many of the gun crimes that are caused in America are from illegal guns, and used by criminals. One of the sad facts that liberals refuse to accept is that criminals don't abide by the law. It's one of the reasons they are criminals.

Of course, if you cling to the idea that criminals are made that way because society has been hard on them and they are merely rebelling against this unjust system, then there is little hope for you. Also if you believe that criminals can be cured by understanding and tolerance, then you're unlikely to be helped either.

We have regular offers by the authorities in high crime areas for the citizenry to "turn in their guns." Various inducements are offered and several weapons are put into crushing machines to end the cycle of violence. Liberals smile, wash their hands of the problem and wander off to "help" some other people with their lives.

But does the area become less dangerous after this fruitless effort? I think not.

It's about as meaningless as Martin Sheen spending the night sleeping on a grate, or Angelina Jolie dolling out helpings of turkey and mashed potatoes on Thanksgiving Day to the poor; a simple case of symbolism over substance.

I became a gun owner shortly after the LA riots. If you remember back in 1991 Rodney King while high on drugs was chased around Los Angeles in a Hyundai. At times it was reported that the car reached over 100 miles per hour. This did the car manufacturer a lot of good as no one believed they were that capable. When the cops eventually caught him they beat him severely, and the entire episode was captured on video tape.

There was some trouble over that as the disadvantaged always want to scream and shout at the unfairness of life and particularly in their sector.

But things really took off when the four white police officers were acquitted of the crime of police brutality. Between April 29th and May 4th 1992, the minorities went on the rampage. It was pretty scary.

We lived about a mile and a half from "the projects" where many minorities lived. There was a small five and dime store in a strip mall at the end of our normally very quiet street.

A gang of mostly young teenagers came into the shop one mid-day. It was noted by the owner that there were a couple of much older men outside encouraging them. These were kids who used to shop here regularly to buy sodas, snacks and sweets. They had no beef with the shop and under their own steam I'm sure they would not have thought of causing the owner trouble.

But at the suggestion of the men outside that they could come in and take what they wanted for free, the kids did just that and broke some displays and other items as well.

That evening, I was concerned at our proximity to the projects and along with some other homeowners; I went outside on the street to make sure we didn't have any unwelcome intruders.

I used to keep a baseball bat behind the front door and I took this with me.

I was standing there with my bat beside me, when it occurred to me that many of the people in the projects carried guns. Maybe a baseball bat is not much protection against a .38 Special! Unless of course, you have an extremely fast swing.

The very next day, I went to our local gun store. Yes, we have actually got stores that sell guns to the general public. Is this a great country or what?

There were quite a few people who were in the same condition as me; people who had never owned a gun, but all of a sudden saw the need of one.

The salesman was very helpful and I decided on a revolver with a five shot magazine, figuring that being a decent shot at school, if I needed more that five shots to down an attacker I probably shouldn't bother.

I had to give all my details and these were then sent to Sacramento to see if I was on any "For God's Sake Don't Let This Idiot Buy a Firearm" list.

Two weeks later, the bureaucrats not being able to find any reason to negate my sale told the store they could release the weapon.

Now I really felt like an American! I had a proper gun; and bullets too.

Perhaps I should now explain why I was a decent shot. I had in fairness not fired a gun since I was 16. I had been in the CCF (ROTC) at school. Part of that activity was that I had a permanent rifle available to me at any time in the school's armoury. It was Number 21.

Above it in this unlocked building at the end of the gravel quad was a webbing pack, and a box of bullets. I was allowed, and even encouraged, to keep an eye on this Lee Enfield .303 and maintain it in proper condition at all times.

The Lee Enfield .303 was the workhorse of the British Army in two world wars and was only changed for the Belgian FN in the mid-fifties.

What we have to ask here is how come there was never a single occasion when a boy or anyone else for that matter entered the armoury and used any of these weapons to cause damage to either property or man?

Gun control advocates always plead, "it's guns that kill people." But here were some 150 fully workable rifles, and no doubt a few other weapons too as we had a shooting range above the armoury that allowed .22's to be shot.

To answer that comment with, well things are different these days, I would simply ask why? Surely people (boys) are not fundamentally different. What has gone wrong?

As soon as I took delivery of my new toy – a Rossi .38 – I wanted to try it out. We were due to go up to Big Bear that weekend so I postponed my enthusiasm in order to wait for a visit to the outdoor gun club there.

On Saturday morning at about nine, I set off with my adoring wife showing some concern that I was going off to play with dangerous weapons for the first time. "You will take care, won't you," were the words ringing in my ears.

At the gun range there were an assortment of people firing off a variety of weaponry, and I joined their ranks with my small pistol.

It was here that I somewhat regretted my decision some nine years earlier to give up smoking, as it seemed the thing to do while one's gun cooled down.

In the bay next to me a man was firing a very large and noisy rifle. It was even too much for my ear defenders and he seemed to be shooting at a target a long way away.

He had paused for the ubiquitous cigarette and I asked him what the gun was. He explained the statistics of it – gun owners are almost as keen on the lettering and numbering of their devices as aircraft owners, and they are totally fanatical.

I noticed that he had a telescopic sight on the gun and as I'd never used one, I asked him if I could look through it at his target. He was obviously a decent fellow and asked if I'd like to shoot the gun. I jumped at the chance. So he set me up at his position and kept an eye on the target through a separate little scope that he had on a small tripod.

Now never having used a scope before, I naturally assumed that it was like looking through a normal telescope. I therefore put my eye to the end of it, lined up, held my breath, and squeezed the trigger.

The gun had an extremely loud retort and also recoil. For a moment I blacked out, as it seems that one does not put one's eye on the actual eye-piece, just a few inches behind it. I had been what the aficionados called "scoped." The eye piece had gone into the skin above my eyebrow and left a semicircle of blood behind. It began to run down my face.

"Oh, are you OK?" He asked. I said I was fine, but I didn't realise you could get hurt. "Well, you do if you get too close," he said. I knew that now, of course.

"Well, one good thing," he added, lighting up another smoke. "You hit the target's center!" Some consolation.

I drove home with the blood congealing around my eye socket, although I knew I hadn't done myself any real harm; but I couldn't resist the reception I was bound to get on arrival home after my first gun exercise.

As I walked through the door, the effect was as good as I had anticipated. I'm not much of a one for practical jokes, but this was just too good an opportunity. The wound was certainly not serious, but to this day, I can still see a very slight scar where the wretched thing hit me.

As for the instigator of this entire gun episode, Mr. Rodney King or "Rodders" as we affectionately called him, he went on to become the man-of-the-year for the NAACP – the National Association of Colored People. Such an honor! It didn't do him a lot of good. He wandered around in a semi-drug induced condition for a few years, constantly getting into trouble. He died in 2012.

There was eventually some jail time for one or two of the officers involved, and the businesses that had been torched were rebuilt. I never quite figured out why the rioters burned their own areas. Another of life's little mysteries.

There are many arguments put forward for the regulating of guns

And of course, some of them make sense. There is no reason for anyone to have a rocket launcher or an anti-tank weapon, although with increased government intervention in our lives one could argue for that need.

But regulating can take some nasty turns. The other day a decent law-abiding woman who had a "license to carry" was driving from her home state of Pennsylvania to New Jersey. She was a single mother of two children and no rap sheet at all.

She was stopped by the police in New Jersey and as with all license to carry people, she declared her gun which was in her purse on the back seat. It was unloaded and the bullets were in the trunk, I think.

She showed her licence to the policeman, who immediately dragged her out of the car and after putting handcuffs on her, arrested her for an infringement of New Jersey's law relating to handgun ownership.

For her sins she was facing up to three years imprisonment,

and before the trial she spent 45 days in prison and could have lost custody of her children. Eventually some type of reason prevailed and she was given the minimum sentence. It is hoped that the new Republican led congress will pass a bill to allow license to carry owners to transport their weapons across state lines without penalty; as they should be allowed.

> *That rifle on the wall of the labourer's cottage or working class flat is the symbol of democracy. It is our job to see that it stays there.*
> — *George Orwell*

> *If frogs had side pockets, they'd carry hand guns.*
> — *Dan Rather*

Chapter Fourteen

THREE TERRORS

Once, [Rabbi Chanoch] Teller was traveling with 16 of his offspring ... while changing planes in Frankfurt, Teller noticed a German woman gaping.
'Are all of these your children?' the woman asked. 'From one wife?'
'Yes, God has blessed me with all these children,' the rabbi replied.
'Haven't you heard about the population problem?' The woman sniffed. 'How many more children do you want to have?'
Rabbi Teller paused and looked the woman in the eye: 'About 6 million,' he said."
— Lynn Vincent

The private sector should have a massively larger role. It is frankly stupid that we are the only country that believes the Soviet system works."
— Iain Duncan Smith (British Secretary of State for Work and Pensions)

There have been two terrible things that haunted my life. The first was Nazi Germany and the second was Soviet Russia. There is unfortunately a third, which we'll look at towards the end of this chapter.

Being born just 14 days before Prime Minister Chamberlain made that sad and dramatic announcement on the radio, gives me a unique aspect towards the Nazis. The 3rd of September 1939 should be a date remembered by everyone, but particularly by the British who were woefully unprepared and had allowed their pacifist leaders to let things just lie in the face of obvious aggression.

Of course, I was far too young to be aware of anything other than the usual bodily functions allocated to infants. But I'm sure something of the angst of those early days must have been transmitted from my parents to me.

I was probably about two and a half before I had any inkling of what was going on around me, and most of that was indecipherable.

We had been "bombed out" of our first home in Hamble. My father worked at Follands who made aircraft and other aeronautical equipment for the War Office. (Don't you think War Office sounds a heck of a lot better than Ministry of Defense, which I've always though a bit whoossy!)

As a provider of war stuff, naturally the Luftwaffe had Follands fairly high up on their dance card. And also considering the early days of such air warfare, they were damned accurate.

They did mess up on one important occasion though and that was when they went after Southampton Docks. Looking through their gun sights, they mistook the orderly lay-out of the High Street of the city and assumed it was the dock area. So Southampton was quite early on the list of urban renewal requirements.

My father on looking back remembered that he had to go over to Southampton on the morning after the big raid, and it was knee deep in glass. Also there was a postman impaled on an iron railing. Not the stuff to see before breakfast.

But our little semi-detached house was done and dusted as the saying goes. No roof, no doors, and no windows. We had to move.

By the time I was close to six year's old, the Jerries had been beaten and as for the Japs, well that was mostly over to the Yanks. We had had our fair share of them in the jungles of Malaysia. It was not a good time and location for the British Tommy.

It had been a beastly business all round. People were whipped and cowed. Six years of the ebb and flow – mostly ebb in the early days too – will suck the resistance out of anyone.

Of course, I had no way of understanding any of this as I had nothing with which to compare our current situation.

Earlier I spoke of rationing; it was the norm for everyone. We heard tales of some people who were able to acquire stuff on the black market, but I have no idea if we ever got our hands on any of it.

By the time I had any idea what was going on "Dunkirk" was spoken of as a great win for us. Of course, it was the reverse. It was a bad case of being caught on the wrong side of the channel with our pants down.

The Battle of Britain had also passed into folklore and I'm sure my parents took time to look aloft at the hand to hand, or rather plane to plane, battles that took place in the clear blue skies of the summer of 1940.

I have heard many suggestions of the moment when it became clear that Hitler could not win. Many people say it was his unwise decision to turn to the east and attack Russia. Others say that by having Rommel beaten in the desert of North Africa, fuel from the Middle East was forever outside his control. Interesting to see that back then in those far off days, the importance of oil was to the forefront.

Not too many people outside scholars of the time consider The Battle of the Atlantic to be the beginning of the end for our foes.

Once again, I remember my old boss Stan talking about The Battle of Britain being the defining moment when Hitler lost.

His reasoning was that the Royal Navy was still in those days the most powerful afloat, and the German navy had not caught up to us.

The average speed of an armada of barges and other assorted vessels crossing the English Channel would be at most one to two miles per hour. Even at its narrowest at 21 miles, it would have taken about, 15 to 20 hours to get across. Of course, in order to do the job, the Germans would have needed to use some of the other launch sites and the journey would therefore have taken a lot longer.

Without air superiority to strafe and worry the Royal Navy, they could never have made it across without strong naval support which they didn't have.

The Battle of Britain ended on October 31st after three months and three weeks. It ended because by then Hitler had postponed the invasion of the country until the spring of the following year and also the Luftwaffe realised that they had failed to beat the RAF and in fact it was a case of the RAF beating them.

This was not due to any inherent skill on the part of our pilots, but more a case of us being able to fight on our own turf and the Germans having only a short time to be in our airspace.

In recent years it has become fashionable to think that the Battle of Britain was never in any doubt, but as in so many cases, it was, as the

Duke of Wellington said after the Battle of Waterloo, "a damned close run thing!"

Once Hitler turned his attention towards Russia we had to begin to assist our new allies. Only a short time before they had been allied with the Nazis but that all changed – the enemy of my enemy is my friend.

Our support for the Russians took the form of running convoys up to their northern ports. It was a dreadful business. The weather was atrocious and if one fell overboard you had a life expectancy of about a minute. Therefore no ship ever turned around.

Being in a naval family, talk was often of convoy work and how many men suffered in the Atlantic and also on the Russian trips.

I think the talk rather poisoned me as it had been hoped I might make the navy my profession; yet another disappointment for my father.

Nonetheless my father would read books about naval life, and The Cruel Sea by Nicholas Montserrat was among his favorites.

Perhaps this involvement, however much on the surface of my young and forming mind, had the effect of me being a little obsessive about the subject of WWII.

I am often to be found watching what S.W.M.B.O. calls the Hitler Channel. In fact there is no such channel, but the History or Military channel does provide a regular "fix" for my constant need to watch this period of time.

My father had lived through the depression of a few years earlier and in that time found himself without work. An advert appeared wanting strong young men to help with the upcoming visit from the leader of the English political movement the Fascists, Sir Oswald Moseley.

Like many young men my father had absolutely no idea what this party stood for and Moseley was a well known figure from the aristocracy.

After less than a week, my father clearly understood what this party was all about and as soon as Moseley left the area, my father was glad to be shot of him.

Moseley became closely allied with the German Fascists and was interred for several years once war began

As a man, Hitler always seemed an enigma to me. Those who met him personally reported that he was a very quiet, rather mealy mouthed individual. His relationships with women were extremely poor.

I think that tells you a lot. Women are very clever at reading between the lines, and particularly through the various guises that men cloak themselves with.

And yet, he had something that lit up the minds of an entire nation. I had a friend in Holland, who explained it this way: "They were a bunch of thugs, like Al Capone and his gang in Chicago in the 30's," was his view of the Nazi leadership. And like those gangsters, they were there when the timing was right for them.

There is no doubt that to have the ability to inspire an entire people into virtual bondage cannot be dismissed lightly. And yet beneath the strange appearance and the fanatical desire to make Germany the leader of the world, there was the cruel and the driving warped philosophy of racism.

Initially once he gained power this was kept back, but it didn't take long before the Nazis began their development of what they desired – a master race. In so doing of course, this meant that other races were to be downtrodden and in the case of the Jews, exterminated altogether.

The German people have never struck me as particularly foolish, and yet if you look at the films of the end of the war and see the devastation, it is hard to understand how the culture that brought us Beethoven and Bach could have gone so horribly wrong.

I have spent quite a bit of time in Germany. We had some business partners who were very smart fellows. One of them was in the Battle of the Bulge. He had also been on the Russian front, so he really had a tough experience all around.

Neither of these men could really explain how it all happened. The other partner was too young and his father had been an economic adviser to Hitler. He would actually "tear up" if the conversations got too deep.

If you look at the top tier of the Nazis they were an odd bunch. Goebbels, Goering, Himmler, Heydrich, Eichmann, were supremely powerful and yet so vulnerable in their devotion to the man with the silly little moustache.

Surely the most tragic of these people was the wife of Goebbels, Magda, who poisoned her six children before she and her husband committed suicide in the bunker at the last days of the war. It is hard to imagine how anyone could be so completely overcome with loyalty.

But then one only has to look at the events of Jonestown with the infamous Jim Jones in 1978.

In this case of course, it was a selected number of devotees who drank the Cool Aid, not an entire nation. That has always been the fascination for me.

Although the extermination camps were erected in Poland and other countries outside the German borders, so that the ultimate crime of genocide was not on the doorstep, there is little doubt that people knew what was happening.

It must have been impossible to ignore totally what was going on beneath their noses. What about the rounding up of the Jews, the constant propaganda about the bane of the master race. Surely it was obvious to anyone with the slightest understanding. How about the drivers of the trains to Auschwitz, the clerks who noted it all; those who "dispersed" the possessions of the Jews? These people had relatives too. People knew!

And yet, when the victorious Allies forced the citizens of various townships to witness the evidence of the crimes committed under their names, most could not bear it.

One of the troubling questions I have always had is would we have been as easily led and taken in under similar circumstances had we been the ones with a Hitler? As a people were the British so very different?

Would we have quietly submitted to a rule of such terror when it seemed that we were to be lead out of the valley of tears.

Pictures of Hitler's reception when he returned so victoriously from his conquest of France with his troops marching down the Champs Elysees, show the crowds ecstatically cheering and applauding as if they would follow him to the gates of hell. Many would do just that, and beyond.

Compare that to the final pictures of him reviewing the few Hitler Youth gathered in the garden of the bunker in Berlin, and the scenes of devastation throughout the country that he led for the twelve years of the Reich that was to last a thousand years.

I came to America in 1982 when the Berlin Wall was still intact. I had never visited the city and only been the other side of the Iron Curtain to such a benign place as Yugoslavia. I had been in and out of Moscow Airport a couple of times, and once looked across the Baltic from Helsinki to the winking lights of Estonia on the other side.

One of the sights I would like to see before I'm asked to permanently hand in my passport is both sites of these infamous regimes; the

Nazi and the Soviet. It would be a sort of victory lap of very modest proportions. Hardly enough to raise a blip on the world stage, but having lived successfully – through no effort of my own – through these two frightening episodes, I feel I would like to stand where the monsters stood and where the horrors of the world I've lived in were planned.

I intend therefore to visit Berlin in Spring of 2015** and walk around the Brandenburg Gate and the mound that was the bunker. I hope to take a walking tour of the Nazi sites and drink in the city. Of course, it's not the place it used to be in 1939. The RAF and the USAF changed the lay-out somewhat, but at least I will have the chance to be there; my own little personal celebration some 70 years after the events.

Also too as a part of that pilgrimage, must be a visit to Poland and the ultimate in man's inhumanity to man, Auschwitz.

Even if you might understand the Germans feeling of resentment at the armistice of 1918 placing them beneath other nations, stripping away their pride and their possession, it is hard to follow the logic of the Holocaust.

It is not just the Jews that were of course, persecuted, but Gypsies, homosexuals, and pretty much anybody that the Nazis and their henchmen the Gestapo felt worthy of a final solution.

Eric Cantor, the ex-leader of the House of Representatives visited Auschwitz about a year ago. Himself a Jew, he stood in the camp and said: "This is the worst place on Earth." It has to be.

I intend going there and don't expect to be overwhelmed as I am quite familiar with most of the facts surrounding this dreadful graveyard. It's all a long time ago, but I think we need to keep reminding ourselves of what can happen when blind devotion overtakes a people.

I have been to the Museum of Tolerance here in Los Angeles. I found it a most unpleasant experience. To begin with the attitude of the staff was extremely aggressive in their custody and their intention of making us feel guilt.

Frankly, having been old enough to be on the receiving end of Nazi aggression, I rather resented the overbearing directions as the attendants pushed groups from one tableau to another. Nonetheless they are there to ensure that the ultimate crime is never forgotten. Sadly there are people who still try and maintain that it is all propaganda. Their logic defies me.

I have never visited Poland before, and I am looking forward to it very much. It was a bad place to be in the war. To begin with it was the first place Hitler struck with his blitzkrieg, and they had no chance of repelling him.

At the end of the war it was not just the Nazis the Poles had to fear but also the Russians. Pausing at the edge of the Vistula River, Stalin encouraged the Warsaw underground to rise up and fight against their German occupiers. Sadly they complied.

As a result and with the Russians just waiting across the river the Germans killed the uprising and the brave resistance fighters who laid down their lives for their country.

It should have been a warning to the world as to the type of man Stalin was to watch such carnage. After it was over and with the Russians still immobile, Hitler gave the order to raze Warsaw to the ground, which the SS did with relish.

It was then that Stalin moved his troops in. There was no resistance left and only a beaten and starving people, whom he readily enslaved.

And so on my visit, I shall look to the east thinking about my second trip to Europe in another year or two. This one will be to Moscow and to walk upon the ground of the second horror of my life – communism.

Back in the 1970's I made my first trip to Japan. At the time, jumbo jets were not allowed over the skies of Russia. They didn't have one, and so they didn't want their people able to see what the west was capable of.

And so the flight I took on a Saturday in February that left Heathrow at eleven in the morning and flew to Moscow was a 707, which was quite acceptable to the Soviets. Here it gassed up and took on as much fuel as possible so that it could make the long haul to Tokyo's Haneda by noon the following day.

I was very interested to see what Moscow Airport was like, but I had been warned to take especial care of the transit card I would be given on my way out of the aircraft.

"Whatever you do, don't lose the bloody thing," was the advice my frequent flyer friend gave me. "You'll see everyone holding on to their cards fiercely as without them you can't get back on the plane. Trust me; you don't what that to happen."

As the plane rolled to a stop, it was ringed with Soviet troops in thick grey coats with furry hats; each clutching a well oiled Kalashnikov. Were they expecting us to invade?

As he had predicted, those of us who left the flight did exactly as he had said. We clutched our transit cards quite visibly and shuffled off into the gloom of Moscow airport's cathedral like interior. We were made to go through a metal detector on our way IN to the terminus. Rather unusual, but not in a society as paranoid as the Russian.

I remember putting my gold cigarette lighter on the table as I walked along the thick tunnel of X-Rays which I'm sure with their clunky technology gave me enough radon's to last a lifetime.

It was there however when I exited. Now a beer, I thought.

Being English, I was used to queuing; and I had seen it practised with great alacrity by my mother during the war. But here in Moscow airport it was an art form. I believe it was the case all over the city, and in fact the country.

In order to get a beer, one had to queue to tell a waitress skulking behind a glass counter, what you wanted. As my Russian was limited to Dah and Niet, I merely pointed, she then gave me a piece of paper and pointed to a small booth to the side.

Here one queued up in order to pay the babushka behind the counter who took your money – not seeming to worry about the denomination or country of origin – I think I paid in the almighty dollar at the time. This harridan then gave you another piece of paper and you went and queued up at another station where the bottle of beer was handed to you.

I don't remember if I particularly enjoyed the beverage, but I do know I was glad to get back on the plane. The entire experience showed me some of the inherent problems that existed with our great foe. These were the people who threatened to rain down nuclear bombs on us if we upset them too much.

I've never forgotten the place and the next time I went through on my way out east, I stayed on the plane and watched the babushkas shuffling down the aisle with hessian sacks, collecting all the trash of our previous three-hour flight. Again, these were not exactly people you would fear; but the generals in their tall, wide caps and fur collars, now that was a different thing entirely.

The flights that left Moscow back in those days went out over the countryside, watched I'm sure by the paranoid military for signs of invasion by a BOAC Boeing 707. They seemed to be quite sure that they were at the point of armed aggression by the west at any moment.

Looking out of the window there was absolutely nothing to see. It was completely dark for the next several hours. Not a headlight not a street light. Were they in some type of enforced "black out" like we were during the war? Nothing so worrying, they simply didn't have any lights down there across that entire continent of land.

There is a night time photograph of the Korean peninsular that's gone the rounds of the Internet. It shows the place from outer space. The dividing line between the north and south is easy to see as the south is full of light and the north lacks any at all, except Pyongyang, the capital, and that's not exactly brilliant.

I sometimes think we light our western cities to the point of excess, as we're always being encouraged to be thrifty with our energy needs, but nothing tells you the state of a nation so much as the condition of their night skies.

I'm sure we were sucking fumes as we coasted down to the islands of Japan, and I was never more glad to enter an airport with people smiling and with normal activity all around.

And so I want to revisit Russia and this time get out into the center of the capital and witness what it's really like.

The lure of communism is still with us. I'm sure our current president has thought happy thoughts about the system in his more introverted moments.

Towards the end of the 19th century it must have seemed a viable alternative to the rabid extremes that most European countries were living under at the time.

I've never read Das Capital by Karl Marx, but I'm sure I would be able to connect with many of the concepts he explains.

If you lived in Tsarist Russia, it would have seemed even more sensible to sweep away the rule of a bunch of tired aristocrats, who believed they were in some way appointed over the rest of the peasantry by divine right. After all it wasn't so many hundreds of years since England fought a bloody civil war about just that same right. But take God out of it and you are left with the question of just who are these people lording it over us?

Of course, what took their place turned out to be infinitely worse. At least under the aristocrats they were mostly left alone with their poverty, religion and their own thoughts. Afterwards they spiralled down into the George Orwell nightmare of a massive secret police and a gulag from which there was no escape, and probably a doubling of the sentence when you thought you were about to leave.

Can you imagine a regime so cruel as to actually tell a man about to leave after seven years that his sentence was to be done over? Such poor souls were called "repeaters," and they were never given any reason for such injustice. Particularly as the original sentence was no doubt trumped up in the first place.

So why doesn't the idea of communism work?

It seems to me that however attractive the dream of complete equality may be, it is fundamentally unnatural to the human being.

We are all so different and our abilities and skills so varied that how can you make us all equal?

The previously quoted Rush Limbaugh if fond of saying that the only difference between communists and socialists is that communists know what they're doing.

To begin with in a truly communist country, there are no property rights. The state owns everything. It then allocates your dwelling for you according to your status. But surely status must be all the same in a truly equal society?

It's that type of question that could get you carted of to the Lubyanka Jail for a spell of "thought treatment."

I particularly liked the Soviets belief that if you didn't completely accept their system, then obviously you were not right in the head and you were put in a mental ward. There is one book by Solzhenitsyn with just that title.

Our current president has recently decided to open the diplomatic doors to Cuba; one of the last bastions of communism. His reasoning is that if something hasn't worked for fifty years it's time to try another method. This is interesting as his basic ideology hasn't worked for longer and yet he still clings to his Robin Hood ideals.

The Castro brothers have held their grip on Cuba for so long that the poor citizens are merely pawns to their wishes. It must be terrible to be so devoid of hope that you decide to throw yourself on the mercy of a battered raft and the capriciousness of the seventy miles of sea to try and reach freedom in the USA.

It's been one of my greatest fears that I would end up on the wrong side of such a cruel system. Here you would be completely helpless, and at the mercy of any small minded apparatchik who decided you were a danger to the state and sent you off for retraining.

Have you ever noticed how the left are so fond of training? Particularly if you have transgressed against any of their so called sensitive beliefs and tenets.

Running foul of leftist principles and needing permission for anything would be like trying to apply for a building permit to extend your garage in Big Bear. And I know of what I speak!

When the Berlin Wall was torn down, there was an almost visible relief in all of us. The great danger had passed. We were finally at peace. We would no longer have to spend all our money keeping up with the Jones-skayas!

And yet, under our very noses, another threat was building in another area of the world and we never even saw it coming – Islam.

I've spent a bit of time in the Middle East. Frankly it didn't impress me too much. It seemed to be constructed along the lines of a bomb site. And they used donkeys a lot.

With this background information, there didn't seem to be much to concern oneself about when the Mullahs began their call to arms.

And yet, this new horror has entered our lives with as much fanaticism and enthusiasm as the Nazis and the Soviets.

I was in Tehran, Iran in early October 1979. It was during that stay that I was nearly killed by a terrorist bomb

I was in a car going to a restaurant for dinner one evening. There were four of us in the car. One of them suggested that as this restaurant was still a few miles away, we should perhaps change our plans and go to one we were just about to pass.

This second one was quite new and very trendy. It was in a basement. I, of course, never having been in the city before had no opinion, but the others all agreed that our original idea was best and we journeyed on.

The following morning we hear that the second restaurant had been blown up, and hardly anybody survived. We didn't know it then but the Iranian revolution had arrived.

I was due to return to Tehran four weeks later to continue negotiations, but it was cancelled. Within four months the Shah had been deposed, the Ayatollah had returned from Paris and Islam ruled the streets.

Tehran was an interesting city with some of the most beautiful women in the world. It was sophisticated and fun. The first thing the regime did was empty the bars of all the finest hotels, pouring the alcohol down the drains. That should be enough to let you know that these people are crazy.

The fact that they are completely bonkers doesn't diminish the risk when you're confronted with some suicide bomber with his finger on the button and his mind on the prospect of a half gross of virgins.

It's not the time to attempt reason. And there are lots of these guys who want Allah to rule the lot of us, or kill us in the process. There seems to be no end to their viciousness.

Our illustrious leaders have no idea quite how to handle this. They seem to believe that when dealing with a semi-civilised culture you can shame them into better behaviour, or put some type of economic sanctions into practise, but this lot are totally outside the accepted realms of normality.

And what after all is the point of aiming a $2,000,000 Cruise missile at a $40 tent!

Eventually of course, after we've played the Munich/Chamberlin game of appeasement, we will have to go to war with them and that will no doubt include nuclear weapons. The technology's out there and it just needs delivery systems to make it possible. We've got ours; a bit rusty maybe, but firstly we'll do the decent thing and let them catch up a bit, I'm sure.

The recent uprising of ISIS, which our beloved leader insists on calling ISIL, is grounds for concern. They make the SS and the KGB look like whoossies.

Currently in Iraq we are beginning "mission creep" á la Vietnam. First a few hundred, then a few thousand. To begin with, pulling out all our troops from Iraq, in order to show the world what a wonderfully peaceful chap he is, made Obama look like a fool

Had we kept a token force of around 10,000 on hand in a decent barracks, we could have jumped on ISIS as soon as they started. But no, we (he) wanted to show everyone how he could end wars. He of course forgot the obvious; you only end wars by winning them, or, of course, losing them. So now in order not to completely lose the whole of Iraq, we will have to go back in there again.

This is not tough stuff to figure out. And meanwhile the Iranians are pulling his nose by wriggling out of sanctions on the promise – not backed up naturally - of not building nukes. Some hope with that.

I have a plan. It simply requires a president of the United States to make this address: *Fellow citizens of the world. We understand that many of you are annoyed with what you perceive as our meddling in your affairs. In our defence, I would like to say that we did this primarily to make life easier for everyone, including us. Democratic and peaceful nations are unlikely to make trouble for us, and they're easier to do business with.*

We have therefore tried very hard to bring you peace, and I have to admit that we have mostly failed. For whatever reason, you don't seem able to grasp the concept of democracy and freedom and seem to respond better to bloodthirsty tyrants and thugs ruling over you. Therefore as of tomorrow, we are making plans to close our embassies in those countries of the world who don't like us. Also we are removing any trace of our military footprint except where such a presence actually guards our direct interests.

We believe that it is best for those of you in the troubled region of the Middle East to sort out your own affairs. And one last thing, we shall no longer be providing any financial aid to any of you. Good Night and Good Luck!

Just think how wonderful it would be not to have to concern ourselves with these truly useless people and then we could concentrate on cultures that actually liked us, or at least didn't actively hate us.

> *How dreadful are the curses which Mohammedanism lays on its votaries! Besides the fanatical frenzy, which is as dangerous in a man as hydrophobia in a dog, there is this fearful fatalistic apathy. The effects are apparent in many countries. Improvident habits, slovenly systems of agriculture, sluggish methods of commerce, and insecurity of property exist wherever the followers of the Prophet rule or live. A degraded sensualism deprives this life of its grace and refinement; the next of its dignity and sanctity. The fact that in Mohammedan law every woman must belong to some man as his absolute property – either as a child, a wife, or a concubine – must delay the final extinction of slavery until the faith of Islam has ceased to be a great power among men. Thousands become the brave and loyal soldiers of the faith: all know how to die but the influence of the religion paralyses the social development of those who follow it.*

> *No stronger retrograde force exists in the world. Far from being moribund, Mohammedanism is a militant and proselytizing faith. It has already spread throughout Central Africa, raising fearless warriors at every step; and were it not that Christianity is sheltered in the strong arms of science, the science against which it had vainly struggled, the civilisation of modern Europe might fall, as fell the civilisation of ancient Rome.*
> — *Winston S. Churchill – written in 1899.*

> *A woman for necessity, a boy for pleasure, but for ecstasy, a goat!*
> — *Old Arab saying.*

** I did in fact visit Berlin. It was fascinating, and there is no doubt that Berlin is a place doing well. The site of Hitler's bunker is now a paved over parking lot outside a characterless block of workers' flats – nothing to see. However just a hundred yards or so away from that faceless asphalt is the monument to the Holocaust. It was hard to ignore the bitter irony.

Chapter Fifteen

WAR

The true soldier fights not because he hates what is in front of him, but because he loves what is behind him.
— *G.K. Chesterton*

War does not determine who is right - only who is left.
— *Bertrand Russell*

In the closing stages of WWII, my mother took me down Church Road to St. Andrew's Church Hall. They had a jumble sale on, and something must have appealed to my mother on this occasion as I don't remember her ever going to one before or since.

I do remember that I was a somewhat demanding child and never had any idea that money didn't just grow on trees or was handed out automatically at the local branch of the National Provincial Bank.

As usual the church hall was crammed with tables stacked high with old clothes and the ever-present musty smell that accompanies them.

Somewhere beyond these piles of old jackets and overcoats, was a table with books of all sorts. For some reason my eyes fastened on a set of very large dark red colored encyclopaedias on the history of WWI.

I don't expect I was very good at reading at this stage, but these imposing books struck my six-year old fancy and I managed to badger my mother into letting me have two of them. The man in charge didn't seem to mind breaking up the set and I struggled back home with my prizes – they were very heavy.

Over the rest of my childhood these two large tomes were always in my room and I often looked at the sepia photos and etchings that were in them.

Most of these pictures were quite gruesome as they showed conditions in the trenches of Flanders and how bleak life was for the Tommies who spilled out their lives in the gore, gas and bullets.

I don't know what happened to those books, as once again with the efficiency of women, my mother "got rid of them" as "you didn't seem to look at them any more!" I expect they ended up with the big heavy microphone to which I was once so attached.

Maybe before they were dispatched to the eternal home of boys' possessions they lit a fire in me for the subject of war. Perhaps it was also the time that I lived through that struck the first spark. As I've mentioned before I don't believe you can endure such an event without it affecting you.

It's not so much the wide subject of war that has always interested me, or I would be reading books on the Peloponnesian Wars or perhaps the War of the Roses. The subject of my original bookish interest too has never been high on my list. In fact WWI is a very complicated affair and hard to understand.

It's the entire business of WWII and how it surged back and forth and how lucky we were to have come out of it on the winning side that has always stayed with me.

Compared to the earlier struggle, WWII was less bruising to the troops but of course, the civil population were to suffer as well.

From 1939 to the end of fighting, over 451,000 British people died in the conflict and 67,700 of those were non participants. (Seven hundred civilians died in Zeppelin raids over London during WWI,) 8,000 were killed by Hitler's secret weapons the V1 and the V2 in the last year of WWII alone.

(Seven years after the war almost the exact number (8,000) of people died in the Great Smoke or Smog as it was called, and not as a result of some maniac's sky born weapons. But at least with this disaster it resulted in the Clean Air Act which eventually caused London to become free of this annual curse.)

In Chino California, there is an aircraft museum, where they have an actual "doodle-bug" as they were mostly we called the V1's. I've seen it several times and wondered at how advanced the Germans had been with this small ICBM.

From January 1944 these flying bombs were launched from the coasts of France and Belgium and aimed at London and its surroundings.

They were rather hit and miss affairs as they had no guidance systems and merely carried enough fuel to make to the target area. But as Churchill once said about London: "It's the greatest target in the world."

The RAF used to fly up close to get under the wings of the V1's and interrupt the airflow which would cause them to fall immediately.

Initially it was the aim of the pilots to try and turn the machines around so that they would go back from whence they came, but that never happened.

By comparison the V2 was truly frightful and was the original rocket that under the guidance of Werner Von Braun became the model for the USA space program.

The V2 was launched from deep inside Germany often on mobile launchers which could not be detected and bombed. They flew way above the range of any fighter and once at their zenith would descend to the city beneath quite silently.

It was said that if you ever heard one, it was the last sound you'd ever hear.

The Doodlebugs on the other hand emitted a growling sound as their engines were jets that pulsed fifty times a second. Everything was fine as long as you could hear that growl. But once it stopped it had all the gliding capabilities of a brick and down it came.

My mother and I were having lunch in our kitchen one day in 1944, when I had the strange feeling that things were not safe. I'm not one of those people who get such feelings so perhaps it was that that made my mother take notice.

We went and climbed into our Morrison shelter which was a box in the corner of the ballroom where we lived – yes, I know it sounds strange, but homes were not that easy to acquire and you took what you could get.

On reflection, I don't think that these little boxes were any good at all in protecting the occupants from a collapsing house; more a place where the rescue crews could find the bodies!

However in the fashion of the day we didn't doubt the authorities and regularly used to go in there when the air raid sirens blew.

On this occasion we had just settled into this six by six steel frame with chain link sides, when the familiar growl could be heard. It seemed to pass overhead and then stopped – Oh boy!

A few seconds passed and then there was a loud Whoomph and all the windows rattled.

It had landed and exploded in a recreation field about half a mile from us and no doubt would have caused a number of the area's windows to blow out if they hadn't been secured with thick gummy stuff to stop such an event. It was weird stuff too.

One day while sitting in my office in Putney in 1973, the Thames River Authority decided to test their early warning flood design. This entailed all the air raid sirens going off simultaneously.

I had not heard this sound since I was a young boy and as they expanded from just a deep vibration in the air and rising up to their full high pitch scream, my skin crawled and I felt extremely disturbed. Such reactions lie deep inside one.

Half a million people dying is a pretty impressive amount, but if you compare that to the number of Germans it is not so bad. They lost nearly two million people with 1.1 being military. At least 500,000 civilians were also lost but that number swells once you include the results of the Holocaust.

A look at any war memorial in an English village tells the awful story of both World Wars. Initially people think that the longest list of names is the sad total for WWII, but that is not the case. WWI was the true horror for Europe.

British deaths from WWI totalled 775,000 and German deaths equalling two million. Once again the numbers are considerably larger for the German population. But in both cases the number of civilian deaths is puny.

It is a sad litany of the dreadful consequences of such wars, and with modern weapons a warning to those in charge of the tremendous danger we all live with.

Having read a great deal about WWII and also watched endless documentaries I sometimes become confused as to whether I actually witnessed the various battles and conflicts or merely saw them from the comfort of my living room

I've never been a great lover of war films such as the John Wayne type, but a couple of others do stay with me. One was the semi-documentary, The Enemy at the Gates, about the two snipers at Stalingrad with Jude Law and Ed Harris. I think it showed how brutal the effects of continuous shelling and ongoing battles can be. The other was Patton.

I'm not too sure how accurate this film was or his role in the battle for North Africa, but the character played by George C. Scott was truly memorable.

I can see how war is for many the defining part of their lives and how many military feel lost when they return home. Having your life in permanent danger must be a nasty way to live, but then with the camaraderie involved there is a reliance on your fellows that is impossible to replicate in civilian life.

There are certain memories that I know are real and not some that I've picked up via the TV or books or even the movies. For instance the never to be forgotten horror of gas masks.

After the use of poison gas in WWI there was naturally a fear that it would come out of the skies after September 3rd 1939. The entire population was fitted up with these nasty rubber masks with flexible glass – pre-plastic days so I don't know what they used. And the round piece that hung under your chin that held the filters needed to screen out the chlorine.

Men were often seen from the earlier conflict who had been gassed and they were always ill.

There was an unpleasant smell associated with these awful things, and they were sometimes uses as playthings by kids who had little else. Toy manufacturers were no doubt converted to bullet makers or some other such war effort, as there were no toys made during the war.

Each gas mask came in a brown cardboard box and was fixed with a long piece of string to carry it over the shoulder. There were regulations that insisted that everyone should have one with them while out. I'm sure the Kardashians would have found some more suitable and elegant container, but I don't remember ever seeing anything but the plain brown box. Even Churchill had pictures of himself complete with the ubiquitous box.

Towards the end of the war we used to go down to see my grandparents by train. It might even have been immediately afterwards. But as the Bakerloo line wound its way underneath the northern suburbs – the line dove down at Queen's Park – we would begin to see Londoners laid out on the platforms. They had no other place to live.

Starting in 1940 the Luftwaffe bombed London for 57 consecutive nights and by the end of the war over one million homes had been damaged or destroyed. Over 40,000 civilians were also killed.

The bombed out homeowners had nowhere to live in any degree of safety and so they took to London's "natural" air raid shelters, the underground – the Tube.

I remember seeing them lined up like sardines and they began to be so well organised that they had tea trolleys being pushed up and down the platforms serving drinks and snacks. There was just enough room for passengers to pass along close to the edge away from people's feet.

This situation continued after the war as although the danger of falling bombs had ended, these poor people had nowhere else to spend each night. Families were conceived, born and raised in such conditions. It's hard to imagine.

Apart from the episode of my first blown out house when I was only a baby, I was lucky to have escaped such difficulties. Although close to danger with his work in the aircraft industry, my father didn't site us in an obvious target zone. We survived.

Often at night there would be conflicting air raid sirens and we would find out that it was not "theirs" but "ours" that were flying overhead. The RAF did most of the night time bombing and the USAF took over in the day. We would hear the roar of the engines as they flew over and I well remember looking up at the squadrons of bombers on their way to Germany with that night's pounding tucked into their bomb bays.

My luck held out again with the year of my birth. I was obviously too young to be called up for WWII, but also for the Korean conflict.

The infamous flatmate, who was two and a half years older then me Dave was called up, but somehow managed to avoid Korea. Korea ended in 1953, when I was 14 and Dave would have been 16 ½.

National Service (conscription) ended a year after I was called up and I was rejected as I'd had a lung problem a few months before the medical. The interest had gone out of the program by that time and so I escaped.

Had I gone in, no doubt I would have been used to help stay the problems of our diminishing empire. There were some nasty little conflicts going on in the late fifties and early sixties.

Friends I met later told me of the fights in Cyprus, and Malaysia. Kenya too produced some particularly nasty terrorism with the Mau-Mau.

But I was fortunate to have sailed through these difficulties and by the time there was any real danger again, I was too old.

In the mid-seventies the Irish Republican Army decided to try for control of Ulster.

Like all terrorists they targeted both the military in control of the province and also the civilians back home.

We were unaccustomed to thinking about safety issues beyond looking out before crossing the road. As a result we were quite vulnerable to the bombs that the IRA would set for us. Initially they set these in Belfast were the streets were regularly damaged, and most of the hotels and pubs were blown to bits.

I had to visit this troubled city several times in this period and I never got used to the feeling of having a two hundred pound bounty on my head once I left the sanctity of Aldegrove Airport.

It was a gloomy place and our business was with the Belfast Telegraph. I met the managing director several times and he explained how the entire terrorist business was built on informers and infiltration.

He recounted the story of how one of his staff, a newspaper delivery man who put out the days bundles of papers first thing was stopped by a couple of men. They climbed into his van and instructed him to go to a certain address.

He argued with them that he had another few deliveries to make and would they just let him do those. They agreed and afterwards they came to an army check point. They told him to drive straight through as they were both wanted men.

He was terrified as it was the rule that any such escape would cause the soldiers to fire on the driver to stop the vehicle. He would be a dead man. He was lucky, as the troops were not quite set up that early in the morning and he was able to drive straight through.

Eventually the population became much more alert and society rid themselves of places were bombs could be stashed or hidden. As Thomas Jefferson said: Eternal vigilance is the price of freedom.

Sadly with the arrival of lone wolf terrorists who are sure to strike as often as they can we will become so prepared out here on our island in the USA.

The conflicts that have arisen in the Middle East are perhaps the most troubling. Not least because we truly don't understand them.

We were about to board a cruise ship on March 20th, 2003 when George W. Bush invaded Iraq. I have to say I was a little concerned at what might happen.

Initially I was worried that we would have problems with the much hyped Republican Guards. As it happened they were no real opponent at all. It was basically all over in three weeks. But then the problems began to develop in winning the peace.

I have to admit I bought into the naïve belief that by ridding the region of Saddam Hussein we would open the door to democracy across the entire Middle East. It was foolish on reflection.

If I had a serious criticism of "W" it would be that his born again Christianity allowed him to think too well of his fellow man. Also, he like most of us, do not understand the Arab mind or the inability to accept western ways.

The fact is that Arabia doesn't seem to have the mental resources to cope with the process and the continuation of democracy. They like the voting bit, but are unable to make it work. The first step of any newly elected ruling party seems to be to execute or imprison their opposition.

As much as I would like us to do the same from time to time, that's not the way it's supposed to work.

On reflection the Middle East can only operate with strong (and thuggish) men. Saddam was a bulwark against the Mullahs in Iran and would have been the first to invade if they had become a really serious threat. Now that has gone and we are left with an Iran likely to adopt nuclear weapons, and no one to stop them. Sabre rattling from our island or veiled threats from a diminutive Israel will not stop them.

I recognised that years ago and so I wonder what plans we all have when the first test is carried out? How soon before Saudi Arabia develops one and then who next? Jordan?

Perhaps this is the best for all. A few nukes going on all over the Middle East might just tamp them down for a few decades. As long as they don't find a way to unload them here! As for Israel, well I'm glad I don't hold any of their investments.

When the wall came down in 1989, I really thought that finally we could end major wars. But it seems that we are incapable of living in peace and harmony. I would like to think that the peaceniks who have spent the last eight years apologising for the USA's so called crimes, would see the foolishness of it being a good foreign policy. Currently we have no foreign policy that I can see.

If the USA withdraws from the world who is to fill the vacuum? We seem to be going down the same road as Europe in 1938. We can easily spot the Neville Chamberlain, but where is the Churchill?

> *God created war so that Americans would learn geography.*
> — *Mark Twain*

Chapter Sixteen

JAPAN

In Japan, I was immensely impressed by the politeness, industrious nature and conscientiousness of the Japanese people.
— *J. Paul Getty*

Japan, not only a mega-busy city that thrives on electronics and efficiency, actually has an almost sacred appreciation of nature. One must travel outside of Tokyo to truly experience the 'old Japan' and more importantly feel these aspects of Japanese culture.
— *Apolo Ohno*

My father used to talk enthusiastically about Japan. He visited there aboard one of the P&O "Strath" ships on which he saw that world. They were the Strathaird, the Strathallen and the 22,000 ton Strathmore, on which he met my mother on her way out to India to work as a children's nurse.

He used to talk about the cities of Yokohama and Tokyo and how many of the men and most of the women used to wear kimonos. I thought it was rather strange when I was growing up as a child.

He was there in the mid-1930's and it must have been a strange sight for a young man from middle-class Hampshire to witness the unusual sights, smells and sounds of that far away place.

I was always rather envious of his experience, and in my unproductive teens and early twenties there was never any thought that I might too journey to that fascinating place.

But life deals out some amazing opportunities and as mentioned in the previous chapter, in the mid-seventies, there I was gliding down to the then International Airport of Haneda, This was before they moved such flights out to the far flung terminus of Narita.

I was met by the sales manager of Dodwell and Company, who were an English trading company that had been active in Japan for a hundred years.

Richard had been introduced to them by a contact of ours in Australia and after a meeting there, he had arranged for them to take our agency. He then bowed out and left me to do what I did within our trio of directors; namely train and manage the sales team until they were able to stand on their own feet.

The sales manager was called Takata, and he was a thin, medium sized, smart Japanese of about 50. He met me at arrivals and took me directly to the hotel.

I had a contact in the UK who was the sales manager for a group of hotels in London. He had been to Japan many times and when I talked to him about it he gave me several pieces of advice.

The first nugget was not to stay at The Okura. "All the greenhorns stay there," he said. "The best place to go is the Palace Hotel. You'll see a nice mixture of both Oriental and Occidental businessmen there. You'll earn points for staying at The Palace. I can fix you up. I know the general manager well."

Our drive into the center of Tokyo was fascinating to me. We seemed to be high up a lot of the time, on roads that went all over the other streets. Also the buildings were strangely shaped and some of them had big nets covering the tops. I was later to learn that these were driving ranges for the Tokyoites, who were mad on golf.

One building, Mitsubishi, had a massive earth mover on the top. It was the biggest I'd ever seen and I wondered how they had got it up there, surely not in an elevator.

We arrived at The Palace which was opposite the royal gardens on a very wide boulevard. There were many black limousines parked outside, with their drivers all standing around smoking; some of them were flicking feather dusters over their cars. All the seats inside were covered in anti-Makassars, which I thought was odd.

As soon as I gave my name at reception, with Takata standing a respectful distance behind, I was immediately greeted by a small man in full morning dress. He bowed to me, and I bowed back, having had a few lessons in The Cricketers pub back home. "Don't bow too low, that's subservient," Alan had told me. It seemed this face thing was all important.

All three of us traveled up in the elevator, with the GM asking polite questions about how Moreton-san was doing, and how was my flight etc, etc. He unlocked a door and bowed me into the room.

It was large. Even large by European standards, and as I was to find out later, stupendous by Japanese ones.

Takata was obviously impressed, as he also was by the huge bouquet of flowers on the sideboard. I was impressed by the half dozen or so bottles of good booze that were on display.

It was quite an arrival I had to admit. Takata asked me if I wanted to rest, and as it was mid-day, I suggested he and I went to lunch if I was not detaining him from his family. He said that would not be a problem, and he would wait for me downstairs.

By now my large Revelation Globe Trotter had arrived and I took out the suits therein and hung them up over the shower rail while I ran a scalding bath to let the steam air out the creases. It was an old trick I used time and time again.

When I returned downstairs, the GM scuttled out to greet me and asked if everything was to my satisfaction. I told him it was very good indeed. He smiled and bowed his way back to his desk.

"Have you been here before Summons-san?" Takata asked me. "I told him that no, but I had a friend make the reservation for me.

"It is a very big room, Summons-san." I realised I had made an impression as big as the room.

As we walked to his car, he suggested that there was an English restaurant close by where we could have lunch. "They have roast beef and Yorkshire cake," he said I could only imagine the horror of such a dish out here, even if it was pudding and not cake.

"Could we not go to a restaurant that you would go with your family, Takata-san. I would really much prefer to eat Japanese food."

And so within a few minutes we were sitting in a small place with a lot of Japanese people tucking into I really didn't know what. But I scored extra brownie points by asking for chopsticks rather than the knife and fork that were somewhat ostentatiously put next to me.

"You use Hashis?" Takata asked me with a lift of his eyebrows. I didn't mention that as I'd been eating Chinese food with them since I was in my teens, it didn't present a problem.

We ate our fill and drank quite a bit too. I didn't know that the Japanese truly liked their alcohol, but that became plainer as the week progressed.

He dropped me back at The Palace and I got a decent siesta in before a quiet evening and the work of the following day.

As I was to find out on my regular travels around the world, sleep is a wonderful rejuvenator, and woe betide the regular traveller who tries to cheat the clock with too much hard liquor. You will surely suffer.

The next day, I was collected by Takata and driven to the headquarters of Dodwell and Co. It was close to the American Embassy. It was a grey building surrounded by cables and poles. The Japanese, like the Americans, were still not burying their wires underground, and it made for a somewhat messy horizon.

As we came into the general office on the second floor, I spotted a big banner proclaiming: "Welcome, Mr. Summons." It was quite effective.

There was a lot of bowing and scraping and a few handshakes before I was led into the boardroom and the lessons were to begin, led by me!

That first day in Japan was unforgettable. It ended with the four "students" and me going out for a drink across the street at a little bar under the watchful eye of a beautiful late middle-aged woman called Sato-san.

She gave me a searching look and waved away her serving girl to escort us to a small room at the back. We slipped off our shoes and worked our way around a small table on a tatami floor. The "boys" stood back and pointed at the corner as my spot to sit cross-legged.

The reason for Sato-san's selection was that our room had two outside walls. This meant that the "gaigin," could lean against the wall and not break it, which was likely to happen with the inner flimsier screens.

I soon found out that her choice was very wise. Sitting on the floor is not very comfortable for English backsides or backs. I also found out that it's not necessary for men to sit correctly, they could lounge. Not so for women. We drank a few beers and then I explained that I would not be spending the evening with them as with my schedule, I preferred an early night. But Friday would be different. They could rely on that.

I may have lost a bit of face, but with the brownie points having built up so far, I thought I could let a little slip.

As usual since I joined the firm I ran most mornings. Just because I was in Japan was no reason to let that habit slide. I carried a red track suit with me and after donning that the second morning I was there, I went out to try the park next to the hotel.

It was the middle of February, but I don't remember it being particularly cold; and the sun was shining.

The grass was brown and the trees clipped, giving them a somewhat stunted appearance. The outer edges of the Imperial Palace were off to my right across the busy boulevard as I wound my way around the well maintained paths.

There were several tramps lying around on the various benches. I was rather surprised at this as Tokyo seemed so well ordered that vagrants didn't seem to fit in. Also they had very dark skins, which was not the way most Japanese looked.

As I trotted on, one clump of rags struggled to an upright position and with a sweeping gesture, called out to me in a loud voice: "And good morning to you, sir!" And then fell back upon his bench. It was a strange experience.

I walked to the office after my run; being so close to the America Taisikan – the American Embassy, it was easy to find. People were very well ordered and small. It was the usual going to work crowd with papers under their arms. There was a total lack of foreigners among them.

Once in a while a gaigin would appear, noticeable by his size and dress. It was hard not to stare at him as the distance closed. It was almost like the famous meeting between Livingstone and Stanley.

This was back in the mid seventies and Japan was only just entering the serious world of commerce. Also few English companies were making it that far out to the East, so I was also, too, a bit of an oddity.

My father would have missed the men wearing kimonos, and the number of women also similarly dressed was reduced considerably. I was to find out that kimonos were favoured for formal times and weekends. There were some men in them, but very few, and usually upon the old.

I still remember my team from those years ago. There was Ito, who was a tall man with very good English. He suffered a tragedy later in his life with the loss of his son in an accident.

Tsuda came from Osaka, and looked after me well when I visited that city on my next trip. Haguchi's English was poor, but he had a wonderful singing voice, and when he sang country and western songs, he had no accent at all.

Finally there was Haraguchi, who was a short plump man, and like the rest in his mid thirties. Haraguchi always requested a second bowl of rice when we ate out. He also carried with him a rolled up love letter from his mistress.

This quirk was discovered one evening when we were lounging at Sato-san's. He had taken his jacket off and this scroll had fallen out of his pocket. The men all laughed and then told me what it was. He read some of it out to me; "*As the tree awaits the sun's warmth in the spring, so I wait for you.*" Now Haraguchi was not the most obviously attractive man. He was round and wore thick glasses. His front teeth protruded, and he had that tough hair that only sticks out more when it is cut short.

It was hard to imagine such adoration being foisted on him – and by a mistress no less.

However it was explained to me that this was not a mistress in the western form. It was a hostess in a bar that he went to after work. She poured his drinks and held his hand and listened to his woes. I asked what would happen if his wife found out, and was told, that she already knew and it didn't bother her. Such was the ascendency of the Japanese male.

Our promised Friday night out no doubt caused almost permanent damage to my liver. These fellows were determined to have a good time and dragged me around a big selection of bars.

I was to find that Japanese whiskey may taste like Scotch, and also smell the same and look the same, but a bellyful of Santori makes for a wicked hangover in the morning.

We ended up in some type of Karaoke bar where the entire team serenaded me. Regretfully, although I was a passable soprano when a boy, once the testosterone hit the vocal tubes, my voice collapsed and I never sing in public. Possibly if surrounded by a full choir of similar croakers, I might enjoy the odd hymn, but not in a tiny Karaoke bar, I can assure you.

The following morning I was collected for my flight to Bombay by Takata-san. He drove me to the airport in the same silver car, and asked me if I had a good time the previous evening. I said it was pretty good as I remembered it. He replied: "Summons-san, you smell!" Oh dear!

I returned to Japan a couple more times over the course of the next year. Each time I revelled in the "foreignness" of it.

Japanese cars were quite different to ours then. We had one or two on English roads, but they looked odd and out in Japan there were thousands of them. Some of them had strange names like "Oscar" and "Cedric."

The antimacassars were on all the taxis, as Japanese men were still wearing a lot of hair oil. Very few people touched, and bowing was the normal form of greeting.

After a year, three of the team came to London to see how we did things there. I made sure they had a good time, and sent them back home via our operations in Amsterdam and Frankfurt. It was a great honor for mid-level people to be given that opportunity. They were always very grateful when I called them to see how things were progressing.

Once I left the company and then moved to America, I thought it unlikely that I would ever go back to Japan again.

Without the raison d'être of business, it is not an easy country to visit as a tourist. But I had not considered that my son, Michael would change that belief.

Having gained his "A" levels, Michael told me that he wanted to go up to the city of London to try and make some money. He didn't fancy university at that stage.

He joined an old fashioned English trading company and then after learning that business went to a Japanese company doing similar work.

Here he met Eiko, who was working in the firm. This was to culminate in a terrific wedding some years later.

After Yamaichi, he transferred to Sanwa bank, figuring that the best product to trade in, if you want to make money, is money itself.

He was transferred to Tokyo and then back to London after a couple of years.

He returned to Japan in September 1998, and he and Eiko lived in a flat on the west side of Tokyo. It was time to bust out my one phrase of Japanese "Can I have another beer, please," and go and see the boy.

Yvonne and I traveled out to Narita and then into the city center. Things had changed in the twenty years since I last visited. I couldn't spot the big earth mover on the top of the Mitsubishi building. But the traffic was the same, and lots and lots of motorcycles and scooters.

By now Japanese motor cars were seen all over the west, so there were few oddities there. Also the number of gaigin had exploded, and over the years they had become a staple of Japanese life, with them speaking the language and doing it well.

Japanese food was very popular in California and so we were very happy to eat the local dishes.

We had a wonderful first visit with Michael and Eiko spoiling us with a trip out to the countryside round Hakone.

First there was a train, then a cable car, then a boat ride across a lake and then we spent the night in a very posh hotel, in the roof of which was a great onsen – a public bath.

Michael and I made our way to this speciality and after the preliminary wash down we entered the steaming water. At this the four or five Japanese men immersed in the hot water decided they didn't want to share their water with stinking gaigin, and out they got. It was really quite funny.

The Japanese are very courteous with visitors, but they don't particularly like to share their bath water with us. Particularly if the visitors are a trifle loud, smoking cigars and smelling of beer.

As a treat to himself, Michael bought a large catamaran, and we have had several momentous sails on it; one where we took my grandson, Evan, when he was 15.

Unfortunately, it was in August, and I had never been there in high summer. Boy is it hot! And humid. But out on the boat, it was bearable and at nights we would sleep on the netting until Michael would wake us as soon as the mosquitoes began to stir. They carry their own knives and forks out there, and it's best to avoid them.

The last sail we did was to move his boat permanently from Yokohama to the Inland Sea and a small marina in a little town called Nio.

It was an adventurous trip of about five days. We had a couple of Michael's friends aboard and also a professional captain.

This fellow left us once we had reached Wakayama City as we were at the entrance to the Inland Sea – what could go wrong from here? It's just like a bigger version of Big Bear Lake, right? Wrong!

Eiko had joined us along with Jasmine, their Cavalier King Charles Spaniel. We set off from Wakayama and had to pass under the Seto bridge, which is the longest spanning bridge in Japan.

Also the currents there are particularly strong with such a large body of water rushing in at high tide and out at low tide.

Suzuki-san, the captain, had warned us that we had to pass through at exactly the right time and also to keep an eye out for the whirlpools.

Naturally we did as he instructed and considered ourselves home free, but then the wind came up and also the high waves; so much for Big Bear Lake.

The final two hours of motoring on the twin Volvo diesels were extremely frightening. The coast of Japan is thick with jagged black rocks, and we had no wish to go too close to them. Michael did stellar work guiding "Milestone" using his i-Phone of all things.

We had a course of South West and the wind and waves were coming at us from the North West – right across our beam. We banged up and down over the crests while trying to hold the boat steady.

Eventually we saw the marina's sea wall and made our way around it and into our reserved berth. It was to be Milestone's home for the foreseeable future.

A check of our equipment showed that the trip had caused the main water tank located above the port engine, to be in danger of breaking free. One of two metal spars holding the tank had fractured completely, leaving only one; any more rough treatment and the tank was likely to break free and foul the engine immediately.

Milestone is a wonderful seaworthy boat, but with one engine gone, I don't know how safe we would have been sailing up that dangerous coastline.

My trips out to the rural areas of Japan have been most instructive. It's said that Australia is the most urban country in the world, with nearly all it's population living in cities around the outside of the continent.

Japan on the other hand is becoming that way too, with the added difficulty that the center of the country is made up of largely impenetrable mountains.

Japan is about the same size as the UK, but with twice the population and half the land that is habitable.

A walk around the little town on Nio showed me a problem that might well become the world's problem over the course of time; the increasing urbanisation of the population and therefore the loss of a rural culture. It's happening here in the USA, as Michael and I find on our long motorcycle rides throughout the country.

As we strolled along the streets of Nio a number of what to my ancient eyes looked like bomb sites were evident. Surely these were not a left-over from the USAF raids of WWII.

Michael put me straight: "They're dead man plots," he said.

It seems that young people can no longer make a living out in the countryside. As a result they move into the big metropolises. Over time they see less and less of their ancient relatives, who ultimately die, and often with no information as to their brood. This is either by accident or design. I suspect it is the latter as the Japanese are pretty canny people.

The house is usually not worth a great deal of money and there is no market with the town shrinking. Therefore the heirs prefer to forget about it and hope they are not found.

The house eventually falls into disrepair, while owing a lot of back taxes, and so the authorities have no alternative but to bulldoze it to the ground, leaving what looks like a bomb site. It's all rather sad.

In this same area too I noticed a number of stickers in the form of a teardrop on the backs of cars. Michael informed me that this is yet another Japanese tradition. When you reach the age of 65, you have to display this symbol to let other drivers know that you're an old fart. As if it wasn't tough enough!

One of the places I am most grateful to have been in my life has to be Japan. It's still a far off and very foreign country, although with the advent of social media and the general shrinking of the globe that aspect is changing.

One of the immediate and noticeable aspects of the Japanese is that they are definitely getting bigger. When they buy a Number One in MacDonald's it may be a Big Mac and Rice, but fast food has certainly beefed them up.

But as they become more and more urban in their lifestyles, they become like the rest of us. It may be more accommodating, but I miss the differences.

I've been to Japan about 13 times. I miss it, but it is a long way away.

The only English words I saw in Japan were Sony and Mitsubishi.
— Bill Gullickson, a former major league baseball pitcher.

Chapter Seventeen

TECHNOLOGY

The first recorded music I ever heard was a small collection of National Anthems on records that were very fragile and if dropped would break into lots of pieces.

The gramophone on which I heard these when I was about eight, was a wind-up device with the loudspeaker being in the lid.

One would wind up the turntable, select the 78 RPM record, and then searched around for a needle. The gramophone was about two feet by three feet by one, and had a hollow arm coming out of the side.

At the end of the arm was a found flattish ball which contained a thin metal diaphragm. Into this would be screwed a needle which was quite expensive – about a penny for three. Then the needle would be carefully lowered on to the record.

Because of the costs we used to use pine needles, which of course were free. The winding up of the turntable lasted for about three records – both sides, and a pine needle barely made it for one side alone. But there were lots of them.

I explain this machine in some detail as for anyone over the age of fifty it's likely they have seen one either at their grandparent's house or in a museum. But for anyone under the age of say 30, it would seem impossible to listen to music on such strange equipment.

If the under-agers think that music has always been just a click away on their I-pod's, then they are very much mistaken.

I have always been quite interested in the development of technology, although with my inability with numbers, it was never likely to be a field I could compete in.

Nonetheless I have enjoyed the terrific changes that have occurred in my lifetime, and in particular with the development of music reproduction.

I've experienced it all with the exception of 8-track which I blessedly managed to avoid. It didn't last long and was primarily popular in the USA.

But in the mid fifties, when I happened to mention to my friend John Fry that I was interested in music, he invited me to his house to listen to his father's record collection, and a fire was lit in me.

His father was a representative with Deutsch Gramophone Company. He was in the midst of replacing all his 78 RPM records with the latest LP's which went around at 33 1/3 RPM. Somehow the forecasted 16 RPM's never made it out of the lab.

I'd never seen so many records in my life, and asked for a list of pieces that my father had given me. I can still remember many of the titles to this day.

This began a time when John and I were to be found "pushing the envelope" of music with more and more difficult stuff. I never did get the hang of Belshazzar's Feast by Sir William Walton. Even when I saw it live at a concert. Very difficult stuff!

His father's music set up was a twin turntable with a strobe light to check the speed against the chequered edges of each one.

We were forbidden to mess about with the hallowed LP's but any of the 78's was fair game. It was here that I experienced all the Beethoven Symphonies, all the Mozart ones and lots and lots of Schubert and Schumann. These still remain firm favorites, although my taste has extended quite a bit further.

Of course, the BBC could always be relied upon to play a lot of different music over the airwaves, and these I listened to as well.

It took me quite a long time before I could afford a record player myself, and I seem to remember acquiring one second hand about the time I was married in 1963. It was electric though and pretty good.

The breakthrough came when I won a lot of prizes with Muzak. One of these was a stereo made by a company we did business with called Parmeko. It was a teak cabinet with all the necessary accoutrements inside and twin teak speakers to give the full stereo effect. I was immensely proud of it.

Hi-fi and stereo equipment had been around for a long time. I was taken to an exhibition of it some time about 1950. I had no idea what I was looking at except the enthusiasts were all men who wore beards, smoked pipes and talked about things I had no understanding of at all.

These were the type who eventually morphed into CBers with "handles" and aerials in their back gardens. Are any of them still around?

At this exhibition I acquire a microphone. It was a big heavy thing and I had it for years. I couldn't do anything with it but I was very fond of it. My mother has a lot to answer for in the distribution of some of my stuff. Just because I didn't use it for a decade or so didn't mean I wanted it thrown out! If not watched carefully, mothers will do this type of thing.

After leaving England, Michael became the inheritor of the Parmeko, and it finished its life as a bedside table with my former wife. On a trip back to England, we stayed with her, and I was pleased to see it again; although it's playing days were long gone.

By then we had passed through the tape stage. These were a great invention for those of us who liked to record music.

I established a quite good collection of music recorded from the radio over a ten-year period. But inevitably, another change was about to come our way – the Compact Disc.

So once again, the billfold was taken out and "records" were back on the menu once more. But now they were the CD variety.

I liked the feel of them more than tapes and the quality was far better. One thing I did miss from the old LP days was the write ups on the sleeves of the covers. The fronts had become something of an art form, but the backs had an encyclopaedia about the music for those interested.

A small compact CD player and a wallet of CD's were my constant companions when travelling, and things looked set fair. But as with everything else in life, one thing that is guaranteed to change is change itself. The I-pod was introduced by Apple.

I was fairly slow to get into this new technology, having built up/ invested quite a lot in CD's but naturally after seeing Michael's set up I couldn't stay away much longer.

I bought the Classic I-pod and a subscription at no charge to I-tunes. Slowly I transferred all my CD's over to this small device, and to this day I still can't get used to the fact that I have about 4,500 tracks loaded onto the I-pod, and it's only about a quarter full.

I bought a program called Roxio which allows one to record tracks from the computer to I-tunes and then transfer them to the I-pod. I still think it's all a miracle.

But then we have to look at the entire business of computers in my lifetime.

My first experience was when I worked at Ilford Limited. Part of my job was to take invoices over to "Powers," where the supervisor would somehow sort them out.

Powers referred to Powers Samos, an American mechanical accountancy company. The department contained about fifteen large green machines bolted to the floor, each under the control of a girl in a pink type of housecoat or overall. The supervisor was similarly clad except she was twice their age.

It was a noisy place with the girls hitting big buttons and bits of card flying around all over the place. I didn't know it at the time, but this was my first experience with computers; or at least the front end of them.

Later on when I was with Muzak, I called into Ilford Limited and just took a short visit to see if the supervisor was still there. Yes, she was. This time however she was in charge of a smart key-to-disc operation.

The room was air-conditioned and it was quiet and had potted plants around. She did remember me, and we spent a few minutes talking about how her responsibilities had changed.

Back in the old days, all the punched cards the girls produced were put into a tabulator and a very long piece of paper tape came out. This was then run through the computer which could read the tape.

In her new abode, she was now part of the office building and not a part of the factory, where she had been before. Such was the noise and dirt of the previous operation that it naturally seemed to be more of an industrial section.

Not now. Here each girl sat at a smart pale blue and grey consul, tapping away at her work. The information she input was sent directly onto a disc in the center of the room and this then was placed directly onto the mainframe next door which you could see through large plate glass windows. It was all very futuristic.

During my time with Muzak, I spent a lot of time in such areas, and I had a customer called English Electric Leo Marconi, which traces the number of mergers and takeovers that had been in its past.

Its headquarters were located over the top of William Whitely's, a department store in central west London.

In the middle of this operation sat LEO III. It was one of the computers that the Lyons Electronic Operation had used for accounting work after the war.

It was a behemoth. It was about 150 feet long and fifteen feet wide and square. It was full of valves and it needed powerful A/C to keep it from burning up. The company still used it for simple operations and there was always a team of white coated engineers pulling out the boards and changing around the various wires that were plugged in. It was a big fellow.

But it was less powerful that any smart phone in the average person's pocket these days. In fact by the seventies, most calculators could beat it in calculations. I often wonder what ever happened to poor old LEO. It must be galling to be so eclipsed.

But there's nothing so dated as old technology. Just look at the old Sci-Fi pictures where discs on computers spin aimlessly and CRT's look clunky and decrepit.

I've seen some differences in car design in my life, but somehow, these can age with grace. And particularly out here where "classic" cars can demand a high price indeed.

It was noticeable in my final travelling days that when entering a rental car, there was little to worry about in locating the various controls. Not so back in my teens where manufacturers were still experimenting with gear lever placement and in fact the way the clutch worked.

I remember driving a Wolsey once. It had a strange pre-selector gear lever on the steering wheel. You put the lever into the gear you wanted and it would not change until you pressed the clutch pedal. Once you got the hang of it, it was rather a good system.

Finding reverse too could be something of a challenge. It could be anywhere. Ford put it in the "first" position on their Anglias and Prefects, very confusing. But then they had some type of pneumatic system operating the windscreen wipers. This meant that when you went up a hill and the car was using all its power, the wipers stopped. Fortunately Ford ended this idea.

I went on a train the other day. Quite a bit different from the ones that used to take me on my commute to London in the mid-fifties.

Back then there were still coaches that looked like the smoking rooms of Victorian gentlemen's clubs. They even had the patina of tobacco coating all the surfaces, including the passengers.

Everyone smoked and not just cigarettes, lots of men puffed away on pipes and filled the atmosphere completely. Talk about second hand smoke.

There were usually a couple of very small non-smoking compartments on a train, as there was the mysterious "Ladies Only."

When I took the Metrolink from San Bernardino to Union Station, Los Angeles, the other day, it was a different experience entirely. To begin with the engine was diesel. Towards the end of my time "riding the rails" to Euston, diesels were beginning to come into use, but most of the engines were great belching steam monsters.

The Metrolink engine was no less powerful, but it was a lot quieter and I assume efficient. The compartments however were quite different. They were double deckers with smart, functional seats and the passengers of course, were dressed totally differently to my old regular companions on British Rail. I didn't see one suit.

One dramatic difference in the passengers was the complete lack of newspapers. On my hour and a half journey, I did not see one paper being read going in either direction.

Instead of papers, I saw electronic books (Kindles), I-pods, and video games. But most of all people were staring at their smart phones. This seems to be an all consuming activity these days.

I have traveled on trains in Japan and they too sometimes have double decker coaches. They also have attendants pushing carts down the aisles to offer food and drink. I wonder if the Californians will eventually provide that.

Both systems are worlds away from Watford Junction and the 7:47 Euston train that I rode for a couple of years.

This current dependence on electronic devices is something I'm sure few people saw coming. And yet, once it arrived, we all embraced it and took it into our lives with very little difficulty.

I have encouraged older friends of mine to get on board with this technological stuff, as I believe it is a lifesaver. If you ignore it, very soon you will be left behind and also be closed off from a form of communication with the rest of the world. I believe it is the wrong time to be a Luddite.

Writing this book has been made a lot easier by access to the Internet. If I need to check a fact or a date, then I only have to have a window open to a portal, check the fact then minimise the site before continuing. The site is available if I need to go back and check it.

With access to such a wealth of information at the click of a mouse, it makes knowledge available to all, even the most foolish.

Perhaps it is just this knowledge that the ancients feared as being detrimental to society as a whole and caused them to try and keep it locked away. Without some training in how to use that knowledge it become a weapon that can be used poorly.

It is barely 30 years since the personal computer was launched by Apple. Looking back on the early models it's hard to see that this was to be the beginning of such a leap forward into people's lives.

I had a small computer on my desk about 1987. It was an odd flattened box, and a new fellow in the company wrote a program that allowed me to keep a record of all our potential sales.

Within a few years nearly everyone had a PC and we began to write all our own correspondence. Until then we used to dictate it. Shorthand was regularly taken by secretaries back then and I wonder now if it's possible to learn either of the two systems that women used – Gregg or Pitman. It all disappeared so quickly.

I've been out of the workforce for 15 years now, and although I do occasionally visit The Sun's premises, where everyone has a terminal on his or her desk, I have no idea how today's offices function.

I do know however, that with so many improvements, efficiency is still hard to acquire for businesses.

In an earlier chapter I mentioned that my mother struggled with housework on a daily basis. It was what mothers did.

In the late fifties a man called John Bloom introduced an affordable washing machine. Up to then women used to boil linen and then wring it out through a mangle, which was a pair of heavy rollers you put the material through. Afterwards, it would be hung out to dry on a washing line in the garden, then ironed and aired it before it could be used again.

There also was the laundry, which would collect items in long flat fiber boxes, take them away and return them a week later. But such a service was expensive. Poorer women used to cope themselves. It was a big job.

John Bloom's product was a twin tub machine. It revolutionised the work of home laundry. One tub used to take the washing with a soap powder, then the second tub would spin the load dry – well a lot dryer than wringing wet. It still had to be hung out to dry of course.

It was a great leap forward, and pretty soon most houses seemed to have one, or a competitor. John Bloom made a fortune, and then he lost it in some other venture. I last heard he immigrated to Southern California and retired.

My grandmother never used a washing machine. Also she never used an electric iron. She had two irons made out of actual iron, and these she would heat up on the gas stove. Then when she believed them hot enough she would test the temperature by holding the flat surface about six inches from her cheek. I never knew her to burn any fabric.

She also never had a refrigerator and kept foodstuffs that might spoil in a pantry – a small white tiled room next to the kitchen and always facing north. And this was only in 1964.

But it's the area of personal computing that is without doubt the greatest area of improvement that I have witnessed in my lifetime.

I am about to take a trip – in fact back to Sanibel Island in Florida to see my friend Paul Everest.

In my briefcase, I shall pack a personal computer to continue with this manuscript. Along with it will be a tablet, an I-pod, an I-phone and a pair of Bluetooth headphones that will link wirelessly to the phone. As well as all this I shall take a miniature pair of speakers in case anyone wants to listen to some music while we dine.

Perhaps the most important piece of electronic jiggery-pokery will be my Kindle. This is truly an amazing piece of equipment that I have had now for five years. I did wonder when I acquired it if I would miss the actual feel of a book in my hands.

As it happens I converted to the format in a few minutes and now I have 180 books of different types in its archives. It only takes a few minutes to have any of these books sent back from the "cloud" to reread, or even send to Yvonne's Kindle.

The only drawback I can find with the device is that it is hard to go back and forth quickly to reread or find a certain page. Therefore it is tough to use as a reference book.

When it's time to cut back more on the number of books in the house, I shall be leaving behind the reference books, but donate the novels. I shall not read them again, and if I get the urge to repeat any of them I'll just pony up the small amount to have them downloaded to the Kindle.

If I think back to that exhibition that my father took me to when I was about ten and was able to show the most advanced of the enthusiasts there what I could pack in my case today, they would be utterly astounded.

I'm proud to say I was one of the first to ever have a bank ATM card. It was back in 1966 and the National Provincial Bank in Worthing invited me to have one. It was a very small grey piece of plastic about 2 ½ inches by 1 ½. It had little holes in it and it was in fact a small punched card.

You were given a PIN as today, and you put the card into the slot outside the bank's premises and hey presto, an envelope was sent out to you containing five pounds, I think it was.

The card was kept inside and eventually after about five days it came back to you in the mail for further use. Primitive but effective.

Similarly about 1975, I had an early beeper. But this one was set off by a phone call from the office – it could only be activated by them. It alerted you to call and thence receive whatever news they had. At the time we had absolutely no way of imagining a phone that was in your pocket. Only Dick Tracy had one like that.

No chapter on technology in my lifetime would be complete without a mention of television. It's yet another invention that has revolutionised lives all over the world.

And yet strangely, if you ask people they nearly always say they don't watch much of it. Amazing as the programs are on 24 hours a day and one assumes the TV executives measure consumption.

I must admit that I've watched a lot of TV over my life. Perhaps because we were late into the game, I've needed to catch up. We put it on the news as soon as we get up and it stays on news for most of the day. I've tried to give up the news addiction but the draw is too powerful to resist.

I have to say that the general TV programs put on by the major channels don't appeal to me at all. Maybe it's the change in culture as I will watch some of the BBC stuff that's aired on PBS.

But there's nothing so interesting to me than to hear proponents of different views explaining their positions. Rather boring stuff for lots of people, I'm sure.

From the early flickering black and white with 425 lines on the screen to today's flat screen colored technology, it's come a long way, but for all that it's people who make it interesting.

A few months back we had a new system installed by the cable company. The box that sits on top of the TV now has a recording device on it that allowed one to record any program and view it later.

Now recorders are not new, we've had them around for decades, but they always required a steady hand in setting them up to catch a particular program. You had to set the timer and the channel it was all a bit complicated and of course, you couldn't watch one program and record another.

This new system is a game changer with the ability to record one program and watch another – even more than one program can be recorded simultaneously.

Many years ago there was a program on the radio in the UK called The Brains Trust. Four distinguished professors would pontificate on subjects listeners would send in for discussion.

I remember one question asking if the panel thought that people would travel more or less in future generations.

One learned academic said that he felt it likely many would never leave their homes, as everything would be available inside them. He said that in the future, each wall would be a screen onto which would be projected any scene in the world. If you wanted to be in Hawaii, then a push of a button would serve up the place on all your walls, with sounds and no doubt smells as well.

At the time we had just about reached the 24-inch color TV stage, so his views sounded beyond believe. But here we are 40 years later with larger and larger screens and I believe "smellies" are pretty close in cinemas. We shall await developments.

"Never underestimate the technological capabilities of the United States!" Said to me by a fellow spectator in New York, while viewing the ticker tape parade held for the returning astronauts (Aldrin, Collins and Armstrong) from the moon in August 1969.

Chapter Eighteen

PUBS

Most people hate the taste of beer to begin with. It is, however,
a prejudice that many have been able to overcome.
— *Winston Churchill*

I miss the banter with friends and family, which more often than
not takes place within the confines of a decent public house. So
I miss the pubs
— *Chris Vance*

I've always loved pubs. From the start of being able to get in them, they've always had a fascination for me. We lived next door to one during the latter stages of the war. It was called the White Horse, and being a child, I never once went in there.

Drink in the UK has always been expensive and I'm sure that is the principle reason for my parents not going there very often. I do remember hearing them talking about a certain Major Cartwright from time to time and on one occasion, when I was about seven, I asked if there was a Mrs. Cartwright. I was met with that sort of dull stare that my father had perfected when a difficult subject was raised; usually by me.

His first line of defence under these subjects was to pretend that he hadn't heard it. But either I was rather precocious or somewhat thick as I would generally bulldoze on.

"Where's his wife," I insisted.

"She died," was the strained reply. No doubt my father hoped that was the end of it; but no, I wanted all the facts.

"Why did she die?"

More silence, but after a repeat or two, came the reply through clenched teeth; "Cancer!"

There were several subjects that were never raised in public when I was growing up. Sex was obviously at the top of the list, followed by cancer and then divorce. I think there was such a fear of these two that even mention of them might cause them to be caught, like some type of infection.

Having found out that the late Mrs. Cartwright's demise was due to this horror, I left it alone and my parents went on about their lives, which included very rare visits to the White Horse and the sadly widowed Major.

English landlords – who are actually tenants of the brewery owned pubs – were very lax back in my growing up days. Basically if you looked old enough, then you were old enough and "old enough" was also a little squishy when it came to going into a pub.

The basic rule was that your father could take you in when he felt you were old enough, generally about 16. The age of consent was 18 in the UK.

If your father was inclined he would take you along with him and give you a lemonade. This is in fact Seven-up.

If you behaved yourself and didn't act up, after a few visits, he might buy you a shandy, this is half a glass of beer with half a glass of lemonade in it. This was heady stuff.

Now as you aged a little more, the landlord would allow you and your friends into the pub, but not to consume alcohol. You would have to wait until you were virtually 18 to do that.

I'm sure that's all changed now, as drinking laws have become quite stringent, particularly accompanied with driving.

At school we were issued with CCF uniforms (ROTC) and that put a year or two on us, so outside of any area where we were known it was pretty safe that we could get in to a pub and even have a beer or two. Remember it was rather expensive, and so that was a governor on the entire operation.

A pub is the shortened name for public house. It was originally a house that was open to the public.

The Romans are credited with introducing the first pub, or tavern, to England sometime around 60AD.

But I'm sure back in Neanderthal times there were occasions when Tog, tired of his miserable cave would stumble over to Gorp's much nicer one. After all it had a fire and some wonderful brew that Gorp made by spitting in a bowl of water and letting it fester!

There is great competition for the distinction of being the oldest pub in England and several of them fight for that right. But without doubt, the Romans had a place on the site of what is now the Fighting Cocks in St Albans, some 25 miles north of London.

It was called the Bunch of Grapes in those far off days, but then St. Alban's was called Verulameum.

The Fighting Cocks is not a wonderful establishment. I went there about twenty years ago, and it had been covered inside with Formica; a favourite material that hides a multitude of sins.

It's in a pretty spot on the banks of a flowing stream with swans and water lilies. But it's very hard to imagine Augustus and Caius, swilling down a pint of vino while celebrating their most recent pillage.

Up in Nottingham is the famous Trip to Jerusalem, know simply as The Trip. It's not the most appealing but at least it can boast that it was a staging post for Crusaders going out to fight the Muslims in the 12th century. It has a large chimney going up out of the back of the main bar, and halfway up is a "priest's hole," which was to hide fleeing pastors during the various inquisitions we enjoyed back in Tudor times. Ah those were the days!

The development of the pub as we know it today stems from the agricultural lives that most of us Brits enjoyed prior to the industrial revolution, around the mid-nineteenth century.

Before the great inventions that brought so many to the developing towns, people lived very simple lives in small villages and hamlets.

There was little spare money and not too many enjoyments to be had outside church festivals and the occasional wedding or funeral.

Keeping warm was always a challenge, as was keeping light in your small, damp hovel. One solution was to visit the one place that always had a fire and candles and company, the local public house.

This was often just the same type of house as yours, but with a front room opened up to allow some benches and also a trestle across the end where the "landlord" would serve up his home-brewed beer. This was usually kept in an earthen cellar and pulled up by a pump.

Visitors to the UK often accuse us of having warm beer. This is not the case, as it is cellar temperature, and until recently not refrigerated. In fact many of the earlier beers were still "alive" with yeast still working. Constipation was never a problem for consumers of such beverages!

The only "live" beer I'm aware of now is the famous Worthington E. In bottles, this stuff was hard to open and pour in warm weather.

There was a residue at the bottom that landlords would be careful to leave out of the glass. I knew one old man however who used to drink that down straight out of the bottle. "I was a slave to constipation in my youth," he told me. "Once I learned about this little trick," he said smacking his lips, "it never came back." You live and learn.

So-called warm beer is not really warm as cellars in Britain are rarely up to summer temperatures. But styles have changed and most beers these days in British pubs are refrigerated at some stage of their keeping.

I remember one little pub near where I used to live just before I left home in the early sixties. I can't remember its name now, but it was tucked away at the end of a country cul-de-sac.

It had a "cellar" that was just a step down at the back of the one room bar. Within sight you could see several cross members holding barrels of beer. Each barrel had a peg in it and a stopcock. Beer was poured out into glasses and brought through to customers. When empty the cask was rolled away and another one hoisted up.

The landlord must have been a strong fellow, and I'm sure today's Health and Safety officers would disapprove of such a system. I would be very surprised if such a pub was still in existence these days.

There is a distinct difference between city pubs and country pubs. The latter were really the beginnings of the trade, but it seems to be the city pubs that have taken up the calling and are thriving. Some country pubs survive, of course, but the number has diminished considerably.

Sadly the same urbanisation of life in the west has happened to pubs as well. Since I left in 1982, pubs have closed by the thousands and it's sad to see their demise.

There are several reasons for this I am sure. To begin with, the industrialisation of agriculture has meant fewer people are needed on the land. A farmer now can manage his spread with his family and some very expensive equipment. There is no need for teams of people to bring in harvests and re-sow the fields.

People who traditionally worked the soil now work computers in the cities. Their replacements in the country cottages are now office workers, who are prepared to make the long and expensive commutes in and out of the cities in order to enjoy the fruits of living in the country.

Unfortunately those fruits are not what they used to be years ago. Firstly the village church lost its congregation and merged with other parishes as people stopped believing in organized religion. Then it was the turn of the village shop and post office. There just wasn't enough business to keep it open. Most of the commuters were home too late to do any shopping which was now done at the weekend in the family SUV at the nearest big town half an hour away, or even further.

Finally, the village pub or even several pubs found they couldn't survive with a decreasing local trade. Some of the better positioned and with the right amount of acumen opened good restaurants with expensive wines that would bring in customers from all around the district. But being a restaurateur is a far cry from being a landlord.

The drink and driving laws also put a serious nail in the coffin of committed drinkers, who now could no longer be free of prowling police cars and the loss of their valuable licenses.

Finally I think that the pressures and the feminisation of the modern workforce took away the incentive for anyone with a need for drink.

It used to be a point of honour that if you had had a "skinful" the night before, you would turn up the next day on time and fully functional, even though perhaps a little pale and stinky. Today, if such were the case, you'd probably find yourself frogmarched down to Human Resources where a stern faced creature would read you your rights, force you to sign a legal form and then enrol you in an after-work AA program (at your cost naturally.)

Also if your breath smelled of booze after a lunchtime cocktail or pint, someone would suggest that you had a problem and bang would go your chance of another step up on the corporate ladder. Those days are gone. I don't know if that is a good or a bad thing. But as someone about to leave the work force some ten years ago said to me: "It's just no fun anymore!"

Some years ago I took a drive along the twelve-mile journey towards my old school. I had made that trip by bus so many times that I thought all the stops were engraved on my memory for ever. Most of them were in fact pubs; The Wagon and Horses, The Bell, the Queen's Arms, the King's Head.

On this recent trip, I was astounded to find many of these pubs were up for sale. Such a thing would have been incomprehensible a few decades ago.

When pubs began to make a reputation for themselves back in the nineteenth century, it was not a big step for the most successful of them to begin to sell to other publicans. Thus began the rise of breweries.

Once breweries began to be successful then it made sense for them to provide their product to a wider and wider area of pubs. Eventually these areas became small fiefdoms, and their range of by now brewery owned pubs were jealously guarded. I lived in an area which was controlled by Benskin's Brewery. This Victorian business was at the bottom of Watford High Street and its fumes used to make me gag on my way to my preparatory school.

I suppose they had at their height at least 150 pubs all dependant on their regular deliveries, some of the nearest being done by drays pulled by a team of either two or four huge cart horses.

In order to be accepted for the position of running a pub, you had to pass a strict interview. Here you and your wife would be rigorously questioned for days to make sure you had the "right stuff!"

As if you were a parson, if you were accepted you would be given a pub in a poor district and if you made a go of that you could move up. I say as a parson as that was the preferred method of seniority for the clergy as well.

The competition was fierce and not everyone made it. There used to be nothing sadder than to walk into a pub under the control of a poor landlord. It was a nasty and depressing experience.

There were a few beers that were on sale that were not brewed by the local and controlling brewery. Guinness and Worthington were two. Over the years it was noticeable that as the population moved around a lot more, and began to develop a taste for certain brands so too did the brewers realise that it made sense to "import" these as well – for a decent cut, of course.

At one time, breweries began to realise that landlords were doing a little too well. Their homes were on the brewery's premises and they lived basically for free with the landlady tradionally offering pub meals which were the entire province of the couple.

One of the bean counters hit on the idea that they could reap most of these profits if they changed these tenanted houses into managed houses. This was probably the beginning of big changes in the licensed trade.

Managed pubs seemed to work alright in the cities, but they were disastrous in the suburbs and the country.

Remember, a pub is a public house. It is someone's home and not the choice of some design student with a hoard of trendy artefacts bought at random in a flea market. A manager just doesn't have the same feeling as the landlord and even worse, if the living accommodation upstairs becomes valuable to the brewery as a dwelling for a complete outsider, then it becomes just a lock-up.

This I think is the problem with many American bars or as they are often called taverns. The famous TV series Cheers was undoubtedly a lock-up, although as a pub it worked pretty well.

The center of the Cheers TV set was a replica of a bar with regulars who all knew each other over many years. Regulars are the most important part of a good pub, otherwise it becomes like an airport bar where the only regulars are the staff, and that's disastrous.

Also it's important to understand that a pub is not somewhere people go to get drunk. That is actually considered "not cool." You can get a little jolly, but drunk no!

Similarly there is a certain etiquette when going to a new pub. You don't barge in and begin to behave as if you're one of the regulars right away. Also don't go buying rounds for people in order to ingratiate yourself. That certainly will not work. If you are going to become a regular, begin quietly and wait until people begin to talk to you and they will be pleased to welcome you into their midst. Good pub people are appreciated.

I have been in hundreds of pubs in my life and some of them have been quite memorable.

Perhaps the first one I became quite intimate with was The Dog in Watford. It had a splendid sign of a bulldog outside. It was as usual in those days a two bar pub. One bar was for the "public," which meant that anyone in any form of dress or condition could frequent it. It was the normal spot for "working men" to go after work to relax before the rigours of home life.

Some years before I left the ring of suburban London, I was out for a walk with wife and Golden Retriever. About a quarter of a mile from a pub, it began to rain heavily. We were ready with umbrellas and raincoats, but were pretty wet by the time we struggled into The Magnet; a very small pub with the sign outside of Billy Bunter. In the twenties and thirties Billy Bunter and his friends at Greyfriar's School were popular in a comic called the Magnet.

Due to our soggy condition, I chose the public bar in order not to dampen their carpet.

As we went in it was pretty obvious that the local lads, hunched over a spirited game of dominoes felt a trifle inhibited, and their voices dropped a few decibels.

We had our drink, and as the storm had passed we were making our way out when the landlord quietly beckoned me over to a corner.

"Next time you come in, sir," he confided in me. "You may find it a bit more comfortable in the saloon bar."

I thanked him and said it was because of our condition, but he said that would be perfectly alright as far as he was concerned. The fact is that he wasn't in the least concerned with our comfort; he didn't want his lads inhibited by our seeming posh presence. Such was the English class system. "Bloody toffs, comin' in our place!" "Yeah right!"

For those Americans reading this and questioning the fact that I had brought George, my Golden Retriever, into a pub, let me assure you that there was nothing wrong in this at all. The English regularly bring their dogs into pubs. We pride ourselves on having dogs that are well behaved and trained. Many of them are far cleaner and better behaved than the humans. Also their conversation is very often more profound.

With the changing times many pubs elected to go the one-bar route, and I can't say it made them any better. Of course, it cut down on the problem of having to have two bar staff on duty, or annoy people with a wait for service while the one man rushed about in between.

For a short time I lived opposite a private hotel, and used it's saloon as a watering hole for a pre-dinner drink. It was OK and was about as close to being a pub as any other hotel I've ever used.

In Cornwall, the pubs were wonderful, if you could get away from the touristy ones. My favourite was the Roseland Inn a couple of miles from the King Harry ferry which took cars and pedestrians across the River Fal to Falmouth.

The Roseland Inn was owned by a man who never drank – well not in public. He would have an orange juice if someone wanted him to "have a drink with us." This arrangement is the norm when wanting to "tip" the barman. Normally drinks are paid for as you go and a tab is not run up. As a result if you want to give the barmaid something then you offer them a drink, which they will often "have later."

The Roseland Inn was a one bar pub a long way down a winding narrow lane and did excellent pub grub before such practise became the lifeline of such places. There was one rule there, however; don't sit on the captain's stool.

This old salt would come in most of the times we were there and he would sit at the end of the bar against the wall watching things happen. He smoked a pipe and looked every inch the seafarer. His boat had come in for the final time though some thirty years prior, now he was a landlubber like the rest of us.

Of course perhaps the best pub I have in my memory is the one where we had our wedding reception all those 30 plus years ago.

The Lamb in Angmering was a fine place that did a little accommodation, good food and had two excellent bars. The only time I went in the public one though was when we went in to cut our wedding cake.

In our more normal saloon, it had an inglenook fireplace and old oak furniture. The bar was "L" shaped and the short arm of the "L" was always known as the "member's enclosure."

When we went back after a few years we popped in to see how things were going. It was amazing how a new owner had transformed the place. He was a Pakistani, and although a nice enough fellow, he had no idea what constituted a pub's atmosphere.

He had thrown all that old fashioned furniture out and put in its place thin Oriental type stuff that didn't look as if it could support even a normal sized man.

For background music he had bought what he thought was western style music. While I was there Willy Nelson was followed by a Big Band, and then some Bach. It was very weird.

We finished up and went up the road to the Spotted Cow, where all the locals had resettled. It was a shame.

Eventually a new owner was found and the last time I went in there it was back to where it always had been. Sadly our very last trip found them in a major overhaul and now I believe it's a very nice restaurant indeed; but what's it like as a pub?

We have had mixed feelings about our Californian pubs, and enjoy them as much as possible. Fortunately in Big Bear we have come off a positive dearth with few places that one could call one's home. That has changed now, and we are very pleased with our choices, and bar staff,

We are going back to England in a few months. We will stay in London and I don't think there will be any opportunity to leave the city. It will be interesting to see how the pubs are fairing.

On my last visit I was rather surprised to find two changes that rather caught me off guard.

Firstly nearly all the bar stools had gone. It was now the practise for management to want people to order from the bar, and then sit at the tables awaiting the drinks to be brought over to them; a rather strange idea. There was no problem with standing at the bar, but nowhere to sit there. Years ago, the little tables dotted around were where you sent the mother-in-law or other undesirables while you sat with your closest at the bar.

The second fact that I found odd was that there were very few English people serving behind the bar. They were nearly all eastern European and frankly not a lot of fun. Mostly they seemed to be Romanians, Estonians and also Polish. When I mentioned this to a friend she said: "Oh, English people won't do that type of work?" Good grief!

I do wonder at the future of pubs in general. In my lifetime they have changed enormously. At one time the most you could hope from the majority of them if you were hungry was a packet of "crisps" or peanuts. There sometimes used to be a large bottle of picked eggs on hand.

Those days have gone with most pubs in England serving very good food.

Out here there are still some places that only serve a micro-waved plate of goo. But they are quite rare. Mostly today in California, the bar is an off shoot of the restaurant and they generally work quite well.

But the tradition of "going out for a drink" seems to be disappearing. Young couples no longer see this as a regular part of their lives, and the old time regulars are fast slipping their cables. You don't see too many old hardened drinkers.

As I live in a resort town, there is always likely to be a number of places that attract visitors, but off the hill it's a different thing entirely.

When Michael and I take our regular long rides out into the country, we are astounded at the emptiness of America. It's the same problem as the rest of the west.

There is no work for young people who naturally gravitate to the towns. They leave behind empty houses, empty villages and of course, empty pubs; a sad end to a glorious tradition of warmth, cheer and friendship.

Beer is proof that God loves us and wants us to be happy.
— Benjamin Franklin

229

Chapter Nineteen

TABOOS

I can resist everything but temptation
— Oscar Wilde

How can we pick and choose which parts of the Bible to follow?
One thing is God's will and another is just cultural differences?
What if it's all cultural? What if homosexuality or saving yourself
for marriage is as outdated as women staying silent in church or
Leviticus forbidding tattoos?"
— Trevor D. Richardson

In the last chapter I mentioned the curious behaviour of my father when certain subjects were brought up. Of course, as I said in immediate post-war Britain, sex was never mentioned, but there were other things on the do not discuss list. Divorce and cancer were complete no-no's.

Before immediately judging this inhibited attitude as merely quaint, we perhaps should look at our own society's quirks about taboos. Because we too have subjects that one cannot discuss in public. But firstly a little history.

The other evening we were watching a period drama. The period was one I had lived through – the early sixties. In it a young girl had been for an abortion and the police were considering raiding the establishment as such a practice was illegal.

I had a friend about this time, who had unfortunately succeeded in "getting a girl into trouble!" He turned to me to see if I could help. I have no idea why he should have imagined that I knew anything about such a practise, but I called another friend who said he might be able to do something. In the end the baby was delivered after a hurried marriage and the couple lived in misery for many years.

This was the state of affairs back then, I'm afraid.

On another occasion, I found my flat mate (the infamous Dave) sitting at the dining table writing a long letter to his boss. He had just been told by his girl friend that she was "late!" Oh the horrors!

Now it happened that this girl was rather nice, but in the way of many of the girls at that time, and not seeing any commitment coming from Dave, she used a little pressure. It was a fairly common procedure.

Unfortunately she had totally underestimated Dave's fear and overestimated his interest. He had absolutely no intention of shortening his lifestyle with the encumbrance of a wife and child. He was rather like an old fashioned Charlie Harper from Two and a Half Men.

His plan was to lock his company car up in a local garage, send his boss the keys and set off on a boat, if he could get one. We lived in the dock town of Southampton and it was not too hard to find a position as a steward back then.

And so this was the third solution to the unwanted pregnancy issue – flight. Firstly there was doing the right thing, secondly, an abortion and finally Dave's way out; and all this on top of no pill, just condoms, which were pretty beastly. How were we expected to manage our hopelessly raging testosterone?

Today however we have a complete reversal of the situation. Somehow men have managed to escape the horrors of unwanted pregnancies, and now seem to be able to have it both ways. More if they are canny.

I don't know quite how this has happened, but it doesn't seem to have made young people any more carefree or happy.

Abortion is one of those taboo subjects that is never discussed and just accepted. The general attitude of most politicians is to say that abortions should be legal and rare. The second part of this is distressingly untrue. Abortions are very frequent and sadly even encouraged by certain organisations.

I do understand that for anyone with a history of the illegal activity in their past this is a painful prospect to recall and perhaps to even allow a relaxing of the current position. But surely there must be a system that we can evolve that doesn't subject women to such a dreadful burden and still encourage them to have some restraint on what is after all infanticide.

Whether life begins at conception or a few weeks later is just an academic discussion. But it is only a monster that believes a nine month old fetus is not a baby. And yet many advocates of abortion insist that killing a baby a moment before it exits the womb is a mother's right to choose.

One moment after such an exit, it is patently murder and the woman would be under arrest, so what are we talking about here? And more importantly why can we not discuss this without people screaming at the others' point of view?

There was a movie produced in the mid-sixties called Alfie. It starred Michael Cain in the title role. He was everything the infamous flatmate, Dave, wanted to be. He was well dressed, with a rascally charm and a serious appetite for "crumpet." The London slang name for females.

In the movie, Alfie has a job as an upscale chauffeur and does his hospitalized mate a favor by running his wife home after a visit to the ward.

Sadly the proximity of crumpet being in the rear seat of his Rolls was too much for him and they succumbed to temptation.

Eventually the bulging price of their sin became evident and the woman came to Alfie to have the problem resolved.

The activity of a backstreet abortionist, played perfectly by a seedy actor named Denham Elliot was everything of which we all had a horror. Afterwards, Alfie looked at the woman and said to her: "You do look old, girl!" Obviously a caring sort of chap!

The scene was unforgettable and no doubt has helped feed the vigor of the pro-choice crowd to never allow such treatment to be meted out to any woman ever again.

Having lived through this time, I would be the last person to want to return to it. I remember seeing Ms. Kate Michelson giving her opinion of her experience before an all male panel, who were there to decide whether she should or should not receive an abortion. It sounded pretty bad to me and I had no idea such panels existed.

If one accepts her memory then it seems to me that this idea is disgraceful and such a procedure would poison one for life; and that seems to have happened with Ms. Michelson. She went on to become the president of NOW – the National Organization for Women, or Feminazis, as Rush calls them. Mainly they seem only to be interested in left leaning ideas with an unhealthy suspicion of men.

I feel that something should be said about this problem of illegal abortions in the past.

Until 1920 (The 19th amendment of the Constitution) women were not allowed to vote. Accepting that this was nearly 100 years ago and after a great deal of fighting, we do not hear arguments along the lines that if not watched, the vote will be snatched away from women. And yet this is very much the attitude of the most militant in favor of unrestricted access to the unfortunate procedure of abortion.

If you accept that the extremes of both sides of the argument represent either total access at any time, with complete government funding, or on the other no abortions whatsoever and punishment for those who provide or submit to them, we have two extreme and unacceptable viewpoints.

As the Supreme Court has decided that abortions should be legal throughout the USA, it is extremely unlikely ever to change this stance.

However, I am sure that even the most battle hardened would balk at the prospect of a new born baby having a sharp pair of scissors rammed into the back of its neck as it exits the womb. Well, obviously some of the most battle hardened are in favour of this. Frankly, I believe it is scandalous.

Our current President has voted in the past that any child who actually survives such an experience or appears alive after an abortion should be killed as a part of the medical procedure.

I believe such proponents should be forced to watch the entire operation and then put forth an argument for its continuance. I also believe they should hear some comments from the mothers of such a practice and see how they have felt about it after some time has elapsed. Without a doubt they must be upset for many years to come and perhaps never quite recover from the experience of knowing that they have allowed their child to be so mutilated,

Then there is the question of adoption. Surely there must be someone who can come up with a plan whereby the thousands of people wanting to adopt babies, can be linked up with the thousands of those who want to abort them. But I'm merely a man, and if Ms. Michelson sticks to her belief, then my opinion must be worthless. As the proponents of "choice" constantly remind us, it's a woman's right to choose, and have control over her own body.

However as the only members of our society who can actually give birth, then that surely must come with some responsibility.

We have at the moment some women who allow themselves to be impregnated and then turn to the government to pay for their abortions time and time again. Frankly I cannot see why we can't put some type of governor on this behaviour by charging them for this frankly immoral activity.

I do not come to this conclusion through any rigid religious belief, just simply that expecting the government (tax payers) to pay for your behaviour, and in many cases commit infanticide – for that is what it is – is objectionable on the most basic moral grounds.

Before my mail box fills up with complaints that it's not fair for poor women to have to pay, I would simply say that some type of deferred payment could be charged over a long period. Something like a student loan.

But since Roe versus Wade was passed in 1975 some 50 million babies have been aborted. How many Beethovens have we destroyed; how many Picassos?

Surely in a society that believes in human freedom, we should allow those most precious of us to be at least given the chance to live. Or at least allow a decent public debate with some good brains to try and find a solution, without Ms. Michelson having conniption fits about the right to choose. Perhaps we could ask the likes of the Reverend Jackson or the Reverend Al Sharpton to lead these discussions as it is their congregations in particular who are destroying the young life of their society.

Which brings us to the other area of taboo we shrink from discussing – Racism!

I have to accept that it took me a very long time living in the country to get my arms around the thorny subject of race. And here, let's not beat about the bush, we're talking black and white.

I think it's always suspicious when a group who are unable to persuade the rest of us to agree about a subject, change the name of the terminology. To begin with black people were usually called black when I was growing up, then it changed to Afros, then to colored, and now African Americans. What is with the name change? Has it helped at all? I suspect it has as little soothing effect as electing a black man to the White House. In other words symbolism over substance.

I knew a fellow down in Marina Del Rey who was born and raised in Johannesburg, South Africa. At age about seven he came to California where he has lived for the last forty years. He is white and now an American citizen. Should he be called an African American?

By the same token, am I an English American, or perhaps a European American? Total nonsense. The fact is that we are all Americans and we should be damned proud of it.

If we have to make a distinction between the races, surely black and white is OK. It treats the two of us the same.

Some years after I came here permanently, I returned to England for a short visit. I was having a drink with a friend of mine in a pub near Windsor Great Park. On the wall next to where we were standing was a brass plaque. It said: *The definition of heaven: All the police are British; all the cooks are French; all the mechanics are German; all the lovers are Italian and the whole thing is run by the Swiss.*

The definition of hell: All the cooks are British, all the mechanics are French; all the police are Germans; all the lovers are Swiss and the entire things is run by the Italians.

When I saw that, after ten years of being in California, my immediate reaction was: That's a bit strong, someone could get offended by that. After a few more moments, I realized that we were in England and people understood the humor in the stereotypes portrayed. In fact it was very funny.

Every one is portrayed equally apart from Italians, and who cares about them anyway! We have been making jokes about such stereotypes for centuries in Europe and people think they're funny, and don't get offended.

Here, humor seems to have disappeared and even people who are not in such groups believe it's their job to speak out against discrimination. But is it discrimination?

Recently the political parties have been up to their old tricks of labelling people and placing them in groups, always on the look out for any form of racism. And yet one never hears of a definition of this dreadful term from which we all shrink. What is racism?

I find different people of different backgrounds fascinating. That includes black people. When I first came here to California I didn't understand the way things were, and actually had to be taught some racism by a couple of black colleagues. It was fascinating.

One of these men had been born and raised in a small town in Minnesota and his family members were the only black people there. He had to be taught the same as me when he came out west. He didn't think he was any different.

There is no doubt that some automatic discrimination does exist towards some blacks from a very few whites. I have witnessed it and it is extremely nasty. I once told a barmaid of whom I was previously quite fond that we were expecting a couple and would not sit in our usual place at the bar. We would need a table for four. Oh, and by they way, you'll know them when they come in, they're black.

She rolled her eyes heavenward, and I found it a most unpleasant business, and it poisoned my feelings for her thereafter.

I think however that most people are not like that and treat everyone equally, which is how it should be.

If I was accepting applications for a position and one of them was submitted from a person I knew to be black and I put him on the rejected side because of his color, then I believe that is racism. If on the other hand I happen to ask a black friend of mine if his color comes off on the towels, is that racism? Frankly I believe it to be curiosity, which is no more racist than to ask a Scotsman if he is unadorned under his kilt.

I truly believe that our diversity is one of the joys of human beings. I also think it is unnatural to believe that we are all wonderfully equal; some are decidedly not. However, I'm damned if just because I disapprove of 90% of the actions of the current President of the United States that makes me a racist. It's his policies that unnerve me, not his color.

One of the most unpleasant aspects of this racism charge that is hawked by the race hustlers is a flagrant disregard for history.

Some years ago one of my foster daughters brought home her then current boyfriend. He was black and went by the name of Shakee. His father had gone the Muslim route in the sixties and renamed his family from Bill Smith or similar, to Mohammed Ishmael or some such.

The young man was a very nice quiet chap and we enjoyed having him with us for a spell.

At one stage in the mid-afternoon I found myself sitting with him on our deck and the subject of society in general came up. He said: "I can never forgive the wrongs done to my people." I was rather surprised at the earnest way he spoke and I replied: "Which people might that be, Shakee, the people of Compton or the people of Inglewood; which people?" He explained that he meant black people and how their lives had been stolen by the whites and how it was all so terribly unfair.

Now I must confess that I might have had a Budweiser or two too many with lunch but this struck me hard on a number of levels.

I said I did understand his problem. After all he surely knew that my own people had in fact also been enslaved by cruel overlords. Firstly it was the Romans, and then we had to live with constant invasions from any hordes on the Continent who could get a boat and crew together before sailing over to our peaceful islands. There were the Visigoths, the Danes, the Vikings, the Saxons and then the final and deadly curse of the Normans.

These beasts not only took charge of the entire nation, but forced us to give up our language and learn their vile ways, including a big slice of the dreaded French language, which is still taught in our schools.

The usual modus operandi of all these racist pigs was to steal our natural resources, enslave our young men, and worst of all defile our most attractive women and leave us over and over again with the ugly ones. It was a true human tragedy. Not only had we got the standard of our English roses up again but there was another pennant skimming across the horizon and another load of beauties taken from us. Is it any wonder that we turned into such an aggressive race? Who wouldn't?

The end result of all this murder, pillage and mayhem was that after we were forced to accept the rule of the Norman invaders we have never been invaded again since 1066, a date that I'm sure he knew.

In view of this sad history, did he think we should pursue an active policy of seeking reparations from all those nations who had done these unspeakable acts on us, starting with the Italians who are of course the present day Romans – there has never been an apology from them, I might add.

Why should the governments of Denmark, Belgium – a particularly odious and unpleasant people – France and, of course modern Germany who have benefited from our young talents and also our naturally beautiful women be allowed to get away scot free?

Is it any wonder that there is tremendous resentment? Would he join with me in fighting such discrimination?

He was a little taken aback, but said he thought that maybe it was rather a long time ago, and that perhaps we should leave it alone.

I said how long should we allow such feelings to exist and what was the time limit or cut off point?

Slowly he began to understand how mankind has behaved over the years and that living in the past of some hundreds or thousands of years was perhaps not as smart as he had thought.

I felt a little sorry for laying all this on him, particularly as he had told my wife a day or two earlier, that apart from a couple of teachers, she was the only white person to whom he'd ever spoken. And then the second one was me! And after a few beers!

I also felt annoyed at what I considered to be the negative outlook on life that had been foisted on him, and one which was hardly going to help his future. As a result I wrote him a letter apologizing for coming on a little strongly, but I felt it was a dreadful thing that such a decent young man should be burdened with so many unreasoned prejudiced ideas that were of absolutely no use to him in the finest country in the world, and the one where blacks were treated better than anywhere else.

I am proud to say that about ten years later and long after I had forgotten the issue, I received a letter from Shakee. He wrote that he had never forgotten what I had told him and furthermore he had consulted my letter "several times, and found it to be of great comfort."

And now we come to the most contentious perhaps of all the current taboos – global warning!

This is a difficult one as in spite of numerous statistics, we have very little actual information as nearly all of the data is based on "computer models,"

I heard an authority on this matter talking the other day and he explained that most of the grants in support of "climate change" study are provided by organizations promoting the idea of this phenomenon.

I should state right off the bat that I believe man-made global warming to be total bollocks. For un-English readers this means nonsense. I believe it is another manifestation of liberal guilt and also another scheme to remove money from the achievers in order to distribute it to the non-achievers. Or socialism as it more politely called.

My father was known in the fifties to complain regularly that the reason the weather was so bad was because of the testing of nuclear weapons. They were always letting them off in some remote portions of the world; Pacific atolls were favourite sites.

Of course, England has never been known for its cosseting climate, and furthermore it was only a few hundred years since the time when the winters were so hard that the River Thames froze completely.

Pictures were painted of the scene where bonfires were lit on it for the amusement of the crowds, who were skating and enjoying feasts.

I am perfectly prepared to listen to the arguments about this man made terror, but currently I prefer to remain agnostic. Certainly while we still have no firm data to prove it one way or another.

Those in control of things assure us that science has a consensus about the matter, but surely science is either proved or not proved. How come there are scientists who refute the other ones' findings and still remain defiant?

I heard a scientist talking about this the other day. He spoke very eloquently about the Middle Ages in England when the grape harvests were so plentiful that an embargo was placed by France, as it was ruining their wine business.

At the time without greenhouses and modern farming methods, the growing of wine grapes was virtually impossible in any quantity.

Now either this fellow was barking mad, or he was lying; but might it be possible to have a meaningful debate about this, without being labelled a "denyer?" Which puts us doubters in the same unpleasant camp as those denying the holocaust.

I am sure that the constant pumping out of noxious gases into the atmosphere is not good for any of us, but where I become suspicious is when arguments that India and China are doing it more than us are met by cries that they've not had a chance to catch up with the greedy west. Immediately there is therefore the taint of unfairness about the whole thing, and I prefer my science to be gleaned without social judgment as an ingredient.

Most of us downtrodden middle class Englishmen were raised to be decent stewards of the earth and its bounty. We were taught to look after the environment before we even knew the term.

Our roads and lanes were at that time tended by old men with scythes and clippers who took their ploughmen's lunches in the pub where they stopped. They would wash it down with a pint of strong cider and then no doubt have forty winks under the same hedges that they were tending.

They did not drive belching tractors with huge cutters that took no notice of potential birds' nests or squirrel's abodes and just forged on.

And yet today, with all our modern devices, we are supposed somehow to be guilty of killing the planet. And all the time our volcanoes continue to put out massive amounts of steam, carbon dioxide and other pollutants which we are supposed to politely ignore. Just tell that to the pilots who were forced to avoid Iceland in 2010 when the Icelandic volcano, Eyjafjallajokull, exploded and caused enormous clouds all over Western Europe. (No I can't pronounce it either!)

I notice that although our weather forecasts are better, no-one in met offices anywhere fancies giving out a forecast more than seven days out. Yet we are supposed to believe that similar scientists can forecast what will happen in a hundred years if I don't tote my groceries home in a non-plastic bag.

And yet this very act allows thousands of otherwise ignorant "low information" voters to feel superior because they are making a difference and somehow saving the planet. Naturally we all want to feel that we lead meaningful lives and perhaps by this selfless act alone, we can think ourselves of worth

It's much the same as wearing a ribbon in one's lapel or plastering a "ban the bomb" sticker on one's bumper. These acts proclaim to the world that at least we care, and therefore we're better than others because of that. It is of course merely once again symbolism over substance.

Back in the sixties when I was in my relatively ignorant twenties a much publicized and well read volume was around. It was called The Doomsday Book. Unlike the one ordered by William the Conqueror, this one was by scientists who were suggesting that we were all doomed due to our life choices. Sound familiar?

One of the phenomenum that was going to cause our demise was global cooling on a massive scale. Due to increasing airline traffic, jet trails were likely to cause the sky to be overgrown with clouds and this would not allow the sunshine to reach us and therefore create this cooling.

I have to say that for a short while the thought caused me some concern, as did my father's worry about nuclear testing. All of this seems to have passed away, but the very same scientists who were anxious to wave a red flag at our behaviour are now at it with global warming; and with the same remarkable degree of certainty.

Therefore as they were wrong then, is it not likely that they are wrong now? Or at least are we not allowed to talk about it for fear of being called denyers?

A few years back, it became obvious that the world was not actually warming at all – in fact I believe at the time of writing it has been 16 years without any increase at all.

As a result, in true liberal fashion, the language was changed. Suddenly, "Global Warming" was not now mentioned. It was altered to become "Climate Change."

As I said earlier, I tend to be agnostic about this as I don't have enough data that has not been corrupted by political ideology; however, I am very suspicious of any belief that has to adopt a name change to adapt to altering circumstances, while still pursuing the same political goals.

These three taboos all share one thing in common, they are rarely discussed and therefore they are allowed to germinate alone in people's minds or worse within groups who seek an ideological solution. This usually means shutting down opposing viewpoints.

Growing up I remember that there were many more unmentionable subjects and so perhaps we are slowly making progress, and years ago, our parents and their parents before them were just as frustrated by things as we are today. I certainly don't wish for those times as they had many problems that we wouldn't want to face today. But if we could just try and listen to the other argument from time to time I am sure it would help us all.

As a postscript to this episode; we had an enormous to-do just the other day. A massive storm was due on the East Coast. Bill "Bolshevik" de Blasio, the mayor of New York came on all the networks complete with gesticulating deaf and dumb interpreter, to effectively close the city down.

Similar cities also had the same restrictions. De Blasio in good keeping with his anti-capitalistic pals even threatened businesses who didn't allow their employees to stay at home. Shame on them.

Come the morning, the weather forecasters were proved wrong in that New York only received about six inches of snow, and everyone wondered what happened.

But then the usual people came out to state quite categorically that such events were just further evidence of global warming.

Was I the only one to see the funny side of this? Namely that the same people who forecasted incorrectly what would happen in 24 hours, were promising catastrophe in fifty years.

Go to Heaven for the climate, Hell for the company
— Mark Twain

They keep saying that sea levels are rising an' all this. It's nowt to do with the icebergs melting, it's because there's too many fish in it. Get rid of some of the fish and the water will drop. Simple. Basic science.
— *Karl Pilkington*

Chapter Twenty

WOMEN

Here's all you have to know about men and women: women are crazy, men are stupid. And the main reason women are crazy is that men are stupid."
— *George Carlin*

What would men be without women? Scarce, sir...mighty scarce."
— *Mark Twain*

Having sailed this ship through the stormy seas of taboos, we now enter the shark infested and decidedly dangerous waters of the subject of women. Very alarming territory!

And yet we have had several women in my family and let me state from the start that they all seemed to be fairly content with their lot in life and I don't remember them being particularly downtrodden or badly treated. There is the possible exception of "Little Vi," who seems to have suffered at the hand of a man – the evil Elwen, if you remember from the first chapter.

All the others had one thing in common however, they ruled their households with very little interference from their men folk.

They also seemed to have control of all the money. Men would work, no doubt pay the bills by check book, but the day-to-day living and spending money was doled out by the women. It was useless asking men for money, they rarely had any. It was the purses of women that would be opened to dispense the small amounts that we children requested from time to time.

Each morning my father would ask my mother for a certain amount, which no doubt he had calculated to pay for whatever expenses he would be likely to incur that day.

I too would be given what was needed in the way of bus fares and perhaps a visit or two to the tuck shop.

Women seemed to exist on their own plane. There was stuff going on with them that the men didn't seem to either understand or want to know about.

On the few occasions when we would meet up with other family members, it was noticeable that the men would stick together talking and smoking pipes or cigarettes - never cigars as they were only used for special times like Christmas.

The women would generally hang out in the kitchen also talking, but they would always stop if a child came in. We children were sent off to play somewhere, usually outside.

Eventually we would all gather around the table and have tea. This was the normal assortment of bread and butter, cakes and from time to time cold meats. The tea pot would be regularly filled with loose tea leaves and a strainer was used to keep these out of the cups.

At this time conversation was of a general type, but occasionally one of the men would branch off with a tale or recollection. If he went on too long or became a little too hearty, then I noticed that his wife would give him "the look!" It was very subtle, but extremely effective. Nothing would be said, just a slight tightening of the mouth, and the definite dead cod's stare.

Having noticed this use of the stare, I worked fairly hard on it myself and have in more recent years found it of great use on annoying children or even dogs. But it's virtually hopeless against women, they seem quite impervious.

We children were not encouraged to talk at the table. We were of course, quite ignorant and we were often told that nobody was interested in anything we had to say as we didn't know anything. Hard to refute.

But childhood eventually turned into adolescence and women began to assume a more important and interesting role.

I had been told the "facts of life" at age about eight, by a friend of mine, Steven Bailey. In the custom of the day he poured these prurient facts into my small ear behind the bicycle shed on a damp winter's afternoon.

I was staggered. It seemed incredible to me that his type of behaviour was what was necessary to have babies. It seemed so bizarre that I reasoned that perhaps decent husbands and wives had to talk seriously about having children before going through this extremely strange and disturbing act. No doubt they would afterwards never mention it again until the need for more children came up.

On reflection no doubt many marriages have indeed been just of this type. One thinks of the many medieval royal partnerships of course. Not a lot went on with Henry VIII and Anne of Cleves for instance.

When I was 15, a friend of mine, Chris Mansbridge, told me he was going to start going to dancing school. The principal reason for this was that they had girls there and you could learn to dance with them. I saw the opportunity immediately.

Now the only problem was an entire lack of funds and that meant talking to my parents. I didn't know exactly how this would play out but I brought it up over dinner as being something that a friend of mine suggested as being of use in later life. Far from being against it, which I fully expected my father to be, he said it was a great idea and gave me the necessary funds to go along.

It was the Star School of Dancing located over the top of Clarke's Shoes in Watford High Street. I lined up with all the other teens and awaited the opening of the studio by the rather fierce looking woman in charge.

No sign of Chris when we streamed in and I took a lonely hard backed chair staring directly at a wall of mirrors. The fierce one put a record on the portable gramophone in the corner and told everyone to take their partners. I didn't have one of those and even if he had turned up I was sure Chris wasn't what she had in mind. So I sat and watched the twirling couples.

After that number she then told one of the girls to go and get me and they would start off with learning the waltz.

The girl was a quite pretty blonde and with some instruction I assumed the position and the music began. I was pretty bad. But time went on and the weeks passed and I got the hang of it, and also I began a quite serious relationship with the pretty blonde. My father hadn't seen that coming and he wasn't very happy about it either. Such is life.

Over the next year, I went every Friday to the Star, and Chris Mansbridge never turned up once. But after the first couple of weeks I didn't care.

It seemed to me growing up in the fifties that there were very strict roles for men and women, and there wasn't a lot of movement between the barriers.

Women rarely if ever wore trousers, and men nearly always wore suits. We were very careful of our clothes as we didn't have a great variety.

When I moved out of the house and down to Southampton, I eventually found a flat. Next door was a fellow called Dave. In time we figured out that it was a cheaper deal to get a two bedroom flat together and share expenses. It turned out to be so.

I therefore came under the influence of the infamous flatmate, Dave. He taught me a lot.

He was a couple of years older than me and was from the upper working class in London. He knew a lot of stuff that seemed to have passed me by.

For instance there was the entire business of "the dance." And that meant public dances where you really met women. But it wasn't as easy as that, there were rules and certain behaviours that had to be learned.

To begin with we always went in separate cars, "in case one of gets lucky!"

We would have a couple of whiskeys while we dressed for the occasion – dark suits and ties, crisp white starched shirts and polished black shoes. Then once we were at the dance, usually at the Guildhall with Bert Osborne and his Band, we would pop downstairs for a final one. Then it was into the fray.

Now the way people behaved here was quite interesting. The women would sit on chairs around the edge of the dance floor while the men would congregate at the back usually with pints of beer in their hands. I naturally steered towards this group, only to be yanked back by Dave, who hissed: "What the hell are you doing joining that group of wankers? You're here to meet women, not hang around with a bunch of losers!"

I therefore trotted dutifully along with Dave, who turned on me hissing again. "What are you doing now?" I replied that I was following him. He informed me that I could bugger off as he was working that side of the dance floor and I could take the other, but whatever keep away from him!

OK, so now we knew the basic rules; it was a difficult learning experience for a total novice.

The other piece of advice he gave me was to never sneak up on a woman, nor if I got rejected to ask her friend or the next one or the next one. The best tactic was full frontal approach and if rejection occurred then complete withdrawal. No procrastination and no sneers. It was a lot to handle.

Now I did have one big advantage; because of the lessons I knew how to dance. Dave only knew the slow foxtrot, which limited him quite a bit. And Dave's slow foxtrot was not the type that would have won him any placement on Dancing with the Stars!

He had learned his skills at the Hammersmith Palais with some very tough competition from London Lads, and he knew how it all worked. Of course, you had to have a lot of confidence as well. I lacked that in large quantities, but I could definitely dance, and that carried me through.

Once Dave had made contact with a "target," he would take them to the very center of the floor and then assume the position which was rather different to the traditional one. He would hold the woman's hand down low and he would put his hand on the back of her neck. Leaning back he would then feed her the story.

His name was Harry, and he'd just come to the area. He was a professional photographer and was doing some confidential work for a London magazine. (In truth he was a rep flogging baby foods.) I would occasionally drift past him and hear this total bollocks that he was trotting out. Amazing, but the women seemed to lap it up.

So I was taught the ethics of dance hall behaviour from a master. But there were other things of which I was woefully ignorant.

We were out one day driving around in his car. He actually had the much sought after A40, and not only that but it was all white, and not one with a black roof, which I never cared for.

We were talking about women I assume as usual, and I told him that although I now had the secrets of meeting them at dances, I just didn't know how to pick them up say in the street or out shopping, which I had seen him do several times.

He said: "Oh that's easy, Trev, I'll show you. We just need to find one." A few moments later he said: "Oh that one'll do, look over there."

Now I think this shows one of Dave's true sides. He was a modern day Lothario or more correctly a real Male Chauvinist Pig. To him women were almost like other creatures on earth put there purely for his enjoyment. They seemed to lack a real soul to Dave. And he was totally fearless of them.

We saw this quite attractive brunette walking along the street and Dave pulled right up to her. Now Austin at this stage had developed a new idea for opening and closing windows. This is long before electric ones, even on luxury cars, and the only types were the ones you wound up with a handle.

But the much desired A40 had windows that you pulled down with the aid of a little glass piece on the top of the pane. As we came to a halt just in front of the woman Dave leaned across me and pulled the window down. "Excuse me," he said in a loudish voice. "Can you tell me where the post office is?"

I thought he must be having some sort of turn as he knew exactly where it was; it was just along the road on the right hand side. He went there most days to mail off reports and orders.

But in one fluid motion he managed to leave his seat and be standing alongside the women, smiling in the afternoon sun without any pause in the conversation.

She told him where the post office was and immediately Dave launched into one of his tales. "My name's Harry. I've just arrived in town. Tell me, what's there to do around here in the evenings?"

Forgetting that he had lived there for over a year and he knew exactly what went on as he'd sampled it for fifty-two weeks, I noticed that the woman's answer was typical.

"Oh nothing goes on around here." She said.

What is it with young people? They always seem to thing that nothing goes on locally. A serious case of the grass seeming greener, I suppose.

The entire episode ended up with the young lady kindly agreeing to show Dave (Harry!) some of the high spots a couple of nights later. In fact he continued with the relationship for quite some time. I think her name was Valerie. She'd be about 77 today! Good Grief!

It was a valuable lesson, but I never in truth ever used the technique as I was rather fearful of rejection. Dave never cared about it. It was all a numbers game to him and he did rather well back in those inhibited days.

His disregard for women in general was shown when we managed to persuade women to come back to our flat. Yet another lesson was Dave's instruction to invite them back for the purpose of cooking us dinner. "Women seem to imagine that two blokes living on their own are permanently starving as they don't know how to feed themselves," he reasoned. "So play it up and have them come round so we can get a decent meal." It worked most times and women that we had met separately would cheerfully agree about the second date to come and cook us up some dinner.

We would collect them and introduce them and let them have at it in the kitchen while we lounged in the living room. Quite extraordinary!

Now Dave would set about his research into the cooks at work across the small hallway.

They would innocently leave their handbags on the sofa or chairs and Dave would consider these fair game. I would have to stand at the door while he blatantly went through them. Unbelievable!

I had been raised to consider a woman's bag absolutely sacrosanct, and had been taught that if my mother, say, wanted an item from her bag I would dutifully go and collect the bag for her and afterwards put it back. The interior was somewhere no man's hand should ever go.

Dave saw it as the ideal feeding ground for intelligence on the woman's habits and if there were letters, and there often were, information on possible rivals. I stood at the door nonplussed while he riffled away, dreading the sudden appearance of one of the women. But as was usual with Dave, he got away with it.

As with so many things to do with the "fair sex" back then there were lots of secrets to do with them. Their clothing was weird, particularly the undergarments. Even teenage girls would be expected to wear a girdle; some type of medieval constriction that would hide any pretence of a belly. Their bras would push their breasts into pointy ice cream cone shapes, and then there were the ever present stockings with accompanying garter belts leaving the small round bumps like bee stings under their skirts on top of their thighs.

Even if left alone in a quiet bedroom, it would take forever to get all this clobber off, let alone with the jerky, sweaty hands of an ardent attendee trying to rush things along. It was difficult stuff and mostly of course, it was carried out in the darkest conditions possible; they tended to be very modest back then.

Of course, as we all danced face to face and up close and personal it was possible to get an assessment of what lay beneath after a few turns of the floor to Bert Osborne's strict tempo. Heady days!

But then we entered the swinging sixties and all bets were off. And that included most of those constricting undergarments.

Once the pill came along women changed; imperceptively at first, but then within a decade women began to be much more assertive – well many of them. Women's Lib had arrived.

I will never forget my father saying to me one day: "Trevor, we'll rue the day we let women into industry." I thought he was crazy. But in fact they did enter and by the late eighties they were heading up many departments and even entire companies. I never paid much attention to the cry of "glass ceilings" as they existed for most of us men too. There is only one CEO to a company and as my old headmaster said: "many are called but few are chosen!"

The question of equality has never been a serious problem to my mind as in the world from which I came, women were in fact treated as superiors but decidedly different. In Japan they acknowledge this and there are even different words that women use – almost a different vocabulary. I was warned there never to learn Japanese from a woman as people will know.

The entrance of women into the mainstream workforce has created some changes and not all of them pleasant.

For instance, business lunches. Back in my early days, it was considered part of the process with fairly high ticket items to take one's client out to lunch. Mostly this would include alcohol.

Obviously this didn't mean consuming large quantities, but a decent lunch with a bottle of wine was the accepted way of building a good relationship. Sales is merely that, building trust on both sides and allowing the relationship to grow in such an atmosphere.

Such is much harder when it you are both confined to the office. Much better to go out to independent ground. It was never a problem when 99% of one's contacts were men.

All that changed when the percentages shifted and more and more women were in decision making positions. Taking a woman out to lunch had different kinds of connotations and not all of them acceptable. Business lunches began to disappear over a ten-year period.

Women bring a set of different skills to the management table. Not all of them enjoyable to fire-breathers from a different era.

My experience growing up was that little boys were encouraged to climb that extra branch on the tree, take another small step out on the ice and other risks. Girls didn't seem to get that encouragement, well not many of them. Tom boys were extremely rare growing up.

As a result when we entered business we were once again prompted to have a go! Obviously our efforts were monitored by the older men and if we showed too much guts and not enough brains then we were pulled back.

My experience of women in the workforce is that they tend to be risk averse and extremely careful, especially when it comes to that ultimate sin – the spending of corporate dollars.

I remember once many years ago on a dark winter's Friday evening at 5:45, driving along a small street with shops on either side. It was a small English town, but it could just as well have been in the USA.

There was a light drizzle coming down and out from a pharmacists came a young lady in a dark suit with a sample case grasped underneath her umbrella. She was obviously a pharmaceutical rep and here she was leaving a call at this time on a Friday evening.

At that precise moment I saw the future, and it was one without me or my kind. Granted it would take a few years, but in fact it did happen. Here was a woman doing a sales job and furthermore doing it at this ungodly hour when all decent reps would be in a pub or at home fiddling their expense sheets. Only a man under sentence of dismissal would be so dedicated.

Women follow the rules and don't try and bend them – well not too much. They also like to build consensus among their peers and have no problem with calling for yet another meeting if it is likely to protect corporate dollars.

In the good ol' boy days, such behaviour was rather frowned upon. It smacked of uncertainty, which was not the way things were done.

I'm sure business has benefitted from this transformation and in so doing my experience is that men have since become more like women and not the other way around.

It is rare these days for a salesman to have a call returned, whereas before the transformation, it was considered a point of honour to return calls, no matter how unpleasant the procedure. Unfortunately women prefer to ignore the requests of people chasing them; men have witnessed that and found they can avoid such discomfort as well.

In turn salesmen, on being asked how things are going with such and such a proposal, can now accurately state that calls are not being returned. Years ago, any fire breathing sales manager would have merely laughed at such an excuse. But the world continues to turn successfully.

The price of the further emancipation of women is that they have lost much of the mystique they used to enjoy. They are no longer allowed by society to merely sit at home awaiting the attentions of a suitor before settling down to a life of domestic bliss (or sadly in many cases unhappy endurance).

I am unable to decide which of the two lives are most tolerable. Today we seem to have elevated women to a level that hitherto they had shrunk from. I am sure some of my early female associates wanted to be engineers, statesmen, truck drivers and other professions that were usually the province of men. I never met any, but that doesn't mean they weren't there.

Today, we are led to believe that women all want to enter the competition of commerce, the military or sports or all the other fields from which in my youth they seemed content to shrink.

If a woman today said her ambition was to marry, raise children and enjoy the twilight of her life with the chosen man of her life, people would think she was decidedly odd. And yet that seemed the path for all my contemporaries on the distaff side.

Comparing the two existences, I wonder which is truly the best. Fifty years ago, virtually any woman was looked up to and respected merely because she was a woman.

It would have been a strange railway carriage indeed where men were sitting and a woman was left to stand. Doors were opened for approaching women, and a roomful of men would automatically rise if a woman were to enter. They would do so again when she left. No man would pass a woman of his acquaintance without lifting his hat. And this behaviour went across all classes.

A crowded elevator's progress would be impeded if a woman was at the back and she wanted to leave alongside all the men. They would hang back while she made her exit. Woe betide any male who tried to get out ahead of her. He would be considered boorish.

From time to time I see a small throwback to those days which I find refreshing. One acquaintance of mine that I used to meet regularly when I visited Dallas would never let his wife order directly from a waiter. He would consult her as to her choice and then give the waiter instructions. Perhaps it's a Texas thing. But at sometime in the past he had been taught that women do not talk directly to outside servants, that is a man's job.

Such behaviour no doubt has gone the way of Dave's slow foxtrot.

But looking back over seven decades it amazes me that the delicate balance between men and women continues. I'm not sure how much the changes have affected people, but they are substantial.

If asked what was the most important invention of the 20th century, my answer would always be the birth control pill. Not computers, not flight, not medicine, not TV, although all these have all had enormous influence on the way we live our lives today. But the pill actually changed the way our society was structured.

In pre-pill days, women really couldn't control their reproductive situation; so much was down to pure chance, unless the woman took a vow of chastity – and some truly did – until the wedding night.

In those days pregnancy happened in spite of people's very best efforts, and if out-of-wedlock, then there were only three answers to the swelling problem; Marriage, Illegal Abortion or Flight! Most people chose the first with often unhappy results. Pre-marriage intercourse was a risky venture, but most of us walked the dangerous path. Testosterone is one of the most powerful drugs know to man!

Today with a slew of contraceptive solutions available how is modern woman holding up with her new found freedom? Is she any happier than her pre-pill sister? Impossible to say for sure as the game has changed quite a lot.

Along with the pill came a reduction and then total removal of one of the mainstays of old fashioned society – shame!

Although everybody knew what was going on, if a woman became pregnant before marriage a great sense of shame descended on her and her family. It was amazing the speed at which a marriage ceremony could be arranged. The couple were not out of the woods even then as curious eyes would be on the bride's belly and also the calendar. Tongues would wag if a child should appear before the allotted nine month time period.

Any casual mention of a premature baby would be met with knowing smiles. I myself was immensely pleased when my son was born 13 months after the wedding. No room for any doubt there! Ha ha!

Today all that has gone away and I wonder if it has benefitted society.

I live in a small community of about 17,000 people. It is noticeable that many of the single women in the age group of between 20 and 40, have children with no accompanying husband. And if enquiries are made they are quite happy to tell you they have never been married.

They seem to be in and out of relationships and there is the old saying up here that in Big Bear, "you don't lose your girl, you lose your turn!"

So who has benefitted from this extreme relaxing of society's mores? Surely working a couple of jobs with a couple of growing children in a small rented house cannot be a lot of fun. And we all know that if the chance of a decent husband was given, they would all jump at it.

No, I'm afraid that the beneficiaries of these changed rules are now not women but men.

No longer is there the need to face up to one's responsibilities. Women now seem able to shoulder the burden of children unassisted by the impregnator, and no-one seems to give a damn. Dave, who now would be about 78 and probably long beyond taking advantage of the situation, would be in his element. The pendulum seems to have swung completely the wrong way.

I've often wondered what life would be like without women to share the planet with us.

Well, to begin with we would mostly live in very large garages. They would be equipped with all the tools and weapons necessary to enjoy life. Our TV's would be at least ten feet by twelve and fill an entire wall of the garage. There would be no Oprah Winfrey Channel taking up room in the TV box that would have extra sports and military channels. One of which would be devoted entirely to Hitler and WWII.

But having lived so many years with women, I now feel that my life would be nowhere near as happy without them. But I do wonder how the life of today's young women is compared to the lives enjoyed by the girls I knew so many years ago. Yet another of life's unanswered questions.

Sometimes I wonder if men and women really suit each other.
Perhaps they should live next door and just visit now and then."
— *Katharine Hepburn*

Chapter Twenty-One
COOKING

He'd noticed that sex bore some resemblance to cookery: it fascinated people; they sometimes bought books full of complicated recipes and interesting pictures, and sometimes when they were really hungry they created vast banquets in their imagination - but at the end of the day they'd settle quite happily for egg and chips. If it was well done and maybe had a slice of tomato."
— Terry Prachett, The Fifth Elephant

...no one is born a great cook, one learns by doing.
— Julia Child, My Life in France

I used to watch my mother cooking a lot when I was growing up. She wasn't the best cook in the world as with a husband suffering from stomach ulcers, she had to be careful with what she put into dishes. But she used to let me stir things around and I suppose it was normal for me when I left home to put things together in a frying pan – the favourite method of all beginners.

When I shared a flat with the infamous Dave, I soon learned that I much preferred to cook than do the dishes afterwards, and so I left the kitchen after the meal was served. Of course, in his inimitable fashion, Dave would pile up the dishes in the sink for our housecleaner; the much underpaid and overworked Mrs. Dimont, to do on her weekly skirmish into our pretty bedraggled place.

By the time I was married I had a few dishes up my sleeve, but in the fashion of the day it was the wife that did the cooking while the husband produced the wages.

Neither of us was particularly good at either roles, but we pressed on doing the best we could.

My friend Peter Jansen, from whom I learned a lot, also had a spaghetti dish in his resume and after I watched him doing it a few times, I also took it on and things began to grow from that time.

In America I started doing quite a lot of cooking after Yvonne and I worked out a few basic rules. She was very good in the kitchen and we had to decide who was cooking and who was assisting. Once we'd done that we were in good shape and we could produce our various specialities without getting in each other's way.

Just for fun, I thought I would add some recipes here – there are three. They are simple and easy to produce and we eat them regularly as we are so fond of them. It's easy to get into a rut as one ages, particularly as certain foods can upset one. But these are ideal for any occasion.

They come from a book I've got on the back burner, called Grub for Blokes. This is one of those projects that all writers have and intend to finish. I don't know if I ever will. It was designed to help men who have absolutely no idea how to cook and shy away from the activity.

Cooking is one of those last bastions of male preserve that men seem to have difficulty with. Along with typing it can seem to some men that it is "women's work," and therefore to be avoided. The fast food chain, Carl's Junior, ran a successful ad some time ago showing men at various stations in supermarkets looking clueless, before finding the welcoming lights of Carl's Junior. The caption was "Without us some men would starve!"

These men seem to forget that most of the top chef's positions in the world of fine dining are filled with their gender and there is nothing wrong with throwing a few things in the pan and getting to it; particularly if at the same time you can get a beer going and have Fox News Chanel on the TV. For me a little slice of heaven!

QUICK COOK CURRIED PRAWN AND NOODLES

Now, this dish is really easy and very quick to cook, particularly if you do a little preparation beforehand. An ideal situation to magically produce something tasty and colourful after getting back from the pub!

Ingredients: Half pack of spaghetti
                     1 Tbs of curry powder

1 ½ Tbs of olive oil
1 package of peeled and tailed shrimp – about a pound
1 red bell pepper
1 tspn of salt
1 cup of coconut milk – shaken well.
2 Tbs of chopped cilantro

Combine the prawns, oil, curry powder and salt in a bowl and set aside. Thinly slice the bell pepper and you can also add a couple of chopped up mushrooms if you like. Get out the saucepan and fill with enough water to cover the spaghetti; get out a skillet and put it on the stove top. Leave for the pub!

Cooking: Put on the water for the pasta. When boiling, add salt and a little oil to stop the pasta from sticking together. Swirl around to separate. Set timer for the amount needed to cook. Heat a little oil in the skillet, and put in the pepper and the mushrooms (if you've opted for the addition). Add the curry and prawn mix – this should be over a fairly high heat. When the prawns are cooked through, add the coconut milk and stir thoroughly. Chop up the cilantro.

When the pasta is cooked, drain it but don't rinse it. Then you can drizzle a little olive oil over it if you like the extra taste.

Add the pasta to the prawn mix and stir well to coat everything. Serve in bowls with some chopped cilantro as garnish. Hot crusty bread goes well with this as well as some parmesan cheese.

ROASTED SAUSAGE WITH
TOMATOES AND WHITE BEANS

Now we're going to stray into that difficult territory of beans. As most people know, beans are full of fibre and they create gas. There is some method of "defarting" the beans which I've tried. It entails boiling them in baking soda, but it turns them very gray, so I don't recommend it.

Better to use Beano or Gas-X, which is a pretty good antidote to gas build up. But adhere to the instructions as it must be taken "before the first bite of food," to be effective.

Ingredients: 1 ready made Kielbasa sausage
1 medium onion chopped
1 large can of crushed tomatoes
4 cloves of crushed and chopped garlic
Olive oil
1 TBSN of Balsamic vinegar
2 Bay leaves
Fresh thyme or rosemary
1 can of white beans

2 servings of pasta such as
mostacciolli or penne
Sufficient grated cheese to cover the dish

Fry the chopped onion in the oil together with the garlic. Remove to a baking dish. Slice the sausage and fry in the oil until lightly browned on all sides. Add the tomatoes, bay leaves, herbs and vinegar. Add the white beans and half of the liquid from them. Add the cooked onion and garlic and cook together for five minutes. Adjust seasoning, and pour contents into the baking dish.

Now this can be served as it is, but for a little extra panache, cover the top with cooked pasta and then over the top pour the grated cheese. Broil until the top is bubbling and brown. Serve with crusty bread. This can be served the next day as it is easy to zap in the microwave.

BREAD

Before you begin this recipe you might like to buy a pizza stone. Now it's easy to buy on line or from any really good cookery shop. They're not expensive and will allow you to make home made pizza as well as bread. Recipes for pizza are with the stone. If you don't have a pizza stone, use an oven pan with a flat bottom.

This recipe for bread comes from the book Artisan's Bread in Five Minutes a Day. It's really easy.

3 cups of hot water
6 level cups of general purpose flour
1 ½ teaspoons of salt
1 ½ teaspoons of sugar
Cornmeal to sprinkle on the stone
2 packets of fast acting
yeast (Fleischmans.)

You can of course also add herbs, or garlic to add flavour, but for the first few times, stick to the basic recipe to make sure you've got it right.

Pour the hot water into a container that has a lid but is not air tight. Sprinkle in the yeast, salt and sugar; stir to distribute. Now add the flour and don't forget to count the scoops. You're going to make a mess here as flour does like to spread itself around, but make sure you give each cup a little shake to fill the container and level off the top with a knife or other flat edge.

What you have now looks like a kid's play time box, and here you have to mix the ingredients with a wooden spoon or alternative. Keep mixing until all the flour is distributed evenly. It will be a little sloppy when you've finished. This is the longest part of the entire process.

Cover the box, and leave it to rise for two hours. You can then put it in the fridge where it will keep for up to two weeks. Once it has risen you can bake immediately if you choose. But it's easier to form rolls and loaves when it's cold.

For baking take a piece of dough out about grapefruit size, and shape it quickly. Roll it out on a flat surface with flour to stop it sticking to you and the board, but not too much. If it has come from the fridge leave it for an hour to rise first. Half an hour before baking put the oven on 450 degrees with the pan on the middle rack. Add the cornmeal to the pan which will act as a lubricant on the surface. Also put another baking pan on the floor of the oven – very important step.

After an hour's rise, pat some water on the top of the loaf and make a few diagonal slash cuts for decoration. You can also add poppy seeds or sesame seeds on the top as well. Get a lukewarm cup of water ready to pour into the lower baking pan. This will create the steam which makes the crust.

Pull out the rack and stone/tin to make placing the loaf easy. Push back into the oven and then pour the lukewarm water into the baking pan. Close door quickly – mind your face with the steam!

Bake for 30 minutes. Halfway through, turn the loaf around 180 degrees in the oven to bake evenly. Enjoy, it's delicious!

> *But since soup mainly involves tossing everything in a pot and waiting, it's one of my better dishes.*
> — *Suzanne Collins, The Hunger Games*

> *For is there any practice less selfish, any labor less alienated, any time less wasted, than preparing something delicious and nourishing for people you love?*
> — *Michael Pollan*

Chapter Twenty-Two
WRITING

Writing is easy. All you have to do is cross out the wrong words.
— *Mark Twain*

Everybody does have a book in them, but in most cases that's where it should stay.
— *Christopher Hitchens*

It's hard to remember a time when I didn't write. Essays and compositions were easy for me at school, and I could never understand why some people had problems with the subject.

I once had a friend who could make video games from scratch. He would visit scrap yards for cabinets, mostly old TV ones, then he'd find electronic boards and fiddle with them until they met the necessary specifications to meet his design. Then he'd plug in a TV screen link it all up and Hey Presto, he had some new game.

For someone who couldn't even name an electronic board it seemed magic and I often told him so. But he refused to accept that he had any special talent and even got cross when I pressed him.

Over the last few years I've met several people who confess that they have problems with writing. It seems there's some type of blockage between the words in their minds and being able to express them on the page.

It's hard to imagine a difficulty that doesn't exist in oneself, but perhaps it's akin to my struggles with arithmetic for so many years. It's very frustrating.

As mentioned in the previous chapter, like most writers I have a number of projects on various back burners, and hopefully these will eventually become published. But in the meantime to give readers a flavour, I am adding two short stories that sit within a proposed book called Passages.

The idea was to write a short story based around all the countries that I've visited; it's on-going, and I quite like these two. The first is based in Scotland and the second in Denmark.

The Problem with Accents

Roger Taylor was a decent chap. Anyone that knew him would say he definitely played with a straight bat. No one could ever remember him not being that way. Even his ex-wife would rarely if ever say anything bad about him. He didn't seem to have acquired an enemy in his 34 years on this earth.

At school, which his father had struggled to pay for, he was a mediocre student, hardly excelling at anything except a decent arm for bowling at cricket. His math left a lot to be desired and his English lacked a certain style according to the masters who taught him.

In spite of regular pep talks from the staff and his parents his reports told the story of a boy who had managed to float just under the surface of average.

Both the institution and Roger were happy to see the back of each other when it was time to leave. As his father's Austin rolled away from the lytch gate, Roger didn't look back, nor was there anyone to wave him off onto a path yet to be decided upon.

He was sorry to say goodbye to the friends he knew, who lived in the other direction, but not the masters and the other staff who had looked after him as best they could during the six years he had been at St. Abbots.

The journey was uneventful and neither male talked much about the past, present or future. Both understood that the boy was about to embark on a new chapter of life, but neither had a clue what that path might be or where it would lead.

The journey was just an hour door to door; it was enough to put a decent distance from both bases, but not enough to warrant boarding, which was a relief to both the occupants of the small sedan. With the burden of school fees disappearing as fast as the Victorian edifice behind them, Roger Taylor Senior daydreamed about perhaps getting a more modern vehicle for the family. It was a frequent dream: but now at least it had some reality to it.

Not being very outwardly emotional or comfortable with that side of life, Roger's welcome home was a little too much for him, but he gratefully sat at the dining room table and ate the tea his mother had made for him.

"Well, that's that then, Roger," his father said. "The end of childhood!" Roger didn't feel that there was much difference to any of the days he'd experience in this comfortable but small home. He just nodded.

The subject of his future was left tactfully alone and also the next day, and a few thereafter, but eventually his father insisted that they really sit down to discuss the future. It was not an easy conversation, as Roger didn't have any burning passion to be any of the things his father suggested.

A number of his friends at school had already decided to become lawyers, accountants, doctors and other fancy professions, but a choice remained beyond Roger's grasp. He simply lacked any true desire to work at all.

It was not that he was lazy as once he felt interested in something he didn't care how much effort he put into it until he was satiated. But the problem was finding such a subject and even more pursuing that subject for his entire life. But he had to choose something as he couldn't sit on his backside forever.

Once he had completed what was generally considered an acceptable period of vacation, Roger founded himself doing the rounds of various businesses in the immediate area. It was a gruelling and gruesome business, but he was accepted in a local men's clothing store. It was the first of many retail positions he drifted into, but it was not a very involving job. He did learn a lot about clothes however before he moved on to a hardware store. Here he learned a lot about making and repairing all sorts of things.

For the next ten years Roger Taylor drifted from post to post and rather like a floating buoy, he gathered barnacles of knowledge, which he never quite understood could be of any importance. He also didn't realise that in nearly every position he was learning to overcome an inherent shyness. In so doing he learned to acquire considerable charm, which was an underestimated resource in dealing with people in every position in life.

He met Glenda at a time when he was worrying about his lack of success with women. It wasn't that he was unattractive, but more that he was unaware of his appeal. He had been told that he was tall, dark and handsome – it seemed he had all the requisites of appeal - but he didn't know that.

His courtship of Glenda was about as normal as it could be. It began with group outings of the local Young Conservatives, progressed to more intimate meetings in the back of Roger's father's car. Eventually during a warm spell in late June, Glenda felt sufficiently relaxed to let him go "all the way." A few weeks later she had the traditional "scare" and Roger felt obliged to do the decent thing and arranged a marriage. The "scare" vanished within a week of dates being set, and had it resulted in a baby the turn of Roger's and Glenda's life might have settled down into one of normalcy.

Sadly it was not to be. Like others before them without a family to direct their affection, they drifted away from each other and began to live somewhat apart.

They stayed together in the same house they had always lived in, courtesy of both sets of parents who had made generous gifts to get them started. But the early attraction wore off and they were left with an emptiness that they couldn't fill.

It was then that Roger ran into a fellow at the bar of his local pub, The Black Swan, always referred to by the locals as The Mucky Duck. He had taken to dropping in on his way home from his job at a store that sold floor coverings. It was the tenth such dead end position he had held in the last fifteen years, but who was counting?

Next to him stood a plump man with a dark moustache and a gold watch chain around his ample middle. The man was dinking gin and tonics in large amounts; he was also sighing repeatedly and turning from side to side.

As Roger leaned across to have his glass refilled, he accidentally caught his elbow up against the man's glass and the contents spilled over the man's jacket.

"I'm most terribly sorry," Roger said, and grabbed a bar towel used to catch the drippings of the drinks sold. "Let me help you, and certainly get another drink."

"That's OK," the man said. "It's a perfect end to a bloody awful day. Don't worry about it."

Roger fussed about the man as they cleaned up the fast evaporating spillage. Neither of them seemed too upset and settled back to enjoying the quietness of the pub's early evening hours.

Having informally introduced each other, they began to talk of the sort of generic subjects used by Englishmen the world over to break the ice; the weather, the disgraceful state of the Test Match at Edgbaston.

Eventually out of a growing curiosity, Roger asked the man, who's name was Donald Edwards – but call me Don, everybody does - what had caused his problems during the day, if he felt up to talking about it, of course.

"Well, Roger," Edwards said. "You've heard of a perfect storm haven't you?" Roger inclined that he had. "Well, I've been at the center of one so bizarre that even after all this time in business, I couldn't have seen this coming; not in a million years. But I don't want to bore you with my nonsense."

Roger said he would be most interested to hear the tale as his day had just been the usual, and that was boring.

As this looked like it was going to be a long story, Roger indicated a small table and chairs at the side of the room where they could talk in more comfort and privacy.

"OK then," Donald began. "I'm in the electronics business – have been for quite a few years; long before it became sexy. And I've built a pretty strong business even though I do say so myself. I had a team of about ten salesmen working for me selling the electronic pieces I brought in from Japan and Germany. Have a few from the States too. But a couple of years ago I really looked at the situation and found that of the ten salesmen I employed I was getting most of my sales from only four. Of the six others, three I was always re-recruiting and three were never much good.

"So I decided to stop and settle for a quieter life. I didn't replace the three who eventually left and I gave big targets to the others. I told them they could make the target and earn twice the usual commission or get out. As I suspected three did very well and the others failed so off they went.

"I had a fellow in Scotland – a real go getter - and a married couple who lived in the Midlands. They split the rest of the country between them. They are terrific. I should say they were terrific. I've lost the bloody lot now and frankly I don't know what to do about it."

Roger took the now empty glass of gin and tonic and went back up to the bar for a refill. This was all sounding a bit beyond him; but he wasn't in any hurry to go back to another bland evening with Glenda in a silent house.

"So what happened to your team then if they were doing well?"

"I'll tell you what happened, Roger. They were caught screwing around that's what happened!"

"Sorry, I don't get it. What happened exactly?"

"Well, it seems that the married woman who looked after all points north from Birmingham was getting banged by the guy in Scotland when she traveled north. And she was up there every week for a couple of nights at least. Used to stay in the Piccadilly Hotel in Manchester, which I bloody well paid for.

"It seems hubby got suspicious and went up there and checked her out. Found them in delecto flagrente, I believe the term is. Christ, I would have liked to have been a fly on the wall in that scene. She's a pretty good looker, and the two men are well set up guys.

"So the next day I get three resignations on my desk. It seems they all need to get some space between them and I've lost the best sales team I could ever have wanted. The guy in Scotland is married too so it's a real cock up all around."

Roger watched his companion down his drink and stayed silent; there didn't seem to be much he could say. Eventually he broke the silence which was becoming a force in itself and said: "What do you plan to do then?"

"Frankly, Roger, I don't know quite what to do. Starting up from scratch is not easy. The best you can hope for in sales recruitment is fifty percent. Not the best odds in the world."

He then launched on a sort of tirade about the unreliability of sales people, and the horrors of interviewing scores of eager young people. Ghastly, was his opinion.

"So, what's your story then, young man?" Donald seemed to buck up with the prospect of something else to talk about.

Roger told him about his latest position. He didn't seem too enthusiastic, but then the job was just one in a long line of fillers and there was no reason to burnish things.

"Ever been on the road, Roger?"

"No, but I seem to have been in sales ever since I left school though."

"Different situation though Roger, lot of difference."

"I guess so."

"Ever thought about making the change?"

And that's how Roger Taylor's life altered, and how his fortunes turned around. It was really that simple.

-//-

With a totally free area of the UK to choose from it seemed quite obvious for Roger and Donald Edwards to select the South of England as Roger's territory. All it needed was a little training at the head office under the current general manager and some small three-hole punched books which listed all the regular customers past and present for Roger to launch onto a genuine sales career.

Glenda showed some enthusiasm for his new potion when he first began, particularly the increase in finances, but then the routine settled down into the rut that it had been before he joined Edwards and Co.

It was typical of Roger's disposition that the end of the marriage came without any recriminations or even anguish. The general malaise that had infected them for the last few years was obvious to both of them, and one evening they talked about what they were both wanting for the remainder of their years.

Neither of them felt they wanted to stay the way they were and with no solution to upping the enjoyment together, divorce seemed the only choice. Papers were served within a week.

There's no doubt that the new job in Roger's life helped him get over any feelings of sorrow and guilt as even though there was no sin, guilt always lurked in any parting of the ways.

Physically they moved to different parts of the country – she to the South Coast and he to London's outer West End. Glenda began a new career of helping old people find homes and financial security – she was very good at it. He developed Edwards's customer base and also encouraged the boss to increase the product range when it became necessary. He also managed to convert Don's cyber phobia and throw away the old books in favor of a couple of laptops

He dated rarely, and when he did he was always thinking about the next day's appointments and what needed to be prepared to be successful. He bought an expensive car and satisfied his interest in the classics of music. His social life tended to be around the King's Head, which had taken over from the Mucky Duck as his local watering hole.

His other indulgence was to own several very good suits, which due to his training in the retail trade were of the best quality and cut. And at fifty per cent off as well!

Don was pleased with his investment in Roger and secretly delighted that this one hunch had paid off so handsomely – it helped eradicate completely the disasters that had come through that method in previous years.

After a year, it became obvious that Roger couldn't do it all; they needed more people to represent the firm. Naturally, Roger was first choice as sales manager, but sadly his charm, laissez faire and youth didn't help him in this position. He was just too nice to handle the difficult area of discipline. But having put him in that job, with a salary increase to boot, Don was loathe to unseat him. It was only a question of time before they had to have one of those little chats so regular and so unpleasant in business.

"It's not that you don't know the job, Roger, it's just that you let them run you around," Don began the conversation. "Also you always end up doing the work for them and then you have to do double duty when it all falls apart."

Roger couldn't argue; he had been a failure in this situation. But having feared the worse, he jumped at the chance of remaining in the company but in a slightly different position.

"I've been handling the sales in Scotland, Roger," Don continued. "But frankly it's not really my bag. However, I have been doing the sales manager job for years. I know how to control the boys and girls, even if I don't have your flare for the selling. So will you take over the entire north of the border? I'll even create a different company to give you a bit more incentive. You'll be fine up there, Roger and if you keep an eye on expenses, you'll make out like a bandit."

Within two months, Roger had exchanged his London flat for one around the back of Princes Street in Edinburgh. He appointed a plain looking middle aged woman called Sheila to run the office and he began to straight away get into the swing of things. He regularly drove the 70 miles to Glasgow to meet with the many customers Edwards had on the west side. He would also go up to Aberdeen and even more remote places in the far north.

He enjoyed the banter of him being a "Sassenach," and his seeming difference, coming as he did from the south. He only had one problem and that was he really hated the Scottish accent. He found it grated on his southern ear and he was totally surrounded by it everywhere he went. There was simply no escape.

He didn't have a problem in his business dealings, they went swimmingly, but when he ventured outside that particular comfort zone, he was very uncomfortable indeed.

He tried going to the many bars along Rose Street and Thistle Street which ran parallel to Princes Street. But he couldn't find a decent pub where he was comfortable. The Scots took their drinking very seriously; he wasn't a prude but in Roger's mind they took it too seriously. The few conversations he entered into petered out and he always found himself wandering outside to look for a fresher pasture.

As for women, it was worse. He'd been out on a couple of dates but he just couldn't get over the way they talked. He began to feel a very shallow person.

Then he met Margaret. She was a flaming redhead and as tall as he was. She was quite simply the most beautiful woman he'd ever met in his life.

He had bumped into her quite literally as he was exiting the Queen's Crown in a quiet part of George Street. He was backing out into the fresh air away from a fellow salesman who was intent on explaining the vagaries of the air conditioning business to him, when he felt his progress halted.

On turning around he was met with a pair of bright green eyes and a smiling mouth. "I'm sorry," he said.

"I think it might have been my fault," was the softly spoken Scottish burr.

Even though he had effectively left the establishment, it seemed churlish to leave the matter at that and so Roger escorted the girl inside, guiding her past the A/C rep who was now fastening his attention on another luckless patron.

Margaret was a delightful woman; educated, funny and attentive to the tales he told. She drank in small sips from her scotch and 7-Up and insisted on buying the second round. As she went to the bar, Roger was fascinated by her rear view as she swayed through the groups of people cluttering there.

The only problem with her as far as Roger could make out was that wretched Scottish accent. It permeated everything she said. Her accent was not as strong as he'd endured before, but nonetheless he couldn't seem to get over the sound of it and how it grated on his ears.

He ended the evening with her phone number and a promise to meet up the following weekend where she promised to show him something of "her" Edinburgh. Roger looked forward to it.

Roger tried hard to focus on Margaret's many qualities over the next two months. They went out several times, and the affair soon turned physical. Even there, Margaret was very vocal and Roger shrank from her rolling "R's" and flat "A's"; it was tough going for him.

She was a fervent churchgoer and to please her, he resurrected a lost interest in the rote of Morning Service and the occasional Evensong. During the hymns the accent was slightly diminished, but her strong contralto still had the flavor of the rich soil and heather of the landscape outside the stained glassed windows.

During one of their post Evensong dinners together she told him of her family and a little of its history. She was something of an outcast. The family was from just outside London and father was something big in banking. Mother has schizophrenic tendencies, and it was these that caused the rift that was to tear the family apart.

Margaret had a twin sister who was called Peggy. With some slight downturn in her voice, Margaret mentioned that Peggy was in fact a derivation of her own name. "We were quite close growing up," she said. "But she tended to follow more along my mother's lines and I followed my father."

It seemed that when it came time to find a school, the rift began. Mother was not keen to let her children go far away, but father wanted the girls to attend a special school outside Edinburgh, which specialized in the arts. Both girls were keen on painting, and this was an ideal place to learn to paint.

They went for one year, but Peggy was so lost without her family that she decided to return home, there was quite a lot of encouragement from their mother. Margaret remained and further more she even stayed over on some vacations. From aged ten to seventeen, she effectively became Scottish. Furthermore, she fell in love with a teacher at the school she attended in the evenings and weekend. "It was quite the scandal," she said. "But it didn't last too long. I was probably infatuated with the attention and he became bored with my ways.

"My family pretty much disowned me," she continued. "I tried to make it up to them but they were stuck in their little separate ruts. Peggy was the worst. She had earned some reputation as a water color artist though. Even has a gallery in Kensington.

"My mother had been institutionalized and my father had become something of a recluse. So I've been up here for twenty years and they've stayed down there.

"I don't miss that world at all. There's a life up here that works for me, and Peggy, although we look alike doesn't enjoy our Scottish ways at all. She stays in her London world and I stay here; we just send each other Christmas cards once a year – not even birthday cards.

"I was happy working in a bank, which Peggy thought was truly awful, but it suited me down to the ground."

Roger was fascinated with the story of the family break up and he particularly found the story of Peggy to be of interest.

The affair with Margaret continued for the rest of the year. There were times when Roger even persuaded himself that he was deeply in love with his Scottish redhead; even started thinking about marriage. Goodness knows Margaret was a wonderful woman who rarely if ever upset him or made too many demands of him.

His business did well and he was making real money for the first time in his life. The only problem was that the south was doing better and he couldn't keep up. Competition began to eat away at him.

For so many years people had tried to motivate Roger. Sales competitions of various sorts came and went, making no identifiable effect on him. They upped the money and still nothing seemed to stir him. What they and he didn't understand was that it was success that motivated Roger. Of course, money was a part of that, but once he began to lose out in the sales pecking order, he began to obsess about it.

He ditched his laptop in favor of a little black book, in which he listed each day the sales he was working on. Some moved, some stayed in the same condition for days, but at every eventuality Roger would pull out the little book and consult it, making notes against each name.

It was this habit of constantly looking at lists that caused a rift in his relationship with Margaret.

"One day, I'd like you to leave that damned book at home," she hissed at him as he returned from the bar with some drinks for them. He had just remembered that one of his contacts liked football and the results of a recent match were posted up on a TV screen. As soon as he sat down, Roger took the book out of his pocket and wrote the score down to help him remember to call the man the next morning.

For some reason, this was the tipping point and Margaret reacted with an uncharacteristic venom she had never shown before. She had had a particularly bad day herself at the bank, and the whole thing rather spiralled out of control.

As Roger sat there somewhat bemused, she poured out her annoyance at having to always share his time with his damned deals; unfortunately she did it all in a seemingly inflated accent with all their accompanying horrors for him.

It was the first of many such outbursts, and rather than being able to separate the infraction from the accent, Roger just heard the annoying sound of her, rather than her complaint.

Roger also began receiving calls from Donald Edwards about the changes going on in his business. It was obvious from the sound of him that Donald was lonely and had no one to bounce ideas off. Over several days, he started suggesting a new deal for Roger. Basically, if Roger would come back to London, there would be a position there looking after the plumb area north of the city, and also an office where he could be next to the big man himself. It was a tempting offer.

If he and Margaret hadn't gone swimming off the cold east Scottish coast that Saturday in late July, he might still be up there. But in a fit of fun he started splashing her. The more he did it the more she shouted back at him and the more annoyed he became at her rousing tantrum. It ended with him pushing her roughly into the sea.

Rather than cry, which is what she felt like doing, she just spat her accent at him and then sulked. It was a miserable drive home and as she got out of the car, she said: "I don't think we should see each other any more."

He didn't protest, which is what he felt like doing, he remained quiet as she slammed the door shut. He drove slowly away feeling depressed and sad that he'd behaved so badly.

After stopping for a few beers in the local pub, he went home and fell asleep with a confused feeling of both loss and relief. His future seemed easier to contemplate. He just needed to call the office in the morning and then hit the road south. It wasn't such a bad proposition.

It didn't take long to pack his stuff into his car and have the rest sent back to the office address to collect later. He paid his landlady in full and left the city of Edinburgh behind him as a sprinkle of rain came down on the grey buildings that had been his home for the last year. As he drove away, he felt that the guilt he'd been allowing to settle inside him was outweighed by a feeling of returning home and becoming the top player once again.

As he merged with the motorway traffic heading south, he found himself humming along to some of his favorite music in the car, and he positively skipped to the food counter at the café where he stopped for lunch. The rain had stopped too, almost exactly as he left the Scottish border.

Settling back into the rhythms of the south took moments; it was like putting on a favorite glove, made even more comfortable by Don's familiarity. It was obvious that he'd been missed.

Don was so keen to spend time with him in fact that he even came out for three days to introduce Roger to some of the best clients in the area.

Summer slipped quietly into autumn and autumn into winter. Even the climate eased up to welcome the returning prodigal son.

There had been no contact with Margaret since she slammed the car door shut about six months earlier. It wasn't that Roger felt nothing for her, in fact he had nearly called her on numerous occasions. He knew it would be useless as they had run their course. Naturally, he harbored guilt about his shallowness, but during a conversation with an older lady one evening, and after a few too many he allowed his heart to pour out.

"The problem was her damned Scottish accent," he said.

"Don't be so daft, lad," the woman said. She was well into her fifties and seemed glad to have someone to talk to and to give her something to think about other than her own rather turgid life. "It's no different than having someone with the wrong smell. Have you ever had that?"

Roger found the suggestion vaguely odd, but he did remember a date once who wore such a strong perfume that it eclipsed the entire evening.

On his way home he remembered the analogy and realized how accurate the woman had been. There was a wrong ingredient, nothing much anyone could do about it.

However he had very fond memories of Margaret and particularly her presence in his bed, which currently was decidedly cold and empty and had been since he had returned.

Of course, the weather was bound to turn. After all it was England. After a long mild winter, the weather gods decided it was time to make everyone pay for the indulgence. It rained, then sleeted, then snowed and repeated the formula for days and days.

Roger had decided to move his flat to a little better area in the Cromwell Road. It was a large building with big airy rooms and high ceilings. He loved it and the space it gave him. He also found one or two nice little restaurants close by. In fact he was on his way to one for lunch one Saturday when a particularly vicious storm cloud broke overhead. He jumped across the road to a green awning stretched out to divert the flow of water.

Cowering underneath he took little notice of the interior of the shop, but as time passed and with no indication of an immediate change in the weather, he turned around to stare in the large plate window.

At first, he didn't take much notice of the works of art inside, but when a shock of red hair appeared above one of the easels he began to get a very funny feeling inside him.

Eventually the red hair came towards him and the door to the gallery opened. It was Margaret. "You can come inside, you know, you don't have to lurk outside getting chilled."

Roger was rooted to the spot; the green eyes twinkled at him on the same level. It was Margaret. But it wasn't. The accent was pure Southern; pure educated English, pure Kensington. Without hesitation, Roger took a step inside.

Too Much of a Good Thing

Tieg Svensen had almost forgotten when he came to Dragor (It was pronounced Drauer). He had never intended to stay as long as he had. It was a very small backwater of Denmark and had little going for it. Clinging to a small peninsular below Copenhagen and across from Malmo in Sweden where all the ferries went, Dragor was home to a few farmers and some people who liked the quiet life, but didn't want to be too far from the nation's capital, which was a little over an hour's drive away.

Tieg had come straight from a successful career in the financial industry. He had a head for figures and could calculate the numbers for all kinds of odds faster than most bookies. He'd made his money – or so he thought – but one or two bad positions on the stock market had depleted his cache and he found he needed to make a little extra to get him through his relatively simple lifestyle.

Driving around one day he'd found this small hotel – The Windmill – and wandered inside for some lunch. It was five years ago, and he'd never left the place.

Lunch was a fiasco. The soup was cold, the meat was tough and the desert when it came was unrecognizable.

The fact that he'd left most of the food on his plate caused the owner to come out from the back office to apologize and ask if he'd like a drink on the house to make up for it.

Tieg drank Bacardi and Diet Coke, and so did the owner. They retired to the bar and sat on a couple of the stools placed there for drinking customers.

The owner, an older man called Pete Hansen, explained that they were short handed and in fact the cook had walked out that very morning. Tieg nodded his way through the explanations, letting the liquor do its calming work.

On a total impulse Tieg suggested that if Hansen was interested, he could step in and run the place. He couldn't remember quite why he'd suggested such a crazy thing, but Hansen leapt at the chance with hardly a question as to Tieg's qualifications.

In fact Tieg was not in the least qualified. Granted he had been a lifetime user of Mr. Bacardi's fine products, but other than that he thought, as many customers of such establishments, that running one was largely common sense.

It proved to be just that for him, apart from a few suggestions from Hansen, who preferred to spend his days at his flat in Copenhagen, and increasingly left the running of the place to Tieg. Soon, Hansen came down just once a week to talk things over and he read the takings update which Tieg sent off daily on his computer. Over time the takings increased two, and then threefold. As usual Tieg was having a record year, and things looked good for the future.

Tieg got up most days around eight. He lived in a small room at the top of the hotel. There were five other rooms open for traveling clients, as they had a number of salesmen and other road warriors who liked a break before they caught the Malmo ferry to Sweden.

Tieg had a go at the cooking as soon as he had arrived, but soon realized that in order to provide full restaurant facilities, he needed a professional. That's when Hanna came to fill the post. She was pert, efficient, and attractive when you could see under her huge hat and glasses.

As a team he and Hanna brought simple but good food to The Windmill, and customers began to return time and again for their regular specials.

Most afternoons Tieg sat around the bar with a number of men who had time on their hands and a desire to play the horses. Tieg off-loaded the bets when large ones were needed, but mostly he carried the risk himself, when the amounts didn't get too heavy.

Tieg had told Hansen in the early days that a pub only really needed about thirty regular customers to make a decent profit, provided they were regular drinkers. In Dragor, the inhabitants were mostly of a Dutch extract and those worthy citizens had no inhibitions about spending their afternoons and evenings pouring down highly profitable drinks. A good time was usually had by all. And if they wanted a little hair of the dog that bit them, Tieg opened up the place usually before nine.

As he bustled about the place dusting and setting the place right from the evening before, he usually had a beer on the counter himself just to start the day. Tieg didn't consider that drinking beer was actually drinking.

He would occasionally go to Copenhagen for a little taste of his earlier sophisticated life. Sometimes he would bring a young lady back to the Windmill. Unfortunately most of those sophisticated enough to live in the capital, didn't appreciate the ways of this backwater, or the simple pleasure of watching the mists rise up from the surrounding fields each morning.

After several such poor episodes Tieg stopped bringing them back and instead, if the relationship looked like it was going to fully develop, he would book a hotel in the center of town.

Tieg had been married once a long time ago, and acknowledged that a long term relationship might well end up at the altar, but so far no-one had filled the bill for such a position.

The days ran into weeks, then months and then years. He was quite happy, and eventually stopped feeling guilty that he was not filling the promise of his early years, and the hopes of his long suffering parents. They had expected Tieg's future to remain in the financials and to go further and higher in that world. His dramatic drop into relative obscurity gave them nothing to boast about; and in fact it embarrassed them when the subject of children came up with their friends.

Tieg didn't care about it, particularly if there was a Bacardi and Diet around to dull the pain. He knew he was close to being what the experts would call an alcoholic, but he functioned well and never had a hangover to speak of. He'd give it up one year, he supposed.

He wouldn't say he was bored, but Tieg did find life to have settled into something of a rut. He ate well, slept well and enjoyed the country life with his regulars and his own little kingdom. So what if he was building the future for someone else and not himself? Like the booze he could always sort that out later on.

Then Traudie walked into the place asking to fill up an application for employment. She was a knockout. A blonde and about five foot four, slim with a hell of a figure; she had the clearest blue eyes he thought he'd ever looked into.

Tieg hired her on the spot and gave her three evenings a week to serve behind the bar. Not only was she a looker, but she could run the bar as well as he could.

The problems occurred in an odd way. He was seriously thinking about a frontal approach to the new blond, when he had a knock on his door one evening. He opened it to find Hanna, the cook, standing there. At first he hardly recognized her. Gone were the glasses, and the hat. Instead she was wearing her hair down in long curls over bare shoulders.

And she had on a small mini dress, showing off a long pair of extremely attractive legs. She was carrying her shoes in one hand and in the other she held a tall glass of something that looked like whiskey over ice.

After standing looking rather blank for a moment or two, Tieg asked her what he could do for her. "Well, asking me in would be a good start," Hanna said.

He opened the door wide and then ran around her to try and make the place a little tidier. It was not the sort of place to fully entertain anyone, but it was warm and fairly comfortable. Hanna sat in the overstuffed armchair; Tieg sat on the bed, trying to keep his eyes off her legs. It was a fruitless battle.

Quite what Hanna's excuse was for the visit, Tieg never fully found out, but it got extremely physical extremely quickly, and both of them fell asleep exhausted in the wee small hours.

At his usual time Tieg woke up and moved across the young girl. She too stirred and then leaped out of bed. "My God, I'm in so much trouble," she moaned. "I should have been home hours ago."

"What's the problem?" Tieg asked.

"It's my father, he'll kill me. I'm never allowed to stay out all night."

"Well, that's crazy; you're twenty-five for Crissakes."

"Yes, but my mother died a couple of years ago and I have to look after him."

"Well, tell him you got loaded last night and couldn't drive. I insisted you stay here."

"I suppose you did, in a way!"

That was how it all began and it was a fine arrangement. She was happy to stay over in his room for one night a week and there was no pressure to change this, as she was devoted to her father and her life some fifteen miles away in a neighboring village. They even managed to keep the affair secret from most of the regulars for a long time.

Things would have been great if he hadn't had such a desire for Traudie. She was fantastic and Tieg could hardly contain himself around her. The only problem was that Traudie was in a relationship with a sailor in the Danish navy. The sailor was however away on duty for long periods and he got the very distinct feeling that the bloom had come off the rose for her.

One afternoon as she was handing over the bar to him and about to leave, he asked her out to Copenhagen for an evening. She agreed immediately, and they made it for the next night.

The evening went really well and Tieg said that as they'd had a lot to drink it would be best to stay over in a small hotel. He knew exactly the right one. And so this became number two on his list of inamoratas.

Traudie was a wild thing. She moaned, screamed and threw herself into their lovemaking like she would never be able to do it again. He had never had anyone like it in his life before and it was like a drug. Two nights a week they went up to town and eventually after hastily consumed take out dinners, they never left the hotel bed.

It was fantastic, but as is so often in life it was not perfect. Traudie was madly jealous, and he only had to look at a waitress and she would become impossible. Sharing a work environment didn't help in that area either. There were not too many female customers at The Windmill, but when there were, if Tieg showed to much attention to any of them he could tell from the sound of her banging glasses down on the bar top that she was starting to boil up. That would then cause crying and sometimes screaming, and not the type he appreciated.

It was a stormy relationship and most evenings that they met in Copenhagen they spend most of the early part of it rowing about some perceived interest that Tieg had shown to some female since the last time they met up. It settled down into a fairly regular situation. Traudie and he would meet on Monday and Thursday nights – the days she didn't work at the Windmill.

Tieg often found himself suffering from sheer exhaustion after his nights with Traudie. She was more demanding that he'd ever experienced, and her innovations were quite beyond him. She had handcuffs, silk ropes, vibrators, and stuff he frankly didn't know the name of. And she wanted to give and receive all these toys in their full measure.

In between these exhausting evenings, Hanna always slipped into his room on Wednesday nights around midnight when he'd closed up the bar and sent the farmers home.

She was a totally different kind of sexual partner. Where Traudie was full of passion, Hanna was more lethargic. It didn't matter what Tieg did, she liked it and sort of went into a dreamy state when it was time to turn out the light – well the big light anyway.

After about four months, it was going along really well and even Traudie seemed happy with the time he spent with her.

She never suspected that there was anything going on with the cook, as Hanna always looked so odd and starchy in her working clothes. She and Tieg also managed to keep their behavior very formal during the day. And he was sure that Hanna had no idea about Traudie. Hanna did not display the same degree of jealousy as the barmaid although he had detected a certain focus in her off-the-cuff questions to him during their nights together.

Then along came Carla. It was a quiet Friday morning; about ten o'clock. Tieg was just finished setting things up in the bar when he heard a car pull up outside. The door to the bar swung open and a tall auburn haired woman of about 50 swept in. She slid onto a bar stool and looked around the place.

"What can I get you, Ma'am?"

"Well for a start don't call me Ma'am. It makes me feel about a hundred." She was wearing a full length mink coat and her slim wrist jangled with a solid gold charm bracelet which she adjusted as she leaned across the counter. "I'll have a Bacardi and Coke if you can manage it?"

"That's what I drink, so I'll join you if I may."

"Suit yourself. So this is the famous Windmill is it?

"Yes, the famous Windmill. We're rather proud of it. Are you passing through or staying in the area?"

"Well Tieg, and I know you won't mind me calling you that. I'm the new owner of the place. I bought it from my brother-in-law Pete Hansen. Sorry if it's a bit of a shock."

Tieg took a long pull of his drink – he was proud of his attitude under fire. "Well, it is a surprise I must say."

"Yes, well, Pete told me you were absolutely a necessity; that you run the place so much better than he did. So you don't have to worry too much."

"That's a relief. I didn't plan to pack my case, well, not this early in the morning anyway."

"So can you give me a tour of the place that Pete made me pay a fortune for?" She laughed lightly and slipped off her stool. Tieg gave her a guided tour, basking in the aura of her expensive scent.

Her auburn hair was most attractive and she swished her coat along as they climbed the stairs, Tieg noticed the slim ankles above the high red heels of her shoes. She might be a little beyond her "sell-by-date" but she was pretty impressive.

Returning to the bar, she ordered another drink, gesturing to Tieg that he should join her. "I'm sure you'll continue to run this place well,

Tieg, if you want to. Oh, by the way I'm increasing your wages, just as a little incentive to stay, as I'm sure I'd be lost without you; certainly in the early days. One other small thing, I'm a complete idiot with computers, so could you come up to town once a week to go over the figures with me?"

They looked at a calendar and Tieg explained the staffing of the Windmill. They settled on Sundays as being a good time to come up to Copenhagen to her flat, to explain the week's takings. The first occasion would be in ten days time at about six in the evening.

A few customers had come into the bar by then and when Carla departed, she left behind a gap in the atmosphere that was not well filled by the jeans and rough jackets of Tieg's usuals. They all made comments about Tieg's new girlfriend and he had to explain that she was in fact the new owner.

Carla's flat was very up market. Located in the more fashionable part of the city, it looked out over a square and was furnished in a heavy German style.

"My husband died a year ago. Most of this stuff is his taste. I'm not fond of it, but I've been too lazy to make the change." Tieg seated himself at a big solid dining table and took out his sheaf of papers. Carla sat opposite him and he was drawn to the impressive amount of cleavage presented to him. Her dress was the same color blue as her eyes and her hair was drawn back above her head.

He leaned towards her and put the papers in front of her. "People have the annoying habit of imagining that I'm not too bright, I'm afraid. I used to be a dancer – classic case of rich man marries dippy blonde, although I'm not a blonde as you can see." Tieg was a little embarrassed at this confession, and felt his face begin to color.

"The truth is that I really loved Karl – Karl and Carla were a real success story for over ten years until he died. I still miss him very much." Her blue eyes began to fill with tears. The effect was staggering to Tieg.

She reached for a tissue and then made a great effort to look at the numbers he had put before her. Tieg was relieved that the moment seemed to have passed. Carla for her part went off to a heavy cocktail cabinet and poured herself and Tieg a drink. "I assume the usual for you, Tieg?"

"Yes please, ma'…Sorry Mrs…"

"You can call me Carla, Tieg; anything else makes me still feel like I'm a hundred."

Far from being the bimbo she said people considered her to be, Carla had a quick mind and a good grasp of what Tieg had come there to explain. She also had some of the reports that Hansen had given her with the sale of the business. She was quick to compare the numbers of the previous year, and the year before that.

"You're doing a terrific job, Tieg. The increase in business shows that."

She explained that in truth she didn't need a business, and she had only been helping her brother-in-law out as he wanted to move away to the north of the country and sever his ties. "I'm quite fond of him and his wife, and I thought this would give me an interest. Frankly, I don't need the money as Karl left me very well provided for. Do you have a girlfriend Tieg?"

The change of direction took him by surprise. He stammered that no, he didn't really have anyone regular. Instinctively, he felt that any mention of a girlfriend would invite enquiries and they might lead to his involvement with the staff back home. Dangerous ground!

"Well, I suppose you're really too busy running the place, aren't you?" She didn't seem to require an answer and mumbling something about needing to get back and tidy up, Tieg made his way to the door, and beat a hasty retreat.

Things would have been easier if about four weeks later he hadn't have mentioned Carla's dead husband as they were wrapping up their weekly session. "What exactly did he do, Carla?"

"He was an industrial chemist, Tieg; one of the best in the country, in fact." She went on to talk about him and how he had died the night they had gone to the Royal Palace to accept an award. "It was such a beautiful event," she said. Tieg was alarmed to see that her eyes had begun to fill up with tears again. He searched for a tissue as she sort of drooped in front of him. It seemed only natural to put his arms around her and then kiss her cheek. From that her face turned slightly and they had their lips on each others.

It was pretty confused. Standing in the living room they grabbed at each other and almost fell over themselves in an effort to get to the nearest flat surface – the sofa. Being of the same German style as the rest of the room, it was edged in solid wood and Carla banged her head as she leaned backwards. It didn't seem to matter. Clothes were torn off and Tieg found himself enveloped in her perfume and her hunger.

"Well, that was fun," she said much later. "I have to admit it's been a hell of a long time for me."

Tieg didn't feel he wanted to go into too many details with this woman some ten years older than himself. He was still a little unsure of his relationship with her and after all he did work for her. The other two worked for him and that was a totally different kind of situation, he reasoned.

The next week, Carla met him at the door wearing a short sort of negligee. And lots of her favorite perfume. Tieg was a little confused but Carla took him by the hand and led him straight to the bedroom. The lights were low and he needed no encouragement to put in what he considered to be a sterling performance.

Afterwards sitting at the dining table with a drink before him, he began going over the week's figures. It was easier now with her wearing a complete cover up in the form of a long house coat.

"It all seems very satisfactory, Tieg. No wonder you don't have a girlfriend, I can see you're far too busy. The restaurant too seems to be getting busier."

"Yes, well we've had a couple of coach parties come in. It makes a big difference. Even though the cook goes mad at the time. But she's trained for it she tells me."

Carla arranged herself on the sofa and let her blue eyes bore into him. "Now tell me, these two females you have working for us, Tieg, is there any hanky panky going on?

Tieg felt his face color a little as he assured her that such behavior was unprofessional and would cause too many complications.

"You're absolutely right, Tieg, and more than that it would cause me to become very concerned. I don't want to pick up any nasty little illnesses, not at my age. Visits to the gynaecologist are embarrassing enough without explaining how I got some horrible infection."

Her voice took on a harder tone and Tieg realized that on this issue she was about as firm as it was possible to be. He made soothing noises and kept a note to keep his life seriously compartmentalized. Not that it wasn't before this extra little bonus came upon him. At least Carla showed no interest in visiting her new investment at all; having them all under one roof would be a little too much of a good thing, he thought.

So far he had played the new ownership of The Windmill down. He'd mentioned it a couple of times but said it had gone to another member of the Hansen family. He hadn't said anything about it being now under the control of an attractive middle aged ex-dancer with too much time on her hands and an appetite for him. No way!

He still met up with Traudie in Copenhagen twice a week and had Hanna slip into his bed on Wednesday nights. Logically he knew it wouldn't continue, but emotionally he pushed that thought down and allowed himself to live in the moment. And there were lots of moments.

He began to look forward to his evening of opulence with his boss in the city. She was quite a treasure and he enjoyed the fun and games they got up to before, during and after he played the role of faithful servant and manager of her business. He was making quite a bit more money too, and he was feeling confident and sure of a better life – maybe one that even his parents might approve of.

Most evenings with Carla included a form of interrogation regarding other women but it was at least subtle. Not the outrageous type of horror of which Traudie was capable. Those sessions although ending in unbelievable passion were almost dangerous. But the drug still drove him to their regular trysts. He played the game for all it was worth knowing that the longer it went on the more dangerous it became, as everyone became more entrenched in their positions.

One day, Traudie called him from the bar. "It's for you!" Very testy! It was Carla. She had never called him before as they always fixed their next meeting before they parted on Sunday evenings. "I have to change our arrangement, Tieg. Can we postpone our meeting? I have to go away for a day or two. Let's make it a week later. Is that alright with you?"

"Oh, Ok," Tieg said. "That'll be fine. Same time?"

Carla agreed and they ended the call. Traudie was right next to him doing some sort of task. Her face was rather distorted. "And who was that?"

Tieg was tired. He'd also had too much to drink – something that was happening to him a lot more these days, he knew. "That was our boss," he said.

He knew he was in trouble by the look on Traudie's face. Unfortunately, this meant that he tried to gloss over the problem and even embellish a few details like Carla was not very attractive, and also very old. "What the hell is the matter with you, anyway?" he shouted at Traudie.

It never occurred to him that Carla in turn was wondering about the female voice that had answered the phone when she called.

Two days later, Tieg had to go into the village. They had run out of lemons, and with a few gin and tonic customers regularly attending the bar, they were very necessary.

There was a small hostelry in the center of what passed for a village and Tieg stopped in there to have a couple of Bacardis before he had to get back; after all the bar was running smoothly with Traudie in charge for the next few hours. He felt tired and he knew the landlord quite well. He needed a break. As things turned out, he spent too long there he knew, but what could go wrong?

He felt a slight apprehension as he returned to The Windmill, he couldn't quite rationalize it, but it was there. At about ten, he entered the place. The bar seemed quiet but then he heard the sound of raised voices. They were female ones.

He pushed in through the swing door and there in front of him were the three of them sitting on stools at one of the high tables. In unison, they turned towards him and their faces told the entire story. Carla's was perhaps the angriest. They all started talking at once. It was very threatening.

Tieg turned around. He returned rapidly to his car. He had had a good run, but he knew when the odds were totally against him.

On the drive back to Copenhagen, he made some decisions. Firstly he had to go to his parents. He needed a base, and preferably one where he could not be found easily. He also knew he needed to make a fresh start, or maybe a return to a previous one. He recognized also that he needed to call the local branch of Alcoholics Anonymous as without a little help, he'd never get back into the financial game. After all, it had been far too long.

--//--

Writing a book is a horrible, exhausting struggle, like a long bout with some painful illness. One would never undertake such a thing if one were not driven on by some demon whom one can neither resist nor understand
George Orwell

Chapter Twenty-Three
HOLIDAYS

My wife and I went on vacation to get away. I went to Colorado,
and she went to Ireland.
— Jarod Kintz

If all the cars in the United States were placed end to end, it
would probably be Labor Day Weekend.
— Doug Larson

To begin with I should clear up a slight misunderstanding. To Americans holidays are actually nearer to their original meaning than the English version. The word "holiday" comes from Holy Day, and therefore it applies to the one day breaks that occur on everyone's calendar. That's another odd one; Americans use calendar rather than the English version, diary. I was told quite early on that a diary was something that young girls scribbled in under their bed sheets using a flashlight – or as the English would say torch!

As Oscar Wilde said: Two cultures divided by a common tongue!

The English do use vacation in its correct form for a spell away from work, but they nearly always say holiday. I used to feel a little superior when Americans would say I was off last Friday, I was on vacation. How strange to call a day off a vacation, but that's the way it is.

I happen to be writing this on perhaps the biggest holiday in America. It is Thanksgiving Day, and everyone takes it off. It is a massive affair and is more like an English Christmas than Christmas Day is. They even have their turkey on Thanksgiving. It is truly an American celebration although many don't know the true account of the very first Thanksgiving.

Over the years the politically correct have rather kidnapped the history as they have done with so much. Most people have a slightly fuzzy idea that Thanksgiving was a celebration for being rescued by the natives before we butchered them. Liberals like to capitalise on any chance to make us feel guilty, even if the facts prove them wrong. But since when have facts got in the way of a good piece of propaganda?

On August 1st 1620, the Mayflower set sail from England. It was a long and dangerous voyage that ended in November that year.

On the way over William Bradford, the leader of the 40 pilgrims among the 102 passengers on board drew up a contract for his band. In it the terms explained that all their efforts and produce would be put into a common store and belonged to each person equally.

That first winter was deadly and Bradford's wife died as did many others. Come spring, the Indians did help the settlers by showing how to grow corn and other produce. They taught them how to fish and skin beavers and other skills that they were lacking.

But they did not prosper; in fact they were in danger of going under. Bradford then did a surprising thing; he gave each pilgrim a plot of land and made him responsible for developing it. Any help from other plot holders would be purely voluntary. In other words Bradford shied away from communism (collectivism) and steered the group towards capitalism (individualism.)

As a result the pilgrims survived. The more industrious and clever of them did well, and the lazy were forced to work to make it through the tough seasons.

Bradford wrote in his journal:... *"The experience that was had in this common course and condition, tried sundry years...that by taking away property and bringing into a common wealth, would make them happy and flourishing – as if they were wiser than God. For this community was found to breed much confusion and discontent, and retard much employment that would have been to their benefit and comfort. For young men that were most able and fit for labor and service did repine that they should spend their time and strength to work for other men's wives and children without any recompense...that as thought injustice."*

The result of this unleashing of the capitalist beast was success. Bradford wrote: *"This had great success, for it made all hands industrious so as much more corn was planted than would otherwise have been."*

Shortly they produced more food than they could eat and they set up trading posts with the Indians and exchanged goods. They were also able to send back sufficient to pay off the debts they had accumulated back in England.

Thanksgiving was a regular festival held in most European countries at the end of the harvest, and other Christian festivals. It was only natural that having managed to not only hang on, but to actually prosper, the pilgrims would hold such a festival and invite their trading partners to join in. They were all very committed Christians after all, and they would have had in their minds gratitude to God for helping them.

I doubt that many children are taught this story of the original Thanksgiving in schools as being under the liberal dictate, the tale would be entirely secular, and with a good load of guilt to wash it down, I am sure.

For myself I was not aware of the true story, until I read Rush Limbaugh's 1992 book, The Way Things Ought to Be. I am sure that his manuscript must have caused much annoyance in the common rooms of academia. But if you doubt the authenticity of the account, the Web will no doubt help you check.

Not having lived for the first 42 years of my life in America, Thanksgiving along with its twin, the Fourth of July, doesn't resonate very much with me. I was told many years ago not to underestimate the difficulties of changing one's culture. In most respects I have not had any true difficulties, but the acquisition of public holidays are ones where it's tough to get into the spirit.

But we always took the holiday and were grateful for the day off.

Returning to the English definition of holidays, there were few of them when I was growing up in the 40's and 50's. A full scale war is bound to dampen any plans for a couple of weeks paddling along the south coast, especially if the beaches are covered in barbed wire and tank traps to deter the invading Hun.

Once it was over no doubt the wealthy began their usual pursuits of summer holidaying in Deauville, and winter skiing in the Alps, but for the rest, it was the normal visit to Grandma's and other relatives who were prepared to put up with our particular form of invader.

I believe some hardy types used to camp, but back in those days with ropes that would shrink in rain and in a climate less than favourable it was a very committed family that would do that.

It was certainly not in our family's skill set, although my father could rustle up a mean eggs and b, on a stove he made. It was an empty shoe polish tin with holes punched in it and containing some cotton wool. This he would place inside a cake tin, also with holes punched around. Then he would cover the small tin with metholated spirits and light it up.

On our way down to Southampton we would stop in Windsor Great Park and the breakfast would begin. It was always terrific.

I knew some people who would rent a boat on the Norfolk Broads, where I have never been, and others who would stay in boarding houses.

These were awful places, where large, angry women with red, beefy hands would let out rooms in their houses at the seaside. They would prepare greasy breakfasts before shooing their guests out in all weathers, with a warning not to return until dinner time at six o'clock. A small flickering black and white TV was provided in a cramped sitting room for entertainment.

My parents did put us through this form of torture one summer and I think it took us years to recover.

We also went to a holiday camp on the Isle of Wight one year. Surprisingly, it was a pretty nice experience. The weather was perfect for the entire ten days and that helped a lot. Also I met up with some tough lads from Walthamstow, and there were some girls as well. I fell for one of them. She had the most amazing walk I have ever seen. Sadly the rest of her was a disaster and the walk's appeal dropped off with the fickleness of youth.

Holiday camps were a phenomenon of the mid fifties. Butlin's were the first and built up a strong reputation. But they also were crowded and loud. I never fancied the idea of being woken up to the shoutings of "Wakey Wakey!" bellowed over loudspeakers at seven, and then joining my fellow campers in a spirited regimen of exercises outside one's hut. I suspect that Billy Butlin must have recruited a returning POW from Stalag 17 to prepare life for the arrivals.

It was Sir Freddie Laker who opened up the entire idea of foreign holidays to us Brits. But that was not until the late sixties and the seventies. By then travel restrictions and currency regulations had been eased, which made it simpler for the average Brit to turn away from traditional destinations like Brighton and Skegness in favour of Benidorm and Lorret de Mar.

A suntan in the UK was quite a status symbol in those early days; that was of course, before we all learned it was actually harmful. If you could acquire the orange type tan from a ski trip in the depths of winter then you earned double brownie points, I believe.

Unlike the Irish, who have very white, almost translucent skins, the English, having been invaded by all types over the years are quite hardy in the skin department.

It therefore became the fashion to get away to Spain, Italy or even Greece – if you could stand the cuisine! The general idea was to drink as much as possible, then collapse on the beach and build up a tan that would last beyond the trip back home. Thousands did it and none of us caught skin cancer, as it hadn't been invented yet.

I had a couple of such holidays and they were fantastic. There is something about the Mediterranean with its cosmopolitan atmosphere and scenery that is perhaps among the most stimulating places anywhere on earth. If you couple that with the sounds of Continental pop music, the pounding discos, and of course, the nakedness, I can quite easily see how some poor Brits went off their collective rockers. But they could always come back next year. Of all the things that remind me of those halcyon days, it's the smell of Coppertone. Naturally the one with the least protection as that would only stop the tanning nature of the atmosphere.

The sounds of ABBA too remind me of hot days on the sands overlooking the blue Med.

My first experience of "going foreign" was soon after my son Michael was born. My first wife, Veronica, came from a family that was quite well off. As a result she had been over to Europe many times.

My only experience was a ten-day trip to Germany with the CCF (ROTC). It was illuminating, but not what one would call a holiday.

My in-laws liked Belgium very much and so late in the summer of 1964, having left Michael in the care of his grandmother, we took the ferry across to Ostend.

It was a package holiday and included breakfast and dinner. It was not the usual hotel on the front that Veronica was used to, but it was OK for young marrieds.

Now my idea of a holiday was to lie on a beach with a book soaking up as much sun as I could to cover up my pasty white English skin. That was not Veronica's idea at all. Whereas she would tolerate some beach time, mostly she wanted to see things. And this entailed organised trips out.

On that first holiday we took a coach trip to Amsterdam, which was five hours there, two hours wandering around and then ten hours back as there was some sort of accident on the road – those Continentals drive like crazy! I know we were all very tired when we got back and I don't remember very much of Amsterdam except the prostitutes sitting in their windows awaiting passing clients; very sophisticated and most un-English.

We also took a tour of the WWI battlefields and the town of Ypres. This place had been completely levelled in the war but had been restored to its original condition afterwards. I can still recall the photographs of the before and after scenes. The tour also included Hill 60, which had been blown up several times and the final explosion was said to be heard in London when it went off.

The graveyards were very moving and also I remember a traffic roundabout, which contained some tall cypress trees. Around their base were several knee high hedges. This was the place where poison gas had first been used and the trees and hedges represented both men and gas.

The overall foreignness of the country fascinated me, and I can still remember a word that was displayed over the top of a convention center. It was "tentoonstelling," and I had to find out what it meant. It was the Flemish word for exhibition.

Ostend is a town much loved by the Belgians themselves and their Royal family have a seaside residence there.

The afternoons were spent watching short fat ladies with their little lap dogs walking along the promenade and dipping into the many fancy businesses for shopping or afternoon tea. Such teas were chock full of the rich chocolate for which the country is so famous. No wonder they were fat.

Using English was not a problem as the Belgians already use two languages to get by; Flemish and French, although it is considered more sophisticated to use French which is the tongue of the capital, Brussels.

Not being too far away from our school days, we both had a smattering of French, which we could use, as the Flemish is quite impossible. It makes the Dutch laugh to hear it as it sounds very baby-like to their ears.

I returned many times to Ostend over the years and also did a car touring holiday of the entire country, which was a great experience.

Veronica's wanderlust came to an end on that occasion when Michael and I had to introduce her to a 'come to Jesus" meeting outside the town hall in Luxemburg. At her insistence we had driven up to Maastricht in Holland and then down to the small country of Luxemburg. No sooner had we arrived there than Veronica wanted to "do" Germany.

Michael, who was about ten at the time, and I had had enough of this gallivanting and after our talk, we somewhat reined in her obsession.

Holidays for the young are perhaps the pinnacles of life. Work is normally not too interesting for their start on the ladder, and the prospect of a couple of weeks away with nothing to do apart from enjoy yourselves is obviously a wonderful thing. I spent a lot of time planning such events and mostly they turned out well and showed me other places in a different light.

Even when we arrived in California, we began a regular trip to Cabo San Lucas in the southern tip of Mexico's Baja. We found a small hotel called the Cabo Baja which was run on quite simple lines, and we loved the three swimming pools out on the rocky outcrop overlooking the Pacific.

In those days the bar was a simple affair with several locals joining the holiday crowd. One evening it turned quite cold and there seemed to be no firewood. Normally with the Mexican climate, such a need was rarely apparent hence the lack of fuel.

No matter, one of the staff fetched an axe and chopped up some of the wooden furniture – Hey, it's Mexico!

It may seem strange to include a chapter on holidays/vacations in a memoire of one's life, but the fact is that if done right they are perhaps the highlight of any year.

All life tends to towards the hum drum – even the most interesting has some degree of repetition which can become mundane. Holidays however are different and bring out the best of times.

I do not include those that have gone wrong or were bound to end in failure like the dreadful experience of a bed and breakfast in a boarding house in Southsea.

At the turn of my 30th birthday, we took a vacation which still remains in my mind as a fantastic adventure.

It began with a flight to Saltzberg, unfortunately arriving well into the dark hours so we couldn't see much. We were taken by a small van to Bad Gastein and checked into a chalet type hotel on the main street. It was by then quite late and we just wanted to go to bed.

Our room was spotless, but the beds seemed unmade. I rang down to reception to let them know and was told by a rather stuffy Germanic voice that in fact they were made up; it just required us to spread the covers ourselves.

It was my first experience of duvets and I naturally felt pretty stupid about it all. We looked out of the window and saw just a few small lights off into the distance as everything was really dark and quiet.

Come the morning, we went and looked out of the window again and that precise moment is when I became a mountain person.

The small lights we had seen the night before were now replaced by huge, and I mean huge, mountains spread out ahead of us. It was the most amazing sight for anyone from a land whose highest peak of Ben Nevis is a puny 4400 above sea level. (I currently live at 6700 feet.)

The scenery was green and breathtaking, and I couldn't wait to go out into it.

It never occurred to me that Veronica was nervous of going up in the chair lift that was the transportation to the top of the nearest mountain. But as we sat one ahead of the other on the individual seats clamped on the cable, I noticed that her hands were locked around the pole and the knuckles were decidedly white. The poor soul was scared to death as we skimmed over the tops of trees and across wide deep valleys. I loved it all.

We wandered around the top of this peak for awhile and had some very strong coffee as we watched the clouds gather miles away with accompanying thunder – a storm was going to hit somewhere in our vicinity later on.

Veronica's fear left her once we boarded the large cable car to descend once more. It seemed to her that it was much more substantial, and she relaxed and enjoyed the view.

I, on the other hand found the experience quite frightening. Somehow the collection of all these people in a cage that had the unnerving habit of stopping from time to time and allowing us to swing in the wind, was far more worrying than the individual chairs. I guess that once again it must be my preference for individualism against collectivism.

Our stay in Bad Gastein was only for two nights and then we were off again for the next leg of this extraordinary holiday.

At about nine in the morning we left for the railway station and caught the train for Villach. Our tickets were all in German and so we didn't take a lot of notice of them as neither of us spoke the language.

We had a delay of a couple of hours at Villach and as by then it was lunchtime we decided to eat in the restaurant on the platform.

There are perhaps only a dozen or so meals that remain in a person's mind as being perfection, and for some strange reason the goulash soup at Villach Station is one of them for me. It was unbelievable and I only wish I could get another helping before I hand in my final ticket stub.

A train arrived and our tickets were inspected by an official in a uniform who informed us that this was not the train for us although it was going to the same destination.

An hour later another train arrived and we boarded that as it was marked for Ljubljana in Slovenia. On our way there our tickets were once again inspected by an official, who, in a language I had no knowledge of informed us with gestures that this ticket was not for this train.

I now had had enough of this continental BS and waving my British passport I told him I was on the train with a legal ticket and had no idea what his problem was but please leave us alone. He decided the fight was not worth too much effort as we were near the end of our connection and he left us alone.

We changed trains at Ljubljana and the next inspector told us in broken English that our tickets were in fact for a special train that had left an hour earlier. It seems the first official we had met was the one who had caused all the difficulties on our journey. But there is no doubt that a red faced and frustrated Brit can still intimidate a lowly Austrian official. I wonder if it still works today?

Our destination for this leg of our holiday was Rijeka in Yugoslavia, which is now Croatia.

A mutual friend had been on vacation to a nearby seaside resort there called Opatjia and had loved it. We were in Rijeka for about five days and as the weather was not too good we took a trip to this seaside place and couldn't see what the friend had found so fascinating.

Like most of Yugoslavia, both resorts were rather rundown. Marshall Tito had managed to keep out of the clutches of Stalin in much the same way that he had managed to exploit the Allies during the war. He was a communist, but among the most mild of the species. However the economy did not allow for too much luxury and most of the hotels were of pre-war vintage, with peeling paint and fading tapestries.

The weather as mentioned was not too good on our five day stay, and this encouraged us to go "off the menu" a few times.

Basically for full board like us, guests were given a different menu to the rest. It was considerably smaller and didn't have a lot of á la carte items.

When the time came to leave I asked for the bill and anticipated a cost for each time we had ordered differently for the full amount of the bill. I was very surprised to find they had subtracted the cost of the table d'hote from the á la carte and only charged us the difference.

Our last full day in Rjieka was a Sunday and we were sitting in the dining room when a family of Italians came in. It was a fascinating sight.

Italy is just up around the bend of Yugoslavia, and I suppose locals enjoy a drive on Sundays like many other people.

There was nothing particularly interesting about the men, but the women were amazing. There was a very old lady in black with a veil – she must have been the great grandmother. She was quite small and noisy. Then there was a sixty year old who was very fat, followed by a forty-five year old who was even fatter, then came the daughters and great granddaughters.

The youngest must have been about 14 and was exquisite, and then the twenty-year old who was just on the other side of the bell shaped curve of beauty. The party must have been about 12 in number and they kept us amused for an hour even though we didn't know any Italian at all.

They ate an amazing amount of food and if one was charged with selecting an Italian woman for her beauty, then it's best to get one below the age of consent, as the sell-by date comes along very fast.

This experience at Sunday lunch should have prepared us for our next leg of the holiday. The SS Andrea Mantegna, which was a small pocket cruise ship that travelled the Adriatic.

It seems the ship now has long gone to Davy Jones' locker as a search on Google doesn't produce much except a black and white photograph.

It was a compact vessel, with quite the most ridiculous captain one could every wish for. He was straight out of an Italian comic opera with a starched white uniform, twisty moustache and lots of gold braid hanging off his shoulders and cap.

He freely mingled with the passengers on our three-day cruise up to Venice and seemed to love the attention that guests always pour on the senior officer.

Mealtimes were quite an adventure as they were purely Italian with emphasis on getting us all to acquire enough poundage to mean off-loading in cargo nets.

The servers would begin to become quite agitated if you refused a second helping of anything they felt would do you good.

Lunch would consist of antipasto, quite a lot of it, then soup, followed by pasta with sprinkled cheese. Afterwards would come some type of veal escalope with vegetables on the side; this would be followed by cheese and then some fruit. As the captain ate with us it was no wonder he was as round as a ball.

We had a day stop at Trieste, labelled as an independent city, although it belongs to Italy. It goes back to Roman times with a large amphitheatre at the end of the long street we strolled along. Before we left the ship we were told that there would be a warning hoot on the ship's whistle which would let us know we had twenty minutes to return; the second whistle would mean we had missed it. We checked our watches often!

After two nights on board this small but delightful ship we disembarked at Venice. It was raining, which was a disappointment. Nonetheless we hired a water taxi and gave the boatman the address which was on the mainland. He was a skilled operator and even managed to dodge most of the heavy showers by stopping under bridges and holding onto their roofs.

On one occasion I produced my bottle of duty free. Neither of us being drinkers, we had bought a very cheap and large bottle of the local brew – slivovitz. It is plum brandy and popular in Yugoslavia.

I offered him a swig and he seemed very grateful, before we headed off to the next bridge and cover from the storm. I gave him another swig. He really seemed to like the stuff, so I tried it as well.

There is a technique for melting the dried paint of paintbrushes by leaving them in a solution for a few days. This stuff would do the job in half the time I should think. It was lethal. But he loved it.

Eventually under a pause in the showers we arrived at our hotel. But the iron gates were locked and a chain swung down with a large padlock. However drooping in the wet was a small envelope addressed to us.

It said that they had closed early for the season but arranged for us to stay at another hotel across the bay on the lido. Our driver grabbed our suitcases which he had already manhandled out of the boat and across the street once before and took us back again. That slivovitz is obviously powerful stuff.

We were now booked in to the Hotel Helvetia and it proved to be a modest but comfortable place for our stay of five days. I paid off the driver who was in a very jolly state. As well as a tip I gave him the bottle, for which he was extremely grateful.

We spent some time walking around Venice and it truly is a wonderful experience; like living in the middle ages. I hope they manage to stop it from sinking as to lose it would be to lose one of the world's great treasures.

We had a small hiccough one day. Veronica was a modest person but in the fashion of the time, she was wearing a fairly short skirt. As we climbed the steps of St. Mark's Cathedral to look inside, we were stopped by a monk at the top, who adjudicated that Veronica's skirt was too short to be allowed inside. It was rather embarrassing, but there was nothing we could do.

Back at the hotel on the second night, a foursome arrived with great noise and interruption. They were middle class English and of advanced middle age. Clothed in tweeds and the two women in fur edged jackets we christened them the Somerset Maugham quartet.

As we were fairly close to them in the dining room we sat in fear of being hauled into their party which jabbered away constantly. We therefore elected to speak only in French and that way managed to keep our distance.

Our final leg was a trans-European train ride via Aachen and thence to Ostend, a place we knew well. We left the station for our long ride – it was an overnight - and this time we knew we had the right tickets.

Early the next morning, we stopped for a spell in some siding and then chugged into Aachen station in Germany.

An announcement came over the loudspeakers which meant nothing to us, but an official came to our compartment to let us know that we had to move to the front of the train as that was the only part going on to Belgium.

Lots of whistles were blowing and from a distance we could hear an English voice crying plaintively: "John, John, hurry up, you'll miss it!"

Running along the platform in silk dressing gown was the eldest of the Somerset Maugham quartet. His face was covered in shaving soap as he rushed to catch up with his companions. We pulled our heads in from the open window.

There was one more overnight in Ostend and then we took the boat across the channel for a final train ride to Victoria Station in London. It was one heck of a vacation.

I list this time abroad as it was a truly wonderful experience for young people to enjoy with so many different places and cultures. We had been gone for about three weeks and here is the amazing part of it all.

I only cost $50! Yes, that's right, for full board, all the travel and hotels; it was just thirty-five pounds. Incredible. Not surprisingly the company went bust within a year.

It would not be possible to write a chapter on holidays/vacations without including the ones that we have taken to in the last ten years or so.

As written about earlier I once went on a very short (three day) cruise in the Adriatic from Rijeka to Venice on a small cruise ship, the Andrea Mantegna. Cruises were something that only the old or very wealthy did back in those days. (The newly wed or the nearly dead, as is sometimes quoted.)

On one of our week long escapes down to Cabo San Lucas, we were awoken one morning by the sounds of a lot of people setting up an outside buffet breakfast and also with mariachi music tuning up.

I wondered what was going on and She Who Must Be Obeyed, who had some knowledge of that type of thing announced that it was a cruise ship's outing from the nearby port.

Eventually buses pulled up and a motley crew of several score poured out and milled around while the trumpets blared and the guitars strummed and generally put on a show to accompany the "traditionally" dressed dancers. I thought it was a bit early for such an event, and I was also not impressed by the cruisers. They all seemed bored and decidedly ill turned out. Well, it was quite early in the morning, I suppose.

Therefore with this limited experience, I was somewhat aghast when S.W.M.B.O. suggested a few years later that we go on a cruise.

I immediately thought of my two experiences and imagined myself locked aboard a floating jail with several hundred polyester clad "crinklies" endlessly dancing the conga! Not my idea of fun at all.

But as all men reading this will know there is little point in refusing to comply with one's partner's desires if that is what she truly wants. A happy wife is a happy life!

Therefore one day I found myself struggling up the gangplank of a cruise ship, destined for the Mexican Riviera as it's euphemistically called. It was to be seven days afloat and after a long boarding process we made our way to our cabin, laughingly referred to as a "stateroom!"

In fact it wasn't too bad with everything you might want within a short arm's reach.

That evening, we found ourselves on a table for dinner with some quite interesting people and gradually and enthusiastically adjusted ourselves to life on the briny!

After a short time, I was hooked and found life aboard a terrific place to relax and even enjoy some of the amusements. I'm not a "joiner" so I merely watched from the sidelines as people made fools of themselves. No conga lines though.

This was to be the first of many such adventures and we have since travelled on about 17 cruises, with a couple more in the planning stage. It is hoped to do the Chile to Brazil cruise in the winter of 2016 when we leave Santiago, call into Ushuaia, go around the Horn, visit the Falklands, than go to Buenos Aires, Montevideo and end up in Rio de Janeiro. It will be quite a trip.

As much of one's life alters in its aspect over the course of many decades, so too does the focus of holidays.

Living in a rather damp climate and working the proverbial 40 hours each week, it's easy to simply want a change to a sun drenched beach for as long as one can get it.

Having left the workforce, and now living in a climate with a guaranteed 300 days of sunshine, such a goal is no longer attractive. Also an exhausting regimen of touring various countries doesn't appeal. And yet having been a traveller all my life there is still the draw of journeys.

Ten years ago, I took a motorcycle ride with my two sons, Simon and Michael. We packed tents and intended to spend a week touring the Sierra Nevadas including Yosemite, which I had never visited before.

It was a great experience, except for the fact that Simon became ill on the trip and had to return home before Michael and I did.

In spite of that Michael and I have repeated the trip to slightly different destinations over the last few years.

It's not an easy thing to travel 3,500 miles on a motorcycle and to camp each night, but it is an adventure that is just about within my aging skills.

So far the longest we have managed is to go up to the Glacier National Park with a stop at Yellowstone, and the Tetons. It was a wonderful experience and we were a couple of miles from the Canadian border before we turned around for the return trip.

There are four necessities for such a ride; an airbed; ear plugs, a fold up chair and lots of water on the ride. I have experienced being without these necessities and believe me it is not amusing; particularly the lack of an airbed.

Our modus operendum on such trips is to leave early – usually by 7:15 – and ride for about four hours. We stop each hour for water as you become very dehydrated on a motorcycle.

We usually have a late breakfast or early lunch about 11:00 and then press on to our destination, planning to arrive about three o'clock in the afternoon.

It doesn't take us too long to erect our small tents – you can't carry too much on two wheels – then we relax before we go out for a cocktail and to buy that evening's dinner. It's a simple and enjoyable life once you get in to the routine.

Our next trip is to be to Sturgis, but not when the half a million maniacs go there. We shall be through the small town a few weeks beforehand. We'll look at Mount Rushmore, visit the Badlands and Deadwood before we head west.

We shall stay in Yellowstone to take a tour of the northern loop and then head back down through Wyoming, Utah, and Nevada before getting back home after two weeks. We will be tired.

Really! Is there anything nice to be said about other people's vacations?
— Amor Towles, Rules of Civility

Chapter Twenty-Four

HEALTH

When you don't have any money, the problem is food. When you have money, it's sex. When you have both, it's health.
— *J P Donleavy*

Money cannot buy health, but I'd settle for a diamond-studded wheelchair."
— *Dorothy Parker*

Growing up in a post WWII/Victorian/Edwardian world there were a lot of old fashioned superstitions and down right bad ideas about life in general. Medicine still had a long way to go and back then the ratio of art to science was without doubt loaded more towards the art side.

Health was as it is today of paramount importance to us all. But it came at a cost, and often that cost was not fully known.

Mixed in with obvious good sense, were a lot of old wives tales and I'm sure many of them were positively harmful. And yet we managed to survive.

Perhaps looking back over seven decades, the biggest difference in the way we considered health matters was the overriding pervasion of guilt into so many aspects of the matter.

Provided we had not been born with some defect, which might in fact be down to some sin on the part of our parents, we were assumed to have all been given perfection in our physiques by God himself.

This was a very Christian society after all, and even if one should be unfortunate enough to be a non-conformist in such an area, then the organisers of most aspects of life were certainly not.

Therefore you were expected to look after yourself, and if you were struck down with an illness, then there was always the inference that somehow it was due to you and the way you had been living. Therefore sickness was usually accompanied by guilt.

Now I'm a big believer in a certain amount of guilt, particularly in the young. Let's face it they have a lot to be guilty about!

But this odd business has stayed with me and there is still that overlay of a bad feeling that if I get sick, which fortunately is not too often, then somehow I've brought it on myself.

I might understand that logically it is not my fault, but I can't shake off the guilt feeling totally.

Sickness in the 40's, 50's and even the 60's was a lot tougher than it is today. A visit to a hospital was a chilling event particularly for a child.

Firstly there was the smell of the place. It was a nasty cloying disinfectant odor, that became the sweet smell of ether the closer you got to the operating rooms. It infected your every pore and was very hard to shake off.

The doctors, who back in those days would make house calls, were very different to todays. A visiting doctor would arrive at your house, a little unsure of the geography and lay out of your room. They always wore suits and watch chains across their waistcoats and had cold and dusty hands.

In the hospital, being their own turf, they had a little more authority and accompanying arrogance. The jackets of their suits were then replaced with a white coat which always carried mustiness about it.

The nurses on the other hand were different. The all wore the same uniform. It was a pale blue skirt and blouse with a white starched apron over the top. They had bonnets of a type of white lace. For outerwear they wore dark blue cloaks with scarlet linings that were held across their throats with silver fastenings.

But the most wonderful aspect of these angels of mercy was that underneath all the starch, we knew that like all women, they wore garter belts to keep up their dark stockings. These made even the most plain of them a magnet for the eyes and dreams of developing teenagers.

Some of the medicine was awful. I remember the dreaded M & B tablets. These were used to bring down a temperature which our parents' generation feared as much as the plague.

These pills may have done the job, but in the process they gave one nasty hallucinatory dreams, and these were not helped by the flickering of the ever present coal tar lamp.

If you've not had the experience of one of these monsters burning in your childhood room, then you have been lucky to have missed one of life's torments together with accompanying delirium.

The concept went back to much earlier times, when illness was considered to be air-born. Much work was done in Florida in the early 19th century to seek out the dreaded miasma, which was thought to cause all kinds of misery and infection to humans. I think the coal tar lamp was a left over from those dark and distant days.

It was about eight inches tall and three inches round. In the top was a porous brick into which one poured liquid tar. Underneath there was a night light which heated the stone and gave off its essence. The lamp also gave off distorted images and flickered all night; if you are at all suffering from nightmares this will certainly increase their potency.

I don't think I was any more prevalent to illness than my peers, but I seemed to have spent an inordinate amount of time with this nasty little companion in my room. I could barely wait until morning eventually came around.

Back in the late 80's and early 90's I drove a 1976 Cadillac Eldorado. It was a marvellous machine; quite the biggest that Detroit made. I ignored the fact that I was the only white man to be seen driving this vehicle in Los Angeles. I loved the car and still miss it.

But the secret to giving it a long life was to put right anything that might go wrong, and to do it immediately. No matter it if was an ash tray falling off, or a dashboard clock not functioning, it had to be repaired right then and there or the entire thing would end up a rusting hulk propped up on bricks, dripping oils and other unguents.

I've tended to treat myself much the same as that Cadillac. If something goes wrong, then the first thing is to see if I have a potion or pill to put it right, if nothing works then I get help. So far it seems to have worked, and I don't spend much time in doctor's offices either.

Back in my youth the prevalent air of "it's your own fault" increased with the severity of the illness.

Colds and flu's were just due to unfortunate contact with ones fellow humans – usually the ones of whom one's parents disapproved, of course. "You've caught that off that bloody little Horace, he's always sniffing!"

If it was more serious then you had no doubt actually caused it yourself. Not sleeping enough - or rather not going to bed early enough.

An hour before twelve was worth two thereafter, as we were constantly reminded!

Taking unnecessary risks was your own fault; although a certain amount of risky behaviour under supervision was believed to be good for developing the character.

Smoking – under the legal age as well as drinking - and the worst of all self inflicted sins, masturbation was virtually guaranteed to produce a sickly person.

I read a long time ago that the character Uriah Heap was portrayed by Dickens to illustrate the effects of such self-abuse. Rounded shoulders, pale countenance, shifty weak eyes, a slight stutter and the ever present clammy hands were the inevitable pay off.

All we boys struggled with this on-going guilt and most of us failed entirely.

Diet was not a big deal in those days. It was expected that you should eat well. That meant three squares a day beginning with a hearty breakfast of eggs, bacon, and fried bread. No one had ever heard of cholesterol.

Most fried food was cooked in the drippings from roasted joints of meat.

This was collected in the pan each Sunday, and transferred to an enamel bowl. Layer upon layer of animal fat was loaded on and used as required. If things ever got really desperate, then "bread and scrape" was the remedy. This was basically a slice of bread with dripping on it.

It was never considered that a balanced diet was an aid to health and we used to pour on the sugar, load on the salt and fry away to our heart's content with the drippings. But were our hearts actually content?

People used to get ill and either recover or die. Because life was a lot more physical, obesity didn't seem to be a problem. In fact it was considered a benefit to be a little on the large side. As Shakespeare said in Julius Caesar: "Let me have men about me that are fat; yon Cassius has a lean and hungry look!"

As mentioned earlier, the worst of all illnesses was cancer. It was so bad that it was never mentioned. Much of this came from a belief that it was in some way a "dirty" disease; one brought about by some behaviour caused by oneself.

As for any type of venereal disease, well, that was so unmentionable that it came as a massive surprise to young men doing their National

Service (conscription), and finding themselves waking up with a decidedly unpleasant rash after a night of drunken sin outside the barracks.

The oft quoted joke was that of the "squaddie" seeing the doctor about a rash he was sure he had picked up from a toilet seat; only to be told that that was a funny place to take a girl!

As we approached the time when we were able to overcome our deep-seated fear of women and approach them, our heads were full of some of the most frightful nonsense that it's a miracle that any of us made it to first, let alone second, or even third base.

And there lurked that greatest of all health fears, pregnancy. Many hours were spent with our closest allies pondering the risks involved and the possibility of infecting girls this way.

There was a vicious rumor of the time that contraceptives (condoms) that were manufactured by a company called Durex, had a department where people actually stuck needles into the products before they were packed. This was so that the government was able to keep the population going. Stories circulated of young men who had fallen foul of this dastardly act with girlfriends who became pregnant "just like that!"

As for homosexuality, it was believed to be so awful a deviancy that it was never spoken of. Those "guilty" of such a terrible sin were actually treated as criminals as it was against the law.

Occasionally a celebrity was found to have make a mistake in his choice of gender for a bed companion, and the papers did all they could to cover it up, while allowing just a hint of the actual sin.

Much was made of the difference between the sexes. Before we were struck with the blight of first name calling that was imported from America, nearly everyone apart from very close friends or relatives was called Mr. or Mrs.

Close friends of ones' parents were called Aunty or Uncle even if they were not related.

Clothes were decidedly different. Women rarely if ever wore trousers; always dresses (frocks) and skirts.

Nakedness was never on show, and great efforts were made by older males to make sure that we youths knew how to behave like men.

No tendency towards effeminacy was tolerated. If, after puberty, you spoke in a high voice, even for a joke, older grizzled heads would swing towards you with a disapproving glare.

Handshakes were taught so that men knew that they were dealing with an equal. Walks like John Wayne's or Robert Mitchum's were remarked upon for their manliness.

Along with visiting American servicemen in the war came the introduction of aftershave. A complete no-no to our masculine world, who believed that the only smell tolerated on a man was no smell – or the slight smell of fresh sweat.

Looking back when the 60's arrived with flower power and outlandish dress, the old men must have thought that we had fallen in to a pit like Gomorrah. What was next? Men marrying men?

I am surprised when I find the number of my fellow citizens lining up at the doctor's office when they have a cold. Surely they must have learned that this is not something that he can actually cure. Better to find an over the counter medicine and keep warm and dry. It's going to pass.

But then this surprise is nothing compared to observing the counselling industry that has grown up around our youth. What type of citizen are we producing that needs to have a complete stranger tell them that things are going to be OK if a tragedy occurs within range of you?

Character building was a part of my growing up, and pretty much any type of horror was seen to be a test of one's resolve. Men didn't cry. If they were upset that much, then the women would rally around to protect them.

It was not in anyone's interest to have a weakling in the family, particularly the so-called head of the family. Mind you, behind closed doors anything could happen and few people would know about it.

Mental illness just didn't occur. I'm sure there must have been a few deranged ones around, but if so they were conveniently taken off to large draughty Victorian buildings and kept out of sight of others.

Occasionally we would hear of women who suffered from "nervous breakdowns." These were never explained, although as a few years rolled by we heard that these affronts were attributed to a change of life. We had no idea what this meant.

On the back of many magazines were advertisements from the Charles Atlas Company who promised developing youths "a body that men were scared of and women would admire."

Most of us longed for such an asset, but none of us had the funds to acquire it. We heard that the form of "dynamic tension" was merely a way of pushing one limb against another, and we tried like mad for several minutes to see if we could gain the coveted physique.

Charles Atlas himself proclaimed that before he became a world body building champion, he had been a seven stone weakling and regularly had sand kicked in his face by bullies. We could all relate.

Part of our regular school regimen was physical exercise. Rugby – a game for hooligans, played and watched by gentlemen, and soccer – a game for gentlemen played and watched by hooligans were regularly forced on us several times a week.

We were made to don huge, smelly, leather gloves and fight in a ring shouted at by ex-NCO's with no sense of fear. Athletics in the summer along with the mind-bending boredom of cricket were all a part of keeping us fit and active. Our days were filled with lessons, and sweat. But it was a system that worked and we rarely became sick, unless it was expected of us.

Before the invention of various inoculations and vaccines, we all fell victim to mumps, measles, whooping cough, German measles, and chicken pox. None of these came with any guilt attached. It was expected that you would get them as everybody did. In other words it was quite natural.

Mumps were particularly unpleasant and it was said if you didn't actually contract them and they appeared in later life, your testicles could become so big and heavy that a wheelbarrow was needed to move them around.

I was one of the few who never became infected and to this day I give the matter some thought. My wheelbarrow is out in the yard and rather rusty too, but it's ready!

It seems a nasty trick by our creator, but at about the time we gain a flood of testosterone and an accompanying lengthening of our skinny limbs, we get spots. Some of these are really nasty, and gain yellow heads on them.

As we are concurrently trying to appeal to the opposite sex, who seem to pass through this stage with less affliction and considerable speed, we find it of some comfort to squeeze these heads as often as they occur.

Not a good idea as the resulting sore nearly always ends up leaving a scar, which remains for the rest of your life.

At the same time as this, and against the advice of ones' doctors, we develop an almost super craving for fatty foods and sugar. Who is responsible for this design flaw, because it is a monster? It's amazing that any of us come out of this stage approaching normal.

But then there was always the salve of cigarettes. I am told that the lure of these horrors is slowly fading with todays young. But growing up in my time, we could hardly contain our need for this prop towards our adulthood.

We would splurge our very limited funds on packets of cigarettes and smoke them until we grew dizzy and nauseous. We would smoke anything if it lit, and in the process developed a habit that would take us years of misery to shake off. It was in the mid-fifties that some scientist, no doubt on a smoking break, dreamed up that maybe it was harmful. Ya think?

Much against the will of the tobacco industry, tests began to emerge that showed smoking to have links to the many diseases of which we were most afraid. This therefore confirmed our beliefs that we were bringing such misery upon ourselves.

I'm sure I was not unusual in that on leaving school I hung up my various boots and settled into a dormant posture for several years. After all with many years of enforced games behind me, why not?

I was brought out of temporary retirement on only one occasion by an invitation to play Rugby one Saturday afternoon for some local Young Conservatives.

It was a decent winter day and I was given my usual position of lock. In Rugby the forwards pack in a group to push the other side in a scrum. By the time I left school the fashion was three – four – one, instead of what had been the way of three – two – three. No matter, the fellow in the middle of the back row was me.

Scrum caps are designed to stop one's ears being shall we say, "resettled" in the crush of having one's head between the two backsides of the men in front. I had never found it necessary while at school, but in this team the two backsides on either side of my head were extremely large and muscular, and they moved constantly.

Our opponents were a very good and fierce team; we were hard put to avoid a degrading defeat. As I left the field, I felt moisture running down the back of both ears, they were bleeding.

As I sat in a hot bath along with some thirty other grubby, sweaty men, I decided that this was not exactly the way I wanted to spend my Saturday afternoons. Let's face it; there were girls out there, and cinemas, where you could sit in real comfort. The boots were subsequently thrown away.

Yet another disappointment for my poor father, who having relinquished his dream of me playing for Wales (or even England) saw his final thoughts of my performing honourably for some good amateur team vanish along with the muddy boots.

And so until I reached my mid twenties I lived on my fat. Or rather gained quite a bit of if. No matter, I was quite underweight to begin with.

About the time my career began to wake up, I went along with the fashion for the Royal Canadian Air force Exercises, which were in a small book.

These were graduated exercises that were easy to perform and lots of young men were doing them at the time. I never found anyone however that successfully made the transition from page three to page four.

The increase in intensity was truly monumental. But the die was basically cast. It was time to get off the couch, and lose some of the fat and get in shape.

Then along came a health problem just before my thirtieth birthday. I had to have a hernia repaired. It meant gong under the knife!

With three months before the procedure, I embarked on a serious attempt to get fit, believing that it would increase my ability to repair and get back to full function earlier.

I began to swim and run. During the last week, I swam every day for about 45 minutes and had stomach muscles like concrete. In fact the worst thing I could have done before an abdominal operation.

Oh, how quickly that fitness disappeared. With one stab of the surgeon's scalpel, I was reduced to a pathetic old man. I could barely walk around my run, let alone jog it.

But I did get better quite quickly and found that I didn't want to go back to my lazy days.

I was talking to an acquaintance some little time ago. He was talking about how he used to live close to an athletic club some ten years previously and how he would run around the track there a couple of times a week. That was it. His sole attempt at fitness.

I thought back and realised that I've been at it for over 45 years, and I'm sure it's helped me to keep well and healthy. But I've never overdone it.

Soon after I went on the road, I had a customer called Henschel. He was a German and a very nice man. But he was obviously sickly. He had the palor of illness about him and he often coughed loudly.

One day I was shown into his office as he was in the middle of a massive coughing fit. I watched him struggle and eventually collapse exhausted into his chair. I asked him if he was alright, and he nodded still out of breath.

He finally apologised for his problem and I asked him again if he was going to be OK.

He then told me that he had been a member of the German Olympic team that raced at the Berlin Games in 1938 in front of Hitler.

He was a sprinter and had raced – unsuccessfully! – against Jesse Owens, the Black Flash.

He said his health problems originated with his rigorous training, where he was convinced that his harsh regime had strained his heart. He very much regretted it, but there was nothing he could now do to help himself recover. The damage had been done some twenty-five years earlier. So you can overdo the fitness thing.

But my old friend "guilt" is always there if I go too long without making the effort. And it is tough on cold winter days to force oneself out on the bicycle (my favourite form of exercise,) when you have to dodge the layers of ice, or the puddles.

I recently was forced to change my doctor - or as they so nicely call it my "primary healthcare provider!"

There are two type of doctors in this world; the ones you see when you're well and the ones you see when you're not well.

Having entered the final quarter of the game of life, I feel that although in good shape I'd like a fellow (or woman, as I've had a couple of female docs and found them to be excellent) who will check all the boxes and keep an eye on me. There is such a one here in the Valley, although he has learned his bedside skills at the school of Doc Martin, if you've ever seen the program.

Unlike the previous guy who was terrific at the regular conversations we used to have, this one is not a health nut. He is overweight and I've recently found out smokes as well. Over Christmas I bought him a bottle of booze, and was invited in to deliver it in person. He was eating lunch in his office. It was a Big Mac and fries! I found out that the bottle didn't last long either. My only concern now is if I'm gong to outlast him.

Like a tailor, a travel agent, an accountant or a dentist, a doctor can make or mar your life. I don't want to have to change again.

No piece on health can be complete without some reference to the payment of care.

Having come from a land of socialised medicine, and having had treatment both under that and also privately, I have to say that my naturally aversion to anything run by the government is bound to taint my opinion.

Obamacare came in in 2013 with a lot of lies and obfuscation – *"You can keep your doctor if you like your doctor; you can keep your health insurance if you like your health insurance!"* Those of us who understand the liberal mindset knew it was nonsense.

You can't give an extra 35 million people health care without someone paying for it. And that someone is going to be us.

The prospects of some bureaucrat in some place earning his pension and enjoying his tax paid benefits deciding which procedure is right for my complaint gives me chills.

But in truth, the situation exists now with insurance companies who make the very same decisions every day. It's not always pretty. But the choice is yours as far as the insurance company is concerned. If you pay more the service will be better, and the health care will also be in a higher bracket. Also the advantage of a private scheme is that if it is a bad one, it will go out of business. The bureaucrat will always stay there and probably get a bonus.

Not that money is any guarantee of success. Let's face it even the most wealthy and important die or are not cured. None of us is going to escape from here alive.

Also I do believe that in a caring society some form of tax should be placed on the healthy to pay for some basic care for the unhealthy. You can't just let them collapse on the street. The problem is deciding how much money, and how much care should be provided.

I appreciate that we do have such systems with Medicare and Medical; I'm not quite sure exactly how they work, but I do know that if we opt for single payer (total government control of the entire system) we'll all suffer.

As Winston Churchill said: *Capitalism is the unequal distribution of wealth; socialism is the equal distribution of misery.*

I don't fancy the idea of the same socialistic dream being able to affect my well-being.

> *Eat healthily, sleep well, breathe deeply, move harmoniously."*
> — *Jean-Pierre Barral*

Chapter Twenty-Five

TIRADES

The truth will set you free, but first it will piss you off.
— *Gloria Steinem*

So you try to think of someone else you're mad at, and the unavoidable answer pops into your little warped brain: everyone.
— *Ellen Hopkins*

I published a daily blog from June 2010 to June 2014. It was called Trevor's Tracks (in So Cal.) You can still find it via Google, I believe. It covered a great number of subjects – pretty well anything that took my fancy – but also each week there were a number of fixed posts.

There was a music track of considerable variety – not always a particular favourite of mine. Then there was the weekly newspaper column and a Right Track, which was a political view from the right.

Then each Saturday was a post called Trevor's Tirade. It always had a picture of a small child in mid tantrum, courtesy of the Web site Morgue File which is a wonderful resource for odd and interesting photos.

Considering that there were 200 of these, it's surprising to me that I could have had so many tirades, but then there are quite a lot of annoying things about life. Some of them are quite big, but most of them are just small irritating things about the traits of one's fellow human beings.

Here are some of the subjects covered, although they have all been freshly written.

Christian Names (Or as Americans call them First Names.)
When I went to my first real job at the age of 17, I asked my father how I should address the men around me. There were few women in

business at the time. He said: "Call your manager Mr. Jones; everyone else you call sir!" Advice that I took to heart and it never caused me any problems. I continued with this habit over the next few years until I joined the American firm 3M based in Wigmore Street, London, W.1.

Having "sirred" my way through the interview, I was taken up to see the big boss, the Sales Director, one Jim Smith.

Up to now, all the people I had met there asked me to call them by their Christian names, a practise that I found somewhat awkward.

Entering "Jim's" office, which was huge, the great man was kicking a paper ball around the carpet and attempting to score a goal into his wastepaper basket. He also had his tie off, which in formal England was extremely strange.

He spoke in a kind of drawl which was also very odd, and the entire interview consisted of him telling me how fortunate I was to be joining this wonderful company and various other platitudes. I was not impressed, but at aged 21, I simply thanked him for the opportunity and left him to his soccer practice.

Over the following years and now living out here, I find the use of Christian names to not be the advantage it was cracked up to be. I believe the general idea of it was that with the dropping of formality, everyone would be on an equal footing and therefore able to relax more. I have yet to see this work out in real terms. Furthermore there is nothing so distressing to me than to see some seven-year old talking to a middle aged person using that person's first name.

One of the last accounts I used to visit in my career was a large insurance company in Manhattan, Kansas; (they called the place the Little Apple!)

I used to sign the visitors' registry T. Summons and then go and sit down. It was a matter of great amusement to me that when my time came to go upstairs, the receptionist was quite at a loss to know how to call my name out over the small Tannoy she had. She tried calling "T," then eventually she hit on just Summons, which had the opposite effect of sounding much too formal. The idea of calling "Mr. Summons" never entered her head.

Hugging

Along with the unlimited use of Christian names has come along the even more distressing habit of hugging. Now not only can this cause a distinctly uncomfortable feeling but it also creates what an old friend of mine used to call "an assault on the person."

I was walking around the condo complex in which I once lived some time ago. One of the directors was there with a new manager who was looking around. I had never met this chap before and as I stuck out my hand to greet him, he pushed it aside and enfolded me in an enormous hug. It was truly an invasion and an assault. As both my arms were pinned to my side, I couldn't even push him away.

I think however that it did set up a sort of early warning system in me. Recently at a party that S.W.M.B.O. insisted we attend – Oh God! I was standing watching things when a new arrival turned up and the host brought her over to us. She went into full hugging mode immediately even before the names were spoken. My radar kicked in immediately and I recoiled quite distinctly. The woman looked fairly shocked. Fortunately the host, who knows me very well said to her: "Oh don't worry, he's not a hugger."

So as far as this hugging is concerned please leave me out of it. I find it totally unnecessary and watching dignitaries like our current President go through the palaver is quite excruciating. I'm told that Bill Clinton is the worst for grabbing your hand, then arm, and before you know it he's got you in the bear grip. Very nasty for anyone hug-averse!

As an aside, one of the senior managers I knew in Tokyo used to relate his horror when a young man, I would imagine in the fifties. He used to have to go to the docks to check the manifests of arriving ships. One was captained by a Greek with a massive black beard. This man would always pick up Hamari-san and swing him around, pressing his face to the Japanese. "His beard used to stink," he said. "I lived in fear of it."

Waving

What it is with people above 5,000 feet? Is there some type of brain app that kicks in once you get past Running Springs? All of a sudden people who would cheerfully drive you off the 405 at rush hour become wavers. These are people who sit in their tinted windowed Lexus's and insist on waving to perfect strangers they pass along the road.

I might be out walking the dogs and all of a sudden there is this hand appearing either behind the tint or even out of the window waving like some tree limb in a storm. Initially I used believe this must be someone whom I had forgotten back in England and who had suddenly turned up. Then I realised it was a total stranger. It's a weird feeling.

Even worse is the fellow up the road whom I see nearly every day. What is it that compels him to wave at me an hour later when he's driving down the damned street? Does he imagine I've forgotten him and need reminding?

But it's the total strangers who annoy me the most. And we all know that these are the same people who let their dogs foul the sidewalks and don't pick up afterwards. "Oh, it doesn't matter, it's the mountains. Oh look let's wave to that fellow over there!" Come on People!

<u>Handshaking</u>

Some years ago at a course on Guerrilla Selling (It might have been called Gorilla Selling for all the help it was) I had a word with the lecturer. We had broken for coffee, and I brought up the point he had been making about meeting and greeting clients.

He had been talking about shaking hands and had made no distinction as to whether it was with a man or a woman.

At the time I was about 50 and there were still a lot of us "old timers" around. I told him that in the world of correct etiquette, a man should never offer his hand to a woman. He should wait until she offers hers to him. He might like to file that away.

In recent years women have become much more outgoing, particularly in the world of business. Nonetheless, I find it interesting when watching groups of people meeting up that the men will all shake hands with not a pause. However if you watch carefully most of the women will merely say Hello, and not offer a hand. There seems to be some deep-rooted instinct there.

But it is important to teach young men to shake hands properly. It's not a natural process and if left alone, they can develop the "dead cod" grip, which is truly objectionable. I taught my grandson to do it properly when he was about ten. We still "shake" when meeting and greeting and he's got it down well.

When he was about 14 he came out with me one day as he often does on an assignment. It was to a local museum locally and the curator, a rather attractive woman, came out to greet us.

She was obviously one of the more forceful types and out came her hand immediately. I introduced Evan to her as being with me for the day, and she put out her hand to him. She looked at me and said afterwards. "He's got a very good handshake." I could see that Evan was thrilled.

Warnings

About two years ago we had an announcement on TV. It broke in to the program and said that a new warning system was about to be tested. In the event of a real emergency we should listen to it and behave accordingly or some such bureaucratic nonsense.

There then followed a very annoying noise with more words that seemed to be recorded on an antiquated, defective system. Eventually having disturbed us for some minutes it all went away. I thought it was quite a good idea to have some type of central alarm that could alert the populace in the event of a hacking attack by N. Korea or the Russians launching one of their ICBM's.

But it didn't end there. Of course, now they had it the bureaucrats knew they could enter our domains whenever they liked and boy do they like!

It now seems necessary to test this vile system every week at assorted times; usually when I'm trying to listen to Charles Krauthammer explaining some arcane political tactic. On comes this horrible siren, then the crackly voice telling us if this was a real emergency, ditto ditto.

Thank God for the mute button; but how long before they find a way to neutralise that?

Table Manners

Both my father and grandfather were demons for table manners. My father would just plain tell you off, whereas my grandfather, the naval man, would use some humor. If like many youngsters, I would stick out my arms to get greater leverage on a piece of meat, he would say: "Dip your oars a bit, I'm coming alongside!"

But it was a very big indicator of the way you were raised, and therefore a slight on your parents if you didn't do well at the table. Therefore the middle class tended to concentrate on how you handled the eating irons.

Considering how efficient the Americans are in their lives, it always amused us Brits at how they ate. "One armed bandits," was a term often used due to the habit of using just a fork. Also it's quite painful to see an American doing that table top dance with the transfer of knife and fork when it comes to cutting food up.

When we came here, I told Simon, who was seven years old, that he could choose which system he wanted – either British or American. I think he favored the former. I'm sure he still does, although at 40 he's somewhat on his own in this matter.

As a child I often heard my elders refer to someone as a "good trencherman." I had no idea what this was. In fact a trencher was a hollow in the dining table into which the food was poured. A spoon would then be used – or maybe you just lowered your head. It was medieval times after all.

It was the Victorians who gave us the concept of table manners and overall genteelness. Until then one used one's knife which was used for other work. I still do that while camping and rather enjoy it.

But as with so many other aspects of manners, which are the lubricant that helps society work more smoothly, eating well is to avoid being a total pig and putting others off their meal.

I was forced to write about this in the blog once after an unfortunate experience at a local tavern. They do excellent food and a lady was working her way through a large steak, which had a lot of "jus" with it.

She naturally went through the transferring routine with knife and fork, but what drew my attention was the use of her paper napkin.

Now for anyone not knowing the rule, a napkin of any type should never appear above the level of the table top, unless it is to dab the lips, whereupon it should be replaced immediately upon the lap.

This woman had used her napkin excessively and it was in a disgusting condition. Instead of adhering to the rule, she kept wiping her mouth and then throwing the paper on the bar. It was a rather nasty sight.

My dilemma was, what would one do if one was attached to this female, who was about 50 by the way. Do you ignore this boorish behaviour, or attempt some advice?

Perhaps if one was the bartender, one could take the offending thing away and offer a replacement.

Humor (or a lack of it)

The other day I heard a barman tell a joke. It wasn't a bad one but what made me take notice was that I realised how few times in

319

recent years I have heard a joke told. Even among friends, let alone to a comparatively strange audience.

Perhaps it's my imagination, but before the days of the Internet, we told lots of jokes, but then along came political correctness and with it the fear that we might offend someone.

Of course, we all get jokes in our daily emails, and many of them we've seen several times. But as for actually speaking them, how often – just think back?

I think that it's a great instinct among us humans that we don't want to upset anyone, but surely we have gone a little too far, in that we have taken away much of the fun of life and in the process have we managed to offend fewer people? I somehow don't think so.

Earlier in Chapter 19 I related a plaque I had seen on a trip to England which described Heaven and Hell if run by certain nationalities.

It was harmless fun, unless you were looking out for any possible chance of offence, and then it would be magnet for such PC Police. I think it's a great shame that we have lost this art and enjoyment.

Traffic Zones

On our recent motorcycle tours, Michael and I often run across road work. We go in the height of summer and that seems to be the favourite time to attack major projects on our infrastructure.

When I first used to visit America in the mid seventies, it was noticeable that road works were large and also very quick. This was done by having lots and lots of men working at it.

By contrast in the UK we would have a road up for weeks while a couple of moody laborers would hang around leaning on their shovels waiting for equipment to turn up.

Now I'm not saying the things have reached this stage here, but there are a couple of annoying things that always catch my eye.

At a time when budgets are always being cut, why is it necessary to have so many people involved in the simple act of directing we motorists.

We drive up and stop at a man with an octagonal sign. He is chatting on some walkie-talkie. Eventually the opposing traffic comes by led by a large (expensive) truck with two men in it. They reverse and then lead us off around what is often a relatively small incursion in the road surface.

Currently, I believe that the going rate for such Cal Trans workers is about $50,000 a year, plus full benefits. The truck I assume is around $50,000 also.

We live in an electronic age and so why can't we erect a simple set of traffic lights – we all know how they work don't we? These could be sensitive enough to gauge the amount of traffic if we want to go the extra mile. What after all is the pilot car supposed to be doing anyway? We all know how to drive – we reached this spot without doing anything seriously wrong after all.

Back in my very early days of driving in a far less benevolent climate than California, the usual rule was that if a road was left overnight with a big hole then a couple of dim flickering oil lamps were left by the departing crew. It was up to you to avoid the thing. We rarely fell in.

Over the subsequent years I'm sure the standard of driving has improved greatly. So why do we need a pilot car to escort us around what is mostly a small impediment?

Twelfth Night

Just down the road is a tall tree that now for the fourth year has a lonely Christmas silver ball hanging from a limb. It was put there by a young lady who had bought one of the condos nearby. She has been up a couple of times since then but very little. And yet the few balls she hung have been dropping off with nature's wear and tear, leaving this solitary testament to her festive spirit all those years ago.

Sadly, she is not the only person to have failed to obey the rule of Twelfth Night, which is that all decorations for Christmas time must be removed by then. And yet the lonely ball still hangs awaiting its inevitable demise, as it has done month in and month out.

Once again it seems a lack of adhering to simple standards and rules allows such deviancy to exist. Do the owners of the small house on my bicycle ride really enjoy the tacky Father Christmas on their front door in July? And yet there he sits, smiling at us in his fading red coat and very hot fur collar.

Then there are the lights that have seen better days hanging from eaves that the owners have failed to empty so that rain and melting snow falls in rivers over the electric bulbs. It's quite fun in January, but not in April.

Sexism

Is it just me, or are you getting fed up with men being portrayed as stupid, greedy creatures in TV ads? So often we see the scene of domestic bliss interrupted by a claim by an ever-so-smart woman that she is saving them hundreds of dollars on their car insurance by switching to XYZ Insurance Company.

The man who is usually stuffing his face is completely unaware of this masterly tactic as he's too stupid to understand simple mathematics.

Or there's the case of the broken faucet/light/roof/cupboard door that he tries to fit with duct tape. Of course his clever wife is on the phone to Angie, yet another smug woman who has compiled a list of competent contractors who can take care of everything. At the right moment of course, all the duct tape repairs collapse. Wouldn't you know it!

Now far be it for me to suggest that perhaps we could employ some dumb blondes to fill these rolls of the foolish, but if done, I can hear the cries of "misogyny," "sexism," and "Chauvinism," from all quarters. But if it's good for the goose why not the gander?

Misnomers

I recently bumped into our new postmistress, and had a spirited discussion after she informed me that she was in fact the new postmaster. Now call me old fashioned, but what is with this gender confusion? She was not unattractive and her clothing was quite feminine, therefore one could conclude that she was not being forced by nature to live in the wrong body as the "T's" in LBGT unfortunately are.

But there seems to be some type of problem with the word "mistress." I've run into it before with a harbour mistress who also wanted to be referred to a master.

Mistress after all is the correct and extended form of Mrs. And therefore should never cause offense. But like the word for a female dog – a bitch – it has become unacceptable because it offends the ignorant.

Perhaps the worst example was a few years ago, when a council member in Washington D.C. was disciplined for remarking that if they cut the budget any more they would be considered niggardly! Oh boy, did that cause problems.

But back to our new post office overseer; I was in there the other day and an envelope of mine had come unstuck. I needed a small piece of tape to close it securely. I asked the attendant to let me have a piece, and was told that the new "postmaster" had removed all tape from the counters. I therefore asked for a staple as a small machine was close by. "Oh no," I was told. "You can't use a staple as it won't go through the system." And they wonder why they lose so much money.

While we're on that, I am becoming increasingly fed up with claims that the post office while losing money is not actually losing tax-payers' money. As they lose billions each year, they are loaned what is needed by the government. Well, that makes it fine then doesn't it!!!!

Bare Feet

What is it with people wandering around in bare feet? Now I appreciate that we are in an age where it's cool to throw off all restraints of civilised behaviour in order make everyone feel relaxed and free, but for heaven's sake bare feet? And that includes outside on the street.

I notice a few shops have signs that warn No Shirt/No Shoes – No Service! But for how long before the shoeless/shirtless brigade becomes so large that businesses are impacted?

Around us we have a number of rental homes to be used by vacationers, while the true owners struggle to earn enough to pay for taxes and pensions for our bureaucrats. I notice many of these guests wandering around in what pass for pyjamas and the obligatory bare feet. I just wonder what kind of condition their sheets must me in!

Compliments

I don't often find myself on the same side as our current president, but I did feel sorry for him the other day as he was caught making a statement regarding our Attorney General here in California. Kamala Harris is an extremely beautiful woman by anyone's standard and the remark he made was to say that she was the most attractive AG he knew, or some such compliment. One would have thought that he'd called her a racial slur as the PC police came down on him very hard.

Within a couple of days he had to come out and apologise for the remark, although in my ignorance I could not see what was so offensive about saying what was after all quite true.

Perhaps that was a moment when he should have stood up and told the PC police that they were the ones out of line and if Ms. Harris happened to be offended by his compliment then she should be the one to call him out, not some bunch of addle-brained harridans who were probably jealous anyway.

I have reached the age where I feel quite old enough to tell a woman she is beautiful without it being misconstrued as a "come-on." In fact as I was leaving a coffee shop the other day a young girl of perhaps about 17 was sitting waiting for her order. She was quite alone and as I left I said to her: "I hope you don't mind me telling you, but you are an extremely pretty woman."

She looked up at me and smiled and said: "Thank you very much," and I left. Considering that most young girls are full of self doubts and spend an inordinate amount of time gazing at themselves in the mirror, I see nothing wrong with letting the occasional one know that she's OK.

New Year's Eve

We were out to our annual New Year's Eve festivity the other evening, and on the way there I mentioned to S.W.M.B.O. that looking back over a rather long spell of life, I could only remember three actual Eve's that were of any note at all.

Perhaps the most memorable was at a very fine house in one of the better inner suburbs of Southampton. I was 21 and had the much sought after company car – a Morris Minor. I can't remember who invited me or where exactly the house was, but it had a very large entrance hall complete with massive Christmas tree. Furthermore at midnight a real live Scotsman appeared with bagpipes and his dirk fully on display!

I didn't drink very much in those days, but obviously on that occasion with all the festivities I allowed my face to be lowered into the bucket a little too often.

Quite how I drove home I don't know, but come the morning, I found my car parked askew on the pavement with the door completely hanging open. The interior light was by now out, and the resulting battery dead as the proverbial.

I spent most of New Year's Day trying to find a garage able to fill the battery up with juice before I was expected to go about my business.

These days our New Year's have settled into a rather comfortable routine. We visit Nottinghams about 5:30 p.m. The owners, Charlie and Evelyn spend most of the afternoon decorating the upper room with all the accoutrements necessary for people to make fools of themselves at the stroke of twelve.

This is the only time I go around to the business side of the bar and serve them as by then they need a break and the band is usually warming up. They open the place at seven, which is usually the time for us to leave, having celebrated the turn into the New Year. Well, it has to be that somewhere on the globe – perhaps Bermuda?

But I gave up the traditional event many, many years ago having realized that it was over-priced, forced bon homie, with poor quality food and service, with usually a lousy band. Not for me I'm afraid!

Traffic

This is an easy one as everyone hates traffic – the congested sort. But since retiring to the comparative peace and quiet of the mountains, traffic annoys me more than it ever did when I used to commute to London.

The problem is inexperienced drivers. We get all types up here and in the winter they're wanting to enjoy the snow. Quite naturally, and I try not to condemn their fun.

Many of the people in Southern California have no experience of snow and ice and naturally they want to let their children experience it. But it would be so much better for all if they could somehow try not to be so damned stupid on the roads.

Even in the summer when driving conditions are excellent, drivers seem not to know where they're going, and totally give up any thought of using those pesky signals the manufacturers so foolishly put on the cars and of course, charged them for.

So here are a couple of rules for driving in the mountains.

A) Use signals – they won't run your battery down.
B) If you're confused, and that happens a lot, please pull over to the side to consult your GPS, smartphone or wife – it's not polite to just stop in the middle of the road in traffic to do so.
C) The chains go on the driving wheels!

D) A four-wheel drive car still slides on ice when the brakes are slammed on.

E) Please don't wave at people you don't know just because you're in the mountains.

F) If the traffic is at a standstill, it's polite to allow someone trying to enter the road to come in. It won't delay you by more than a second.

G) If you and your five small children do need to play on the side of the street in our blackening snow when it's dark, it's a good idea to dress them in something other than black.

Junior

One of the main distinctions between the Brits and Americans is that Brits never refer to their offspring as Junior. Back in the old days if there was a duplication of names at school, age would be the determining factor and the eldest would be called Major and the junior would be called Minor. At least there was some dignity in that.

But Junior is a rather derogatory term I think, and particularly when the person is well on in years. We have a very prestigious Mercedes Benz dealer out here in Orange County. The owner is somewhere to the north of sixty and he regularly comes on TV to promote his cars. He always refer to himself as Fletcher Jones Junior, when the old man must have slipped his cable years ago. Is he going to his grave with this demeaning title?

Grief

Growing up I hardly ever saw an adult cry. I think I remember my mother in tears a couple of times, but basically adults didn't cry. Also it seemed to be the responsibility of every adult within range to tell me not to cry and to be brave when I hurt myself and tears began. Reaching that goal of manhood and bearing up under difficulties was thought to be in everyone's best interests.

And yet today we have reached the stage where if you want to see an adult in tears and even better truly distraught, then you only have to turn on any local TV news program.

The other day a condominium caught fire. Two people, a mother and child died as a result. That was the news and quite sufficient, but no. The TV crew had located the father of the woman and they had encouraged him to say how he felt at the loss of both daughter and granddaughter. Naturally the man was almost catatonic, but the camera still rolled. Why? What was the point of such a broadcast? Nobody could learn anything from such a spectacle. As was shouted out in the McCarthy trials in the 50's: Have you no decency, sir?

Bureaucrats

Throughout this missive bureaucrats have come off rather badly. My overall dislike of them is that they are able to inculcate themselves into society, and then build so many rules and regulations around themselves that they are never fired or even disciplined. Without any competition around they are able to do pretty much what they like and we have to pay for it. And their pension and benefits are the envy of the private sector.

One of the peculiarities of this branch of society is the behaviour at announcements to the press and the rest of us in general.

We recently had a new dam built at the end of the lake. Well, it wasn't actually a new dam, more a new routing of the road that used to go over it. It had been finished for some time before it was officially opened, and remained so until some high up bureaucrat was available to cut the ribbon – no matter, we all managed quite well with the old one until that magical date!

On the appointed day, roads were policed, traffic re-directed and a full scale platform was built to hold the dignitaries. It might even have been Arnold Swartzenegger, but I don't remember.

Now my two beefs with all this, and frankly I don't see any harm in the principal of a grand opening – we had after all paid for the work - but to begin with we have a foolish spectacle. Namely that the Gov. had to mention by name all the people involved with the project at a management level. There then follows a general shuffling of feet as each of these civil servants is made to identify themselves to muttered applause by those in the know. The rest of us have no clue who they are and wonder why they get a mention for doing what is after all only their jobs – like the rest of us, but without the accolades. Can we not dispense with the role of honor, and get straight onto handing out the cake, or champagne?

The second nonsense which has become "de rigueur" for any public official holding a conference is to have one of those truly annoying "signers" waving their hands and arms right next to the speaker.

Now before you all get to the keyboard and fill up my in-box, let me state that I have all the sympathy in the world for those lacking the ability to hear. But most TV's these days have a subtitle option and I'm sure that those afflicted with hearing loss have already figured out how to use it.

As for the deaf people who want to attend such an event, then cannot a written script be handed out to them on demand?

I fear this employment of signers, who are always there when the funds come out of tax dollars, is just another way for politicians to show that "they care." And the hand waving is really annoying, so please can we just stop it or at least find out how many of the hearing impaired actually use the facility. I bet it's very, very small!

Denial has rented a room in my head and frequently stomps around slamming doors.
— Sarah Noffke, Awoken

Chapter Twenty-Six

DOGS

The better I get to know men, the more I find myself loving dogs."
— *Charles de Gaulle*

When the Man woke up he said, 'What is Wild Dog doing here?'
And the Woman said, 'His name is not Wild Dog any more,
but First Friend, because he will be our friend for always and
always and always.'
— *Rudyard Kipling*

Once you have had a wonderful dog, a life without one is a life
diminished."
— *Dean Koontz*

I had a conversation with my 19 year-old grandson the other day. He is trying to figure out what to do with his life. His parents and other grandparents are all nurses and they are pushing him in that direction. "But the problem is, Grandad," he said. "I just don't fancy spending all my time with people. I'd rather be with animals; so I'm thinking - a vet."

I quite understood him and said so, but also that the choice was very much with him. I would have gone in the opposite direction however.

As I wrote about in Chapter 20, I was raised in that Victorian way that blames oneself for ill health. I know of course that this is a poor idea, but the guilt remains deep within me and always has done.

We should be careful of inputting such ideas into children's heads I think, or they will turn out like me!

But my logic is that I could stand illness in humans as perhaps they had in someway brought about the condition themselves, but as for animals that's a different matter. Their suffering is too much for me to bear. So the vet job is definitely out for me.

I'm fond of nearly all animals, with the exception of creepy crawlies, and snakes; I don't much care for them. But the rest fascinate me and I love watching them.

Cats, I think of as some of the most beautiful creatures ever created, but they have one problem for me and that is I have absolutely no idea of what is happening in their heads. Cat owners tell me that they don't know either, but can live with the enigma.

When I was growing up we had a tortoiseshell cat called Teddy Bear. I was about four or five and it was during the war.

My father had a trick I loved to see him do. We had a kitchen cabinet with a pull-down cutting board. My father would open this and lay a small sprat so that its head would protrude just over the edge. Then he would pick up Teddy Bear, who would extend his arms and claws and my father would hook him on to the board. Then he would push him gently so that he'd "swing for fish!" After a few minutes Teddy would be unhooked and given the fish.

I'm not too sure what happened to Teddy Bear, but there was talk of "fits." There was a similar problem with a cocker spaniel we had called Charlie at about the same time. It must have been the pressure of the war!

I had a ginger cat that I shared with the infamous flat mate Dave. It was totally bonkers and used to chase around the living room and try and get up the chimney. I think he let it go with the flat when he transferred the lease.

But dogs, now they are a different matter entirely. I understand what they are thinking and can relate completely.

Our first dog after Charlie was a Welsh Pembrokeshire Corgi, called Barney – or when he misbehaved, Barnabus!

My father was well into his Welsh thing hence the breed I think, and there is no doubt that Barney was a terrific little dog. He was like a fox with a narrow head and pointy ears and a red colour. He was a little on the treacherous side and would definitely bite. But that was back in the days when if a dog bit a child, then it was considered to be the fault of the child. "Stop bawling, Trevor, you probably deserved it!" Was the response.

Today the poor creature would probably be put down or given away, which I have seen happen several times here. I learned what ticked Barney off, and either paid the consequences or stopped doing that type of thing. It was not a difficult lesson to learn.

Barney and I got along just fine. And so I did with Lady, another corgi who was sent up to Paddington on the train in a tea chest.

I don't know if my parents thought they might breed these two but once Lady came into heat, Barney was driven mad by the scent and howled to be let out of his end of our "L" shaped flat.

This continued each time Lady came into season and we had to keep them apart. There seems to have been no effort to neuter either of them.

Lady was a bit of a disappointment. From the time we got her she was immensely lazy and never ran around at all. We didn't even take her out on walks as she much preferred to stay at home in front of the fire. But she was an amenable animal, although somewhat greedy.

When Barney was about two, he contracted distemper, which was a very bad illness from which most dogs did not recover. My mother and I stayed up a couple of nights to nurse him through it will bread and milk to keep his strength up, and he came through with no after effects. But he would still bite me.

Perhaps as I learned not to upset my father, who was also quite bad tempered, so I learned not to upset Barney as well. It was maybe good training for later in life, as few dogs have tried to bite me since.

I had left home when Barney and Lady died. I'm sure it must have been a very sad time for my parents but they never bought another one, although they were ideally situated to do so. They didn't travel much, so one would have thought that another dog would have been ideal. But no!

Once Michael was about four, and was able to rigidly stand on his own two feet some friends of ours bought a boxer called Harry. This prompted us as good Yuppies to buy a dog too.

Now I was particularly fond of Harry. Boxers are huge fun and Harry was a great fellow. He would roll around with his owner and me and we loved to play games with him.

Veronica had a West Highland Terrier when we were married and on our arrival at our wedding night hotel, she shed a few tears that she might not see "Bunny" ever again. Perhaps it was more likely the tears were because of her realisation that she was now landed with me.

Bunny and its companion a nasty little Yorkshire terrier, called Timmy, did see their absent mistress many times as it happened on our many visits. She didn't cry about it any more, I'm glad to say.

So we had to decide what type of dog we should get, and I can't remember how much input I gave to this decision, because as in so many things I was quite ignorant. We ended up with a Golden Retriever.

We visited a breeder in Leatherhead and chose from a litter of about eight. We told the breeder that his name would be George, and his papers thereafter stated his name as Lord George of Boscarne. He was to become quite the aristocrat.

The choice of name was a little unfortunate as both our fathers were called George. Of course in defence we never called them that so it just seemed a great name for a dog. I think my father-in-law eventually forgave us, but my own father was never keen, calling it forever, just The Dog!

At the time George was doing quite well with my amateur training, my boss Stan had discovered a dog training class held in a church hall in Bagshot. I decided to invest the small amount and took George along.

Looking back I can truthfully say the hours I spent there each week were among the funniest I can ever remember.

Most of the people at the class didn't have a clue. Nor did their dogs; although I think the dogs had more of an idea than the humans. I can still remember some of them quite clearly, although it must now be over fifty years.

To begin with there was "Laddie." He was on the end of a leash held by a feeble old lady. He was a mixed, fairly small terrier, but what he lacked in stature he certainly made up for in energy.

Charles the instructor, who had obviously been trained by the British Army, used to fix his beady eye on the pair as they walked around the outer limits of his circle. "Down boy, down boy," was the constant refrain from the owner as Laddie jumped and tried to do figures of eight up to her waist.

"Give 'is 'ead a good pull," was Charles' instruction. "Go on, if you pull 'is 'ead orf, I'll buy you a new one!"

Eventually Charles could stand it no longer and strutted over to the unfortunate woman and grabbed the leash. She watched amazed as Laddie immediately came to heel and trotted obediently beside his temporary new master. Charles never said a word to the dog and didn't seem to exert any kind of force. Perhaps Laddie knew better than to try his shenanigans and didn't fancy 'is 'ead being pulled orf!

The moment he was handed back to his rightful owner the jumping began again.

Then there was the Doberman. This animal was in need of some serious counselling, but Charles never attempted it. The dog sat growling softly while displaying a huge erection, which never seemed to go away. On the one occasion when the command "leashes off," was given, the Doberman rushed off, peed in the corner of the hall and then attempted to mount a docile Yellow Labrador.

Charles and many of the rest of us were hard pressed to separate the pair.

I also remember a wonderfully quiet Mastiff called Dolly, who lumbered around and only ever wanted to lie down. Pulling the dog into an upright position proved too much for the fat man who had somewhat unwisely bought her when she was a manageable puppy; she was therefore allowed to lie down as often as she liked.

I spent several hours in this old church hall and learned a lot while enjoying the fun and games. It's such a sad thought that none of the canine participants are still alive; they lead such short lives.

About the time that George was fully grown and as trained as I could get him, we had a sad event with Veronica's best friend splitting up from her husband. She moved in with us, which was a tight fit in that we only had one spare room and she had a boy of about six; she also had Ivan.

Now Ivan was a full grown 140 pound Newfoundland and I loved him. Black as coal, he fitted into our household as easily as a hand into a glove, and George who was a very amenable animal enjoyed him to.

There were only two problems with Ivan; one was that he was as dumb as a stump and two, that he could not resist water. If anyone ran a bath, Ivan's ears would prick up and he would prowl around outside the bathroom door. If you were foolish enough to leave the door open or ajar, he would rush in and climb in as well. It didn't matter if there was a human in the tub, and because he was so big it was very easy for him to climb over the edge of the bath.

Then came the difficulty of removing him. He would deliberately sit on the plug hole and because his fur was so dense it would block any water from escaping. Lifting a reluctant 140 pound soaking dog out of a bath takes a lot of strength. I know Ivan loved the struggle.

We attended a Newfoundland rally once somewhere in the Midlands. They were everywhere in the grounds of a stately home. Some pulled small carts with kids having rides, but the highlight was the water rescue event.

Here an owner would swim out to the middle of a small lake, while the dog would be restrained at the edge. At the command the owner would begin waving frantically and begging the dog to "save me!"

There was never any difficulty in getting the dog to plunge in and begin the swim, but truly these dogs are not very smart and their powers of concentration are limited. Soon after beginning the trek, many of the dogs would lose focus and start to swim around in circles or just go off, while the owner tried desperately to attract their attention. Some of these people would be left with no alternative but to set off and try and rescue the animal who had quite forgotten where or why it was there in the lake. Hilarious!

I went to another one-breed meet once with Stan my boss. For some reason he had found out that a Rottweiler gathering was taking place near where we had some business. We turned up at this fairly small semi-detached house near Camberley, and were welcomed in.

There must have been some two dozen of these big strong guard dogs roaming around the limited space of this small house, and they all seemed to be having a wonderful time. We managed to find somewhere to sit, having dislodged a couple of drooling beasts and watched events.

There was a lot of drool as there was a lot of food, and Rotts are permanently hungry. I have to say that seeing so many I was rather tempted to add one to my canine collection of one, but I knew that there would be trouble on the home front if I did.

Dogs are not an impulse buy or they never should be. Taking a trip to the local dog pound on a rainy Sunday afternoon is not for the weak minded. In fact for the dog snob, it's not even on the radar.

Sadly I fall into this category. I put it down to my country of origin. Only those at the extreme bottom end of the social strata have dogs of mixed parentage. You rarely have to ask what that dog is when out for a stroll. Being English we know our breeds, and if it's not one we recognise, then we can tell if it's just one we don't know or if it's a MONGREL!!!!!!

Now I have known a few mongrels in my time. There was the famous Bonzo, who lived next door to a friend called David up the road from my grandparents in Southampton. His heritage was buried so deep that it was impossible to fathom any links apart from Alsatian, which is German Shepherd out here. He was quite big and the king of the street dogs in the area.

When I was about twelve or so, a small gang of us used to meet up and roam around the nearby park, which was called Mayfield. We used to like to take Bonzo along with us as he was such a great animal.

His owner, who was also David's Aunty, would allow us to take him provided we didn't "get him into some awful condition."

She knew of what she spoke as on several occasions we had returned Bonzo to her with a thick coating of marsh mud all over.

I don't quite understand the mindset of young boys. I was one, so I should understand, but there is a type of drive that allows us to go ahead and do something which we know is wrong and for which there will be consequences. However we seem quite able to overcome the thought of the inevitable payback while we live every moment of the forbidden activity. My experience of girls has led me to believe that they lack this gene, except when it comes to pregnancy, but we've covered that elsewhere.

So off we would go with Bonzo trotting at our sides. No lead was ever used as Bonzo had all the incentive he needed. He was with his most favorite person in the entire world, Colin!

I never figured out what the attraction was between these two, but it was large. Colin lived several streets away but he could summon the dog with a piercing cry whenever the dog was out and Colin was within earshot, which in a dog's case is quite a long way off.

"Buuuuuooooooooonzooooooooooooo!" would be the call and a few moments later the great hound would appear with tongue lolling and tail rotating like a propeller.

As we made our way to the park, one thought was on all our minds. We had to get Bonzo into the swamp.

This was a large circular area of marshland that was usually covered with leaves and branches. To our eyes it looked a hard surface, but we knew it to be otherwise.

At some stage we had to get Bonzo occupied with some type of game, while Colin placed himself on the far side of the swamp. This was not easy as Bonzo tended to keep his eye on his hero.

Sometimes we failed entirely, but we were dedicated in our pursuit, and often we managed the deception. Out of the blue would come the piercing cry, "Buuuuuooooooonzooooooooooooo!" The dog would search around and if we were lucky he would make for the most direct route to his hero, which was straight across the muddy marsh.

The thick oozing nature of its consistency would not deter Bonzo from his goal and eventually he would make it across, having acquired a liberal coating. Once we had achieved our objective however, remorse would immediately set in.

Our return was full of concern that David's Aunty would be so furious that she would not allow the dog out again. Perhaps we could clean some of the filth off him? Perhaps a quick dip in the pond we came near to on the way home? But there were swans that lived there and we were scared of them.

Eventually we would arrive and sit the dog at the back door while we escaped to avoid the wrath that would surely be visited upon us.

In fact, David's Aunty would no doubt have simply washed the dog off with the garden hose she kept at the back door for the purpose. And Bonzo did need a fair bit of grooming to get him in any type of respectable condition.

As stated earlier, dogs are not impulse sales. However I have been sorely tempted on two occasions. Firstly there was a Dalmatian that I fell in love with in Richmond Park. A woman breeder was there with about four of them and one took my fancy. He was a noble animal and seemed to take a liking to me. I believe I had to be gently led away before I made a fool of myself.

Dalmatians are notoriously difficult dogs. They are very independent and hard to train, but they are gloriously elegant. Their history in the US fire departments across the land goes way back.

They were used firstly to warn the public outside the fire house that an engine was about to come out, and secondly they would run alongside the galloping horses to warn others of their approach.

Once they reached the scene of the fire, they would guard the equipment from other fire companies against any theft or tampering. Fire fighting was a very competitive business back in those days. To this day several fire departments keep a Dalmatian as a mascot.

My other close encounter in the impulse buy arena was at Crufts, the International Dog Show held at Olympia every year since 1891 – it moved not far away to Earl's Court in 1979.

Here I met and really fancied a smooth coated Retriever - out here they call them flat coated. He was jet black and a twin of George apart from the color. Again I had to be led away, this time with threats.

Impulse buying of any pet is silly and there have been many a family regretful of that decision to buy a cute little ball of fluff for Maisy for Christmas. "Won't she love it?" Well, maybe for a few weeks. But then when it grows into a ravenous, slathering brute, which can drag Maisy along the road on the very few occasions the child can be persuaded to take it for a walk, buyer's remorse is bound to set in.

And yet I can't think of any dog of any stripe that I have not liked, and even loved to distraction.

In my new life in California, we were so busy trying to make things work and with a young boy to raise that dogs did not enter our thoughts very much. We used to enjoy our neighbors' dogs when they were out walking, but we had little time for the luxury of dog ownership.

However, once Simon left the nest, we soon began to think about a dog. It had been about a decade since we had one and we felt up to it now.

We sat down with the Observers Book of Dogs and talked about the type of breed we should consider.

Yvonne had left "Angus," a West Highland Terrier behind in the UK with some people who spoiled him rotten!

We agreed that terriers could be a little on the difficult side. Angus had an annoying habit of depositing a rather large "motion" on the kitchen floor most mornings; it's not the best way to start the day!

So we kept terriers off the list; similarly hounds, who are very self-willed and can run off at the slightest opportunity. On and on we went crossing this breed and that breed off our list.

We lived in a "condo" with no garden and surrounded by lovely grounds upon which one could not in all fairness allow any dog to wander.

It would mean regular walks, which we could manage with few difficulties, but also we could not imagine a large dog in such circumstances.

Also the climate is quite mild and even hot, so moulting, or shedding as it's called out here had to be considered. Eventually we ended up with only one choice – a Poodle. What? A bloody French Poodle?

Yes, it seems a strange choice but it turned out to be very sensible. Also I found out that there was some history there, of which I had forgotten.

When I told my former wife about our choice, she reminded me of an episode on our first foreign holiday, to Paris.

We were sitting in the Tuileries not far from the Louvre, and a man came along with a pair of black Standards. I loved them and made a fool of myself until I realised that their French was fluent and mine only up to poor middle school standard.

Nonetheless, I vowed that when we returned home I had to have a pair just like them. Fortunately, my memory faded and switched on to the latest stereo or something equally foolish once home and the desire left me.

But once the decision had been made some thirty years later, we set about finding one.

Looking in the paper we found an ad that was asking for buyers at a Poodle rescue. Yvonne called and spoke to the lady.

After a fifteen minute conversation she hung up and looked rather upset.

"The woman was almost rude," she said. "Wanted to know where the dog would sleep and I told her on the kitchen floor, she reacted badly and said that Poodles have to be with people, they have to sleep on the bed!"

Now neither of us has been a proponent of dogs sleeping on human beds, but once we owned it that would largely be up to us, wouldn't it?

A few days passed and we had heard nothing from the woman. So I decided to get into the game. The phone was answered by a firm female voice and I reminded her of the previous call with Yvonne. Our accents are a big help in people recognising us, and the woman said she remembered.

I asked her what might be the problem. She replied that she was busy and she wasn't quite sure if we would be suitable.

Now there are not too many things that are guaranteed to upset a red blooded Englishman, but the suggestion that we might not be "suitable" to own a dog, is pretty much up there at the top of the list.

My hackles were raised as I answered her questions about earlier dogs I had owned. Barney and Lady were dismissed as "not counting." She was also a little concerned that I wasn't able to tell her exactly why some dogs I was involved with died.

Eventually she said: "Oh well, OK you can come along."

I suggested the following Saturday. "No, that's no good."

I said, "OK, you tell me when it's convenient." She suggested the following Sunday afternoon, "about two!"

She gave me directions and we began to think about the upcoming interview.

Now it should be mentioned that in her youth Yvonne had the nickname of "Spitfire!" For the gentlest and most ladylike of women, nonetheless it's advisable not to piss her off! I was concerned at what might happen on our visit.

From the tone and tenor of both our conversations with Sally Perkins, we imagined a somewhat dishevelled, overweight woman in a long hand-knitted cardigan, smelling slightly of puke (dog's of course.)

We arrived a large iron gate in the Hollywood Hills and as directed rang the bell and waited. The gate slid soundlessly open and we drove up a slightly curved drive to a large single storied house overlooking the LA basin. Thoughts of dishevelment began to vanish with each yard of the well manicured entranceway.

We were greeted by a late middle aged woman who had obviously in her prime been a great beauty. She apologised that she was just finishing up with another buyer and would we be kind enough to sit in her living room for a few moments.

The long hand-knitted cardigan was nowhere in sight.

The room was sunny and full of original works of art. I'm sure I spotted a David Hockney on the long wall behind the grand piano.

Ms. Perkins plonked a tiny white tea-cup Poodle on our laps with the suggestion that we might like to think about this one to be getting on with.

It was very tiny and not at all what we wanted. It also had a deformed hip, and I'm sorry, I'm far too selfish to take on a known problem before we even get down to house training.

Eventually we were taken outside and sat down on a couple of hard chairs. Ms. Perkins brought out a very nice miniature black Poodle called Molly. It was quite a lot of fun but somehow, it didn't set us alight, and I don't know why.

Then after we'd talked awhile, and found out that Ms. Perkins had been an opera singer and was married to Barbara Streisand's theatrical agent, we were introduced to another miniature black bitch. Yes, bitch, which is the correct term I have to remind my American friends!

This little dog came and sat right next to us. She was quite a bit smaller than Molly although well in the range of being a "miniature."

There was something about her and soon she jumped up on Yvonne's lap. A bond occurred and we gave Ms. Perkins a check. After some hints including one to let her sleep in a crate next to us at night, we left with the new member of our small family.

We stopped at a pet store on the way home and bought a travel crate, together with some other items necessary for the well equipped dog.

The dog's name was Whitney, which we thought was rather silly and so we intended to change it. We never did.

Soon after we arrived home, we sat looking at this little Poodle who seemed quite happy with her choice. We then looked at each other and said: "Can we ever love this?"

Well, for the next ten years we loved her exceedingly. And she loved us too. Unless I had been bad when she made it quite obvious that she didn't love Daddy. Normally, if I asked her that when I picked her up she would plant a small lick on my cheek to confirm her affections. If naughtiness had occurred, like telling her off, she would deign to plant one and instead would turn her head firmly away.

When she had to be groomed and it was time to have her nails done, she would lift each leg for attention. She was in truth a real Beverly Hills bitch, but in the nicest possible way, of course.

When she died it was perhaps the saddest day of my life, and for several months afterwards, I would get what I called Whitney moments.

Within a week we had made a call into a groomer that we used and ended up buying another black miniature Poodle bitch.

It eased the grieving as "Cora" was a dear little creature although not of the same quality as Whitney. Sadly after only nine months with us she jumped off the sofa one evening and suddenly was unable to walk properly. It was her heart and she died the next day at the vet's. Another sad loss.

This time we decided we would not be in a rush, and leave a decent pause before making another commitment. But that was before Simon made a call to us.

Now several years before, Simon had done exactly the thing I always counsel against. He'd gone to the pound and made a purchase.

This animal was a disaster. It had been manufactured at the doggy factory late on a Friday afternoon, just as it was closing. Obviously a worker had searched around and found a few bits and pieces lying about and decided to make one last dog before going home.

We were told it was part Corgi, part Beagle, and part Shar-pei! It looked like one of those Mexican hot rods where the front end had been lowered.

Yvonne loved her and Whitney thought she was cute, primarily because she could boss Sharpie, as the dog was called (naturally!) around.

Simon and Caroline were about to move to a flat where dogs were not allowed and so they immediately thought of their dogless parents. Naturally we would love to take this creature into our empty lives. Ya Think???

Yvonne was thrilled – me not so much. But up she came and settled in. She had not been very well, but the vet gave her a clean bill of health and she thrived under Yvonne's care. We all do!

There is no doubt that she much preferred her life with us in constant attendance to being left alone in the busy house of young professionals. She did have an annoying tendency to come in and pass gas in the middle of the night right next to my side of the bed. Enough to poison the sweetest dreams! In the end I had to resort to leaving all my shoes around the floor so there was nowhere for her to settle.

After a couple of years the lack of a Poodle began to build up in me and we started to talk about another. We saw no point in changing the game plan and therefore looked for another black miniature female. It was very hard to find.

However we did find a breeder in lake Arrowhead who had some dogs (in American that means little boy dogs!)

We weren't really interested but thought we'd go down there anyway. Looking back I think it was a Sunday afternoon, which if you've read this far you know is the very worst time to go out dog searching.

The woman breeder had three puppies with one bitch (little lady dog!) But this had been promised to another breeder in Florida. This left the two boys, one of whom looked perfect right off the bat. I took to him immediately.

The other dog was slightly smaller and the breeder said he was a little crazy. There had been a very bad hurricane in the South East of the country some few months earlier and it had been christened Juan – John. It was the name she had given to this other little puppy – Hurricane Juan. What fool is going to buy a dog that the breeder says is "a little crazy?"

Now apart from not going out on a Sunday afternoon to look at dogs, one should not take one's soft hearted wife along with one!

"Oh, we can't leave one alone here," was Yvonne's reaction to the thought of buying the first dog we liked. "He'd be all alone. We should buy them both!" The breeder warmed to her very much.

So with Juan as one name, it was easy to call them Frankie and Johnny and they came to us at the end of 2004.

They were only four months old on their arrival and we knew we had quite a lot of work ahead of us. We had bought a large fold out cage for them to live with us in the living room as well as two crates for night time.

We brought them in and put them in the cage which took up about an eighth of the room. Sharpie looked up from her bed in front of the fireplace, where like all old ladies she liked to warm herself. She waddled over to the corner of the cage and squatted down and peed on the carpet, something she had never done before or since.

In doggie speak it was the equivalent of telling the new arrivals: "OK fellahs, welcome, but just remember whose top dog here, or there'll be trouble."

As they grew up the boys, as they were always known became very fond of Great Aunt Sharpie and she of them. When they had their little thrashes around the living room chasing each other, she would rouse herself and waddle after them with what seemed a smile on her face.

She died when they were about eighteen months and I'm sure they missed her greatly, we rather did too.

Poodles are often thought of as lap dogs which or course they can be, as can any others. I knew a Great Dane once who liked to sit on the sofa, preferably on your lap if you'd allow it. He would walk in front of the spot he had chosen and then carefully he would back up, allowing his rear legs to fold up while leaving his front legs still on the carpet.

But Poodles are in fact of German origin and not French. Their name derives from "pudelhund" which means water dog, and they are in truth hunting dogs.

The rather strange bobbles of hair are floatation devices and also to keep the joints warm in cold water, but usually left these days purely for the show ring.

The ball on the tail is said to be a raised digit to its rival the British Bulldog.

There have been other dogs my life, mostly belonging to friends and relatives. I have been fond of them all. I don't like to diminish their importance by just a brief mention but time and space demand it.

Firstly there was Harley, a cross between a mastiff and a boxer, whom Simon and Caroline loved for many years, then his replacement, George – yes, another in the family. He's fairly new but shaping up beautifully. He a pure breed Boxer, who reminds me so much of my old friend Harry.

Michael and Eiko have a wonderful little King Charles Spaniel called Jasmine who is quite the deep water sailor. She is a joy to be around.

The other day the Pope decided to ease a young boy's mourning for his recently deceased dog. He told the young man that yes, he knew that dogs did really go to Heaven.

Up to now it had been a certainty that they did not, which rather put me off the entire Heavenly experience.

But now the Pope has perhaps changed his mind and maybe I'll have to start making amends. I would hate to miss the chance to meet up with all my four-legged loved ones.

I append the end quote as I think it's funny. However Poodles do get a bum rap.

I wonder if other dogs think poodles are members of a weird religious cult.
— Rita Rudner

Chapter Twenty-Seven
WEATHER

But who wants to be foretold the weather? It is bad enough when it comes, without our having the misery of knowing about it beforehand.
— *Jerome K. Jerome*

Pray don't talk to me about the weather, Mr. Worthing. Whenever people talk to me about the weather, I always feel quite certain that they mean something else. And that makes me quite nervous.
— *Oscar Wilde*

Weather is perhaps one of the most boring subjects in the world. There's nothing we can do about it unless you're a liberal and feel that things have taken a substantially better course ever since we banned plastic shopping bags.

However, perhaps in my case it's a genetic flaw, inherited from my grandfather, the naval one.

He was obsessed with weather. In fact when he died his diaries contained nothing but reports on that day's weather. Believe me, if the subject turns you off, then you'll be in no rush to find out how things were on Sunday, the 15th of April, 1948!

Now one has to accept that he served his time on board sailing ships and keeping a fair weather eye out must have been mandatory for anyone anticipating a climb up those rope ladders to keep watch.

Transferring to steam ships later on must have been no different as a storm out on the ocean is no funny thing, and the technology was not exactly perfect before GPS – how do you fancy working a sextant after all?

He used to become particularly concerned if the weather came out of the east. I can't see any reason for this as most of the bad stuff came out of the west with the Atlantic storms landing their final efforts on England's green and pleasant land.

I suspect that this eastern thing that he had was a hold over from very early times. Let's face it we had enemies over there and they wanted to get their hands on our island. A wind from that direction would assist their efforts no end; and certainly when there was nothing but a tacky old square sail to help them.

We never had anything serious to fear from the west. The Irish could stamp out a mean coracle, but they only held one man plus perhaps a skinny woman. One could hardly work oneself up into a state over a fleet of coracles.

Grandad also didn't believe in taking chances with weather. I lived with them for about nine months when I was sent down to look after the territory of Sussex, Hampshire and Dorset. Southampton was a perfect spot to live, being right in the middle. Naturally at 19 years of age it never once occurred to me that this might be a disturbance to their well ordered and simple lives. They never complained however.

Before I was given the ultimate joy of joys, a company car (in fact a rather nasty flashy van) I had to use public transport. We lived in the small adjunct of Woolston across the River Itchen, but there were buses that ran quite regularly around the long way.

There was a "floating bridge" that had centered on much of my early childhood when Grandad would take me on a couple of turns across and back. It was an old bulky thing that ran on a chain that the boat would pick up from the river bottom on its way across the three or four hundred yards. In its hey day there were actually two such ferries that crossed mid-stream; quite exciting if you're about five.

Fourteen years late it was mostly a pain as you had to hang around on the other side waiting for a bus there. It was a dismal and murky area too and one known to succour ruffians and hooligans. I don't know what it is about proximity to docks but they do seem to encourage the lowest of the low.

Southampton doesn't get a lot of snow, but one evening we had some. I had arranged to meet a friend over in the city, and as I was putting on my things, my Grandad asked me where on earth I was going. There was by now about quarter of an inch of snow on the ground. He simply couldn't believe that anyone would actually go out "in this weather!" He also thought that the transport authorities looked at such matters his way and that no bus driver worth his salt would actually risk the city's expensive equipment in such conditions.

I think he was stunned when I made the trip there and back and seemingly without incident. He didn't have to worry beyond his bedtime as I was never a "late bird," believing that if I couldn't get done what needed to be done by say nine, then it probably wasn't worth doing. I therefore returned to report that all had been well.

To this day when I go out in poor conditions then I think of how he would speak and how he would try and warn me of the dreadful risks.

Having said this, I do believe I have a little of Grandad's genes in me because weather is rather important to me, and I've noticed it in Michael's attitude as well.

The last address I had in England was almost exactly in the center of the "sunshine triangle." That triangle is roughly from Ventnor in the Isle of Wight up to Heywood's Heath in Sussex and then down to Eastbourne, if you know your English geography.

We did get more sunshine than the rest of the country, but not by a great deal.

If my opportunity to come out to the States had been located in Minneapolis, I suspect I would have given it a lot more thought, but Southern California? Now you're talking; sunshine, beaches – endless summer!

And in fact when we had been out here for a year we hardly registered winter at all down in Marina Del Rey.

There was one occasion in our first September when it rained quite heavily for a few hours. We had a balcony overlooking the extensive walkways and swimming pool of the apartment complex, where this unaccustomed downpour caused it to splash everywhere. We stood there and watched as the Del Reyians actually danced in the rain and sang in it as well – we were after all only a few miles from Hollywood!

Logically the Marina was probably not the most sensible address for a national business just starting up. But fortunately Richard's wife Edmeé, had spent a winter in Fairfield, New Jersey and having arrived in Southern California announced to him: "Well, Richard you may think you're going back to New Jersey, but I can assure you that I am not!"

I shall be forever grateful, even though New Jersey would have been a much more sensible center of operations.

Unfortunately Southern California is not considered a serious place by much of the rest of the country, as I found out after one presentation in New York.

Having done a reasonable job in front of a roomful of people in introducing our methods of improving productivity, I came to our list of references. I spoke of Crocker Bank (long since defunct,) Wells Fargo, (still going strong) and I think Barclays Bank who were just starting up out here.)

"But they're all California banks, don't you have any out here," was the question from the boss, a dark, gloomy man hunched in the center of the room.

Yes, we've got Manufacturers Hanover ((you bet we did, they'd loaned us a lot of our start up costs and they no doubt wanted to see that we were kosher!) "But that's in Brooklyn. I mean here in Lower Manhattan!"

I suspect I might have been a bit flip in mentioning that as far as I knew this was all one country, and the people they employed were no doubt much the same as his. I don't think the negotiation progressed far from then on. Let's review: a limey, telling a New Yorker that some outfit in God knows where the other side of the Rockies…!

Afterwards our agent at the time said to me: "You know it might be a little difficult convincing people here, if they think you're working in a beach community." He was right and a couple of times Richard and I did discuss the potential of moving to New York. The talk usually lasted about a minute after I asked him if he was going to move there, and him suggesting that perhaps I might. Not a chance!

I'm firmly convinced that it's the northern areas that make things happen the most. A look at Europe shows that the lower countries are the ones who take most of the summer off and invented the siesta. They also seem to have more saints and virgins all of whom claim a day off as well.

If the world is constantly raining, cold and damp, you have to invent houses and not just clamber into a nearby cave while enjoying another elk horn of Rieja before taking a nap.

Strangely enough however it's the northern lot who seem to struggle most with alcohol and seek out its warming effects. Moscow regularly has to drive trucks around picking up the drunks in winter to stop them from freezing to death. They don't have that problem in Madrid.

You take your life in your hands walking along Sauchiehull Street, Glasgow on a winter's Saturday night, whereas you'd solicit nothing more than a pleasant "buenas noches," outside a bar on the Paseo de Castellana in Madrid.

England has weather. It's a permanent feature of the culture in ways that it never is in other countries. The English are rather obsessed with it, as they are always surprised when it is poor, which it mostly is.

And yet when it turns out to be wonderfully sunny and dry, they panic that there could be a drought coming, or if after a long weekend of it they might already be in one.

I remember some time back in the mid-seventies that this occurred and the government had to appoint a Minister of Weather to begin to make arrangements to ration water when the time came.

As I remember, this individual was so effective that it began to rain after a couple of days of his appointment and it didn't stop for a year or two. No matter, the poor chap didn't lose his job, pension or benefits, he was made the Minister for Sport! We certainly needed one of those. (Please refer to Chapter Ten and the section on bureaucracies and governments.)

Good weather is one of those little bonuses in life that you just accept as normal. You don't make a big deal of it, just enjoying the day and occasionally remembering that if you're to meet people outside for an event, you don't have to append to the invite "Weather Permitting."

I believe that there are a couple of negative aspects with good weather that don't always strike you once you have it. For instance, I noticed that people out here in Southern California didn't seem to forge really strong bonds with their friends.

Most friendships seemed to be rather casual, and I wondered about that for some time. In the end I came up with this theory. In the UK or other northern countries, you would almost certainly meet up in their homes; out here it's restaurants or bars, and rarely back at people's houses.

Many houses here are quite modest, and even if there is a meet with people it's held outside on the deck or patio with a bar-b-que. If you have to spend a few hours in someone's house, then it's far more intimate with their possessions all around.

I have noticed that people who hail from the East Coast, where the weather is quite changeable, will invite you to their houses, where most native Californians prefer an outside venue. From a personal viewpoint, that suits me fine.

The other problem with constant good weather is that people lose the ability to drive in any other type.

If you ever go to Madrid, and it rains, watch out at cross roads. Madrileños expect their cars to stop immediately if they stamp on the brakes. They don't understand that after several months of hot dry conditions a rain squall makes every road a skid pan.

And then there is the fun of watching Mexicans drive up the hills into the snow and attach chains to the wrong set of tires, or carry on as if four-wheel drive stops them from skidding. It doesn't!

After 17 years of living in the Marina Del Rey area we retired and moved to Big Bear Lake. It never crossed our minds to do otherwise as we'd had a home there since 1989.

Now here we have WEATHER! Mostly that comes in the form of snow in the winter. At the time of writing we had an overnight storm from right out of the Arctic and it dropped about six inches of snow overnight. Furthermore it left behind a great swath of cold, freezing air to follow.

It was eleven degrees this morning and we're not talking about some whoosey Centigrade here, but good old American Fahrenheit.

But up at 6,750 feet above sea level in the San Bernardino Mountains, we do have 300 days of sunshine, although on days such as this it's not the sort you want to sit out in wearing a bikini.

Winter storms here are not truly the type of winter that the northern states enjoy. This stuff is baby winter, not the real men's stuff like they have in Montana.

I haven't talked to Michael yet about which is his favourite state in the USA, but I bet Montana comes very high on the list. I wish I could fully explain the draw of it as for seven or eight months it's unliveable in,

However, although we only spent a few days there in the middle of August I can quite easily understand how people endure the harsh climate that begins to set in at the end of September and doesn't let up until early May.

The majesty of the place is amazing and accepting that you can barely go outdoors for most of the winter, the size and scope of the place is addictive. No wonder they call it Big Sky country.

Our winters are the same as Montana's in the same way that our summer Hummingbirds are like their Bald Eagles – attractive, but not exactly dangerous.

However on checking this morning our six a.m. temperature was one degree higher than West Glacier in Montana, although Missoula clocked in at one degree F. Pretty chilly.

You can't take chances with Mother Nature even in our benign climate. There are ancient sepia photographs that show the old trappers and miners leaning up against ten foot tall snow drifts here.

A few winters ago my big gas-powered snow plough just couldn't handle the six feet fall that came in. We had to hire a back hoe and driver, who labored away for an hour to allow us access to our driveway. We even had the joists crack on our garage roof and they had to be strengthened by a friendly contractor as the one who built it did not do enough. All roofs up here have to be able to support an eight foot fall. But is that wet snow or the dry stuff that fell on us recently?

It can strike at any time from mid-December to early April, but once you get around the bend of mid-January the days begin to lengthen even though imperceptibly.

Both Yvonne's mother and mine had birthdays at this time and once that passes I check a little calendar I have in my desk to see how much extra daylight we get each day. It's only a couple of minutes a week to begin with, but it's surprising how it builds up. You can tell by the elevation of the sun mid day that by February we're getting on with the season.

Although I marginally prefer winter here to summer, once we get in to March or April, a late snow fall and corresponding drop in temperatures causes all of us locals to somewhat groan. Although the ski slopes love it.

Skiers are a fickle lot however and I have known several years where we have had good ski conditions but no customers. By Easter they've usually skied themselves out and are looking to the beach for their fun and games.

The best times of the year in Big Bear are spring and autumn. This is the time when the flatlanders stay away for some reason, and the warm air is full of the sound of the whining of hoteliers and merchants.

Like farmers with the weather they are never satisfied with the flow of visitors and complain annually. Those of us not in business however revel in the silence and the lack of traffic.

Summer can take awhile coming and there is an old saying up here not to put your bedding plants in before Mother's Day. A couple of years ago even that date of around May 10ᵗʰ was too early as we had a late frost that caused all the nurserymen to cheer with repeat and miserable clients a week or so afterwards.

Once summer is here and we can don our shorts and T-shirts Big Bear can be truly wonderful. Even when the lake is down there is plenty of water and boats are out there from dawn to dusk. Cyclists are exploring the mountain trails and chancing their skills on the 15 mile around the lake ride.

One advantage of coming to California has been the virtually complete absence of hay fever. I suffered from this beast from the age of 21 when it hit me one day while I was in Portsmouth. It is like a bad head cold with accompanying chills.

I managed a couple of years off with a series of injections that I had to give myself as they had to be administered daily. The idea was that you started off with a 20 strength dose and gradually built up to 20,000 in strength. It was the final one that cured you. Unfortunately the effect wore off with each year and by the fourth one it was no good at all.

I used to search around for computer rooms for some relief and many of my customers in the industry were kind enough to let me spend a few hours working in them.

Being allergic to grass pollen, once I arrived out here I found that there was little of it that would last beyond a day or two. I did get it a few times but never as badly as I used to in London, which seemed to act like a magnet for the stuff. Up in the mountains the season seems to be a few days in April. In England it starts about May 23ʳᵈ and there's very little variation in the date. It also lasts through July and sometimes into mid-August.

Don't knock the weather. If it didn't change once in a while, nine out of ten people couldn't start a conversation.
— *Kim Hubbard*

Chapter Twenty-Eight

SPORTS

Sports is for morons!
Bill Handel, Early morning LA talk show host

If winning isn't everything, why do they keep score?
Vince Lombardi

Because I was always tall for my age and of course, slim – nearly everybody was after Hitler's attempt on our lives – my father had great hopes for me as a sportsman.

The few short fat people around were never expected to exceed in sports as they were simply the wrong shape. Also the "delicate" ones were usually let off.

We had a couple of those at school and they were never bullied I remember, although they would have made easy targets. Rather they were known to be very good at chess and stamp collecting which the rest of us rabble never attempted.

I did have a go at stamps once, but as my heart was set on one of those mysterious triangular ones and they cost a fortune, once again the lack of funds put a dent in my plans.

I'm sure that such disappointments in one's youth are a very important part of growing up and forming one's character. It's not surprising that the offspring of exceptionally wealthy people tend to go off the rails. Particularly those whose parents have had a windfall like winning the lottery or starring in a James Bond movie.

But sports turned out for my father to be yet another disappointment in his one and only son.

It's not that I was bad at sports, but it was more a lack of commitment to the goal of winning at all costs; and that I'm sure is what takes precedence over any natural talent. Of course, if you've got both then you're likely to end up on the rostrum of a big event.

The first major upset came in the squat form of Constantine. My father foolishly had insisted that I enter for my prep school's boxing tournament – "it would be good to do Trevor!" Naturally, as my father was the fount of all knowledge, I overcame that odd little feeling in the stomach that one gets when looking over a very high point or knowing that something is definitely not right.

We were paired with our opponents by weight, and I weighed about 65 pounds I guess, as I was only about seven years of age.

Constantine however was 13 and looked it. He was short but built like a fire plug. I think he had begun to shave twice a day; he had the look of a pugilistic nightmare. He entered the ring, snorting like a bull and pounding the air in front of him; no doubt to intimidate me, which he did most effectively.

I was pushed into a pair of fading leather gloves about the size of my head and made to sit down on a stool in one of the corners.

Now both the gym master and my father had given me the rudiments of the noble art – right arm tucked across the body, chin behind the right glove and the left hand up to strike a mortal blow.

I suspect that Constantine might have been a southpaw, but at the sound of the bell, he shuffled forward across the canvas and ignoring my outstretched left arm completely, he hit me in the nose and then followed that up with a second to the stomach.

I hadn't experienced such pain in my life and fell back against the ropes. Some lunacy inside forced me to go back for more punishment whereupon Constantine repeated the medicine.

He was the archetypical shuffling powerhouse with fists working like pistons and a type of breathing that resembled a farmhouse animal. I back-pedalled; he advanced; I backpedalled more; he still came on.

In the end I had no other recourse, but to turn away from him and actually run around the ring. It may not have been a pretty sight, but it was damned effective, as his squatness was no match for my fleet footedness.

Eventually the bell thankfully sounded and I was put out of my misery as the ref disqualified me. The humiliation of the event didn't strike home for several hours. On the way home on the bus it struck my hitherto innocent mind that maybe in the future I should be wary; wary of my father's enthusiasm for joining in activities in which I had never witnessed him partake.

Apart from some oft repeated story about a try out on the tennis court for the county, I had only actually ever seen my father run on one occasion. He was pretty good at it during a sport's day at his firm's summer party. He came over the finish line of the 100 yards all of a sweat and actually won a pair of gold cufflinks. But that was it. From then on his sole contribution to the world of sport was as a spectator and even that was relatively short lived; well in the flesh.

Soon after he was forced to draw a line through the "International Boxing Champion" in my future resume, he decided to light the fire in me of a possible place in the country's football team. By this I mean the game of soccer. It was nowhere near as painful or as humiliating as my shortened bout with Constantine, but it was pretty bad.

For several Saturdays he would take me off to Vicarage Road where Watford would pit their defective skills in the third division against all comers.

We were a bit short in the financial department and so we had to stand in the terraces. These were concrete steps with iron bars located at intervals so that men could take some of the weight off. Sadly at eight my face came up to about the level of the bars and they therefore didn't work too well.

My memories of this special time with my father were that it was mostly raining. I also didn't get the feeling that he was enjoying it a lot more than me. It rained with that persistent English drizzle that soaks everything, and especially a gabardine raincoat which was the uniform of choice for all of us under the age of about 15.

He was well into his Welsh phase and therefore would become quite agitated when a forward called Dave Thomas ever got within a few yards of the ball. Even with this divine skill, Watford rarely rewarded my father with a win.

A few years later, the league in its wisdom formed a fourth division and I think Watford was sent into it immediately.

The game seemed to go on for ages and with no watch – children didn't possess such things - I had no way of knowing how much more of this misery I had to endure. But then there were the half-time shenanigans of the brass band.

Old and generally limping men would march around the field with a sheet into which we young lads would be encouraged to throw a penny or two. That was it. The famous half-time show!

As we staggered into the second half, my entire being was focused on how early I could persuade my father to leave before the always disappointed crowds started streaming out of the gates.

By now the future of the game was rarely in doubt and there seemed little point in prolonging the misery. There were a couple of occasions when having left the ground, trudging along on our way to the homeward bus, a roar would go up announcing the miracle that Watford had scored. I really didn't care as I was out of there.

I have always felt sorry that our time together at these matches was not a lot of fun. I know my father wanted to have his son enjoy his interest, but it was not to be so. But it did give one little gift to me and that is a profound hatred for the game of soccer.

Some time ago I returned to the UK to visit my mother for a visit. There was a TV in my room and on the Sunday I turned it on to be met with every channel spouting information on the previous day's games. It was amazing to hear so much talk about such a boring game.

It is of course, much the same here. But at least the game is far more interesting with so many opportunities for actual injury.

I am a member of a local gym and it never ceases to amaze me how many of the men there spend their time talking about the results of games past and future. It is sometimes endless with speculation and often tinged with pride or humiliation. Humiliation is something I know about after my extended time in the boxing ring I can tell you!

I quite like American sports and slowly I have learned a little about football with all its many rules and regulations.

The one problem they all have in common is that they last far too long. Perhaps it's my lack of concentration but to me three hours plus to watch any game is tedium in the extreme.

I rather like baseball, but it seems to me that nine innings is far too long. If it were say five, I could get into it more. Football has caught me on several occasions postponing a trip to the bathroom as there were only three minutes on the clock. After twenty-five, my need has reached alarming proportions and I have had to leave believing that I'll miss the result. But no, on return there was a time out, and an overturned call.

This season, appealed calls are now reviewed by a team of specialists in New York. For Heaven's sake what's next, a couple of Philadelphia lawyers on hand to sort out discrepancies?

I can't see the appeal of basketball at all and yet once the Super Bowl is over sometime towards the end of January, there is nothing on apart from this game. It seems to have been designed exclusively for seven-foot tall Negroes with pituitary gland problems.

I don't see the point of having a net at the same height that these fellows can reach. Why not stick it up another couple of feet and let the little guys have a chance. Surely in this fair-minded liberal world of ours, it's just not fair that only giants can get into the game. Can't we have affirmative action for shorties?

What the heck is going on with ice-hockey? Here we have perhaps the most contrived of all sports. To begin with it's inside on man made ice. I have written about ice rinks for my column a couple of times and I can tell you it's cold inside there.

I was dragged along once to watch a match. It was in 1968 and it was between Russia and Czechoslovakia. The former had invaded the latter's country some four weeks before and it would be fair to say that this was a grudge match.

It was a great experience if you like an all-out brawl. For that is what it was. I'm not too sure how many referees are involved in an ice hockey game but they needed all of them to separate the many fist fights that were going on all over the place.

Once again I think the game could be shortened as it's far too long. Also there is nowhere near enough scoring. I would like to see midgets used as goal keepers as the goal is currently far too small. You can't make the goal much bigger as it would make that great little manoeuvre around the back of the net impossible. But if you had a midget in defence, I think it would increase the scoring and make for quite a lot of entertainment, particularly if you took away all the padding.

If there were a lot of applications for this position from the vertically challenged community, I think we could certainly use them on the soccer field as that too suffers from too small a target area. Hence the lack of scoring, and no doubt this is responsible for the general ambivalence of the country here to really get into the game. We prefer decent sized scores – like our portions of fries!

My father eventually gave up visiting Vicarage Road and instead poured his enthusiasm into the football pools.

Now these devices to get you rich quick appeared sometime in the forties I think. They must have been a great comfort for the middle-class gentleman who had a recalcitrant son and a declining interest in watching the local team get thrashed.

At about five-ish, my father would turn on the radio set and allow it to warm up. That would take about five minutes. Then knobs would be turned and much tuning would occur.

I seem to remember that brass band music would be playing right up until the time of the awaited announcements. Then the voice would begin. "Here are today's football results." Until it was over, my mother and I were warned to keep absolutely silent.

My father would have his multicoloured piece of paper at the ready with a pencil in hand. The object of this weekly religious ceremony was to pick eight draws – that is games where the two teams were unable to score a win. There were three or four divisions with about fifteen teams in each so there were a lot of games.

Usually quite early into the proceedings my father would throw down his pencil and write off this week's dream of wealth beyond our wildest dreams!

Like a regular churchgoer however, his faith would remarkably return for another shot the following Saturday evening. I believe his sum total of winnings over several years was a paltry few pounds. But his hope was kept alive. We had a passing interest as well, because "someone has to win it." I have learned in the forthcoming years that this is a poor excuse for gambling.

At the time the magic number for winning the pools was 75,000 pounds – about $120,000 in today's dollars. Sadly this is just about the amount you'd need to live in Los Angeles and buy a house. Inflation!

Back at school I was expected to do all the various sports, no matter how unsuitable they might be. We didn't do wrestling, which was delegated to a TV spectacle on a Saturday afternoon, and boxing was not high on the agenda. I was glad of that after my episode with Constantine.

But we had indoor activities in a well equipped gym and an entire bag full of outdoor stuff to help us develop from miserable little whimps into grown up champions.

We had an annual "standards" athletic activity, where you were expected to do all the track events within a standard time and your results were put into a chart so that your house might win a cup. Oh Whoopee! It was here that I was accused of not having any "house spirit." I don't know who accused me, but they were right.

As in my reticence to get inspired at the progress of the cardboard Alfa Romeo car around the track at The Crusaders, I couldn't get excited at how well Swifts did at standards.

I did however want to achieve what was necessary as I saw it as a little personal challenge and joined in with the few who would run the 440, 880 and the mile in one go. It was quite hard, but we managed to do it and then swaggered around watching the rest run it in three separate races.

I succeeded in learning how to high jump and did that for the school, but that was my only time as a school representative.

I did have one other special race, and that was a challenge to a boy called Alan Dunningham. I'm not quite sure what the problem was as he was a fairly decent chap, and lived quite near me.

But he was sports mad and used to rather swing his weight around. He also had every conceivable piece of kit for every sport, and used to brag quite a lot. I've never liked bragging.

I got fed up with it and one day I threw the gauntlet down. I challenged him to a race around the castle, which was about a third of a mile.

Now Berkhamsted with a "ham" and a "sted" in its name shows that it was a quite important place for the Romans and they had left a castle there. By the fifties it was just a large mound of earth, but it was much visited by academics interested in the subject.

To my shame I have to confess to never having visited it during my time there, but it did make for a decent amount of running track.

We set off and Dunningham stayed close to my left shoulder. It seemed impossible to shake him off, but as we came down the final stretch I noticed that he was no longer quite with me. He had overdone it and had broken. I was the winner and felt pretty good about it.

Dunningham didn't show off in front of me after that and tended to give me a wide berth. But the adrenalin rush of the win soon left me and perhaps that is one of the secrets to my slight aversion to sports in general.

I never found the joy of winning to be anywhere equal to the pain of defeat.

Also I much preferred individual games to collective ones. This was to follow me throughout my life in lots of different activities.

Perhaps that's why I prefer American sports to English ones, apart from perhaps cricket, which I came to enjoy in my last few years living there.

Granted cricket is billed as a team game but it's very much an individual activity when you look at it, with a bowler pitted against a batsman - as in baseball.

When I had to play the game I was so poor that I was always delegated to some outer fielding position, where there was little chance of the ball ever reaching me. Unfortunately this only added to the boredom and I used to go into a sort of self induced doze, whereupon if the ball did make its way to me I had to be shouted at to "WAKE UP!!!"

Rugby too has a certain element of individuality when you see a three-quarter charging down the field. Soccer on the other hand has always been for me twenty men running around with a soggy ball on a muddy field. Yes, I know there are twenty two, but two of them just hang around the goal mouth. I was given the chance to do that once, but the call to "WAKE UP" reached me too late!

She Who Must Be Obeyed has recently become a devotee of ten pin bowling. I've had a go at it several times and I can claim to have bowled 197 on one occasion. It was pretty heady.

So far SWMBO has not quite reached that score, but I know it's a goal of hers and the day will surely come.

She attends a league twice a week with some old people. I have tried to explain that the reason I don't go along to support her is that like all old people her fellow bowlers spend most of their time dwelling on their health problems.

What is it with old people and illness? I know that for them it can be the single most important thing in their lives, which is quite understandable, but can't they see the eyes glossing over in the faces of their unfortunate audience?

I have had to tell her that not only do I dislike such discussions, with my Victorian upbringing I believe fervently that such "old people's" talk is contagious. And I might catch something.

On her return from the local Bowling Barn however, she tends to tell me of the latest health disaster to have hit one (or all) of her team.

There are tales of diabetes injections into the stomach in order that the game can go on. I have to disabuse her of straying outside the confines of the actual game. Such illness might be transferred through a carrier after all.

SWMBO is quite sporty in fact, and will watch most games on TV, if left alone.

Her particular speciality was show jumping, at which she was quite a champion. We have several silver cups to attest to that. In truth her real event was dressage, but she was steered off that path by her mother, who didn't much fancy sitting around watching a horse going through its paces in a ring and where you really have to be a rider to know what the hell is going on. So show jumping it was.

I too had some experience with horse riding or horseback riding as they call it out here. Why is that by the way? One can hardly horse neck, or horse belly ride can one? It's pretty much the back or nothing. But I digress.

I had a friend who liked to ride and invited me to come along. It was quite good fun, trotting along, once you'd learned how to "post." If you couldn't do that it was quite uncomfortable. Much better to move up a gear or two and go for the canter or even better the gallop.

I did have a couple of occasions where the horse got into the spirit of things a little too much and got away from me. We were not far from the stables and on both occasions they ran back there with me gamely hanging on as best I could.

Then there was Kirkland.

Yvonne had been looking after this magnificent ex-racer at the local stables in Playa del Rey. He was a large chestnut and we both enjoyed him very much. Yvonne had done the dressage stuff with him and I have to tell you that anyone who had only a slight knowledge of horsemanship would know that SWMBO knows her stuff when it comes to riding. Kirky would pretty much do anything she wanted including that crossing over of the legs on the diagonal. Funny thing was Yvonne didn't seem to be doing anything but sit on him. "It's all in the hands," I have been told many times. But SWMBO also reminds me it's mainly the muscles in the seat and legs. And I just thought you got on the beasts and rode them.

One day I said I'd like a go on Old Kirky. She said OK, but he'll know if you can't ride. I brushed such nonsense off and mounted. I have to say that in the intervening few decades, the height of a horse appeared to have increased dramatically. But off we went around the ring. See, no problem here at all.

I thought we'd done fairly well in first gear, and suggested to Kirky that maybe we could move up a notch. He misinterpreted my slight kick to his sides and went straight into third and then amazingly he went through fourth and right into fifth – the full stretch gallop. I could feel the wind blasting through my unhelmeted hair; it was exhilarating!

It didn't take long to realise that we were going a little too fast and I tried to put on the brakes. This didn't seem to work and by now Kirky was going around the track at a fearsome rate. The ring was edged by telephone poles cut to about four feet above the ground. There were large ropes in between. I could hear these swishing past as we galloped along. Kirky was having the time of his life; me not so much.

SWMBO had never let him seriously have a go at a good run before, and here was this spirited fellow on him loosening the reins like in the old days at the track.

But it was bound not to end well. Back in my mind I remembered at about the fifth lap that the way to control an out-of-control horse was to gently turn him into ever decreasing circles. I began this manoeuvre and I was quite pleased with the initial results. We reached a circle of a few feet, at which time Kirky got fed up with the game and dropped his shoulder and came to a full stop.

I had not been expecting this and with nothing to grab on to I sailed over his head and landed flat on my back – fortunately onto the soft sand.

Kirkland then trotted over to Yvonne, who no doubt was showing some concern for the safety of her husband. He shook his head and nuzzled her with no doubt horsey language that said: "That was really great. You can bring him by any time!"

For several nights I had visions of those poles whizzing by me and the horror of perhaps Kirkland jumping them and careening off on to the Richard M. Nixon Expressway which under the renamed moniker of route 90 was quite close by.

A day later my misery of the entire episode was to be repeated when a conversation broke out in the office about riding in general. In her most English and imperious tone Yvonne announced: "Well I thought you could ride, but Kirkland proved otherwise!" My shame was complete!

About the only "sport" that I managed any true proficiency in was snooker. And that was at a time when it was said that snooker was evidence of a misspent youth.

In fact towards the end of my time stretched over the green baize snooker became accepted into polite society.

The BBC needed a short twenty minute spot to fill a blank in their up-market channel BBC2,

A man called Ted Lowe managed to convince the management that snooker would fit right into their needs. It started very slowly and then built a substantial audience.

Lowe was one of the regular commentators and is legendary for saying back in the early seventies: "For those of you watching in black and white the pink ball is next to the green!"

With a strict dress code of formal wear – dinner jacket removed to expose a waistcoat – the scene was reminiscent of a gentlemen's club, and not the stained tables of a beer hall, which had always been the usual venue.

My exploits never amounted to very much and when I left the front line of sales to join the management of Keyboard Training in 1972, I had to have one of those little "come to Jesus" meetings with myself. I knew that I didn't have the talent to be a real success at the game and now that I had been given an opportunity to advance several rungs up the ladder, I better put my cue in the rack and concentrate on a career.

I still enjoy seeing the occasional game of pool on TV, but it lacks the finer points of snooker. Perhaps it's the overall dimensions of the table and the game. As I've often told people out here, in the UK we have smaller pockets, but the Americans have bigger balls.

If you want to see the most perfect example of a game of snooker – it's a little one-sided - then ask Google to find you the 147 break of Ronnie O'Sullivan. It takes about 10 minutes and without doubt lifts the activity to the level of pure poetry. Not a single poor shot or accidental stroke.

I would have thought that the knowledge that you are going to be leapt upon by half-a-dozen congratulatory, but sweaty team-mates would be inducement not to score a goal.
— Arthur Marshall

I think my favorite sport in the Olympics is the one in which you make your way through the snow, you stop, you shoot a gun, and then you continue on. In most of the world, it is known as the biathlon, except in New York City, where it is known as winter
— *Michael Ventre, L.A. Daily News*

Chapter Twenty-Nine
PROGRESS

The reasonable man adapts himself to the world: the unreasonable one persists in trying to adapt the world to himself. Therefore all progress depends on the unreasonable man.
— *George Bernard Shaw*

The test of our progress is not whether we add more to the abundance of those who have much; it is whether we provide enough for those who have too little."
— *Franklin D. Roosevelt*

I have on several occasions written of my dislike for all things bureaucratic and socialist in nature. However it would be churlish of me not to acknowledge that some government agencies do good work and also that if it were not for some form of socialism, all the marbles might well end up in the pockets of the very few.

In the case of governments, I can report that my dealings with Her Majesty's Government have been extremely good. I can't believe that their public servants are any more efficient than the ones out here.

I recently wanted to renew my British passport and having done the requisite form on line, I mailed off the old one, not quite out of date, plus a new photo and hoped for the best. To my amazement, a new one was sent back to me via DHL International in 13 days. Pretty good all around.

Not so much luck however with Yvonne's request for the same service. For some reason hers was more out of date and an old "blue" one.

It had four different hand written signatures and other script and the officials didn't like it at all. They send back an email saying that she had to apply as if she's never had one before.

They had tried to combine two forms in one which made for some confusing instructions – it was to do with counter signatories in the case of a passport for a child that caused the muddle.

Also she had to have her picture signed and dated by a person of some substance in the community – not easy to find in Big Bear!

All this was completely absent from my application. Anyway we've sent it all off and will await the response. They've cashed the check anyway!

As I have such a dislike of bureaucrats and their power, I'm probably not the best to judge how effective all their policies have been.

Just recently an agency here reported that in the last two years 49% of the world's wealth is now in the hands of one percent. This has increased from 48%.

If you accept that total liberalism leads inevitably to totalitarianism, and total conservativism leads to anarchy, then we should try to find some way of meeting in the middle.

And yet there has been some definite progress in my life of 75 years.

To begin with let's look at material wealth. My great grandfather, who ran a couple of collieries in South Wales before he retired, and whom I knew until his death in 1950 at age 94, never owned his own house. He always lived in rental properties.

Both sets of grandparents bought the houses that they rented when they were about 65. I remember the family discussions that went on for hours about the pros and cons.

My father bought his first house when he was about 46. And I bought mine when I was about 34. When I married Veronica, her father put us into a house but never turned the deeds over to us. This resulted in all kinds of tax difficulties later on.

I was still in that condition when I decided to try for some independence and bought a second home down at the beach in Selsey. It was quite modest, but we enjoyed it very much. I like to think that had my father-in-law not been so generous I would have made the move a few years earlier.

Michael bought his first house when he was about 21 – precocious lad. He now owns houses in three countries, all bought by himself over time.

Simon and Sue similarly got into houses quite early on out here. I've always counselled young people to take this first step as it's really important if you want to build any wealth.

Unfortunately, the way things are going at the moment it seems to be much more difficult to do all the things that were possible just twenty years ago.

I've always thought of opportunities in life a bit like a string held between two hands. It seems the hands have been getting further and further apart and the string is getting tighter. No one knows how tight it really is, but with 18 trillion dollars in debt and no attempt to stop the reckless spending, I fear it's getting very tight indeed. Without funds opportunities will dry up.

When we arrived here in 1982, it was quite possible for an average salesman to earn sufficient money to buy a house, run a car and put away money for his children's college. Naturally this assumes he also had a wife helping out as well.

Over the last six years, salaries have shrunk by an average of between two and three thousand dollars a year. Correspondingly inflation still continues and basics like food and healthcare have increased. No longer could that average salesman do what he could thirty years ago.

Recently a young lady of our acquaintance told us that she had been to the hospital's emergency room a few months ago with a breathing problem. She was dreading the bill and as it hadn't arrived she called the hospital. They told her there was no charge as it was covered by the new healthcare laws. These were brought in against the will of the populace and with not a single Republican vote in favour.

She said she felt very awkward as although she knew it would be a struggle, she was prepared to cope with it. In her words: "The treatment was free." But the fact is that someone has to pay for it somewhere along the way. I fear that now we have bred another person with a dependency attitude. Is this by design or accident? I wish I could answer that worrying question.

Progress has been dramatic in so many ways in my lifetime and I do believe I have been very fortunate to have lived in such a period.

The advances in medicine, transportation, entertainment, housing and overall technology have been so remarkable that only a generation or two back would be bewildered at how much improved life has become.

And yet are people any more happy; or grateful. Gratitude seems to me to be lacking in our wealthy society, and I wonder why.

The second quote to head this chapter says much. As one of the liberal icons of the last hundred years FDR tried hard to make life easier for the people at the bottom of the pile. But was he successful? It's very hard to say.

LBJ announced the Great Society in the mid-sixties and having poured in billions since the level of poverty is still about the same. Mind you many of those so listed have cars and color TV sets in their living rooms. But we don't seem able to resolve the problem of the income gap.

Perhaps I have a little of the bolshie in me, but I have never quite understood why a CEO can make literally millions of dollars in salary and benefits while the janitor is scraping by on minimum wage. And yet it's the way of the world and all the economists and socialists can't seem to figure out the solution.

We have reached six years of the administration of the most left-wing president ever. With promises of Hope and Change, most of us were pleased to have the first back man in the White House.

I don't believe Obama to be a bad man, in fact perhaps he suffers like so many on the left with an overdose of altruism. But beware an altruist who only wants the sacrifices to be made by you.

We are now worse off in our racism ideals and the middle classes are a lot worse financially. And yet we don't seem to have any solutions even from the ultimate do-gooder himself who only mouths the same promises of a Robin Hood society.

But if a governor is not put on the abilities of the clever and already wealthy they will end up as I said earlier with all the marbles.

And yet I can certainly attest to people being a lot better off than in my earlier life. Also I think they are a lot more secure with safety nets being larger and more widely spread.

I worry about the declining standards in education as although children have an enormous advantage in learning with the Internet available to all, they don't seem to have the necessary discipline or curiosity to capitalise on it. I doubt I would have either when I was a child.

Without some discipline exerted in the classroom and also at home, only a clever and well motivated child will succeed and end up with more marbles than the rest. And so that appears to be the crux of the matter —motivation and self discipline. Two things that I couldn't claim to have in my early years. But I had the advantage of a system that literally beat some sense into me when I regularly failed. Detention was a class I had to attend regularly.

My bedroom windows regularly had ice on the inside of them when I got up on a winter's morning. You could see the evidence of Jack Frost quite plainly. Such a situation today for a growing child would probably place them in some governmental care program. But did it do me any harm?

The idea of watching morning TV news or playing a video game on a laptop was out of the question through the 40s and the 50's and was hardly even the stuff of science fiction. And yet how quickly we have adapted to these wonderful inventions and how soon we forget how it used to be.

Most Saturdays my father would make the trip down to Watford High Street to the National Provincial Bank to cash a check to give money to my mother. It was an unpleasant journey and ended up with us being in a line along with lots of other men doing the same thing.

Today, we have plastic cards that can be swiped in a variety of slots and money, if we actually need it is readily available, if you've got it in the bank to begin with of course.

How long before we have a magnetic strip inserted in our persons and that will allow all kinds of transactions – also it will allow the authorities to keep track on us every minute of the day. Remember the system in Brave New World, by Aldus Huxley?

In Chapter 15 I covered many of these technological advances in my life, but in this chapter about progress it's more about how we as a species have improved. And I fear it's not too much.

Back in the seventies I met a man called Dr. Christopher Evans. He was the chief computer scientist for the British National Physical Laboratory.

He was a genuine scientist and quite an interesting chap. He turned up for our meeting wearing a jeans suit, open necked shirt and carrying one of those aluminum briefcases. Richard was somewhat slighted at this appearance. But we pressed on.

Over lunch in a Greek restaurant opposite I asked him what he thought was our future – the future of the human race. He replied that he thought we were doomed. Unless we could develop computers fast enough to take decisions away from us.

His reasoning was that mankind had not developed it's intelligence in the last several hundred years, however we had developed machines and methods that were becoming far too advanced for us to control them.

He continued that at one time, the worst we cold do to an opposing civilisation, was to throw rocks at them or perhaps shoot arrows. Today we have the technology to destroy an entire country with nuclear weapons.

I don't see Dr. Evan's pessimistic view having improved in the forty years since I met him. In fact it seems that instead of just one adversary – the Soviets – we now have many, and none of them too reasonable.

So for the future I am a little glum. We have more that enough labor saving and technological devices – most of them we don't really understand completely. What we seem to need is an improvement in human nature.

How do we continue along a path where bad people still get into positions of power and then threaten all of us?

What does one do for instance with a man line Putin or the Ayatollah, who seem impervious to our threats or pleadings?

From our side, on the one had we have the "Bomb the heck out of them" brigade and on the other there are the "We just need to talk to them to get them to understand." The problem is that there is not common ground with either of these positions.

Ayn Rand was once asked about such a situation. She said it wasn't a choice between living or dying it was more a choice of being killed or committing suicide.

I look at the world these days and am amazed that our so called enemies can't see how wonderful their opportunities are compared to their ancestors. But of course, if your dwelling is a tent and you live by herding goats, there isn't much improvement from 1000 years ago.

But their leaders of course enjoy their TV's and DVD's and the best medicine, if they can break out from under the threat of drones.

It was noted that when he was finally found, Bin Laden wasn't in some hole in the ground, but in a many storied house with lots of TV's. Was this what the Prophet expected from his disciple?

I still can't take these bearded fools seriously as what they have delivered has only been a series of pin pricks. Yes, I know I wasn't in the twin towers on 9/11 – although I had been to the top of the north one years before – but from a statistical point of view I think we've killed more of them than they've killed us.

A look at the Chapter 15 on war will show that if you can keep that up you will almost certainly win. Ask any German history scholar.

But it is not all bad news. My grandson is 19 and I've spent quite a bit of time talking to him about issues. I find it refreshing that he seems to have no problem with race. He has many friends of different cultures, as do his parents.

I am convinced that if we could strike out that inbred repugnance that many of the previous generations had for people who are different, we could at least make a start to living harmoniously.

However, the human race is slow to truly change and maybe I'm being overly optimistic.

Life can only be understood backwards; but it must be lived forwards.
— *Søren Kierkegaard*

Chapter Thirty

AUSCHWITZ

Man's inhumanity to man makes countless thousands mourn!
— Robert Burns

I am keenly aware that the security we enjoy is frail, and could easily be disrupted. Secretly, a nagging fear gnaws at me: what has really been learned from the lessons of Auschwitz and the Third Reich? Do we really understand what happened there and how we might prevent such events in future?
— Daniel Waterman,

In Chapter Thirteen I wrote about the three terrors that have struck fear into mankind in my life. They were the Nazis, the Soviets and in these modern times the Islamists.

All three attempted to take our freedoms away and enslave us with their ideologies.

Because of the proximity to my early life it is perhaps the Nazis who most seemed to threaten us; they were after all on our doorstep across just 21 miles of Channel.

The Islamists require total submission to their medieval ways and their religious beliefs. I can't somehow see three English middle class people adapting to the Burkah, long beards and five times a day prayers to a god we had no true belief in.

The Soviets would have wanted the same goals with total submission but not to a Diety, but to a political ideology that would have been completely foreign to free thinking Englishmen.

But the Nazis had one other bestiality, which puts them above the other two. It was hatred.

There are certainly those in Islam who would destroy large swathes of people and have actually done so. The communists under Stalin and

Mao Tse Tung collectively destroyed some 80 million people. Stalin thought it was politically expedient – he after all said: "The death of any human is a tragedy; the death of a million is merely a statistic."

Mao starved to death some 19 million; Stalin used his Gulag archipelago to do the same thing; millions who got in the way of their complete control and plans for a workers paradise.

But the Nazis went about such behaviour for the reason of pure hatred.

Whereas one can see the logic – granted pretty flawed – of not being able to fully sustain large numbers of people who don't agree with your political beliefs, or are in the wrong part of the country to help swell the ranks, sheer hate is quite another thing.

Furthermore that it occurred within a so-called civilised country that had produced some of the most important cultural minds and philosophy, not to say some of the most beautiful art in the history of the world, has always caused me tremendous concern.

Also, the Germans are our first cousins and more than any other Europeans have shared our history and many of our monarchs.

Always at the back of my mind has been the question: Could we apparently peace loving Brits have been encouraged to do the same hideous crimes against an entire people? Or like many of the Germans themselves would we have just looked the other way.

I have met several Germans in my life who have felt the scar of their culture's crimes very badly and seem to have taken on the blame of the sins of their fathers.

But had I been born twenty years earlier and five hundred miles to the east, might I have ended up in a black uniform with a skull and crossbones on my peaked hat, and polished jackboots? Would I have sworn a personal oath to the Fuhrer and stood enraptured in the stadium in Nuremburg?

"The Conspiracy" is a movie starring Richard Branagh in the role of the arch Nazi, Reinhardt Heydrich. I saw it for the first time in the nineties and I found it most profound and moving.

Whether or not Heydrich flew to the meeting in his own Storch airplane may have been the stuff of fiction, but the way he slowly introduced the concept of genocide to the nation's bureaucratic leaders is truly chilling.

Some efforts at reason and decency were tried out by a few of these men, but it became obvious that the heads of the Nazi movement had no interest in modifying their plans for a "final solution" to the Jewish populaton.

This chapter is written in two parts, the first part is in the sanctity of my comfortable home office looking out on an exceptionally peaceful country road. These are thoughts about how such evil could happen and why such people could be led down this dreadful path, which thankfully ended in complete failure.

The second is the article I wrote for the Los Angeles Newspaper Group following my European trip in March 2015.

On the surface these Nazi leaders don't look particularly fearsome. In fact Hitler looked odd and so did Himmler and also Goebels. Fat Herman Goering looked jolly and had been a fighter ace in the First Wold War.

Heydrich was an outstanding athlete, a talented musician and family man. He worked tirelessly towards his goals, but those goals were evil in the extreme. Were they sociopaths? Psychopaths?

I don't think Hitler ever visited a death camp and so perhaps he was able to somehow neutralise himself from the actual events of his planning. His immediate staff went out of their way to insulate him from the actual crimes that were being carried out.

Himmler certainly visited camps, and there are newsreels of the former chicken farmer doing so. It didn't seem to bother him in the slightest.

Without doubt Heydrich knew exactly what was to happen as he oversaw the beginnings of the plans before he was assassinated in Prague.

Eichmann obviously knew what would occur as he was the actual designer of the methodology needed to murder up to 13 million people.

The movie shows that a few department heads tried to reason with Heydrich, but there was no way to succeed as all of the top men knew exactly what must occur in order to succeed in ridding Europe of the estimated eleven million Jews that lived there. They also wanted to rid the Continent of dissidents, homosexuals, gypsies and many intellectuals.

Such official doctrine was bound to lead to extremes, but the total destruction of an entire race, which was the eventual goal of the Nazis, seems madness. And yet the men and women who instituted such monstrous plans seemed on the face of it quite sane. They certainly set about the task with a dedication and efficiency that would put into question any defence of insanity.

And yet we see with the rise of radical Islam and the denial of the holocaust that people are still of the opinion that some of us don't deserve to share the planet's resources and joys. Have we learned nothing in the last 70 years?

As I've mentioned a couple of times in this memoir, one of my favourite quotes is: *The world is a comedy to those who think and a tragedy to those who feel.* It is attributed to the statesman Horace Walpole from the 18th century. I think it describes two distinct types of people and how they address difficulties. I'm proud to say that over the years, I've ended up on the thinkers' side of the fence, as I don't think it helps to over emotionalise situations.

But the disgracefully categorised "Jewish problem" in the eyes of the perpetrators is something that demands an emotional judgement as it cannot be answered logically.

Imagine leading your life happily, working to succeed and provide for your family. Imagine having fought in the First World War as many German Jews did, of course. Then the rumours begin. You hear of old acquaintances disappearing. You find that people no longer speak to you openly, and then some of your relatives begin to make inquiries about leaving Germany.

Then those same relatives find that they are not allowed to leave. Then you hear of shops being taken over and looted; then your boss tells you that you can no longer work at the firm. You realise you and your family are trapped.

Soon your house is requisitioned and your treasured possessions are confiscated by the state. There is nowhere you can turn, no authority to whom you can appeal. You are a Jew!

The road inevitably leads to the railway yards and crammed cattle trucks to haul you away, separated from your family, friends and everything you have known. You spend hours and even days being jostled in this hell hole with no food or facilities. And then you arrive at your destination. Here you stumble out on to a platform with German guards shouting at you and Alsatian dogs snapping at you. You are confused, and terrified.

Undoubtedly most of the people who visit Auschwitz hope to understand the reason why a highly civilised society would set up an industry entirely devoted to the systematic elimination of an entire people – the Jews.

There follows the article I wrote for the Los Angeles Newspaper Group on my return from our European trip. It was published on May 10, 2015.

Having lived all my life with the horrific stain on Germany's recent history, perhaps my compulsion to understand the reason was that English and Germans are first cousins, and so perhaps deep inside there is the fear that we as peace loving, cricket playing, tea drinking English could also commit such atrocities.

My four hours guided tour of both the Auschwitz One and Auschwitz-Birkenau sites did not erode my concerns.

During the bus ride from Krakow to the site a thirty-minute film was shown. It introduced us to the situation as it was discovered by Russian troops when they liberated the camp in January 1945.

The videographer, who was much decorated for his work filming the war for Stalin, said something that struck a major chord in me. He said when he and his colleagues entered the camp and witnessed the dead and dying human skeletons they were overcome with a deep feeling of shame. That for me put the last link in place.

It was not a question of Germans or English: east or west, left or right it was humans that had created this epicentre of atrocities for their fellow man's suffering. Therefore by association the perpetrators in some way infected us all.

Although we may never fully understand the why of this ideology of cruel racism, it is the how and the scale that makes the sin so monumental.

An entire organization was created to collect, transport, process, murder and recycle 13 million "undesirables" from the length and breadth of the expanding German Empire. Had the war continued for another few years, they would almost certainly have achieved their goal. As it was at least 6 million were murdered – a staggering number by any measurement.

The appetite of this machine was insatiable. Once set in place German industry capitalised on this ready made slave labour. Many of these factories may have pretended they did not understand the truth and preferred to look the other way. But almost certainly many did know.

In their defence there was little they could do about it. Any serious attempt to complain would almost certainly put the whistle blower straight into a camp together with his entire family.

The Nazis were masters of deception. They played a game of normality for those sent directly to the gas chambers. Many of these unfortunates had been shipped across Europe in overcrowded and unsanitary cattle cars. They travelled without food and water.

On falling out onto the sandy ground of the arrival area the prospect of a hot shower would have been overwhelming to them. They went willingly to the changing rooms where they left their belongings with their new masters, who told them to remember where they left their clothes.

When they were crowded into the chamber no doubt most of them were expecting water to come out of the apertures in the ceiling. Instead SS guards posted on the roof threw down crystals of Zyclon –B.

It took up to 20 minutes to die. The sounds of the screams overcame the revving of motor cycles designed to mask the noise.

The Sonderkomandos - those prisoners whose jobs were to clean out the chamber - then entered and took the dead bodies away for incineration in the ovens next door. Finally the ashes were turned into fertilizer or dumped in an adjacent pond or the river Vistula.

During our tour of Auschwitz we passed into a room with one 30ft wall of glass behind which was a mountain of human hair which had been shaved from the recent arrivals. This included the 20 percent of arrivals who were initially spared the gas chamber and were designated to a 12-hour day slaving for the regime.

One of our party was overcome by this human evidence.

Another room displayed thousands of confiscated spectacles; shoes and personal belongings.

The display that resonated with me particularly was one where hundreds of suitcases were piled floor to ceiling. Each one of these cases had been carried by a person who had been robbed of all processions, and who hoped and believed that the little they carried would be something to start their new lives.

The Nazis stole even this along with their names. It was those slaves who naked, shaved and terrified were given a number in place of their names. This number was tattooed on their arms. They now owned nothing, not even their names.

The 80% of arrivals who were sent directly to their deaths were not tattooed and were not entered into the Nazi accounting system. They had ceased to exist from the moment they boarded the trains. Their possessions were taken away to a separate area in Auschwitz-Birkenhau to be cleaned and sold in order to pump much needed funds into the economy.

Human hair was sent to make blankets, uniforms and insulation for submarines.

The area where things were sorted and categorized was called Kanada after the country that seemed to embody everything that was bountiful. Any job in this area was considered the most desirable. It was indoors, and contained opportunities for scraps of food hidden in transportees belongings. Jewellery and currency had no worth in the camp apart from bank notes that were much valued as toilet paper.

When the Russians arrived in the camp they found 300,000 men's suits and 600,000 women's dresses ready to be sent to Germany for selling on the market.

By the time of liberation between 1.2 million and 1.5 million people had been slaughtered in this one camp alone.

I had hoped that my visit to this center of an evil world could cauterize a wound that had been with me for over 65 years. My early life had been marked by several attacks by the Luftwaffe as our homes were located close to aircraft plants where my father worked. But the experience of being on the right side did not provide a thick enough insulation for what my fellow man had created across the English Channel.

I shall never forget my day in Auschwitz-Birkenau. But I shall never return.

Currently there is a renewed anti-Semitism in Europe. The eloquent Dr, Krauthammer recently posited that in fact it had never really gone away, just paused for seventy years.

His fear is that eventually all the Jews will be forced to leave Europe and they will have to settle in Israel, where they will be easier to destroy with nuclear devices.

I believe that this is firmly in the minds of the mullahs in Tehran, who I have read already have plans for accepting the price of such an attack with reprisals from their hated enemy.

And yet, if this should occur, and if all the Jews are destroyed, what will it benefit mankind? We will surely all be the poorer.

A good big 'un will always beat a good little 'un
— J.G. Summons (My father)

EPILOGUE

Sometimes, it is the people no one imagines anything of who do
the things that no one imagines.
— *The Imitation Game*

A woman has to be intelligent, have charm, a sense of humor,
and be kind. It's the same qualities I require from a man.
— *Catherine Deneuve*

It is perhaps fitting that the final chapter in this missive of a charmed life should be about the most awful time in my history. As mentioned before such evil is beyond belief, but if circumstances had been different, then could a child born of British parents just as easily have been introduced to his life just a few hundred miles to the east and therefore been on the wrong side.

And then there is the matter of timing. It's all just coincidence in a way unless you are a deep believer in religion where somehow everything is mapped out ahead for you. As my favourite relative, my paternal grandfather, was fond of saying: "There but for the grace of God go I."

A charmed life or not? Having written down so much I believe I have to agree with my friend Paul Everest, and accept that I have been exceptionally lucky.

To begin with I was born at the right time – a decade earlier would have found me slogging my way through Nazi occupied Europe in the bloody final scenes of WWII. Those Jerries just didn't give up, did they?

They kept on fighting right up until the Fuehrer shot himself after crunching down on a cyanide pill. He wasn't going to chance it, was he?

A recent tour of Berlin showed the infamous Fuhrerbunker to be now nothing more than a parking lot outside some ignominious workers' flats. The Holocaust Museum also being just a few hundred yards away.

Even entering the war five years earlier would have been far more traumatic for a growing child. As it was I was six when it ended with the final two years probably not being in doubt, once the United States came in and began to make inroads.

My luck was also good in that I was born into an intact family that cared for each other. Not too many of those around these days it seems.

I was in my late teens before I came into contact with an unhappy couple. It shocked me and made me realise that I was fortunate not to have lived in that environment.

Also too my family did not have to endure the absence and possible loss of my father. His profession in the aircraft industry allowed him to stay at home and although it caused considerable financial hardships through a truncated career, at least we didn't have to lose him.

Even the lack of money might be said to have benefitted me. I appreciated wealth and although I could never be considered to be wealthy in the American sense, I have gone through my life with no periods lacking food, clothing or housing.

Perhaps I would have appreciated a more structured mind that would have allowed me more choice in employment. But had that occurred then no doubt I would have been stuck on a ladder that lacked the free range life I acquired.

It's a very unusual firm that will let you jet off to a country just to have a go at making something happen. What about the budgets? The five-year plan? I never had any of that.

As it happened I was fortunate to find a company whose leadership welcomed my particular style and where it worked to some extent. And it allowed me to meet Richard who eventually brought me out to America where I have enjoyed the life and particularly the climate!

The other day a local asked me which was my favorite place in the world. He was shocked when I said Big Bear. "But what about the people here?" He asked.

I told him that in my experience people didn't alter much. Half the world is below average intelligence after all, and one group of people differ little from each other once you get to know them.

I've lived in many places in the world – Spain, Holland, the USA and lots of places in the UK. What is different about them is just that they are in different locations. The people, when you get to know them, are much the same.

And so we are left with climate, and politics.

The climate in Big Bear is superb with 300 days of sunshine a year. We have four distinct seasons and the opportunity to go outside whenever we want.

Having lived for 40 years in a rainy damp climate, to be able to make plans for say a motorcycle ride in four days time without having to add – weather permitting! Is a great bonus.

As for the politics, well, I enjoy the American system. It's rather a large canvas which for someone who only wants to watch and has never succumbed to "making a difference," there's a lot to witness.

Mostly once again I came here at the right time. Ten years later and it would not have been easy. Not that it was ever easy. It was a struggle, but today it would have been near impossible.

Arriving in 1982 and once having adjusted to living in a foreign country, we had a chance to get our hands on some "keeping money;" something that had become impossible back in Europe. Today, I'm not sure it's possible at all if you start with virtually nothing.

And we did start with very little – just a salary and the small amount Yvonne was able to raise selling her house in England. That was enough to help with a deposit for a house here.

From an early age and possibly encouraged by my father's and grandfather's tales of the sea and their travels I had a strong desire to repeat their adventures. I was once again lucky to have fallen into a profession that allowed me to keep on the move, and also the great good fortune to meet up with firms that actually encouraged me.

It's very hard to see how much of all these occurrences are merely happenings, or in fact opportunities that perhaps others would not accept. I think back to the offer that my father received to relocate to Buenos Aires to join a man called Christopher Edes, who was building the Argentine civilian air fleet.

I was about eight at the time and Christopher Edes was a man that had worked with my father and obviously rated him and liked him. I don't think my father gave the matter a lot of thought and always said that he didn't want to raise me in a foreign country. I was never sure if that was the true case or if he really didn't like the idea himself. I certainly can't fault his decision although I always believed I would have loved the experience. At least I would have been able to dance the tango.

Such few opportunities that have come my way I have grasped with both hot little hands; I have to admit that it never seemed to require much courage.

Earlier I reported my experience of offering to resettle workers from Glasgow to the south. Not one volunteered to make the move. They preferred to remain in Glasgow where their future was not at all certain. I believe in the UK that this is the norm, where my seemingly devil-may-care attitude is not. I am grateful for that particular gene as it has allowed me to make moves in my life that did not require much courage. Perhaps that is being lucky – or charmed!

Talking to people regularly, I am struck by how many of them seem to have sired (or dammed) geniuses. I'm glad to hear it as we do need to have as many of them helping struggle out of the mire and keep our civilisation growing. It must be a very big responsibility to have to care for such budding intellect.

I once heard the retiring conductor of the LA Symphony Orchestra, Carlo Maria Guilini, answer the question was he a genius as many people considered him. He replied that he considered a genius was one who created such a presence that when he died he was totally irreplaceable. He believed he was competent, but a genius, no.

I am very pleased to say that none of my three children were ever geniuses, but I'm proud to state that they have all made their way in the world and have forged good and lasting relationships.

I believe that everyone, being unique, could say that their presence in the world has importance but none of us has ever craved the huge responsibility of being other than happy.

My mother was a kind and gentle woman. I learned a lot from her in how to diffuse difficult situations as she had to deal with the rather choleric personality of my father.

My first girlfriend followed in that gentle English middle-class way and perhaps that set a standard. I have been exceptionally lucky in never falling under the spell of bad women and only those who have been kind and gentle with me.

My first wife Veronica was of that ilk and she was a great mother to Michael and looked after her small brood with great skill and tenderness.

Unfortunately my travelling and sales life meant that we drifted apart and separated, for which I have always been sorry.

I have once again been exceptionally lucky in meeting and marrying Yvonne who took the great chance of changing her name, culture and country with someone whom she had only known for six months.

She has been my constant companion and by far the most important part of my life. Perhaps that unplanned moment when I chanced to walk in the door of The Lamb in Angmering, Sussex that Saturday lunchtime in early October 1981, was the luckiest thing of all. It has certainly been the most important contribution to what I will admit has been a charmed life!

Printed in the United States
By Bookmasters